THE MYSTERIES OF HEALING

THE MYSTERIES OF HEALING

Dialogues with Doctors and Scientists

GAYLE KIMBALL Ph.D.

Balinese flower, photo by the author

Waterside Productions

Printed in the United States of America

First Printing, 2020

ISBN-13: 978-1-949003-58-1 print edition
ISBN-13: 978-1-949003-59-8 ebook edition

Waterside Productions

2055 Oxford Ave
Cardiff, CA 92007
www.waterside.com

The most beautiful thing we can experience is the mysterious. It is the source of all true art and science. Albert Einstein

Medical materialism is ... too simple-minded. William James in *The Varieties of Religious Experience*

Endorsements

Gayle Kimball's intelligent and probing interviews become a fascinating excursion, tracking the insights of a remarkable collection of scientists and seekers pushing the limits of what we know. This trilogy will become a prime source for future historians of science. Gayle Kimball has tapped into the experience and wisdom of the world's top researchers working to reveal the subtle but powerful reach of human consciousness.
Roger Nelson, Ph.D., Director of the Global Consciousness Project

For hearts and minds hungry for more knowledge, this trilogy offers a kaleidoscope viewpoint on truth—who we are, why we are here, and how the universe functions. Kimball draws out the healing essence of leaders in the field, weaving together threads of insight through many facets of human experience, like the many faces of a diamond coalescing into the making of healing miracles.

Barbara Stone, Ph.D., author of *Invisible Roots* and *Transforming Fear into Gold.*

The Mysteries trilogy conveys a roadmap to the future! Humanity is continuously redefined by our relationships with each other and the cosmos, and these remarkable testimonies speak of how consciousness provides a key to understanding that the Mind is not limited to the body, but is the pathway to exploring life's infinite possibilities.

Drs. J.J. and Desiree Hurtak, The Academy For Future Science

Dr. Gayle Kimball has succeeded in bringing together a great variety of viewpoints, in a variety of fields, all lively while deep, through her interviews of

many professionals. The Mysteries Trilogy has taken a lot of effort, energy and vision. I am sure they will remain not just a testament to emerging truths but also an amazing way to gather information, belief systems, and everyday life stories of many remarkable people, while keeping high professional standards. She herself is a remarkable individual and the hard work she carried out shows in the writing.

Meanas Kafatos, physics professor and author

As we stand at the threshold of an emerging paradigm in which consciousness becomes fundamental in science, historians and philosophers of science will find these words and thoughts essential to understanding how that paradigm shift occurred.

Stephan A. Schwartz, author and researcher

Getting scientists of any ilk to admit to anything mystical or spiritual in their lives is quite a task—as you might suspect since scientists are so logically and usually materialistic-minded in their views. Gayle Kimball has done just that, and it makes for some interesting reading as to what drives the scientific inquiry. I'll give you a hint: It's not logical.

Physicist Fred Alan Wolf, Ph.D., aka Dr. Quantum®

How often are we privileged to enter the minds and hearts of visionary scientists working at the cutting edge of exploration? Dr. Kimball offers this gift to all of us, including the scientists who participated in the dialogues that deserve to be celebrated and widely read.

Gary E. Schwartz, Ph.D., Director of the Laboratory for Advances in Consciousness and Health at the University of Arizona. His recent books include *Super Synchronicity, Is Consciousness Primary?*, and *Extraordinary Claims Require Extraordinary Evidence*.

Throughout history, there have been visionaries able to "see" further than others. Many have been spiritual mystics or those with great dreams and the will to pursue them into manifestation. Some have been scientific pioneers including Einstein, Planck, Tesla, Wheeler and Bohm. In this timely, far reaching and deeply insightful trilogy, the visionary clear-sight and wisdom of 65 leading-edge scientists and in their own testimonies are remarkably synergized by Gayle Kimball. They reveal a visionary science seeing beyond a material world-view, based ultimately on the oneness of all creation and the naturalizing of non-local awareness and supernormal phenomena. And founded in an emergent and yet ancient perception that mind and consciousness aren't something we have but what we and the whole world are.

Jude Currivan Ph.D., cosmologist, healer, futurist, author of
The Cosmic Hologram and co-founder WholeWorld-View

This informative trilogy offers a treasure trove of personal reflections and insights from many of the leading figures in the modern scientific awakening to deeper understanding of consciousness, the brain-mind connection, and the ultimate healing force of our free will.

Eben Alexander MD, neurosurgeon and author of
Living in a Mindful Universe and *Proof of Heaven*

TABLE OF CONTENTS

Introduction: Scientists Discover Reality is Consciousness

Many of our scientific beliefs are limited in that they can't account for the evidence that consciousness exists beyond the brain. The dominant materialist paradigm denies the power of spirit, the miracles of mind and feelings over matter, unconscious access to information, and the possibility of other dimensions beyond what our physical senses tell us—including life after death. The dominant worldview is like the *Flatland* novel published in 1884 about a two-dimensional world. When the hero first discovers a three-dimensional place, he is only able to see a flat circle. When he sees more and reports back on his discovery, he's persecuted. It's also like the story of the Emperor's New Clothes where the crowd applauds the lie that the naked emperor is wearing beautiful new robes until a small boy has the courage to speak the truth. The dominant worldview often ridicules those with the vision to see other dimensions beyond Flatland, while visionary scientists see the denial of anything but the physical as dogma that ignores extensive research and inhibits our access to subtle information.

Courageous scientists, physicians, and psychologists are creating a new non-materialist scientific paradigm as they struggle to define consciousness. Professor Chris Roe* explained, "We don't have the remotest idea of what we mean by consciousness," but "working on the fringes of the anomalies starts to give us answers." He has the courage to put his head "above the parapet and say the evidence is quite strong," so he has moved from trying to prove psi to researching the process of how it works. [*An asterisk indicates that the scientist is featured in a chapter in the trilogy.] Shamini Jain* defines consciousness as the "source and substrate of creation. It is beyond mind, emotion and the physical. It's what gives rise to the physical."

The visionary scientists say consciousness doesn't originate in the brain and use synonyms like One Mind, spirit, energy, the Force, matrix, hologram, meaning fields, biofield, cosmic intelligence, information, panpsychism, beyond space and time, substrate, non-physical web, spiritual computer, and fifth dimension. It's basic language is mathematics and patterns like fractals. This implies there is another dimension beyond space and time, which may enable psi phenomena like clairvoyance, precognition, and distant healing. The scientists liken the new understanding of reality to the huge effect of the Copernican revolution that challenged the belief that our earth was the center of the solar system (although about one-quarter of Americans still don't know this, according to National Science Foundation surveys.)

These cutting-edge trailblazers persist despite denial from those who don't bother to read their scholarly research studies with results thousands of times beyond what chance would predict. Recognition of the importance of our consciousness, intent, and emotions has major implications for health care, morality, and goal achievement. Bernardo Kastrup* views materialist dogma as making us collectively mad, enmeshed in a collective trance that leads to immorality. The condition of our environment is proof of this insanity. Larry Dossey* observes we face a "horrible crisis in ethics and morality." Madonna's 1984 song "Material Girl" spells out the belief system that Mister Right is the man with "cold hard cash."

I interviewed 65 visionary scientists, leaders in the Consciousness Movement, to ask about their personal development, as well as to learn what their research findings reveal about reality, and to discover why they're so brave. The three books in the Mysteries Trilogy explore how consciousness shapes reality, enables healing and provides access to knowledge from beyond the physical senses. These visionary scientists conclude that we are more than our physical bodies with more potential than we realize and that science needs to expand to account for consciousness. "The new science embraces all of science, but it's reframing it to have a bigger perspective. This means that we can make sense of data that doesn't fit and we can make new predictions that can be tested, confirmed, or disconfirmed. It's an expansion of science that reverses and changes the way you experience what you know," explained Gary Schwartz.* He added, "This perspective turns everything on its head. It's like realizing that the sun no longer revolves around the earth" and encourages reuniting science and spirituality (as discussed in Edward Kelly et al., *Beyond Physicalism: Toward Reconciliation of Science and Spirituality*). The scientists are concerned that the prevailing materialist paradigm limits our abilities and has devastating consequences, including polluting our planet. As youth climate activists say, there is no planet B.

Reality is not what we think it is—that's what I learned from the visionary scientists.[1] Common sense erroneously tells us that we live in a solid material world, that atoms are like billiard balls with definite locations and time is a one-directional arrow. This is all false. As physicist Max Planck said in 1931, "I have spent my entire life studying atoms and molecules and I'm here to tell you that they don't exist." He explained in his book *The New Science* that there is no matter as such because atoms vibrate and are held together by a force that indicates a "conscious and intelligent mind. This mind is the matrix of all matter," thus, matter is derived from consciousness. The materialist belief is that all information comes from the physical senses via the brain although many people experience ESP, telepathy, a precognitive dream or intuition, awareness of being stared at, or a dramatic near-death experience (NDE) that reveals other dimensions, as it did for neurosurgeon Eben Alexander.* Animals also have these abilities, as evidenced in Rupert Sheldrake's research on dogs that are aware of when their person will come home, even at an unexpected time.[2]

The materialist model of science has, of course, produced a great deal, as evidenced in technologies that can send a person to the moon or create artificial intelligence, but it hasn't succeeded in learning very much about our physical surroundings. Over 95% of the universe is invisible dark matter and dark energy that repels gravity.[3] These mysterious forces have been measured and their effects described but not understood. Various theories try to explain gravity but none are definitive. The observable universe made of atoms comprises less than 5% of the universe. One interpretation of quantum physics predicts multi-universes beyond the known universe that remain a mystery to us.[4]

Neither do we know much about the earth under our feet, revealed by Robert Macfarlane in *The Hidden Depths of the Underland* or the 2019 film *Fabulous Fungi*. The mycelium that rises to the surface as mushrooms are intelligent in that they solve problems, just as slime mold does. The "secret lives" of trees and how they communicate is revealed by biologist Monica Gagliano in *Thus Spoke the Plant*. The classic *Secret Lives of Plants* by Peter Tompkins and Christopher Bird also reveals mysteries around us.

Similarly, genes with a known coding function make up only about 1.5% of our DNA structure, while the non-coding genes are called "junk" and dismissed as useless.[5] In regards to their function, computational biologist Ewan Birney said, "It's slightly depressing as you realize how ignorant you are. But this is progress. The first step in understanding these things is having a list of things that one has to understand, and that's what we've got here."[6] Biologists are learning about epigenetics, discovering that gene expression isn't fixed but changes in response to our emotions and our environment. Our limited knowledge applies to the whole scientific belief system. William Bengston* concludes, "I can tell you there is nothing more liberating than realizing everything you think is true is wrong."

The Visionary Scientists

To find out about the creation of a scientific paradigm that acknowledges we have access to more dimensions than the Flatlanders, I interviewed Ph.D.s and M.D.s who write books and articles that contribute to our understanding of reality and consciousness. This book includes 19 of the scientists; the others in the trilogy are represented in the book on reality and the book on knowledge beyond the senses. I was inspired by attending the Canadian Energy Psychology conference in Toronto in 2018 where I was struck by the unusual coupling of highly educated scientists talking about spirit and personal experiences of the paranormal. As a feminist academic who does clairvoyant work, I find them very intriguing.

The trilogy explores the scientists' life stories and the influences on their beliefs and personal courage, along with their understandings of our purpose as humans and how the universe really works. I could identify with what Larry Dossey* pointed out; "It takes a rabble-rouser to actually develop the courage" to take on the establishment. He added that most peer-reviewed medical journals won't touch papers on topics like the efficacy of prayer in healing. Like these visionary scientists, curiosity and truth-telling motivate me to point out that the Emperor is naked, there are multiple dimensions, and we have access to information and guidance from beyond the five physical senses.

Using snowball methodology, I asked each of the visionary scientists I interviewed to suggest others. I knew of some whom I researched for my book *Essential Energy Tools: How to Develop Your Clairvoyant and Healing Abilities*. Others were speakers featured at conferences I attended: Science and Consciousness, the International Society for the Study of Subtle Energies and Energy Medicine, and Energy Psychology. The video interviews were conducted on Skype and most were posted on my YouTube channel for you to see in entirety. (A few interviewees didn't want their videos made public.) The generic questions are listed on the book webpage. Each scientist and I then edited the written transcript to forge a chapter in the trilogy. I added questions for the reader to ponder and references to themes that repeat in other chapters, as noted in italics.

I attempted to interview psi skeptics including Chris French, Richard Wiseman, Arthur Reber, and James Alcock, as well as the Skeptical Inquirer organization, but only Susan Blackmore* accepted. Reber and Alcock responded to a well-documented article on evidence for psi by Etzel Cardeña by stating they didn't read the studies because they knew they violated the laws of physics, i.e., pigs can't fly so why study flying pigs?[7] They're forgetting quantum physics, as discussed by Steve Taylor.*[8] Psi researchers point out that replication is a problem for many scientists, so they rely on meta-analyses of many studies. Physicist Ed May, who worked on the Star Gate program, described himself in an email as a "total physicalist" and suggested reading his Laboratories for Fundamental Research website, which he founded to study "anomalous cognition." Some of the trilogy scientists respond to the skeptics in their book *Skeptical About Skeptics.*

Common themes that surfaced about these pioneers indicate that the visionary scientists are highly intelligent and did well in school and university, as you would expect. The majority were first-born in their families (35 compared to 26 latter-born). Most of the US scientists grew up on the East or West Coast or live there now, with a few exceptions, such as some born in the Midwestern states like Ohio. Others grew up in the UK or Canada and one each in Germany, Brazil and the Netherlands (Kastrup), Italy, or Greece. Some are first generation with parents from India, Latvia, Palestine, and Ireland, demonstrating the rich contributions provided by immigrant families. Some had health or family problems in their youth that motivated their search for understanding.

Some visionary scientists had unexpected and transformative mystical experience, like physicians John Ryan* and Richard Moss,* physicist Jude Currivan,* psychologist Steve Taylor,* and linguist J.J. Hurtak.* For a few, an NDE was transformative, such as for Eben Alexander,* Joyce Hawkes, and Marilyn Mandela Schlitz.* Family influences included visionary mothers for James Carpenter,* David Lorimer,* Judith Swack,* Christine Simmonds-Moore* and John Kruth,* or an influential sibling like Marjorie Woollacott,* David Muehsam,* Mary Rose Barrington,* and Larry Burk.* Psychedelic drugs influenced scientists like Susan Blackmore* and David Luke.*

Having his "bad back" healed by a man he met while lifeguarding at a swimming pool led William Bengston* to research healing and an injury led Richard Hammerschlag* to study acupuncture. Overall, curiosity about reality and the willingness to study the data was the main motivation to follow the evidence, however much in conflict with the materialist belief system.

The scientists are often spiritual rather than religious and many went through an adolescent rebellion against religious dogma. More of them have a Jewish background than would be predicted by the small percentage of Jews in the world population. Jeffrey Mishlove* interviewed over a thousand visionary scientists for his video show "New Thinking Allowed."[9] He reported, "I've discovered that quite a number of prominent people in parapsychology have a Jewish background. Jews are a tiny minority but Jewish people are prominent in every cutting edge activity in which I've ever been involved. I would say 95% of the people who explore these areas scientifically do so because, like me, they've had powerful personal experiences. The other 5 to 10% do it out of intellectual curiosity." Les Lancaster* explained, "the combination of the value placed on learning, the leanings towards mysticism, the eschatological idea of promoting a golden age to come, and the pressures of being in exile was hugely formative for Jews entering the modern era. This is a potent mix that breeds pioneers!"

Most of the psi researchers are older white men, as is true of the trilogy authors. John Kruth* reports that when he started doing research at the Rhine Research Center at age 48, he was considered a youngster. Of 60 scientists included in the trilogy, only two are people of color and only 18 are women. The women have fewer children the 1.9 average per woman in the US and UK, with 16 children between them.

The visionary scientists are intuitive types rather than sensing personality types on the Keirsey and Bates scale (available online to compare your scores with the scientists.)[10] Only two men scored sensing rather than intuitive. They're more extroverted than the typical research scientist: Our group profile is Extrovert, Intuitive,

Feeling, and very close but slightly more Judging, called "Idealist Teachers or Champions." Some are interested in the Enneagram as to tool for self-understanding, like Charles Tart* and Judith Swack.* (More about their typologies is on the book website.)

Some readers wondered why I included astrological types in a book about science: Their most common signs are Sagittarius (10), Aquarius and Libra (both 8). One reason is astrology is a shorthand to personality type for those who find it useful and, second, I was curious how they'd respond to a controversial topic. I've found my natal chart accurate: For example, I have fiery Mars strengthened by its position in the constellation Aries the ram in my 10th house of occupation, indicating I've focused on work. The visionary scientists enjoy their research and get grounded by being in nature. An unusual number are also musicians or singers. "Curious" is the most common word they use to describe their drive to understand reality on a deep level and they like being on the cutting edge of discovery.

The New Non-Materialist Paradigm

Although researchers like Dean Radin* report on thousands of double-blind studies with results in some cases trillions of times beyond what you would expect by chance, the findings are often dismissed as pseudoscience or "woo-woo." Radin suggests, "What is needed for a new paradigm is a more comprehensive model of reality where consciousness becomes just as fundamental, if not more so, than materialism." Actually, idealism is very old, defined as the belief that reality is mentally constructed. Ancient Greek philosophers, such as Anaxagoras in 480 BCE, emphasized the primacy of mind and consciousness although his contemporary Plato's idea of ideal forms is better known. Ancient Hinduism, Buddhism and Jainism also recognized that the material world is *maya,* illusion, and through meditation, sages develop psi abilities called *siddhis,* such as clairvoyance or bilocation. More modern siddhis are described in *Autobiography of a Yogi* by Paramhansa Yogananda. The Bible is full of references to healing, prophecy, prayer, and what Paul calls "gifts of the Holy

Spirit" in 1 Corinthians 12. Many of our scientists were influenced by Eastern religious thought and are meditators, while some participate successfully in their own experiments with ESP, etc. They realize the impact of experimenter expectations and value qualitative research such as case studies—including their own first-person psi experiences. They encourage openly sharing data online.

Psychic remote viewers led by Russell Targ* in the Star Gate government programs during the Cold War sketched secret Soviet missile silos, a huge new secret Soviet submarine, the location of a downed Russian military plane before it was discovered by the Soviets in North Africa, and drew targets before they were even selected. The remote viewers were only given numbers with no hint about the target, paid attention to their perceptions, and drew pictures of the target while in their offices. Stephan Schwartz* worked with remote viewers to discover archeological finds such as Cleopatra's Palace and the Lighthouse of Pharos—one of the seven wonders of the ancient world—as well as sunken ships and a lost Mayan temple. Working in the military as a remote viewer, Paul H. Smith* found the location of drug contraband in a huge container ship while working in his office. Charles Tart* suggests that remote viewers also could be used in therapy to explore the roots of psychological problems. Medical intuitive Caroline Myss' well-known work with Dr. Norm Shealy in his medical practice can be considered a form of remote viewing of a stranger's body.

It follows from materialism that death ends our awareness, but rigorous triple-blind experiments with mediums who accurately communicate with disembodied spirits are conducted by Ph.D.s Julie Beischel* (Windbridge Institute), Gary Schwartz* (University of Arizona), Chris Roe* (University of Northampton), and others. Over 2,500 well-documented cases of children who remember their past lives were collected by Ian Stevenson and Ed Kelly at the University of Virginia.[11] Over one-third of the children had birthmarks and/or phobias representative of death traumas such as wounds that caused their past deaths, or fear of water caused by a drowning death. Millions of people with NDEs often report undergoing a life review with a loving being where they feel the impact of their lifetime actions.[12] Denying the long-term consequences of our actions (karma) leads to over-emphasis on "eat, drink and be merry for tomorrow we die." Some of the visionary scientists had communication with a dead relative, like Russel Targ* whose daughter gave a message of love in Russian so he would know it was her and Fred Alan Wolf's* son communicated with him after being killed in an accident.

The old view is that time only moves forward, although Albert Einstein explained that space-time is relative at the speed of light. It seems like fantasy to think that precognition and retrocausality could exist or that intention in the present may change the past. Yet, Dean Radin's experiments connecting subjects to physiological measuring devices, while they are shown slides, found that their bodies reacted even before an alarming or arousing slide was selected by a computer. Even more astounding, the past output of Random Number Generator machines could be changed by intention—but only if the output hadn't been read, as Roger Nelson* found in his PEAR laboratory at Princeton. (RNGs are computer devices that generate random 0s and 1s.)

The academic bias against psi research means that it's neglected and underfunded to our detriment. Psi is a Greek letter and the first letter of the word "psyche," meaning mind. Psi is used to refer to anomalous or extraordinary experiences, parapsychology, and the paranormal. However, James Carpenter* argues in *First Sight* that "para" should be dropped because we often use these often unconscious intuitive abilities to stay safe. Since the materialist paradigm is so limited and harmful, clearly more research is needed to enhance our physical and emotional health.

The old paradigm believes that scientists can be objective in conducting research, but psi researchers recognize the inevitable effect of the intention and beliefs of the experimenter. Garret Moddel* tried to get around this effect by designing an experiment with two RNGS and two computers with no human involvement. The first round achieved the effect he and his students were looking for. When they ran the experiment again later, there was no effect, leading him to realize that what had changed was his attitude and intent, which the machines reflected. Psi research indicates that we have free will, as opposed to the determinism of the materialist model that says all is determined by chemical interactions, etc. Some quantum physicists also believe the determinism of physical laws denies free will (*See Ruth Kastner**).

The list of psi resources on the book's webpage shows few pertinent college courses. A few donors stand out like Henry and Susan Samueli's 2017 gift of $200 million to the University of California at Irvine to research integrative health care such as acupuncture, naturopathy, homeopathy, and herbs. The gift evoked criticism and the fear it would "threaten to tar UC Irvine's medical school as a Haven for quacks."[13] This article quotes Professor David Gorski as saying the only reason for integrative medicine is "to integrate quackery into medicine." (The Samueli's former institute also funded Shamini Jain's* research in energy healing published in scientific journals.)

To counter this academic bias, visionary scientists established the Scientific and Medical Network (SMN) in the UK, and in the US they organized the Academy for the Advancement of Post-Materialist Sciences, the Society for Scientific Exploration, and the Consciousness and Healing Initiative. SMN member David Lorimer* explained, "The original Network was set up because it still is very unfashionable and perhaps even dangerous to hold a non-material worldview." These organizations also publish and organize conferences. A distinguished and well-known professor who turned down my request to be in the trilogy explained, "I agree with Dean Radin's observation that rigorous scientific psi research is dismissed, but I do not want to become embroiled in public controversy about that." In contrast, this book's scientists have the courage to be embroiled and we'll learn why.

Useful Applications of the Consciousness Paradigm

If our common sense simplistic notions about material things, locality and distance, time, sources of information, death, and the power of belief are wrong—at least on the quantum level, what are the implications? We need training in how to accurately access non-sensory information and use thoughts and emotions to manifest goals. It's helpful to learn to pay attention to seemingly unrelated synchronistic events, especially what Gary Schwartz* calls "super synchronicity" when we experience six or more related events. They suggest that some form of helpful guidance exists and that we can learn how to access it more deliberately.

Visionary psychoanalyst Carl Jung developed the concept of synchronicity when his patient was describing a dream about a scarab beetle as a similar beetle appeared on the window. Dawson Church gives many more examples in his chapter on synchronicity in his book *Mind to Matter: The Astonishing Science of How Your Brain Creates Material Reality.* He quotes Jung's definition: "Synchronicity is a meaningful coincidence of two or more events, where something other than the probability of chance is involved." As we grow on a spiritual path, it happens more often, suggesting a subtle intelligence at play.

The old paradigm values logic and analytical thinking but is uncomfortable with emotions and the content of the unconscious, while the multi-dimensional approach includes what intuition and dreams reveal from the deeper mind. Larry Burk* writes about people who accurately diagnose their own diseases, such as cancer, by paying attention to their dreams. Getting their doctors to pay attention to these dreams was often problematic, or actually led to death that perhaps could have been avoided if the dream diagnosis was taken seriously. Stephan Schwartz* got involved in studying Edgar Cayce's channeled information when a stranger arrived at his house to tell him she dreamed that he should be involved in the Cayce Foundation's A.R.E (Association for Research and Enlightenment). He went on to study there for five years. Henry Reed* leads Dream Helper Circles where members commit to dream one night in a therapeutic way for a target member of the circle and discuss their dreams in the morning. Many of the scientists have precognitive dreams themselves.

The materialist paradigm believes that consciousness only exists when manifested by a physical body and a brain since the physical is all that exists. The new (but actually ancient) view acknowledges that other dimensions may exist. Influential psychologist William James warned against "medical materialism" as being too "simpleminded" in explaining mystical experiences of the Christian saints as purely biological. More recently, neurosurgeon Eben Alexander* was astounded to experience multiple-dimensions when meningo-encephalitis caused severe damage to his neocortex (the outer surface of the brain, most related to our human awareness) and wiped out his memory. He experienced similar visions as Robert Monroe, founder of the Monroe Institute, whom he knew nothing about at the time. Because of medical advances, an increasing number of people survive to tell about their NDEs and many report mystical experiences that change their understanding of multiple dimensions and the long-term consequences of their actions.

In the old paradigm, since only the material world is viewed as real, useful non-physical communication is often dismissed. This includes ESP, studied by psychiatrist Diane Hennacy Powell,* and telepathy. Many Ganzfeld studies conducted during relaxation or sleep, and in James Carpenter's* men's discussion group, succeeded in influencing what the subjects were thinking about. Hundreds of the Ganzfeld studies are viewed as the "flagship of experimental parapsychology."[14] In these experiments, a computer selects a video clip or photo that is later shown to the subject along with three other images and she or he is asked to identify the target image. The accuracy in hundreds of studies is above the 25% rate predicted by chance. As Dean Radin states, "Materialism entails a certain set of assumptions that are perfectly fine for understanding the physical world. But those assumptions (as we understand them today) cannot easily account for all aspects of reality, especially consciousness and psychic phenomena."

The Flatland worldview is that illnesses are cured by drugs and/or surgery, certainly not by prayer from a distance or by healers, although focused intention impacts machines, cells, bacteria, seed growth, plasma, photons, etc.. Practical applications of the multi-dimensional understanding of our abilities include health care, which mainly recognizes the physical dimension. For example, bio-chemist Joyce Hawkes does effective healing work from a distance, as discussed in our video interview.[15] The health care of the future will utilize treatment modalities from the East and the West, pre-dicts Richard Hammerschlag*, co-founder of CHI. Already many medical schools include integrative health, wellness, and spiritu-ality programs, as discussed in the International Congress on Integrative Medicine and Health.

William Bengston's* skeptical students routinely cure mice injected with mammary cancer (which kills control mice in about 27 days), while the healed mice live out their normal two-year life span. Interestingly, biology students who are embarrassed to be sitting in a lab with their hands around a cage full of mice don't have the same curative outcomes, indicating that the attitude of the healer makes a difference in the healing outcome. In what seems like a resonance effect, some of the mice injected with breast can-cer and placed in used healing cages didn't die of breast cancer, even when the healing practice wasn't consciously directed at them. Bengston is researching duplicating the results by recording healing frequencies while a group of people that he trained heal the mice. The goal is to transmit the inaudible frequencies through speakers for healing others. When cancer cells were placed by the speakers in Bengston's lab, 68 significant genomic changes occurred in 167 cancer genes. He reports, "Certainly the cells were able to recog-nize that something was going on here and they responded."

We've known for a long time about the power of placebo to heal, about spontaneous remission of terminal illnesses, and how a person with Dissociative Identity Disorder with multiple personali-ties ("alters") can have diabetes with one alter and not the other. One alter or personality is allergic and the other isn't; one alter needs glasses and the other doesn't.[16] They can react differently to medication, have different blood pressure readings, heart rate, and EEG readings, which indicates the influence of mind over matter.

Seemingly miraculous occurrences, such as the growing percentages of pharmaceutical trials where the placebo is almost as effective as the drug are dismissed by researchers as irritating. However, logic indicates they should try to figure out how to stimulate the use of suggestion or belief to heal. Placebo has an impact even if the subject knows it's a sugar pill, especially if the pill is colorful and large, as researched by Harvard Professor Ted Kaptchuk. Hypnosis can also produce biological effects. For example, telling a subject a pencil touch is a lit cigarette can raise a blister on the skin.[17] Prayer can assist in healing; see Larry Dossey's* chapter for an explanation of a flawed Harvard study that discounted its effectiveness.

Psychologist Chris Roe* points out that the evidence "suggests our current psychological model of what it is to be a human being is incomplete." Psychiatrists Robert Alcorn* and Mitchell Gibson,* along with therapist Barbara Stone,* were surprised to discover the negative impact of other-dimensional entities on the mental health of their patients. These three therapists proceeded to develop techniques to remove the invading energies, which improved the lives of their patients.

Some healers found that the energy field is the template for the physical body, and work with the meridians, chakras, and the auric field. John Ryan, M.D.,* for example, uses chakras in his healing work, as I do in phone sessions as I view them as subconscious memory banks. I also use energy psychology tapping on meridian points, such as Emotional Freedom Technique. Yet very little research has been invested in discovering how these phenomena work and how to apply them to healing. The National Institutes of Health (NIH) budget for the National Center for Complementary Health (established in 1992) should be much larger. Only $126,081,000 was allocated for fiscal year 2020, compared to $43 billion for the NIH.

These scientists report that factors that may influence psi abilities (like ESP) include: previous experience and belief in psi phenomenon, experienced mediators, artists, musicians, creativity, fantasy proneness, relaxed rather than anxious, extroverted, open, able to focus (measured by the Absorption Scale), boundary thinness, positive schizotypy (sometimes called "magical think-ing"), bioeccentricity, and being left-handed or ambidextrous. Psychiatrist Diane Hennacy Powell adds: genetics, history of severe trauma (especially in childhood), history of an NDE, ADD, Bipolar Disorder, autism, and being a mother (in part because of the brain remodeling that occurs under the influence of hormones during pregnancy).

Business and finance are often interested in future forecasts and could utilize psi research and remote viewing to identify future trends, as in Stephan Schwartz's* work, or as explained in Julia Mossbridge's *The Premonition Code*. She suggests that "precogs" could help NGOs predict famines, help patients, guide new college students, etc. Some remote viewers applied their skills to earning money on the Commodities Market. Patrizio Tressoldi* works with devices that respond to intention, hoping that, "Our studies of practical application of mental interaction from a distance are rep-licated by investigators to convince people that our human poten-tialities are much more than we experience in normal life." Menas Kafatos* concludes, "The message of all the different spiritual tra-ditions is we are more than we think we are." The materialist dogma limits our abilities to only what's believed to be common sense and dulls awareness of long-term responsibility for our actions.

Quantum Physics is the Foundation of the New Paradigm

Quantum mechanics is often relied on to explain psi phenom-enon, which makes many physicists uncomfortable. There are a variety of quantum theories such as the Russian scientists' torsion field theory[18] or Ruth Kastner's* development of the Transactional Interpretation. A fascinating, and one might say mind-blowing, hid-den universe beyond space-time is revealed by the invisible world of quantum physics. It doesn't follow the classical laws of physics, leading physicist Anton Zeillinger to observe, "The world is even weirder than what quantum physics tells us." When two photons are entangled or bonded, even though they appear to be separate, if one is sent to another solar system and its spin is changed, the other instantaneously reflects it. This non-local connection bothered Einstein who dismissed it "spooky action at a distance." He also said, "Concerning matter we have been all wrong. What we have called matter is energy whose vibration has been so lowered as to be discernible to the senses. There is no matter." Scientists have observed entanglement not just with tiny photons or atoms, but with macroscopic objects like diamond crystals.[19] This could explain how psi is possible, perhaps one of the reasons quantum physicist Henry Stapp suggested that non-locality may be the most profound discovery in all of science.

Physicists have no definitive explanation of this non-local distant connection of entangled pairs. How can seemingly separate and distant particles be so connected since Einstein taught us nothing can move faster than the speed of light? Imants Baruss* suggests the existence of intelligent meaning fields beyond space-time. Some relate this dimension to consciousness or the ground of being. It's very appealing to point to quantum non-locality as an explanation for distant healing prayer, ESP or precognition. However, physicists don't know if there is an information field or even what consciousness is or how it could arise from matter. This is referred to as "the hard problem of consciousness" that can't be explained by the materialist paradigm. Some of the visionary scientists think of consciousness as benign and helpful, while others don't attribute feeling to it. They agree it's the ground of being, the source of the material world, not the other way around, and that it's difficult to define.

Physics Professor David Kagan warned in a personal communication:

If you hang your hat on today's unresolved mysteries of science, you will likely look foolish because eventually these mysteries will be solved and new ones created in the process. Physics is a false god for those pleading their case that their work is valid. Physics changes all the time. It is not The Absolute Truth. It is but one

*"way of knowing," albeit, it is a powerful way of understanding the
structure of our universe from a physical perspective. Nonetheless, it
can't be the absolute truth because it is an infinite onion, one layer
peeled back at a time revealing yet another layer—ad infinitum, an
image suggested by Richard Feynman.*

Some physics theories suggest there are more than three dimensions of space and more than one time dimension. Some scientists believe that the invisible quantum world exists in potentiality and a wave collapses into a particle only when it's observed or measured. It doesn't exist in space-time until then, in a realm beyond our reality. Another theory is that multiple states of potentiality exist at the same time, as in the popular Many-Worlds theory of Hugh Everett. Over time, the Copenhagen interpretation of Niels Bohr predominated, stating that a quantum particle exists in all possible states at once. Trying to understand what potentiality is before it's measurable, physicist Fred Alan Wolf* explained to me, "Before collapse, only mind stuff exists in the guise of possibilities. Possibilities are potentially able to be something. Atoms are ideas we use to map out what we observe with sensitive instruments." What we know for sure is that we know very little about our world and therefore should be humble and open to new ideas. As Niels Bohr said to Wolfgang Pauli about his theory of elementary particles, "We are all agreed that your theory is crazy. The question that divides us is whether it is crazy enough to have a chance of being correct."[20]

Theoretical physicist Sean Carroll explains that versions of quantum mechanics agree that the universe is composed of wave functions that when measured collapse into either particles (a "cloud of probability" like an electron or the photons in light) or waves.[21] "The world is wavy," he says. Fields (such as electromagnetic fields researched by CHI members like David Muehsam* and Beverly Rubik" for healing potential) are created by waves. The version that makes more sense to Carroll is Many-Worlds where atoms are in superposition of every possible position until observed, hence there are "many copies of what we think of as the universe."

He reports that scientists also agree they don't really understand the quantum realm, hence the well-known saying, "Shut up and calculate."

Many people assume that the effect of quantum physics was to open scientists to the mysterious as Einstein suggested in the book's opening quotation. To the contrary, Wikipedia, YouTube, and journal articles still attack or censor our vanguard scientists as pseudo-scientists. Wikipedia's first sentence about brilliant researcher Dean Radin* is, "He has been Senior Scientist at the Institute of Noetic Sciences (IONS), which is on Stephen Barrett's Quackwatch list of questionable organizations." Another example is Larry Burk,* M.D., who reports, "I gave a TEDx talk, which got censored with a disclaimer by TEDx," regarding his research about women whose dreams revealed their breast cancers. Russell Targ's* TED talk about psychic abilities was banned but you can see it on YouTube. It's still rare to get psi articles published in scientific journals or to fund research. Although Brian Josephson* is a Nobel prize winner in physics, he reports that Cambridge University graduate students are steered away from him by faculty, slowing his research, despite Nikola Tesla's prediction, "The day science begins to study non-physical phenomena, it will make more progress in one decade than in all the previous centuries of its existence."

My Motivation

My interest in the topic is both a personal and academic interest in spirituality, with a Ph.D. in Religious Studies from the University of California at Santa Barbara. As a teenager, I had my pivotal "aha" experience. The chapter on Hinduism in Huston Smith's book *Religions of Man* (back in the old days when people didn't use inclusive language) explained cause and effect, karma and reincarnation. This gave me the vocabulary to understand the purpose of life as attracting experiences to grow and blossom. When I ask my workshop participants to pick one word to describe them, I often start with "curious." (My typologies are E/INFJ, Enneagram Type 1, Gemini, and first-born.)

I could best understand the notion of an unseen intelligence shaping the important events in my life as similar to physics. When an atom is missing an electron, it attracts the electron it needs to be complete. Very few major events in my life were orchestrated by my conscious mind, except my choice of undergraduate university at UC Berkeley and my first teaching job. I was guided to other milestones since I didn't know enough to ask for them, as when I ran into professors from California State University, Chico at a conference who were looking for their token woman instructor.

I never dreamed I'd switch from teaching high school history to university Religious Studies, to Women's Studies, and now to teaching clairvoyance and healing and doing individual sessions in countries ranging from Japan to Canada, as well as writing books about global youth. I learned clairvoyant techniques when I was on a sabbatical from my university and decided I wanted to focus more on spirituality. I'd experienced snatches of psychic information, seeing snapshots of men I would meet in the future and repeating to a boyfriend his thoughts or conversations, but only in anxious moments. I took classes for a year from the Chico Psychic Institute's clairvoyant program. It's useful to be able to turn on my inner vision at will rather than waiting for some emotionally charged situation to turn it on and to be able to assist others to get to their core issues. Researchers debate if psi abilities can be taught: In my experience, the answer is yes, it can be taught like most skills, as explained in my *Essential Energy Tools*.

The scientists report on how they stay centered and inspired, as well as their research findings. Meditation or prayer, exercise, being in nature and looking at challenges as opportunities for growth keep them in the flow. I wanted to know how they cope with difficult challenges and also how they enjoy life. Most would agree with what Dean Radin said, "I find it exhilarating to explore the edge of the known." Or as Christine Simmonds-Moore reported, "I've always been fascinated by mystery."

Concerned about climate change, growing economic inequality, and the increasing number of autocrats, I asked if they are optimistic or pessimistic. In thinking about the future, some scientists are pessimistic, especially about the harms caused by climate change. Civilization as we know it may not survive, warns Stephan Schwartz. We're the only self-destructive species, says William Bengston. We're in some ways devolving and creating disasters, agrees Mitchell Gibson. Capitalism is messing us up, points out Brian Josephson, and James Carpenter agrees the wealthy elite has too much power.

The optimists believe that we're seeing a global awakening of spiritual awareness, especially among young people, and that part of the transition is exposing the broken systems and injustices like racism and sexism. We're seeing an uprising of sanity, believes Larry Dossey. Some pointed to Steven Pinker, author of *The Better Angels of Our Nature,* who argues that violence and wars have decreased. Others believe we're part of a divine plan and have non-human helpers. Advances in technology will be helpful, although side effects such as job loss or too much time spent in front of screens are problematic. The bottom line is will we turn around climate warming? Does it take a pandemic? Please comment and stay current on the book webpage where this introduction is available to share.

Resources

Bibliographies about psi research:

Eben Alexander (http://ebenalexander.com/resources/reading-list)

Charles Tart (http://blog.paradigm-sys.com/links-and-resources)

Dean Radin (http://deanradin.com/evidence/evidence.htm)

David Luke (https://visionaryscientists.home.blog/2019/03/13/psi-resources-online-articles-books-compiled-by-david-luke-ph-d-for-his-course-psychology-of-exceptional-human-experience)

Trilogy webpage: https://visionaryscientists.home.blog

Characteristics of the Visionary Scientists: https://visionaryscientists.home.blog/2019/12/11/characteristics-of-the-visionary-scientists-featured-in-the-mysteries-trilogy/

This Introduction: https://visionaryscientists.home.blog/2019/11/11/what-is-reality-the-new-non-materialist-paradigm/

Interview Questions: https://visionaryscientists.home.blog/2019/11/11/interview-questions-for-visionary-scientists/

Psi Resources: Journals, Groups, Universities, Conferences, Websites: https://visionaryscientists.home.blog/2019/11/11/psi-resources-journals-groups-conferences-websites/ (A historic list of para-normal researchers is available online.[22])

Psi Research: https://visionaryscientists.home.blog/2019/12/11/psi-phenomena-research-by-visionary-scientists-in-the-myster-ies-trilogy/

Video Interviews: https://www.youtube.com/channel/UCYQz9QMYs2b1R1uAKnMzWQQ

Abbreviations

AI:	Artificial Intelligence such as robots
EFT:	Emotional Freedom Technique
EMDR:	Eye Movement Desensitization and Reprocessing
ESP:	extrasensory perception
IONS:	Institute of Noetic Sciences
Kundalini:	Sanskrit word for "coiled energy" involved in some mystical experiences
MIT:	Massachusetts Institute of Technology
NDE:	near-death experience
OBE:	out-of-body experience
PK:	psychokinesis (the ability to influence a physical system with intention)
PTSD:	post-traumatic stress disorder
QM:	quantum mechanics
QP:	quantum physics
RV:	remote viewing

RNG: random number generator computer, also called random event generator

Definitions

Entanglement: A pair of particles are bonded so that they influence each other instantaneously from a distance. Harald Walach* expanded this concept to a Generalized Entanglement model.

Panpsychism: everything material has individual consciousness, in opposition to the dualist belief that material and mind are separate, or the materialist belief in only the physical.

Parapsychology: The British referred to this as psychical research, the scientific study of the paranormal such as precognitive dreams, telepathy, mind influencing matter, etc.

Photon: a particle representing a quantum of light or other electromagnetic radiation.

Psi: A Greek letter used to refer to anomalous experiences, parapsychology and the paranormal. Dean Radin's list of psi categories is: Healing at a Distance, Mind-Matter Interaction (PK or psychokinesis), Physiological Correlations at a Distance, Precognition & Presentiment, Survival of Consciousness after Death, and Telepathy and ESP.[24]

Quantum mechanics/quantum physics: The study of subatomic particles like photons and electrons. They don't follow the same rules of physics as the visible world.

Non-locality: Action from a distance implying a universal connectivity.

Presentiment/precognition: Knowledge of a future event.

Synchronicity: Associated with Carl Jung, who defined it as, "meaningful coincidence of two or more events, where something other than the probability of chance is involved."

Endnotes

1 Thanks to physicists Fred Alan Wolf and David Kagan for correcting this section. Thank you to transcribers Manisha Hariharan, Joshua Herrera and Nicole Hobbs and of course to the courageous and kind visionary scientists.

Ten science questions and results: https://www.businessinsider.com/science-questions-quiz-public-knowledge-education-2018-5

2 Our video interview: https://www.youtube.com/watch?v=6rsmIcnmISc&t=117s

https://www.nationalgeographic.com/science/space/dark-matter/

3 Katia Moskvitch, "Troubled Times for Alternatives to Einstein's Theory of Gravity," *Quanta Magazine*, April 30, 2018.
ttps://www.quantamagazine.org/troubled-times-for-alternatives-to-einsteins-theory-of-gravity-20180430/

4 Ethan Siegel, "The Multiverse is Inevitable, And We're Living It," *Medium,* October 19, 2017.
https://medium.com/@startswithabang

5 Nessa Carey. "Junk DNA: A Journey Through the Dark Matter of the Genome" 2017. https://www.discovermagazine.com/health/our-cells-are-filled-with-junk-dna-heres-why-we-need-it
"Help Me Understand Genetics," NIH. https://ghr.nlm.nih.gov/primer/basics/

6 Stephen Hall, "Hidden Treasures in Junk DNA," *Scientific American,* October 1, 2012.
https://www.scientificamerican.com/article/hidden-treasures-in-junk-dna/

7 Reber, A. S., & Alcock, J. E. "Searching for the Impossible: Parapsychology's Elusive Quest," *American Psychologist, 2019.*
http://dx.doi.org/10.1037/amp0000486
https://skepticalinquirer.org/2019/07/why-parapsychological-claims-cannot-be-true/

8 Steve Taylor, "Scientism: When Science Becomes a Religion," *Psychology Today,* November 13, 2019.
https://www.psychologytoday.com/us/blog/out-the-darkness/201911/scientism

9 https://www.newthinkingallowed.com/Listings.htm

10 https://www.strategicaction.com.au/keirsey-temperament-sorter-questionnaire/
Journal of Contemplative Inquiry
https://stats.stackexchange.com/questions/129684/statistical-significance-of-birth-month-of-professional-boxers
https://personalitymax.com/personality-types/population-gender/

11 https://med.virginia.edu/perceptual-studies/publications/books/
"Dr. Ian Stevenson's Reincarnation Research,"

https://www.near-death.com/reincarnation/research/ian-stevenson.html

12 "Key Facts About Near-Death Experiences," International Association for Near Death Studies
https://iands.org/ndes/about-ndes/key-nde-facts21.html?start=1

13 Michael Hiltzik, "A $200-Million Donation Threatens to Tar UC Irvine's Medical School as a Haven for Quacks," *Los Angeles Times*, September 22, 2017.
https://www.latimes.com/business/hiltzik/la-fi-hiltzik-uci-samueli-20170922-story.html

14 "Ganzfeld," *Psi Encyclopedia*, https://psi-encyclopedia.spr.ac.uk/articles/ganzfeld

15 https://www.youtube.com/watch?v=aHlXRERp2pc&t=7s

16 http://traumadissociation.com/alters
https://www.quora.com/Can-someone-with-multiple-personality-disorder-develop-different-physiological-characteristics-allergies-for-example-for-different-personalities

17 Gordon Paul, "The Production of Blisters by Hypnotic Suggestion"
http://citeseerx.ist.psu.edu/viewdoc/download?doi=10.1.1.484.79&rep=rep1&type=pdf

18 Claude Swanson, "The Torsion Field and the Aura," ISSSEEM.
http://journals.sfu.ca/seemj/index.php/seemj/article/view/425/386

19 Edward Frenkel, "The Holy Grail of Quantum Physics on Your Kitchen Table," *Scientific American*, September 27, 2013.
https://www.scientificamerican.com/article/the-holy-grail-of-quantum-physics-on-your-kitchen-table-excerpt/

20 Sean Carroll. *Something Deeply Hidden*. Dutton, 2019.

21 Ibid.

22 https://psychicscience.org/researchers.aspx

23 Karl Tate, "How Quantum Entanglement Works," *Live Science*, April 8, 2013.
https://www.livescience.com/28550-how-quantum-entanglement-works-infographic.html

24 http://deanradin.com/evidence/evidence.htm

SECTION 1 HEALING WITH HANDS

William Bengston, Ph.D.
Healing with Hands and
Frequencies

Photo by Margaret Nies

Questions to Ponder

How did sociologist William Bengston get interested in healing mice with mammary cancer?

What techniques does he use? When hasn't the technique worked?

When pressed, what theory does Dr. Bengston offer about how the healing might work?

How is he measuring the recording of healing frequencies and how could it be used? What's the resonance effect?

What do each of the materialistic and non-materialist paradigms lack?

I was born a long time ago in a place far far away, in New York City, March 14, 1950. *Do you identify with being Pisces two fishes?* I was a competitive swimmer if that counts. I still hold a New York City record. I'm an ENT/FP on the MBTI.

What was there about your childhood that led you to earn a Ph.D. in sociology and to have the courage to explore hands-on healing? I've never tried to connect those two together. They are two completely different questions to me. As a kid, I never thought of getting a Ph.D. in sociology or to look into hands-on healing. I had a good upbringing, raised on the outskirts of New York City in Douglaston in La La Land in a peninsula with a wonderful childhood. *What about siblings?* They had wonderful childhoods too. We share the same parents. I have an older sister and a younger brother.

Did your parents emphasize the importance of getting good grades and going to college? I never had problems getting good grades so, that wasn't an issue to me. *Sometimes middle children don't have as much focus on them as the first and the third.* No, I have no real issues or hassles growing up. I frolicked about as a normal kid. *You didn't have any teen experiences of angst or feeling you didn't fit in?* Oh heavens, no. I was a swimmer. I was a reasonably good athlete and reasonably good at most stuff I tried.

Where did you attend university? I did it on a swimmer scholarship at Niagara University. I started in chemistry and math but it was boring because I never met an integral equation I couldn't solve. Differential equations were kind of obvious to me. I needed something a little more complex, so I switched to a more interesting area. *Your area is statistics and research?* Yes, the complexity was pretty interesting to me. Physicists have the illusion that they can explain chemistry whereas they can't. If you knew everything about physics, you wouldn't know anything about chemistry. If you knew everything about chemistry, you wouldn't know anything about biology. Similarly, if you work your way up to people, individual human studies won't lead you to understanding group behavior. That's as nutty as saying I studied frogs and I can say something about people. The first humans, unless they are born without parents and never came into contact with someone else, always group bonded and were products of group behavior.

I can tell by your questions, you don't believe in individualism. That's a good thing. Asking about siblings and upbringing is a group question. *I taught Sociology.* Even way back then, I was probably not a reductionist. Individual psychology doesn't mean anything unless you understand the group boundaries and groups from which all behavior arises. There are no isolated individuals. It would be as crazy as saying someone has an individual identity. You're different depending on who you're with: You're different at school and you're different at work. You're a different person with a mate versus a friend. Who's the real you? If you're not a reductionist and you're interested in the complexity of people, then sociology makes a lot of sense.

Did you go right on to grad school? No. I whittled a little bit and hung out. I went reasonably soon because nothing really attracted me. I didn't have any grand plans. It was a way of avoiding making anything approaching an adult decision. I would call that avoidance of reality: Reality is clearly overrated. *Where did you go to grad school?* Fordham because I was interested in crime and that's where the money and production was. *You were interested in preventing crime?* I was interested in trying to understand the phenomenon. If you're going to study something, what you're really interested in is the cause. I was more interested in what was thought to be the causes and in the changes in attitudes over time. What's of particular interest to me is how ideas come into and out of fashion. How is it, for example, that people thought the cause of crime was genetic and then, after a while, they thought it was this, that or the other? I looked for the social context in which these beliefs change as subsets of the sociology of knowledge. One of them is sociology of science. I was interested in what today would be called paradigmatic shifts in thinking. For example, if you came out of a place talking about weird stuff, under what conditions would the weird stuff be accepted and under what conditions would the weird stuff not be accepted. What's the relevance of factual information in that transition?

What's an example of differing contexts of weird stuff? You went to a weird stuff [*energy psychology*] conference. What would make the weird stuff acceptable to people or not? Is it a lack of evidence that makes it weird? What makes the paranormal normal? *You must have read Thomas Kuhn?* Even more interesting than him would be folks like Michael Polanyi and Karl Popper who take it a little bit farther. Kuhn's basic model was based off natural sciences and its transition to social sciences. It turns out that people use paradigms. It's like a buzzword now, almost like saying "quantum." You hear the word quantum all over the place although it has no meaning the way it is commonly used. If you read Kuhn's writings after the second edition of *The Structure of Scientific Revolutions* his thinking evolved. Right now "paradigm" is just a loosely held idea like people talk about quantum collapse of the wave function. There's even something called "quantum healing." I know it's bizarre, but some folks actually go for this.

Can we say that a paradigm is a worldview? What do you think is a more precise definition of a paradigm? A paradigm is a set of untestable presuppositions through which theories are derived. *Do you agree with people like Larry Dossey* that we're in a transition from a materialist paradigm to a non-materialist paradigm, a new way of viewing science?* I don't know. I organized a Society for Scientific Exploration (SSE) conference on that and Larry was one of the speakers in this scientific exploration. Our 2019 conference focused on *consilience*, which means taking divergent ideas, fields, thoughts, and knowledge and trying to bring them together. People talk of "post-materialist."' Just like "post-modern," the term has very little descriptive power. To say that something is not materialist is not to say what it is, only what it's not.

A consciousness model is a better term but the idea that it magically gives rise to stuff is not helpful. We don't know what consciousness really is. It's a belief like the Big Bang or "In the beginning was the Word." They're mysteries. Consciousness collapses the wave function? If everything is consciousness collapsing something it's not particularly scientifically useful. *And some scientists believe there are multiple universes.* Reality is always bigger than we think. Einstein thought the universe always existed without a beginning and there was only one galaxy. Now we know there are a trillion. Maybe this is one of a trillion universes and they're all doing different things. It makes your head explode. The current unexplained "miracle" is dark energy and dark matter.

Some of us in the SSE have been doing studies for 35 years on scientific anomalies and have shown that the materialist way of thinking about the world is questionable at best. So, I said let's see what we can come up with to reorganize. How do we put Humpty Dumpty back together again rather than tearing him down? What is the alternative model? Tell me what's right—that's what I'm trying to get the Society for Scientific Exploration (SSE) to move to. I don't think there's been a scientific revolution for a long time. *What were the themes?* Look at the abstracts and the videos of the talks online. I'm enamored with Imants Barušs'* idea of meaning fields.

His stuff is beautiful, worth paying attention to. He does bring consciousness into a model of how the world might work.

Consciousness comes first and then it manifests the material? I think it's too simple. If you look at the data, if you have materialism and non-materialism (or post-materialism or amaterialism or whatever you call it), sometimes the materialist models work. I don't think it's an either/or. If you take a materialist orientation and look the data, I think it's reasonable to say that it doesn't work because there are too many holes in it. To say that consciousness comes first is may be emotionally satisfying, but it's not really descriptive. If you take the two paradigms of materialism and post-materialism and look at my healing data from several hundred studies, including 18 mice studies, both approaches are relevant. I have compelling data—even to me as a skeptic, with replication in independent labs, that healing doesn't diminish with distance. How would a materialist respond to this? Confused, I would think. Non-materialists, or post-materialists, who are more amenable to non-locality, would be pleased.

I've found a resonance effect that is similar to the placebo effect. Students hid mice I didn't know about and they healed from breast cancer apparently due to resonance with all the mice in the study. We've produced the same resonant effect in cell cultures. All of these studies have a minimum dose response so that materialists would be pleased by the fact a minimum dose is required but confused about the apparent non-local resonance. As we go through data from the healing experiments, sometimes materialists are more comfortable and sometimes post-materialists are more comfortable but no camp is ever entirely comfortable. Consider this: Healing occurs in non-linear bursts. Nothing happens and then suddenly there's a change, the tumor gets bigger and bigger then suddenly disappears. The more aggressive the cancer the more quickly it's cured. The more mice in the study the faster they collectively heal; for example, 75 mice heal faster than 25 mice. Who would be comfortable with this finding? Who would have predicted it? *Could this be because there's more energy in a larger group and more aggressive cancer?* We don't know. The moral of the story is we need consilience so no current model makes these findings predictable.

Do you have any wild ideas of what would be more descriptive as an alternative to a materialist paradigm? I have a couple of ideas. We have a materialist bias. People who advocate for the primacy of consciousness still do conventional studies based on a materialist set of assumptions. I think most working scientists are a bit bipolar in that we pretend that the materialist model doesn't work but do studies as if it does and then we're not sure so we call it post-materialist. We say consciousness is primary but nobody knows what consciousness really is, so you can't use it as explanatory. We should beware of belief. I go under the working assumption that everything I believe is wrong. I'm comfortable with that because I've done so many studies, and every time I do a study I find out that I'm wrong about something. At first, you fight that and then after a while you embrace it. I can tell you there is nothing more liberating than realizing everything you think is true is wrong.

It's kind of a Zen state of mind. Yes, I'd even say the Zen people are wrong. *But doesn't quantum non-locality tell us that there is an information field that connects entangled particles so there is something that is tangible that is non-material?* Yes, photons and electrons. That's different than frogs. *But entangled particles can influence each other non-locally.* I'm perfectly fine with that and have written papers on that. *What allows that connection?* I don't think it's entanglement. I think it's resonance, but I quibble. Entanglement tends to be a one-directional process whereas resonance is fluid. I certainly accept non-locality, but there is also locality. So, that's what I mean by it's not all or one. I'm pretty sure this is here and it's not there. But could it be in resonant communication with another one someplace else? Probably, but that doesn't mean there's no locality anymore. It means that sometimes it's this and sometimes it's that. I don't think it's an all or nothing situation at all.

We do have brainwaves, material things. Material exists. On the other hand, I have a paper where I show two brains at a distance going into phase lock, as do hearts. The cross correlations we did found the connection in hundreds of places in the brain in all sorts of frequencies when the brains go into phase locking at a distance. I've done it using EEGs and fMRIs and seen the brains of the healer and healee become phase-locked with each other but not in a particular part of the brain, as it floats around the brain. But even here we can't say that this effect causes healing. Cycling has an interesting frequency in the brain, a harmonic. Of course, I accept non-locality and of course, I accept resonance between macro structures like people at a distance. That means you can probably function locally and non-locally. The latter is probably not all that connected to the conscious mind. I suspect that bodies and parts are going into resonance at distances on a regular basis.

This goes back to your question, "What is consciousness?" I'm reasonably confident that I'm at least semi-conscious part of the time, but I'm certainly not conscious about most things that I'm doing in any meaningful way. If you study biology and physiology, you're studying with your conscious mind (the little dinky part you're aware of which is not particularly strong. People have diffi-culty remembering a phone number for crying out loud). This little pea brain is trying to understand the real you. It's the real me that knows how to do many things. I already know how to reproduce the cells in my hand when I scrape some off and how to get my proteins to fold but my conscious mind doesn't know how to do these things. My conscious pea brain is on a need-to-know basis and the real me keeps a lot of secrets from my conscious mind. Which part of you is conscious?

What's necessary for the phase lock of the human brains? Is it that they set their intention? No, I have a gimmick technique that I use in heal-ing and all sorts of experiments that involves very rapid imaging. It causes a harmonic in the brain that as far as I know has never been seen before. I can put that signal into your brain just in a passing thought. If I'm going to go into a phase lock with your brain, I don't make that a big deal, not any mystical state of consciousness. It's like walking. You can't dissect your walking to satisfaction. You just walk. You can spend the rest of your life studying the physiology of walking and not be able to understand it, but you're still going to walk to work.

Which part of that is you? The one that walks or the one that studies walking? *As you said, it's not either/or.* Which one is your consciousness? *Consciousness is the one that is aware of walking.* That is the little pea brain: The one that is aware does not know how to walk. If waking and aware consciousness is primary, we're in trouble because that consciousness doesn't have a whole lot of juice connected to it. *Do you think that the unconscious is conscious in its own way?* Oh yes. *There are many communication systems of cells talking to each other discussed In your book* The Energy Cure *and in* Hands On Healing: A Training Course. *Do you spell out the visualization that you use to get into that meditative state or whatever it is?* It's not a meditative state. I'm doing it right now. You've actually never seen me not doing it.

You're thinking of an image? No, I'm just going through the images. When I came up the stairs I wasn't thinking about walking up the stairs. I'm not thinking of doing the imaging. I've practiced it a lot so it's second nature to me. Anything that you're good at becomes mindless. Mindfulness will diminish efficacy like if you pay attention to your walking, you'll trip. Just walk, which means let it go and be mindless. Healing is the same way. If you're paying attention to your healing you're missing the point. If you're going into some zoned-out state you're doing this for your own amusement, but it has nothing to do with healing. Healing happens.

Could you say something about the kind of imagery that you use to get into the healing state? I'm not in a healing state. My system has nothing to do with healing. My system has to do with extremely rapid imaging of things that you want, which are very concrete and recognizable. For a silly example, let's say I would like a thumb drive. So, my image is me holding a thumb drive. *If you're working with the mice, the imagery is the mice are healthy?* No, the imagery is I want a thumb drive: I want, I want, I want. My entire system is utterly based upon selfishness. I'm selfishly imaging those things that I want very

37

rapidly. I'm not distracted from what I'm doing now any more than when I'm walking down the street.

I'm assuming that those are enjoyable or pleasurable things. Yes, I want the things on my list. And once I get them, I've got to take them off my list. *What you're doing is putting yourself in a state of positive enjoyment?* No. *If you're thinking of Tahiti, you're not enjoying it?* No, I'm not thinking about Tahiti at all. I'm going much too fast for that. When I say rapid imaging, I'm talking very rapidly. Without practicing it, you would be unable to comprehend how fast I'm going. I just did a thousand images, I'm not just daydreaming about Tahiti. I'm perfectly here, present, and this stuff is going on in the background. When you're walking down the street, you're doing a thousand contractions of your muscles and nerves are firing and all that but you're not paying attention to it. There is nothing "positive" about what I do. You're not trying to believe the stuff. You're just doing it. I don't believe I can walk but I can walk.

Do you think what you're doing when you're healing the mice is keeping your conscious mind busy so that your unconscious can do the work? I don't know. What I actually think the most likely thing, but I can't back this up, is I'm going into a future where the mice are cured. That makes the most sense to me, but it's of no particular use because I can't demonstrate it, prove it, or test it in any real, meaningful way. *You said that healing probably happens not because of the healer but because of the need of the healee. You do visualize energy coming down the left hand through the mice out your right hand so at least in the beginning you did some kind of visualization.* I've done some sort of imagination, but there are people who don't experience that at all and they heal just as well. The sensations that you feel or don't feel are optional and they're just likely to be gimmicks. There are probably a zillion other gimmicks that'll do whatever those gimmicks can do and all gimmicks can be made better. I've had sufficient numbers of people take part in my experiments, including students and faculty. They're all non-believers so I don't know whether believers can heal, but they're all non-believers and inexperienced. We see a pretty good range between people who are sensitive and experience things to people who are insensitive bricks.

I think what we have done in healing land is we've mistaken the causal sequence of healing. I think we've looked at the sensitives who will feel things coming out their hand and they'll see glows. Are sensitives able to heal? Yes. I say this from experiment but you can take the continuum and have insensitive bricks who you ask, "You feel this?" and they say, "What?" "You put your hands around a cage, what do you feel?" "What do you mean?" They heal just as well as the people who are flopping on the floor and getting all this crazy sensitive stuff and think that is the trick to healing. It has nothing to do with healing. And then you get these other gimmicks converted to manuals on how you can heal. Can you imagine anything so crazy?

You suggested that you may not have to have a human healer. If you found the frequency that the humans are generating that healed the mice, you could replicate it and send it to the mice to heal just as well. I published a paper a few months ago in a traditional biology journal which shows we've captured healing (I don't know if it's a signal) but we have a very elaborate system. We had 38 different kinds of detectors inside of a Faraday cage while three trained people inside the cage were doing my technique on charging cotton. We collapsed that to a particular signal and then we played that recording to cancer cells through small speakers. Anomalous bursts occur in the recording at extremely low frequency—3½ to 5 hertz. Humans don't hear anything at those frequencies and the amplifier and speakers weren't designed to play at those low frequencies, but healing occurs when the recording is played. In-vitro, there were 68 significant genomic changes in 167 cancer genes examined. Certainly, the cells were able to recognize that something was going on here and they responded.

This is not subtle because the cancer cells can recognize the signal and spleens grew by 500%—these are monstrous effects from the recording. But does it result in a cure? I don't know, nor do I know how it changes the genes. If you put an RNG or a geomatic probe in the room with mice without cancer, nothing anomalous happens to the devices. But if the mice have cancer and are being treated with healing intention, a mean shifts in the bell curve x-axis. *You suggested that what happens in healing is the mouse's immune system gets triggered.* That's what we think. The preliminary data on the blood suggests an immune response, but I'm pretty conservative in what I say so I don't know for sure. It's a little premature.

In-vivo, we played the recording to cancerous mice. As in our previous hands-on studies of cancer in mice, the tumors grew and then ulcerated. The animal rights folks freaked out when they saw the ulcerations, even though I had shown them the previous results where the tumors healed and the mice lived out their normal lifespan of two years. Even though an on-site vet said they were apparently healthy despite the large tumors and ulcerations, the animal ethics folks killed the mice and shut down the experiment in Rhode Island. We're in the process of finishing our studies on the blood and the tissue samples we retrieved and this will come out in a future paper. What I can say is that something clearly happened from the recording. We couldn't take it to survival of the mice to see if we had a scalable cure. We're working on finding a more flexible lab.

When you talk about a signal is that like a brainwave? No, I don't think there is any energy in energy healing. I think there is information riding on some sort of energy system. The analogy would be a radio station. You've got a power transmitter but a power transmitter in and of itself doesn't do anything for you. You've got to put information on it. So, I get on the mic and say something. Think of it like an information packet riding a wave. I think of healing as an information packet. I think that the information packet is coming on the request of the healee. You would need a method of delivery and you need the information packet. This is better as a metaphor than it is anything of substance because the bottom line is I don't know. My recommendation would be to run from anybody who thinks they've figured out how all this crazy stuff works. *You said you don't like believers or belief systems.* They scare me. Some people actually believe their own beliefs. I approach anybody, no matter who I'm talking to, and assume they're wrong. So, everybody can relax because I am too.

Is this signal a frequency? Do you deliver it electronically? There is a frequency involved that your ears couldn't pick it up. In some of our detectors, there is no frequency at all. I don't know what's there but we had two scalar detectors and those seemed to have helped. With the scalar field detectors, if you put it on a gizmo to try to figure out what the frequency is, there's no frequency there at all. *But you can still replicate it.* Yes. *Your job is to figure out what works in the midst of all these measurements?* Yes, and the real job is to figure out what really is going on but I'm not even close to that. I have speculative ideas. *But "information" does suggest something?* Kind of, sort of, but I don't know if we're even asking the right questions.

I would think there would be a lot of interest from cancer research institutions in your work. There's interest. I've spoken at a bunch of medical schools at Oncology Departments. I've done experiments at the medical schools in those departments. There is head scratching trying to figure out what to do with it, but there is a whole gamut of response. "A priori, you're nuts" to "Wow, this is the most amazing thing I've ever seen. I don't know what to do with it." The healings happen in the medical school. You've got a choice then. Do you turn around and walk away or pay attention? Well, most people have other things that they are trying to work on too. They have lives and weird stuff like that. I wouldn't say it's been universally antagonistic.

I would say it's been equally antagonistic from the alternative healing community. They don't believe it. It's too much for the people doing alternative healing to believe what we seem to be able to produce routinely. *That you could do it without a human being?* I think they are equally close-minded. They just believe different stuff. My effect sizes are too strong. They don't believe it. *Replication is obviously the gold standard. Have other scientists replicated in their labs the same kind of outcomes with their cancer-injected mice?* I have 16 replications but I don't know of anyone who has tried to replicate it. I've certainly had requests and encouraged it. My methods aren't secret. I have some grant applications out now to see if we can do that and get it going in multiple labs.

Do people succeed in healing the mice if they don't use their cycling? If they just think, "I'd like to go out with Suzie and I'm hungry." They've tried that and the mice died. *That's profound. Is it your guess that it's some kind of information that passes to the immune system of the diseased animal?* I think in the case of cancer, yes, but I don't think everything involving healing is related to the immune system. My method seems to work on this, but there are all sorts of other illnesses it doesn't work on. I don't know of anybody who has done comparative research to see does this technique versus that technique. That's an open area for research.

Your technique may just work on compromised immune systems? No, we got way past that. Our approach seems to work best taking away things that you don't want rather than stimulating things that are missing. For example, we've had virtually no effect on Parkinson's disease where you're missing something. *Dopamine in the brain?* Yes, and on the other hand, we have tremendous success with Alzheimer's because you've got crap on the brain and the crap goes away quickly and dramatically. All forms of inflammation go away. We're very good with depression, bi-polar, cataracts, irritable bowel syndrome, cancers, any inflammation. We've fixed aorta problems that are not all immune based. *Those are not just in mice but in humans as well?* Yes, in humans, so it's interesting.

I read that for some of your embarrassed student healers, some of their mice died, but the mice they took home didn't die. That suggests there is something about the intention or the belief system of the healer. Intention is fleeting. If you're doing anything like having your hand on the cage you're intending. Acting as if you want to heal the mice is the intention. None of them were believers, but some of them felt uncomfortable doing it. The ones whose mice died were biology students treating mice in the lab who were embarrassed. They didn't believe in healing but nobody in my experiments believes in healing. I don't know for sure whether a believer can heal. I've never tested one because they scare me. *So the embarrassment was the problem for the biology students. It was a negative thing they were sending out.* I think so. Healing is boring, no matter what you're doing. I don't know if there is anything more boring than healing. *Ordinarily, you would do a session for an hour with hands on the cage?* It depends on the protocol of the experiment. Sometimes it's an hour. We've done half hour experiments and 45-minute experiments. *What did you tend to find in terms of who was most successful? Are women more successful because there is not as much ego involved?* No. *You didn't find any differences except in embarrassed people?* When they are embarrassed they are shrinking, pulling inward. That seems to retard the healing.

The way this all started for you was when you met Bennett Mayrick who healed your back when you were 21. How did you get involved meeting him and did you think it was freaky? Yes, it was extremely freaky. I met him at a pool where I was lifeguarding. I watched him and tested him and tried to make the effect go away because I didn't believe this crap, but failed trying to make it go away. Mayrick morphed into a healer and fixed my back. I could either walk away or pay attention. For better or for worse, I paid attention and tried to figure out what in heaven happened to me because I certainly didn't believe it, but I can't deny it happened. I used to have a chronic bad back and I don't have one anymore.

What got you started doing the research with the mice? Frustration at doing people. You don't learn enough from people. We did a few hundred people. You have whatever health problem they have and go hocus pocus and they don't have it anymore. With people, I couldn't know if the healing was going to happen anyway, or it was grapefruit or a multivitamin. There are too many factors in people I can't unravel. For example, we fixed gangrene, which doesn't spontaneously remit. I know that something happened, but I don't have a lot of gangrenous people to keep testing.

You and Mayrick put hands over the problem area? Yes, we just kind of winged it. We found that some things didn't work and still don't work. Some things work quickly. Malignant growths work very fast. If I was going to go test this, I would want to go with something

I've seen reliably in the real world and that's how I chose cancer as the topic to study. I wanted a model where there was no chance that it could be a coincidence. If you get a human, there are very few things that don't spontaneously remit. Gangrene is one. There are people that, no matter what cancer they have, it sometimes goes away. There are compilations of people who have spontaneous remissions [*as studied by the Institute of Noetic Sciences*]. On any individual case, you could say it was going to happen anyway. In the mice, that's not the case. *You've been working on these experiments since your 20s?* Yes, I have 35 years under my belt of doing experiments. *How did you find university labs that would let you do hands-on healing?* They usually come to me. I just wait and funding and labs come to me.

What is banana mummification? It's an interesting phenomenon discovered by the great Bernard Grad. He discovered decades ago that there was a guy who when he held stage one or stage two bananas, very green, they would bypass the normal autolytic process and turn into wood. On the mantlepiece at home, I have a 35-year-old banana. There are actually wood-boring insects inside of this banana. Grad simply discovered this phenomenon and I took it a little over the edge with a buddy of mine, a biologist living in Washington State. We've done 44 different banana mummification experiments. A lot of people can do this but the banana has to be at stage one or two. I was looking for a down and dirty model that would be an alternative to mice because it's a pain to set up an experiment with mice. We recently discovered some interesting things. Among them, you can't change a banana from a distance although you can heal a mouse from a distance. We've done mice experiments at 2,000 miles in successful healing, but you can't even be an inch away from a banana. It won't mummify. You actually need to make contact.

Do you set an intention that it mummify or do you just hold it? If you're holding a banana, you've already set the intention. *The intention could be I'm going to eat it.* I don't know if it would mummify then. *Your purpose was to see if the intent could change the chemistry of the banana?* The purpose was to see what are the parameters under which bananas will mummify. *Can you un-mummify them or it's a done deal?* I've never tried. Too bizarre for me to try. *You could take some mummified bananas on a trip and when you're hungry you can un-mummify and eat it.* In the meantime, I can use them as doorstops.

You wrote that you know how placebo studies work, which I think is really important. I think placebos are an example of non-locality. They are actually resonantly bonded groups. If you have one group taking an active drug and another group getting a placebo, if these groups bond together, the stimulus of the drug-taking group will actually stimulate a real physiological effect in the placebo group. I think that placebos are a function of group resonant bonding. I get placebo effects also in mice and cell cultures. I don't think cell cultures have a whole lot of psychological stuff going on in there. I don't think we have to suggest to them you had the little yellow pill or we have to go in there with white coats. The cells bond together and if I stimulate one group, another gets stimulated. If I bond mice together and this group gets treated, the control group also gets treated. We can also unbond them by removing mice.

Do they get bonded just by proximity? I don't know enough about the rules. *How do you bond them?* That's one of the things I'm trying to unravel. What you're really asking is how come on Monday you love your dog and on Tuesday you hate your dog? It's not the dog, it's the bond. We've all felt an attraction to and a repulsion from the same thing. That's the bond and it's a tough problem. *If you have these cells and you do this procedure to them, the cells that are in proximity will respond the same way even if they don't have that thing done to them.* Yes. *Can you do it where they are not in the same room?* I can certainly heal mice that are not in the same room. *Do they have to be near each other or have been in proximity at some point?* I don't know. They all have been. You order a hundred mice and you split them up into groups. I don't know whether the bonding is due to the consciousness of the researcher, the shared experiences of the mice, the consciousness of the mice—this is all past my pay grade at this point in time. *You could get mice that were from a different batch in one building and mice from a different batch in the other building and see if they responded.* My guess is that they wouldn't. *You could set intention that the control group responds.* We could try that too. There is a lot of stuff to do.

You say believers can retard healing. Is it because their ego gets involved, as in "I want to be a successful healer." I think all other things being equal, belief does not add to the equation. Just do the stuff. People who believe stuff have a tendency to go out of their way to try to reinforce their own beliefs: "I believe this. I have to prove this. My identity, my self-respect is tied up in this." Relax, just do stuff.

What are your current and future interests? Whether I can make a widely scalable cure for cancer, Alzheimer's, etc. We're hoping to start some Alzheimer's mouse studies and to see whether or not the experimental recordings mirror what happens when you do it live. *How do you give mice Alzheimer's? Do you put plaque in their brains?* They're bred. *Do they have it as pups or do they only get Alzheimer's as they age?* I think symptomatically, they are only going to have it as they age. There is no known cause of Alzheimer's. There's a whole bunch of diseases like that too where we just don't know.

Have you had health issues where you could apply these techniques to your own healing? Oh, sure, yes. A couple of years ago playing tennis, I shattered, stretched, and destroyed my hamstring. I was supposed to be in rehab for six months or so. I treated cotton and wrapped cotton around my leg at night, then played in a tournament five weeks later. Just a couple of weeks ago I tore my meniscus playing tennis. I just had an MRI and learned I tore some ligaments and the meniscus. I'm supposed to be on crutches but I'm walking fine. *When you treated the cotton, what did you do to it?* Just normally as you hold a piece of cotton. We teach this in the workshops. People treat cotton and we mail it around the world. *Is this explained on your CD* Hands-On Healing *so someone could get that and learn some of the basics?* Yes, I get emails from all over the world. They say they've listened to *Hands-On Healing* and did the hocus pocus and they are claiming this and that. I don't believe it of course, but they're claiming they've cured all this stuff. *You should keep track of it; It's good data.* I should, but I don't. *It's anecdotal, but it's juicy.*

Do you have lots of people asking you to heal their disease? Yes, I refer them to people I've trained in workshops. Some people learn the technique from my CD and post results on the website's community forum. *John Kruth* uses your technique with his healing group at the Rhine Center with good results.* A man with a life-threatening illness treated water, drank it, and no longer has the illness.

Let's look at research institutes. You mentioned being president SSE. I didn't even know about it until 1999 when one of my partners in healing research said, "There is this crazy group of people doing this weird stuff. You have to come and present our mice data." So I went there and found these people were all crazy. It was fun. That's where I met Larry Dossey and Jacques Benveniste and friendships were born. Now, I'm the president. It's a great group of people all around the world investigating, doing research into weird stuff. *What about the University of Virginia? They are doing consciousness after death studies.* One of the founders of the SSE was Ian Stevenson at UVA who looked into reincarnation: There is an Ian Stevenson Library now at the UVA. They're doing a lot of EEG experiments looking to see how bonding occurs at a distance. They have some data there that's really quite extraordinary that is essentially a proof that consciousness is not the brain. Bruce Greyson, in particular, started that. We have proof of flatlined people who have awareness at a distance. Their work is top of the line.

What about the Edge Science Journal? *Edge Science* is the magazine for the SSE, a magazine that does unorthodox pieces. We have a traditional peer-reviewed academic journal titled *Journal of Scientific Exploration*. There's Larry Dossey's journal *Explore* and *IANDS*.

The world situation looks bad with the autocrats around the world, climate change, and climate change deniers. Do you feel pessimistic or optimistic that we'll get through this dark period? I don't connect the two. I'm fairly optimistic that the species is an evolutionary mistake and we will likely eliminate ourselves, but I don't see that as pessimistic. We're the only self-destructive species on a grand scale. The thinking cortex doesn't fit with the amygdala. The territoriality of the reptilian brain, if you superimpose the thinking cortex on that, is self-destructive. I hate you: You hate me: We throw rocks at each other. After a while, we got nuclear weapons and it's the same emotion. The tribalism is all reptilian. I suspect that most species last for a little while and then they're gone. I think we're going to take care of ourselves. I don't see that as pessimistic. I think it's nature weeding out.

What do you do for fun as a person who has a family, does research, teaches and writes, and is president of SSE, besides tennis? I have to keep healing myself because I'm an idiot and I keep playing tennis. I think just about everything I do is fun. *Do you have kids?* Yes. *Do you have grandkids?* Yes. *Are they fun?* Sure.

How did you cope with difficult times? Cycle and you wait. *What's an example of a big challenge in your life?* People you know getting sick. *You just wait it through?* Wait. *Do you meditate besides the imagery?* No. I've tried it. I'm not very good at it. I don't do it as a regular basis. *It sounds like as an academic you've been able to keep any skeptics at your university at bay in terms of a sociologist doing this kind of work with mice.* I've had bad times there too. I've had administrators, deans, and provosts give me a hard time. They have to go through life being idiots so you feel bad for them, but that's why God invented tenure.

What do you teach besides statistics? I teach research methods. I supervise theses. *Do you find that your students are different than they were decades ago? Some critics say these are entitled, narcissistic, fragile teacups with helicopter parents.* I think that's accurate. I think the worst thing that could have happened to the generation is the invention of the iPhone. I think that may be part of the world re-setting itself and clearing it out but I think it's harmful. I see all those things you described are there, plus you have an addicted generation. If anyone wants a good business model it would be Cellphone Enders, a 12-step program that claims, "I'm powerless in the face of smartphones." There is increasing work coming out of folks like Martin Pall that indicate that the radiation from these electronics is destroying the genome. That may be one of the contributing factors to our demise. We shouldn't take ourselves so personally.

Beethoven, Michelangelo, Jesus, and Buddha are examples of creative, incredible beings so it would seem sad to lose those kinds of humans. There will be others. Nature will rebound. *Do you think there are humanoids on other solar systems on other planets?* I don't know if they're humanoid, but I would assume there is life.

Is there anything else you would like included about your work? If folks are interested, check out my website bengstonresearch.com. We've got communities all over the world playing with this stuff, folks who like to help people. My job is to save rodents but everybody else is going out and helping the uprights. I don't know why, but if you want to join in with us, we're having fun. Remember, nobody knows what they're talking about. Don't latch on to simple ideas and patterns. The more I know, the more I know I don't know.

Books

The Energy Cure: Unraveling the Mystery of Hands-On Healing, 2010
CD: *Hands On Healing: A Training Course in the Energy Cure*
Articles:https://visionaryscientists.home.blog/2019/11/18/william-
    bengstons-articles-about-healing-cancer-in-mice-etc/

Richard Hammerschlag, Ph.D.
Acupuncture as Biofield Medicine

Photo by Connie Boykan

Questions to Ponder

How did Dr. Hammerschlag get interested in studying acupuncture? What explanations does he give for how it works?

How does he define "biofield science?"

I have been graced with a Gemini "dual nature" as well as a large measure of luck, manifesting as fortunate choices and propitious timing. Born in New York City as the world was bracing for a Second World War, my younger sister and I were raised in an ample rent-controlled apartment by comfortably middle-class parents. My father was a manufacturer of lingerie, my mother a special ed teacher of grade-school children with poor eyesight. I developed a fascination for science at the High School of Music and Art (Gemini nature at play), where I continued classical flute training and experienced the great pleasure of immersion in a symphony orchestra. My senior year arrived with a major disappointment. Preparation for a career in science required my taking a physics course, which was only offered at the same time as my dreamed-of course in orchestral conducting.

College at MIT began as the Russians were beating us to the moon and my courses demanded an unappealing drinking-from-a-fire-hose style of learning and use of a slide rule that I never quite mastered. But courses in biochemistry and in Eastern wisdom traditions caught my interest and I would pursue both paths in the coming years. *Why biochemistry?* My interest was kindled by a sense of awe during a lecture on the wonderfully complex structure of Vitamin B_{12} and the research strategy that had revealed it. Also by a similar feeling of excitement from a chance reading of early pharmacological attempts to treat mental illness. I found Paul de Kruif's *A Man Against Insanity* on a used-books table in a small-town general store while purchasing supplies for a canoe trip. Add the influence of the profoundly sad death of my sister Lois from a brain tumor. What was crystallizing was a sense that research, with its focus on probing the unknown, was calling me in a way that medicine, with its emphasis on applying the known, was not. I also had inklings that brain chemistry would be the area I would explore.

What got you interested in Eastern religions? The lectures of Professor Huston Smith, the compassionate scholar of comparative religions, opened new perspectives on the nature of reality for me, which filled a spiritual need I had not found in the Reform Judaism of my upbringing. The Hindu and Buddhist cyclic rather than linear Western view of time and existence, the Taoist interconnectedness rather than separation of living things, and the Zen value of intuition as a way of knowing, were among the concepts that fit. These gleanings, plus another reality glimpsed from the required reading of Aldous Huxley's *Doors of Perception,* provided a counterbalance to the reductionist world of the biological sciences I was entering.

I was fortunate to have Professor Smith serve as my undergraduate thesis advisor as I sought to review the scientific and anthropological literature on the ritual uses of the mescaline-containing cactus in comparison with the psilocybin-containing mushroom, as well as to review the biochemistry of hallucinations. By great good luck, the project included attending a remarkable small gathering at the Manhattan home of R. Gordon Wasson, the investment banker and amateur mycologist. Wasson had recently authored a *Life* magazine cover story describing his encounters with the psilocybin mushroom culture in the mountains above Oaxaca, Mexico. I had written him requesting information germane to my thesis and he had agreed to a meeting.

What I didn't know was that Wasson had persuaded his Mixtec contacts to give him a large sample of the psilocybin mushrooms, which he had sent to Albert Hoffman, the Sandoz-based Swiss chemist, for analysis. Hoffman, in turn, had successfully isolated, synthesized and named psilocybin and had sent samples to Wasson. To my surprise, the evening of my visit was to be a test of how the effects of synthetic psilocybin would compare to Wasson's Mixtec village experience of ingesting the intact dried mushroom. Given the choice of observing or participating, I opted for direct experience, adopting the rationale of the added value it would bring to my thesis writing. That encounter with an expanded reality—my initial venture into what has come to be called the entheogenic state—has had ripple effects on how I have viewed the strengths and limitations of the Western scientific worldview.

I entered graduate school at Brandeis University during an exciting time for biochemical research. It was the immediate post-Sputnik era and, while the U.S. space program was in overdrive catch-up mode, the Kennedy administration also made it a priority to generously fund most areas of basic science research. It was a time when the genetic code (the triplet series of "bases" in the DNA that determine each amino acid of a protein) was being deciphered and the cellular mechanisms responsible for protein synthesis were being identified. I was in the young and vibrant Biochemistry Department, fortunate to have a Ph.D. advisor, Dr. Susan Leeman, who worked in the nascent field of neuroendocrinology, one of several interdisciplinary areas to come that would redefine the body as an interconnected whole instead of a collection of parts. I audited a groundbreaking course offered at nearby Harvard Medical School by the newly-created Neurobiology Department under the visionary direction of Dr. Stephen Kuffler (one of several Hungarian-born scientists who would enhance my career, my thinking, and my pride as a fourth-generation Hungarian-American). I still have several of the mimeographed hand-outs from those lectures, presented by the neuroanatomists, neurophysiologists, and neurochemists that Dr. Kuffler had recruited to his first-of-its-kind, interdisciplinary research team whose aim, by studying the "simple system" of the sea snail, Aplysia, was to understand how nerve cells regulate behavior.

Although I was learning forefront concepts of neurobiology as well as standard-fare metabolic pathways and enzyme mechanisms of biochemistry, my Ph.D. dissertation research project was floundering. My initial aim of isolating corticotropin-releasing factor, a key brain hormone known to trigger the stress response cascade, was proving elusive. Even my trip to the Swift and Co. slaughterhouse in St. Paul couldn't provide me with enough brain tissue to separate out sufficient hormone to allow determination of its chemical structure. But the mouse assay we were using to test for stress hormone activity unexpectedly (my "luck" again) revealed the likely presence of two other hormones. One was later found to modulate pain signals, the other to regulate female health, and together they formed a sufficient basis for my dissertation work. I reminded Dr. Leeman of the important lessons she taught me in how to "think physiology," in order to recognize when nature is telling you something different from what you had set out to test.

With a freshly minted Ph.D. in hand, I crossed the Atlantic to a post-doctoral position at University College, London (UCL), where my research goal was to explore whether glutamic acid, one of the common amino acids in proteins, might also have a key role as a neurotransmitter of incoming information carried by peripheral nerves to the brain. The UCL Department of Biophysics, under the leadership of Professor Bernard Katz (soon to become a Nobel laureate as well as knighted), provided a heady and collegial environment, even as my attention became divided between research and the exciting socio-political happenings of the late 1960s.

From London, I accepted an offer to join the new interdisciplinary Division of Neurosciences at the City of Hope National Medical Center (COH) in Southern California. But before heading stateside, I secured a small research grant to work in Tanzania to contribute my skills and to experience the social transitions in a part of the world where independence movements were successfully freeing countries from colonial rule. The project aimed to learn how an increasingly prevalent neurological syndrome, marked by progressive blindness, deafness, and compromised balance, might be related to long-term consumption of cassava, the dietary staple starchy root crop. After four months, two Tanzanian physicians and I had preliminary evidence that subclinical levels of cyanide from cassava alkaloids were being converted by human metabolism to the neurotoxin, thiocyanate. After four months, my grant and my bank account had run dry and it was time to head for Southern California.

The Division of Neurosciences at the COH was similar to the Harvard model in bringing together researchers from many disciplines to study the complexities of nervous system function. Rather than everyone studying the same organism, though, each lab at COH focused on a separate project: neurophysiology of arm motion, genetic basis of behavior, and biochemistry of neuronal inhibition, to name a few. As I puzzled over the role of glutamic acid in the nervous system, the frequent stimulating inter-lab discussions facilitated everyone's progress.

A few years into my project, luck again smiled at me. In setting up a system to examine how enzymes that synthesize neurotransmitters undergo intracellular transport to the nerve endings, we began—first by chance and later by design—to learn important features of the transport process itself. After experiments with many bullfrog sciatic nerves, our findings on the internal workings of normal nerves were applied to increase understanding of how the nerves in our limbs regenerate following injury.

In parallel with the 1970s growth of neuroscience research, the emergent Human Potential Movement, with retreat centers like Esalen and community-based weekend workshops, was hitting full stride. One such workshop that I attended at UCLA included an in-depth session on OBEs. Although intrigued by the phenomenon, the control freak part of me worried over the possibility of not being able to get back in. I was relieved to hear the speaker's perspective that rather than actually leaving our body, the OBE involves moving from one part of the body to another. I remembered a talk I had attended in graduate school days by Alan Watts, the counterculture guru. He railed against our cultural concept of a "me" existing inside my body. This had led him to dub the misguided way of thinking as the "chauffeur theory of existence," viewing a major function of the body as to carry "me" around—an unfortunate consequence of which is the all too prevalent sensations of individual beings feeling separate and alone. But the Watts dilemma, as well as my worry about getting locked out after an OBE, could be dissipated by the workshop's expansive idea that my body is inside of me.

Ten years into my neuroscience research career, I began learning Tai Chi Chuan, the traditional meditation-in-motion form of exercise. One morning, while practicing outside my home, I felt a sudden pain after performing a slow kick. On the second kick, the pain radiated down my leg and I had to call friends to help me back inside. Recognizing the irony that this injury—likely an acute form of sciatica—could be seen as a "revenge of the bullfrogs" whose sciatic nerves I had been studying for two decades, was, was of little comfort. In the next few days, a neurologist and an orthopedic surgeon took x-rays, independently agreed there was nothing wrong with my spine and offered prescriptions for pain meds, which I declined at least until the source of my injury was determined. Soon after, I received a call from the advanced Tai Chi student assigned to teach me the basic form, wondering why I had stopped coming to class since I had been making good progress. "OK, Mr. Western Scientist," she chided me, "it's time for acupuncture" and proposed to drive me to her acupuncturist, Master Hua-Ching Ni, recently arrived from Taiwan. I went to the appointment in part from curiosity, but mainly from a strong desire for pain relief. I had little idea of the career and life changes the experience would cause.

As I would soon learn, a large portion of sciatica cases results from a buttock's muscle spasm that produces pressure on the large nerve trunk. This pressure, in turn, triggers a radiating pain sensation that often reaches the foot. As I learned from direct experience, practitioners of traditional Chinese medicine know where to place a needle to induce relaxation of the pertinent muscles, with the greatly appreciated side effect of relieving the pain. I was also given a collection of dried herbs, with instructions for brewing and drinking, that would correct my underlying imbalance so that a future life stress would be less likely to trigger a sciatica episode.

My introduction to acupuncture in the late 1970s coincided with initial reports describing several endogenous pain suppressing molecules, collectively called endorphins. These findings, I was intrigued to learn, quickly led to studies in Beijing and Toronto, suggesting that acupuncture analgesia is mediated by the release of these opiate-like molecules. A dozen years later, researching how electrical activity traveling along the surface of nerve cells can affect the intracellular transport of proteins, I was introduced to two Chinese brothers who had recently formed an acupuncture college in Santa Monica, my home base at the time. After learning of my interest in bridging traditional Chinese medicine and Western biomedicine (and realizing to our mutual surprise that my first acupuncturist was their father), they encouraged me to create a research-based course that would help their students be better prepared to talk with patients and hopefully become better accepted by the dominant medical community. By the mid-1990s, after 25 years of basic research and having reached the position of Associate Chair of Neurosciences, I approached a career crossroads.

The field of biochemistry, with its emphasis on separating individual components from living tissue and examining their interactions in a test tube, was, for the most part, giving way to the fields of cell and molecular biology, with their new approaches of identifying and manipulating genes in intact cells. To remain competitive for research grants I would most likely need to learn an array of new techniques. Or, I could retire and accept a recently offered position at the new acupuncture college to start a research program. In retrospect, the choice seemed easier than it actually was. I was already familiar with the adrenaline rushes and the frustrations of biomedical research. I opted to trim my lab sails and head for new challenges in the largely uncharted (by me) waters of acupuncture. Nautical images are appropriate since I had learned that acupuncturists refer to the energy pathways of the body as meridians

But life at the acupuncture college was not all that I had hoped. My Academic Dean position lost its appeal once I got the hang of it. The national and local politics of moving acupuncture toward acceptance as a mainstream healthcare option were complex and I found it difficult to identify an effective niche for myself in this effort. And, my not very hidden agenda of starting a research program ran aground on the limited finances of the college. In short, I lasted three years before resigning and awarding myself a six-month sabbatical to regroup.

Two fortunate events happened during that first half of 1999. In light of my research experience in both biomedicine and acupuncture, I was asked to participate in a Seattle conference that hoped to better define the newly emergent field of Integrative Medicine. I agreed, mainly from a strong curiosity: The name Integrative Medicine sounded good, but what did it mean? While the conference didn't provide ready answers, during a lunch break I met an intriguing woman who had come with a similar question and who would become my life partner. The second event was a job offer from the Portland-based Oregon College of Oriental Medicine. Dr. Elizabeth (Liza) Goldblatt, the long-term president of the college, heard of my unemployed status and convinced her board of the value of starting a research department, with me to create it. My decision was a no-brainer. This was not only the career opportunity I had hoped for but a move to Portland would mean living in the same city as my daughter and her family, which included two very young grandchildren.

My richness of luck was further enhanced by an announcement of major research grants to two Portland-based healthcare institutions, Oregon Health and Science University (OHSU), and the Kaiser Permanente Center for Health Research (KPCHR). The grants, from the recently created NIH National Center for Complementary and Alternative Medicine (CAM), would fund collaborative research projects between OHSU or KPCHR and the Portland-area colleges of acupuncture, chiropractic, massage, and naturopathy. Of additional interest, the grants would also fund programs to train CAM practitioners for participation in research. My task of creating a research department and the administrative infrastructure to support it was certainly made easier with this federal grant support and the accompanying assistance from the research teams at both conventional medicine institutions.

The experience of cross-medical system research deepened my appreciation of the uniqueness of acupuncture's explanatory model. While chiropractic, naturopathy, and massage are based mainly on the biomedical model of bodily structure and function, traditional Chinese medicine sees and treats a different body. As Buckminster Fuller might have said, biomedicine is based mainly on nouns, recognizing distinct tissues, cells, and molecules, whereas Chinese medicine is a system of verbs, describing flow, balance, and process.

My new research environment required a quick learn of human clinical trial design and how it differed from the basic research on cell function from my prior career: What set of clinically relevant questions could be asked? What length of time would be needed to get answers? What guidelines were in place to govern research involving human subjects? The challenges were exciting as we designed clinical research that reflected clinical practice, puzzled over what might constitute sham acupuncture for "treatment" of a control group, and expanded our research protocols to test the "whole system" of Chinese medicine that a patient receives in usual care (including acupuncture, Chinese herbs, and Tuina massage using pressure and compression to remove blocks) rather than testing only acupuncture.

My immersion in acupuncture research found me of two minds with regard to Chinese medicine. Much of my attention remained on how best to design research that might reveal the benefits of acupuncture to the broad healthcare communities of providers, consumers, and insurers. But I also enjoyed keeping track of and mulling over acupuncture research findings that might not have ready explanations within the biomedical paradigm:

- Changes in endorphin levels correlate with acupuncture analgesia, but what events occur between needle insertion and endorphin release?
- Initial attempts to map the acupuncture system onto the nervous system have not produced a grand scheme. Will

emergent research on connective tissue offer a better ana-
tomical and functional substrate for acupuncture's meridians? While the meridian pathways are well known, there is
no generally accepted correspondence to connective tissue
or any other well-defined biomedical system.

- Have correlates of acupuncture action defined by brain
imaging revealed any fundamental information about how
acupuncture works? Or is the brain simply monitoring physiological changes induced by acupuncture?

My favorite conviction is that research on acupuncture will reveal
key new information about physiological regulation, perhaps even
in relation to Chinese medicine's theory on the flow of Qi. My vision
was of an explanatory model that would blend the metaphors and
the treatment modalities of healthcare, East and West.

After 10 productive years of conducting acupuncture research,
infusing a research perspective into the culture and curriculum
at the Oregon College of Oriental Medicine, helping to create a
national-level Society for Acupuncture Research, and approaching
my 70th birthday, it felt like time to retire from my second career.
But, as it soon transpired, retirement again would be not so much a
phasing out as a phasing in of new challenge. Dr. Brian Berman, a
family medicine physician and research colleague who had built an
Integrative Medicine Center at the University Of Maryland School
of Medicine, spoke with me about an exciting new project. He was
creating The Institute for Integrative Health (TIIH), with the initial
aim of catalyzing innovations in healthcare. Would I join the newly
formed Scholars program at TIIH? "Yes," was my quick response, if
my project can focus on Energy Medicine.

Two trips to Baltimore each year to share ideas with a group
of colleagues from wide-ranging parts of the healthcare spectrum
proved to be pure mind-massage. In developing my Scholars'
Project, I had found Dr. Beverly Rubik's* seminal (2002) paper
on the Biofield Hypothesis. The concept of biofield had appeal, in
Dr. Rubik's phrase, for its perspective beyond "life as chemistry."

In its guise as part physics and part biology; part conventional medicine (with its clinical applications of EEG and ECG); and part alternative/complementary medicine (with modalities of Reiki, Healing Touch, and similar biofield therapies); the biofield perspective seemed an excellent starting point for my energy medicine project. I opted to focus on defining a biofield physiology that could parallel the well-established disciplines of cell and molecular physiology. Even molecules themselves, in my schema, would be depicted as vibrating biofields rather than in the outmoded manner of sticks and balls that still appear in medical and biochemistry textbooks.

In 2012, when the biennial International Research Congress for Integrative Medicine and Health announced its call for symposia, I decided to test the waters and submitted a proposal for a session on Biofield Science. Happily, I received a positive response, but it came with the surprising proviso that I pool forces with another researcher who proposed a session on the same topic. The symposium, which was a standing-room-only success, was not only how I met my fellow-biofielder, the psychoneuroimmunology researcher, Dr. Shamini Jain,* but the interest our joint session generated led her to propose that I join her in creating a new organization, the Consciousness and Healing Initiative (CHI). As its initial effort, CHI would host a broad multidisciplinary workshop on Biofield Science and Healing that culminated in a published series of white papers and established a niche for CHI as a collaborative accelerator.

Now, fast approaching my 80th birthday, and continuing to serve as a core member of CHI, I keep up with a mere fraction of the dizzying array of advances in neurosciences. I follow with interest the intriguing developments in acupuncture research and delight in research studies on biophoton activity [see John Kruth,* Patrizio Tressoldi,* and Robert and Suzanne Mays*] and other new findings that are relevant to biofield physiology. I greatly appreciate my network of colleagues who send me links to articles on quantum-this and non-local that, which I persistently struggle to understand. The quote from the Colombian visionary, Paolo Lugari, that sits under my email signature continues to fill me with pleasure: "If you aren't dreaming, you must be asleep."

Journal Articles

Hammerschlag R, Zwickey H (2006) Evidence-based Complementary and Alternative Medicine: back to basics. *J Altern Complement Med* 12(4):349-350.

MacPherson H, Hammerschlag R, Lewith G, Schnyer R (eds). *Acupuncture Research: Strategies for Establishing an Evidence Base,* 2008. Churchill Livingstone/Elsevier, Edinburgh.

MacPherson H, Hammerschlag R, Coeytaux RR, et al. 2016. Unanticipated Insights into Biomedicine from the Study of Acupuncture. *J Altern Complement Med.* 22(2):101-7.

Stux G, Hammerschlag R (eds). *Clinical Acupuncture: Scientific Basis,* 2001. Springer, Berlin.

Hammerschlag R, Jain S, Baldwin AL, Gronowicz G, Lutgendorf SK, Oschman JL, Yount GL (2012) Biofield research: a round-table discussion of scientific and methodological issues. *J Altern Complement Med* 18(12):1081-6.

Hammerschlag R, Marx BL, Aickin M. (2014) Nontouch biofield therapy: a systematic review of human randomized controlled trials reporting use of only nonphysical contact treatment. *J Altern Complement Med* 20(12):881-92.

Hammerschlag R, et al. (2015) Biofield Physiology: A framework for an emerging discipline. *Glob Adv Health Med* 4(Suppl):35-41.

Jain S, Hammerschlag R, et al. (2015) Clinical studies of biofield therapies: Summary, methodological challenges, and recommendations. *Glob Adv Health Med* 4(Suppl):58-66

Shamini Jain, Ph.D.
Consciousness and Healing

Photo used by permission

Questions to Ponder

What's the attitude of traditional academics to study of the biofield? What's the purpose of CHI (the Consciousness and Healing Initiative)?

What healing techniques work to reduce fatigue in breast cancer survivors?

How can the effects of intention and group meditation be measured?

What evidence exists of the effect of emotions and beliefs on health outcomes?

I was born in Greenville, South Carolina, to an East Indian family. My parents were the first Indians to settle in Greenville and now there are thousands of Indian families here. My birthday is the end of January and I am an Aquarius, Virgo rising, Taurus moon. *You have that earth to balance your air.* I have no water in my chart, which is interesting because I love the water and I naturally gravitate toward the water to balance things out. *Do you have family members that have water that you attracted to balance?* My husband is a Scorpio and my daughter is a Cancer (both water), while my son is air and fire like me.

What about your family background led you to be a Ph.D. in psychology? I was always really deeply interested in consciousness and metaphysics. I was a huge reader when I was a kid and we had amazing books on our bookshelves, wild books with titles like *Easy Journey to Other Planets.* I used to read those books and tried to understand metaphysical concepts of the soul, karma, consciousness, and yoga. I was curious how these books could make the assertions that they did about how meditation and yoga affected the body. Why did alternate-nostril breathing affect the central nervous system and how did yogis know that was true? It set fire to my curiosity, although in school I realized that we didn't talk about spirituality or its intersection with health. Growing up in the 80s, people didn't know about psychoneuroimmunology—it was just beginning. That ended up being the field of study that I pursued for my Ph.D., along with clinical psychology. Being raised in the Jain East Indian spiritual tradition juxtaposed with our modern education system set me on the path because I realized there is a huge gaping hole of understanding the effects of consciousness on our healing. It wasn't even discussed.

What was it like being a pioneering Indian family in South Carolina? We were blessed because there were a lot of European immigrants at the time. My mom was at a party with a lot of immigrants, most of them European. A Russian woman came up to her and said, "You're my daughter" and my mom said, "What?" She actually lost her mom when she was seven. The Russian lady said, "I'm adopting you. You're going to be my daughter." She became my mother's godmother and we grew up with her as "Grandma." She knit us sweaters and baked the best birthday cakes. She was a mother to my mom, who came here with no family. Greenville has been very good to my family. From the beginning, everyone was super welcoming. My mom would give sari-tying lessons to people in the community. My parents have been active both within the Indian community and the community at large. My dad was president of the Rotary Club and spearheaded conferences on Peace and Conflict Resolution which involved many community members including the Rotary.

I grew up with Baptist Christians so I had an interesting time when I went to church with my friends. I heard the preacher say, "If you don't believe in Jesus as a Baptist Christian, you're going to hell." I thought, "Maybe I shouldn't come to church anymore. I don't want to upset anybody." At the same time, my friends were really interested in Jainism, which is the spiritual tradition that I grew up in. They would ask us questions, loved to try our food, ask us why we believe in certain things and why we were vegetarians. *The Jain religion is traced to Vardhamana Mahavira, The Great Hero 599-527 B.C. I visited a Jain temple in India where they took in all kinds of wounded or orphaned creatures, a sweet, humanitarian place. Have you been back and forth to India?* I have a lot of family in India so I like to go and visit when I can. We took a delegation of scientists to India in November of 2018 where we visited several ashrams in Tamil Nadu. We collected data for a project called "The Power of We." It explores the question, "How does meditation not just affect my body and brain, but also our collective fields? How does meditating in a group link our biofields?" We measured brainwaves to analyze potential brainwave coherence between people while meditating and have some provocative initial data suggesting that brainwaves can come into coherence during deep states of meditation. We're trying to follow that work up now robustly so we can publish the data in a mainstream scientific journal. We also took some measurements of possible conditioned space and we're analyzing that data now.

The Transcendental Meditation (TM) people did an experiment where they correlated the percent of people meditating in a city with a decrease in crime rate. Our study piggy-backs on that and tries to extend it by asking more questions: Does this work only for the TM *siddhi* program [*paranormal effects of meditation like levitating*]? How does that happen? If they showed over and over that when you have thousands of people who are well-trained in the siddhi program meditating, showing correlations with things like crime rate, the questions we might ask are, "How do we explain that? Do we see alterations in conditioned space? Do we wire together? Does our global well-being increase when we get together and meditate together in groups the way people do all over the world?" Maharishi had a very specific formula that he used to try to determine how many people you need to affect an outcome like crime rate, but no one's really ever tried to replicate that. There should be many more studies in this area to explore it further. [*Stephan Schwartz* describes his unsuccessful attempt to replicate the TM experiment in Los Angeles.*]

Did you have people hooked up with skin sensitivity measurements or how did you measure the effects of mediation? Muse is a great company that makes portable headsets to measure frontal EEGs with a head-band. We were able to add an EKG electrode to the Muse headset to collect that frontal part of the EEG with six people and synchronize their data. The hard part is making sure if you've got six people, collecting their EEG to look at coherence, you've got to be able to adequately timestamp everything so that you know that you're look-ing at the brainwaves happening at exactly the same point in time. We did that. Dr. David Muehsam,* who is the Consciousness and Healing Initiative's (CHI) Research and Innovation Director, fig-ured out a clever way of doing that low-cost on the ground. We were in the ashrams, not in a big fancy lab with huge EEG equipment. We had to figure out how to take the study to the field as opposed to bringing people into the lab.

What kind of meditation did you study? Were there different kinds in different ashrams? Yes, we went to one ashram, a very typical Bhakti devotional yoga type of practice. This was the ashram of someone who is an avatar, an incarnation of the main Hindu goddesses, known as Sri Shakti Narayani Amma, who is said to be an incarna-tion of three deities or goddesses. *A man?* You're probably familiar with Amma [*Mother*] who is the hugging saint with an ashram in Kerala, very well known for her amazing energy and her philan-thropy. This Amma comes from a different tradition. The temple, known as the Golden Temple in Vellore, Tamil Nadu, pays homage to the goddess Lakshmi but they revere all the goddesses. In Tamil Nadu—the land and the people—the presence of the goddesses is so strong and particularly so in this temple. We did some measure-ments with the chanting. We couldn't measure the priests who were chanting because they were moving their mouths and that would disrupt the data, so we got measurements on people who were sit-ting in the *puja* room while the chanting was going on.

We also went to the Sri Aurobindo Auroville ashram near Pondicherry. *I was there when people from around the world were building it.* Amazing place. We were lucky to be given such beautiful treat-ment by the scientists there as well. We explored the impact of the meditations. Some of our dialogues are posted on our website CHI.

is, where you'll see a button called "The Power of We," with our summary of our research in India. It includes a video with one of the teachers in Auroville, Sraddhalu Ranade, who grew up around the Mother. We had some great conversations about distant healing, physics, and the cosmology behind Sri Aurobindo's teachings. *Mirra Alfassa, the French woman, is the Mother for them? I still have in my mind the lovely picture of her feet featured in Pondicherry.* It's beautiful. The whole space of the giant temple, called the Matrimandir, at Auroville was downloaded by the Mother. If you have a chance to go and meditate there; it's amazing. Our delegates were able to experience different ways to connect with the divine and explore scientifically those conditioned spaces where a healer or contemplative person can go in and feel the difference in the energy. We wanted to see if there was a way to explore and capture that effect reliably.

How can you measure the resonance of the space? We used a device called the Sputnik, an attachment to Konstantin Karotkov's machine, the Gaseous Discharge Technique (GDV), that he pioneered several decades ago. It's gone through several iterations. The GDV is now called the Bio-Well and measures biophotonic emission from a finger. Another Russian pioneered a very simple device to measure capacitance in a room or outside. It is very sensitive to ionic fluctuations like an antenna. Is that the best measure? We don't know. These experiments are very exploratory. I haven't seen many studies of Sputnik yet.

We have several scientists in CHI, including Beverly Rubik* and Tiffany Barsotti, who use Bio-Well in their exploratory research so we thought, we'll give it a try. We explored bringing in the RNGs as well. Arnaud Delorme, a researcher at IONS, has done great work in many of these areas and is also involved in this study, where he is analyzing the EEG coherence data. We had a long discussion with him about the appropriateness of using the RNG for this. When using something like the RNG to draw any meaningful conclusions, it requires having repeatable on and off periods. But that would prove difficult in this setting where you can't direct, "Meditate for two minutes. Don't meditate for two minutes."

We wanted to go into the temple with our tools to capture the essence of what was going on without disrupting the flow. This is the way "field research" should be done. As it was, given the way things generally run with Eastern and Western world relationships, the priests were wondering how arrogant we would be and how much we would impose our thinking and designs on them. Those Indian priests were checking us out. We have only two people of color in our CHI group. However, we were a group of scientists, healers, and medical doctors who are devout in their seeking both as scientists and as professionals on their own spiritual path and they felt that. By the end, we moved from priests crossing their arms and frowning at us to them putting on the headsets and saying "Take a picture of my finger" and engaging in real dialogue. The most important part of the trip was opening those doors to collaboration. *It would be interesting to take the mice William Bengston* injected with breast cancers and keep them in the temple with a control group in a non-temple and compare their longevity.* What a beautiful idea. I think he'd be game for that.

How did you get to graduate school in California from South Carolina? I went to Columbia University for my undergraduate studies in New York. I graduated with a BS in neuroscience and behavior. In my senior year, a new major was launched and I decided to switch my major from psychology, where I was already studying cognitive neuroscience. I was working with a professor looking at event-related potentials (ERPs) in the brain, studying memory. I was always really fascinated with healing and started learning about neuroscience, but didn't want to be an MD and didn't want to do animal research. I realized that the Neuroscience and Behavior Major with a focus on cognitive neuroscience would mean that I wouldn't have to dissect animal brains. I graduated with that degree but started to think, "How do these spiritual practices, how does vibration, affect us all the way down to the physical level?"

In the early to mid-'90s scientists were wrongly saying there is no plasticity in the brain after age seven. As a senior, I was talking with my undergraduate mentor, a wonderful guy. He said, "I don't understand why people are still studying things like skin conductance and heart rate since we've got the brain." But I was thinking, "Wow, this is an interconnected system. Why is that you have to study the brain and now heart rate isn't important?" Eventually, I found my way to mentors who understood approaching healing from a systems-based level. My first mentors in the biofield space were Drs. Gary Schwartz,* and Iris Bell, at the University of Arizona (U of A), who were so supportive in so many ways. I helped write one of the research projects for the Center for Biofield Research which was awarded to Gary's lab in the early 2000s and began my graduate work at the U of A.

However, I also wanted to be a clinical psychologist, but that wasn't possible under Gary's lab at the time. They asked Gary to leave the clinical track in the psychology department because they felt some of his research was too controversial. That meant that none of his direct students could be in the clinical psychology program. I took my deferment at the UCSD and San Diego State joint-doctoral program in clinical psychology and started working with Dr. Paul Mills in psychoneuroimmunology. Paul is a dear mentor, colleague, and friend. I learned how to use those approaches to study healing, the focus of my work at UCSD; I learned so much from Paul about how to flourish in the academic setting without losing your soul.

Let's define psychoneuroimmunology. I associate it with Candace Pert's cell receptors influenced by emotions and Bruce Lipton's epigenetics indicating that gene expression is influenced by our environment. Psychoneuroimmunology studies the effects of the psyche, the spirit, the emotions, the mind on the nervous system—the neuro part—and the immune system. There is also the endocrine system so some people say "PNI" for psychoneuroimmunology, while some people say "PNIE" for psychoneuroimmunoendocrinology. It's a fancy term for understanding how our spirits, minds, and emotions affect our health and bodies, studying the interactions between these systems.

Coming into the field, it was hard to find mentors and programs that supported these questions and perspectives. I wanted to know what does consciousness have to do with healing? How can I study healing modalities like Reiki or other energy medicine? I still get emails from students all the time asking me these questions. We don't have really solid answers for them in terms of looking for opportunities in academia. I realized that the folks I did meet, who were pioneers in this field, had chips on their shoulders because they had been battered for studying what they wanted to study. I noticed that a lot of the ones who were in really high positions at universities were scared to talk about their work and didn't feel like they had community.

Just after graduating, I presented my data, funded by the National Institutes of Health and published in the journal *Cancer,* a very well-respected journal for oncologists, at the Psychoneuroimmunology Research Society meeting. I was selected as one of the more promising researchers so I gave this data blitz on my findings on healing. Later that evening, one of the leading researchers in psychoneuro-immunology, very well respected, sat me down. He said, "You've got to stop. People are not ready for what you're doing. You're going to ruin your career if you do this." I was just about to go into my post-doc at UCLA. I thought, "If my goal was to be an academic professor and be highly respected, then I get what you're saying, but my service is to the work. It's to follow a path that I feel is going to help elevate humanity and understand our purpose and our potential. Why should science not be a part of that? Why should we be afraid to ask those kinds of questions?"

That was a difficult transition point for me going to UCLA, which is was one of the best centers for psychoneuroimmunology, working for very prestigious professors. In the end, it wasn't a good fit. I stayed there for a year. My family was in San Diego so I either had to move the whole family up to UCLA, on a post-doc salary with no guarantees of future funding or think of a different option. So I just had to trust. What I have found to be really helpful in general, and definitely in times of transition, is to trust guidance—whether you call it your spirit guides, God, or your own soul. Give in to that higher purpose and know that it's not about you, your ego, your career, being famous, or making money. It's about your service and your allegiance to what you want to bring to the world. If you stay with that in a non-attached way, everything works out. [*David Muehsam* and Fred Alan Wolf* had similar experiences of surrender.*]

As it turned out, when I realized I was going to not continue my post-doc after being there for a year, they said, "You either need to move the family" because I was commuting, "or else you're not going to be able to stay here." I had two very young kids and my husband had a job in San Diego. I knew that it wasn't easy to find places and opportunities to do work in energy medicine, but I just gave up and trusted. I said, "This is clearly not the right path. So, I'm going to leave UCLA and trust that something will happen." It was hard and I cried. Two or three days later I got an offer to be a senior scientist with Samueli Institute that had funded my previous research study—completely out of the blue. Not only that, but with the Institute being based in Washington DC, they said, "We think it is useful to stay and keep your position at UCSD," because I had just enrolled for a faculty position there. "Be with your family and do your work in energy medicine and work with us remotely."

Who funds the Samueli Institute? A couple of years ago they closed the Samueli Institute, which was funded by Henry and Susan Samueli. Henry was the co-founder of Broadcom, a big company. They've done a lot of different wonderful things in integrative medicine. They donated $200 million to UC Irvine in 2017 for a giant center with integrative medicine approaches. You have some forward-thinking, smart people who understand that this is the future of medicine and understand the role of consciousness in our healing process. Part of our role is to make sure that the work we are doing is really strong and that we share and align with people like that.

Was it difficult being in grad school and having little children? Not really. I had my own funding. Most people didn't even do their own studies; they would just get a data set from their mentors running these giant studies. They would take a part of the data set, analyze it for their dissertation, and be on their way. In my case, because I was so passionate about researching energy medicine, I applied for a grant and got funding from the NIH and the Samueli Institute to conduct a study on hands-on healing for fatigue in cancer survivors. Since I had my own funding and I was still working part-time, it wasn't a problem. It took longer, but it was super rewarding.

The sleepless nights are the hardest part when the baby is waking you up every three hours. Yes, that is hard. After my kids got a bit older, everyone said, "You look younger" because I was sleeping again! I was seeing patients at the La Jolla VA Hospital when my second baby was born. I only had about three months with him before I had to go back to work in a very 9 to 5 situation. At first, he wasn't feeding with the bottle, which was really hard as I was pumping every couple of hours. I remember sitting there sleep-deprived, needing to be there for my patients and then needing to come home and be there for my kids. You definitely have to have a lot of energy and eat well.

You did find that the cancer survivors who worked with hands-on healers had better outcomes? We took breast cancer survivors who were experiencing debilitating amounts of fatigue, the number one complaint for cancer patients. A lot of survivors, even when they're done with cancer treatment, are so wiped out they can't engage in self-care activities like exercise or meditation. I went to my healing teacher Reverend Rosalyn Bruyere and said, "If you were going to work with fatigued breast cancer survivors, what would you do?" She said, "I would do chelation." It's a hands-on healing practice that is incorporated in Healing Touch and there is a very similar practice in Reiki and other methods where you simply place your hands on the body and stimulate vital energy. You work from the feet all the way up to draw out potential toxicities and to stimulate bone marrow chi. That's how Rosalyn would describe it. So, we did that in a randomized placebo-controlled trial, published in the *Journal of Cancer* in 2011.

We conducted three arms of a randomized control trial with our "sham" scientists who were skeptical of energy healing and didn't practice yoga, meditation, or healing. We trained them in the hand positions. All the sessions were in silence. I was really interested in these placebo elements and whether they could explain results. We asked patients after they received a session with a healer or mock healer to rate: How friendly did they feel their practitioner was? How connected did they feel to their practitioner? How much did they feel like this treatment was helping them? Did they feel like it was hands-on healing or touch alone by the skeptics (because both are shown to have beneficial effects)? We set up the study to keep expectations the same.

We found that those who actually received the hands-on healing by trained healers dropped to levels of fatigue that you'd expect for a regular person walking down the street within a month. With eight treatments, the results were not only statistically significant but highly clinically significant. For the actual healer group we found that their cortisol rhythms improved throughout the day. The literature reports that in fatigued breast cancer survivors; It's not just that the cortisol is too high or too low but it's the rhythm of cortisol throughout the day that gets altered. One study by Sandra Sephton and colleagues at the University of Louisville found that disruptions in cortisol rhythms in breast cancer actually predict increases in death. So it seems like an important biomarker for these women, one that we should study.

Is that because of the effects of chemo? We don't know if it's related to chemo, radiation, surgery, stress, or all of the above. But one thing we do know is that fatigue and depression in breast cancer survivors are associated with abnormal cortisol rhythms throughout the day. Normally, when you wake up, your cortisol level peaks for about 30 minutes and then tapers off throughout the day. In these women, it could be totally disregular—too flat, too high, or too low. For the survivors who got healing, their cortisol rhythms normalized. They had more variability throughout the day, which means the slopes of change were more regular. We felt like that was an important outcome in the study. I put in every placebo variable I could to try to explain away those results, including clinical variables like chemotherapy status and body mass index to see if those explained it.

They didn't. It would be great to replicate that study with hundreds of patients as we had about 80 or 90 total.

Did the patients with untrained healers have better outcomes than patients who didn't have any hands-on? Yes. Those who came twice a week every day, laid down on the table, and were touched by a caring person reported that they felt connected. Their fatigue levels dropped too, significantly. Not as much as the ones who got the actual healing but, notably, they dropped to levels what you would expect a breast cancer patient to experience right before they went into chemotherapy—significantly less than they had before.

Was there a correlation with feeling friendly and connected? Did they have better outcomes than with unfriendly "healers"? No, interestingly, both groups had the same ratings of friendliness and connection. It turned out whether you saw a real healer or a sham healer, you found them equally as friendly and connected and felt they helped with treatment. *I can't imagine that all the healers were perceived as friendly because people have different personality types.* There weren't any significant differences between the groups on friendliness and connection. We found that quality of life is a hugely important indicator in cancer. Sometimes it predicts mortality in certain kinds of cancer patients. We found that if you believed you were receiving healing, your quality of life was more likely to improve. So, whether you were seeing an actual healer or not, if you believed you were receiving healing, your quality of life would improve. That is related to the Placebo Effect but makes much more sense if you explore placebo from a consciousness-based point of view. It's a super important finding because it suggests that if you believe in the treatment you're getting, you're more likely to get a positive effect. You might ask why don't pharmaceutical studies ask patients whether they think the drugs they are taking help them or not? Maybe it would be an early indicator of whether they would help them or not.

People who are told "This is a placebo," even though they know it's a sugar pill, have better outcomes than a control group. Ted Kaptchuk and his colleagues at Harvard are doing wonderful work on placebo. They got a huge grant to study this more in-depth with a large group of patients. They've shown this placebo result for reducing fatigue, pain, and IBS. It's amazing. Placebos do not have to mean that you are duped. I think we need to re-frame placebo and I have suggested that placebo should be replaced with the term HEAL, holistic elements that activate life force.

Most of my scientific colleagues will not like the term "life force." You can say holistic elements that activate salutogenesis—the process of healing. If you think about what we're learning with placebo (we just talked about the perfect example in the open label placebo study), the old models of understanding placebo are based on a physicalist or materialist framework. It suggests that placebo is an inert substance that has no effect. But placebo is a mind-body-spirit phenomenon. So, if you approach placebo from a consciousness-based point of view, you can deliver better medicine. *What are the elements that comprise what we call placebo?* It's expectation, conditioning, ritual, meaning, your presence, and the presence of the provider in interaction with you. That is all consciousness-based. Your healing response, or what has been called the placebo response, is all based on consciousness.

Another recent study published by researchers at Stanford University looked at positive therapeutic interaction with a doctor and a patient on immune outcomes. There are so many studies about this interaction, which stems from consciousness. Presence stems from consciousness, how connected you are to your inner self, to God-consciousness, or your divine consciousness. We talk about rituals in medicine—whether a helper is wearing a white coat or whether you're seeing a Reiki healer—what is the effect of that ritual? [*See Charles Tart* on unplanned remote viewer ritual at SRI.*] You're setting the stage to open consciousness to the healing. Whether you're setting the stage to do prayer and connect with the divine or you're setting the stage to open your belief that the medicine is the active agent—this is your own consciousness. You're creating a whole ritual calming the nervous system and opening your consciousness so you can foster healing on a deeper level.

If you start with a consciousness-based framework, you start with presence and expand to therapeutic interaction. You consciously create rituals to foster healing, which is done in almost every healing tradition I know of worldwide. That's what ancient medicine practices have been doing forever and still apply to modern medicine. You deal with the aspects of conditioning, which is how does my body feel when I go to the doctor's office? How does my body feel when I lay on the massage table? That is your body-mind conditioned by past experiences. Then you get to the level of conscious expectation, which is what are my thoughts and beliefs around this medicine that I'm taking? Materialist-based viewpoints do it backward when they start with the mental and the cognitive. They start with the belief that expectation is everything and they neglect other consciousness-based aspects of placebo that are driving the effects, such as personal interactions. *Is that really at the level of medicine?* Yes, it is. *What is the substrate there?* It's the interaction of the mind, the consciousness, and the emotion, not a physical pill.

Please define consciousness for us because this is a consciousness revolution we're talking about in the new paradigm. Consciousness means different things to different people. I would say it is the source and substrate of creation. It is beyond mind, emotion, and the physical. It's what gives rise to the physical. In Eastern tradition, this is the basis of our cosmology, while in the West many argue that it's not scientific. You have all these concepts like panpsychism saying very similar things. *Some people suggest that when an electron decides to jump this way and at this time, that is a form of consciousness and free will. You can take it way down to the quantum level.* In Jain metaphysics, we talk about the nature of the soul which is considered to be pure consciousness. It is considered not even a subtle substance, but a non-physical substance.

Do you believe that the soul survives the death of the body? I'm a Jain, so I would say yes. If you ask me scientifically, I would say we need to do more studies like the studies that are being done at the Department of Perceptual Studies (DOPS) at the University of Virginia where Jim Tucker [*following Ian Stevenson*] and others are studying the possibilities of reincarnation. Not an easy thing to study, but he does provide some provocative evidence that suggests that there is something beyond the existence of the physical body after death. *They've studied over 2,500 children who remember their past lives.*

Is it too simplistic to say that the illness can be a kind of metaphor and breast cancer indicates a lack of self-nurturance? Have you found any emotional patterns? I always shy away from black and white thinking in anything. I'm not a fan of someone making blanket statements that every breast cancer patient doesn't express emotion or whatever. I know a lot of psychologists do that as with the discussion of Type D personality traits in the breast cancer patient, for example. I don't agree with that. What I've seen in my clinical practice, as well as in the research, is that there are all kinds of people and different types of stressors and ways of dealing with them. We may see certain patterns that emerge with certain populations, no doubt.

Depression is often described as anger turned inward. What happens to the body when we turn anger inward? If that's your propensity, there's likely going to be some inflammatory response. Even that is conjecture to a degree, although we know that hostility is associated with inflammation and certain symptoms of depression are related to inflammation is as well. But we can't just make blanket statements without strong evidence, or we shoot ourselves in the foot. What I encourage people to do is not try to look for blanket statements but go within your own body and notice what happens when you process emotion. I think the more that we can tune into what is happening in our own bodies when we experience sadness, depression, happiness, joy, and contentment, the more we'll know how to regulate our own health. Of course, as we start doing that more on the subtle level, we get more skilled at it.

Tell us about your first book. The book is about the biofield, about the exciting evolutions we are seeing in science that integrate non-materialist with materialist perspectives, particularly the biofield— the field of energy and information that guides our health. What does the research say? How do we understand it in a way that we can foster healing for ourselves and others? *Is it the same as the aura?* Some people would say the aura is part of the biofield, but we wouldn't say the biofield is just the aura. The truth is we're just beginning, from a scientific point of view, to understand the nature of what we call the little "b" biofield. So, you can talk about the biofield of a cell or the biofield of the earth. If you want to say the aura of the cell or the aura of the earth, you could, but what we think of as the aura isn't well understood. If you ask a Jain nun what she thinks of the aura and you ask spiritualists what they think of the aura, they may give you different answers. *But you can do Kirlian photographs of the aura.* The Gaseous Discharge Visualization Technique measures biophoton emission from the finger but how that is interpreted is a whole other question.

Is the biofield that which is acted upon in a healing process? Biofield is a fancy term that Western scientists coined at a National Institutes of Health meeting about two decades ago. It includes concepts of prana, élan vital, qi, subtle energy, and bioelectromagnetics. It includes both what we consider measurable and immeasurable right now. Maybe one day the immeasurable will become measurable and maybe it won't. All of these factors play a role in healing and involve a description of energy and information that can be felt, sensed, and understood by a healer. So, absolutely, when we study the biofield we talk about practices like Reiki, Johrei, and Healing Touch as being biofield therapies. That's the term that's in vogue these days with scientists.

You wrote about neuromodulation using electromagnetic currents like one I know—Harry Oldfield's electrocrystal machine. There are these subtle devices like the one you mentioned and the Rife machine-type of devices. There are lots of subtle energy devices and there are ones that aren't subtle, meaning that they put in a very specific frequency that can be measured. Pulse Electromagnetic Field Simulation, for example, is a popular type of bioelectromagnetic or biofield device that is said to foster healing. Some studies suggest it's useful for pain and wound healing. There are some biofield devices that include Transcranial Magnet Stimulation (TMS) because you're using electricity and magnetism to generate changes in the biofield of a person. That is supposedly going to lend itself to healing. But is TMS at all anything like Reiki? Most Reiki healers would probably say no. I don't know if we can really lump them together except to say that they are working with the body's energy field to provide a healing response.

How have you trained in the biofield therapies? You worked with Rosalyn Bruyere. I'm enrolled in the Crucible Program with her. I learned from her for many years and consider her a mentor. Before I met her, I was initiated into Reiki levels one and two. If somebody asks me what I practice when I lay my hands on a person, I don't really know what to say. It's probably more of what I've learned from Rosalyn because that seems to be what comes through. But I am often guided to work with specific mantras that I've learned when I do healing. Rosalyn's book *Wheels of Light* is about the first chakra, very in-depth, and she still teaches—I highly recommend anyone to work with her. She is a living master of healing.

When I'm doing a phone session with someone I read their chakras and we balance them. What do you think is the mechanism that allows energy work from a distance? Is it the quantum information field and non-locality or the Akashic Records? I'm not sure we have a solidly agreed-upon explanation in Western physics for how distant scanning and healing can work. If you go to our "Power of We" page, we have a video with Sraddalu Ranadde where he shares his perspective on how this works. He explains some of the cosmological frameworks from Vedic points of view that help us understand distant healing, including descriptions of the different types of subtle energy bodies, some that can travel. That could be a potential explanation based on those frameworks. I don't think a lot of people in the West understand the level of description of some of these subtle bodies that exist in the Vedic and Jain literature and in other indigenous cultures. From the Western point of view, we're still exploring and we are still excited about quantum physics, including the de Broglie-Bohm theory, which is quite different from the reigning views in quantum physics.

Why did you start the nonprofit collaborative, the Consciousness and Healing Initiative (CHI)? I came across different scientists who had trouble publishing their research in the frontier areas of medicine and biofield science. They didn't feel like they had community or the funding to move forward the work. I said, "This is crazy! This work is so important for humanity and science and medicine. We have to provide a platform and a gathering space for people to learn from each other, to support each other and the work." CHI was born from a gathering of scientists where we talked about what we knew in the field of biofield science in healing in late 2014. One of the outcomes of that meeting was a decision to start a collaborative. CHI is not an institute, it's a collaborative where we engage in collective alchemy to foster a deeper understanding of healing and its effects on humanity.

We bring together scientists, educators, healers, medical professionals, and artists to bring their wisdom to the table to help understand how healing works. We write scientific publications and we published a special issue in *Biofield Science and Healing* which was published with *Global Advances in Health and Medicine*. It's available by signing up as a free subscriber on our website to get access to 13 articles that lay out where we are with biofield science. We also do public gatherings such as a conference at the Institute of Noetic Sciences conference in 2019. We explored all of the ways we don't end here with healers and top-notch scientists like Larry Dossey,* Dean Radin,* Richard Hammerschlag,* and Bruce Lipton. *(I attended and put a few clips on my YouTube channel.)* Finally, we translate the evidence behind healing therapies to our colleagues and stakeholders in policy, education, and healthcare so that we can bring healing to more people.

What do you do for fun? My lifeblood is singing. I sing everything from Joni Mitchell to Iron Maiden and love performing. I also love to be in nature and will surf and hike with my family any chance I get. My joy is my children, goofing around with them, and my husband is definitely a huge source of fun.

Are you optimistic or pessimistic about our human future on the planet in the face of climate change and increasing inequality? It's hard not to feel depressed given the onslaught of negativity we are handed these days through the media. What makes me the most sad is the needless suffering we see from a broken healthcare system. Besides that, there are the trillions of dollars and quality of lives that are lost to completely preventable chronic diseases such as chronic pain, cancer, heart disease, and other ailments, as well as a huge mental health problem. The US has decreased in life expectancy for the third year in a row, due to suicide and opioid overdose. This has to end. It all comes down to consciousness, which is what makes our work so important. We have to come together to lead humanity to heal ourselves.

Publications

http://www.shaminijain.com/scientific-publications
http://www.shaminijain.com/new-blog

Endnotes

1   https://www.culturalindia.net/indian-religions/jainism.html
2   https://www.ncbi.nlm.nih.gov/pmc/articles/PMC4045099/
3   https://www.health.harvard.edu/blog/transcranial-magnetic-stimulation-for-depression-2018022313335
4   http://www.rosalynlbruyere.org/
5   https://plato.stanford.edu/entries/qm-bohm/
6   https://www.youtube.com/watch?v=sbKraO447dE

John G. Kruth, M.S.
PK and Healing Research at the
Rhine Research Center

Photo used by permission

Questions to Ponder

What's the origin of John Kruth's interest in healing and how has he evolved his practice over time?

What does his research with photons indicate? What characteristic is associated with a big jump in photon emission?

Why did he conclude that human emotions or intention can affect machinery?

How might Quantum Physics be useful in understanding psi phenomena?

I grew up in Pittsburgh in the '60s and '70s and made my way to college in Philadelphia in the 1980s. I am an Aries. Like most people, when I read the zodiac characteristics they seem to match me pretty well and I tend to group with other Aries—we recognize each other. *What are some of those characteristics?* One is natural leadership qualities. It seems that every job that I have, whether I like it or not, I end up in a leadership role, managing projects and people. I am also very active, always running around doing things. It seems I've been doing more things than most people around me for most of my life—that means I have to relax really hard too. *How do you relax?* I'll try to spend a lot of time alone because most of my professional life and most of my interactive social life is with many people. I recharge by spending time alone to get my thoughts together. I also relax very well when I am around friends. I am not the kind of guy to go rock climbing but I do like to spend time with people. *On the Myers-Brigg you're probably an E.* I'm ENFP.

How does your P-ness allow you to be organized, structured, do budgets and be a manager? One of the first things that you have to consider is the people you are with. That's very much related to compassion, understanding and working with them rather than ordering or using people for different processes. As the Rhine Research Center executive director, when something doesn't get done, I have to do it. I am running around and learning things because I want to be able to support the organization and keep it going. Because of that, we end up being able to succeed and get things done. I talk about the Rhine in terms of three pillars: research, education, and community.

I am asking the scientists about their birth order. My parents were Catholic and had six kids. I have an older brother and sister and three younger siblings. Four of us were born within four years and I am the oldest of them. So I am in the middle of the whole group, but I am the oldest of the youngest group. *Was your mother a stay-at-home mother who could devote her time to her six kids?* Yes, but when I was ten my mom passed away. My mom's family was a very strong Catholic and Italian family so there was a lot of support from them. I was raised by my grandmother, my aunts, my sisters, and my dad, of course.

How did her death impact you? A lot of people ask about this because I know that there are a lot of theories around trauma with young children and how these traumas can spur people to start exploring other avenues. I didn't get that feeling at all because I was raised in a family where different types of spiritual experiences and ESP phenomena happened from the time I was very young. It's just how we communicated with each other. We were always having connections and experiences and the idea of survival after death was natural to me growing up. So when my mom passed, I didn't feel like she was gone.

Did you feel her presence? I definitely spent some time with her, as did other members of the family. *What was her message and how did she convey it?* We had lots of conversations, which seemed a very normal way of communicating. Sometimes it would be dreams, but sometimes I was out doing something and would hear, "Stop, don't do that," as a warning. Because of these experiences, I follow my impulses because I trust them and feel I am being guided.

I don't associate healing with traditional Catholicism, because you're supposed to have an intermediary of the priest or Virgin Mary. In the way the church speaks you're exactly right, but in my community and family and other places where Catholicism is really strong, you'll sometimes find that there are integrations of different cultural aspects. They allow certain people to have these abilities to communicate, to heal, and to help people understand their problems. This ran in my mother's family where my mother had been trained in this, going back for generations. *So this is Italian culture?* Yes, very much in my family, although I can't speak for everyone from the same background.

My grandmother and mother did healing with people. I would sit in my grandmother's kitchen when I was a little kid eating breakfast and people would gather there. They would start talking to her in Italian and she would sit back and start thinking. Then they would say, "Thank you very much," and they'd leave. I remember turning to her and saying, "What did you just do?" She looked at me and said, "What do you think I just did?" This is how I started to learn to perceive and start to understand what was going on. It wasn't just me, it was all my siblings and family who were curious. I'd say, "I had a dream about aunt so and so who passed away, what do you think that means?" and I'd hear, here's how you can deal with this and how you speak in these situations.

Are you a healer like your mother? Yes, I grew up as a healer. In my family, it was very common that we would do healing work. My sister is remarkable, with a magic touch, but there's a number of us who do healing work. So this is where my research focus is strongest—with healing.

What did you study at university? Originally when I was at the University of Pennsylvania, I studied physics and then I quickly changed to psychology for a few years, and then I ended up studying philosophy. I went back later and studied psychology research and analysis methods with an intention to do research in parapsychology. I studied at Capella University, where I was able to convince most of my professors to let me do my research projects with parapsychology literature. I was lucky because I was able to study the research techniques and analysis methods in the context of parapsychology.

Do you mostly use intention like your grandmother or do you do hands-on healing as well? My approach to it has changed over the years, as with any healer who has done it for any period of time. At first, it was very intentional, very directed, focused, but I found through time that I was working a lot harder than I needed to. Now I allow more. Bill Bengston's* technique is completely unintentional. You set an intention but then when you're actually doing the healing, you don't even think about it anymore. *He mentally cycles his future wish list.* We have a healing group that's been meeting at the Rhine weekly for six years with the same eight people, which is a remarkable achievement. We learned the Bengston method six years ago and discuss how it's changing over time. Some of the group come from a background of Reiki, Qi Gong, Healing Touch, or religious healing. I come from a cultural healing background. Some people have no experience with healing at all, but we all learned the same technique.

We try to understand exactly what it is. The way Bill describes it is you choose goals that you want for yourself and you get very strong impressions of them. Sometimes you visualize them, sometimes you develop them into a feeling. You continue to move from one wish to another to another, going quicker and quicker, until it eventually seems like you are not doing anything at all with up to 20 items. For me, it turns into a tapestry of a life. I can experience and feel what it's like to be in that life. Once I'm there, that's when the healing happens. I don't make the healing happen; I let it happen.

Let's say Mary comes in with a gallbladder problem, but when you're doing the cycling, you're thinking about your goals. Personal things are what start the cycling but then those things completely disappear, changing into an optimal imaginary view of what life can be. Rather than think about the problem, the focus is completely goal-oriented towards where you want to be. I think this technique is one of the more advanced healing techniques that I've encountered.

Perhaps it keeps your left-brain busy so your whole brain and your unconscious can work on the issue and if you're thinking about positive goals, that sets a template for the healee to match the positive thoughts. Yes, a lot of people discuss it in terms of getting your logical thinking processes out of the way. To me, it's much more emotional, more feeling-based, because once you get the basic technique, you're not thinking about cycling anymore. *Bengston says he does it all the time, as when I was interviewing him.*

Do you have an example of a healing outcome as a result of your group meeting for six years? Defining what healing is a very important thing for me because people look at it in so many different ways. It's obvious if someone has a sprained ankle; if they get up and walk away you know there's a physical healing going on. Sometimes it's not about physical healing, such as finding a way to emotionally deal with end-of-life issues. After about six months of listening to the Bengston tapes and reading books and trying to learn the technique, we got a feeling we were doing pretty well. One of the group had suffered from sciatica problems for the past seven years, which kept getting worse. He's a dancer but it got to the point where he couldn't dance. The healing was six years ago and he hasn't had a recurrence since. So this is something that made us feel, wow, he's dancing and having no pain and it disappeared in one session. Part of my research is related to the experience of being part of a healing group and doing qualitative research. We talk to each other and learn from each other to better understand what healing really is.

Do you do long-distance healing? Yes, a woman was about to go into knee surgery because she had a mass behind her knee. We did a distance session with her the day she was to have the surgery done. They did a last examination of the knee and the mass was gone. But I'm not working with mice in controlled experiments like Bengston. *The placebo effect tells us that mind, thought, and attention are very powerful, but the medical establishment doesn't seem to understand the significance of it.* From my perspective, our group may be doing nothing but activating the placebo response. It's helping people although I may not be able to measure it.

How did you get to the Rhine Research Center? I moved to Durham in the 1980s because the Rhine was here but it took me about 20 years before I actually walked through the doors. After I went back to school and got my degree in research, I realized it's about time. I spent a lot of time learning management skills and then I worked in technology for almost 20 years. These were skills that were needed when I actually walked through the door. If I had come through earlier, I might have not developed them. I met Sally Rhine Feather, the executive director at the time, and John Palmer, who was one of the researchers. They invited me to a research team meeting and here I am 10 years later.

What are the most difficult challenges you faced in your life and how did you cope? There are always some struggles. I studied philosophy. There's not much need for street-corner philosophy these days, so I was always trying to find a way to make my way. If I stayed in a place for a period of time, I ended up moving towards leadership positions, and I haven't always been comfortable with that. I think some of the challenges I faced were how do I make the best steps? I feel like I had a good path when I got into parapsychology but it became much more challenging for a few reasons. You notice that the field tends to be an older demographic and I came into the field when I was in my late 40s. I was a new guy after I'd been working for many years. I still am, in many people's eyes, the new guy, although I've been doing this for ten years.

The Rhine carries weight in the field because it's been around for so long; people know I'm maintaining that integrity. Academic parapsychology was started here by J.B. Rhine, so trying to maintain that reputation sometimes prevents me from doing healing on my own or talking about other things. I went back to school to learn the language of science, methodology, analysis, statistics, so I can speak to people who understand those words. I can teach them about the experiences that I had growing up and the experiences people come here to talk about. I try to translate back and forth between the experiencers, helping them to understand what the scientific field says about these experiences, and also teach the scientific field that these experiences are real and we have to consider them when we're developing a worldview.

Do you find that synchronicity increases as you are more centered on your spiritual path? Synchronicity is a term that people use to mean so many different things, but what I do notice is that there are certain times in my life where it seems like things are clicking. For example, we needed to get a desk for the librarian and within a week I got a call from someone who said, "I have J.B. Rhine's old desk. Do you want it?" I thought: this is a sign. Next, I needed coasters for the desk and an acquaintance posted on Facebook, "I'm making coasters in any design." I sent her a bunch of Zener cards used to measure ESP, so now we have J.B. Rhine's desk with a bunch of Zener card coasters on it.

What about other parapsychology organizations? The Society of Psychical Research was founded in 1882 in London. J.B. Rhine brought this kind of research into a university setting and established the laboratory at Duke in 1935, which was successful for 30 years. Other research was done at Stanford, the University of Pennsylvania, and at Harvard—usually a research project. By 1965, when he was 70, J.B. reached mandatory retirement age. He knew that the Psychology Department wasn't going to support ongoing research because they changed into more biological bases of behavior and conditioning, which was very popular in the mid-'60s through the mid-'80s and continues today. J.B. pursued independent study funding and started The Foundation for Research on the Nature of Man that included the Institute for Parapsychology, which we now call The Rhine Research Center. He also published the *Journal of Parapsychology*, maintaining the highest research standards using the latest analysis techniques. Probability and statistics were just developing in the 1930s, so he was using the latest technology at that time and developed a lot of new ideas.

We also run the Rhine Education Center, an online school where we teach people the science of parapsychology (www. RhineEdu.org). We don't teach people to be psychic, but we have professional researchers who are their professors online. We offer certificate programs to teach people to become parapsychologists. It's pretty unique. Some programs have 20 different researchers talk online over a month. Some universities like the University of West Georgia [*Christine Symonds-Moore**] or the University of Arizona [*Gary Schwartz**] offer one or two courses on parapsychology but we have a complete program, everything from introductory courses to qualitative and quantitative research analysis techniques, and ways to research each of the individual phenomena that we study. It's a complete system, including history and anthropology.

How many certificates have been earned? The school started seven years ago and the certificate program started four years ago with different levels, such as the introduction to parapsychology. The more complete academic certificate requires 14 courses. We haven't had anybody get all the way through that yet but we have people making good progress towards it. The students are from all over the world, including Africa, Australia, Europe, Asia, and India. I see some of them presenting at conferences, doing research work, and it makes me feel like we're making little parapsychologists. Since this is an aging field, the more younger people we can bring in the better—one of my primary goals in this field. *A lot of the visionary scientists are in their 70s and 80s.* We need to do something about that.

How did Rhine get interested in this research? Louisa, his wife was also involved, as is their daughter Sally. In the 1920s, Sir Arthur Conan Doyle came to the United States—not to speak about Sherlock Holmes—but about the work he was doing with the Society for Psychical Research in the UK. He gave a talk in Chicago on work he was doing with spiritualists and mediums. Rhine was at the University of Chicago and so was Louisa, where they were both Ph.D. botanists. When J.B. saw Conan Doyle speak, he said to his wife, "I think that we might be able to study this in the laboratory." He was always trying to find a way to balance his spiritual view with scientific work and thought maybe this was the avenue to take.

He reached out to different people around the country who were studying this and got in touch with William McDougal at

Harvard, who was running research looking at mediums. He told him, "I'm going down to North Carolina where they're starting Duke University. They want me to be head of the Psychology Department. Maybe you can come down and teach psychology and we can talk about this more." So in 1927 J.B. and Louisa took their last $300 and drove to Durham where Louisa said, "You've brought me to a town that doesn't even have a bookstore."

J.B. started studying mediumship in the Psychology Department. He thought, before I can tell whether there is actually a spirit speaking I have to know, can people do telepathy, clairvoyance, or precognition? What are the limits of human ability? He started studying these phenomena and found that they have these abilities. It never made him say, "The spirits don't exist," but he said, "We can't demonstrate this in a laboratory until we first find out what the limits of human ability are." Fortunately or unfortunately, he never found the limits of human ability and thus was never able to make the jump to the spirit contact.

What was Louisa's role? She raised the children but wanted to do something to help the lab. J.B. told her, "We get correspondence from all over the world and I don't have time to respond. Would you be interested?" She read the reports about psi experiences so she started doing what botanists do—they classify things. She wrote a number of books based on the reports that she got in the mail. She started doing interviews with *Reader's Digest* and writing articles, drawing in people to send thousands more reports. Now we do it electronically through the website at www.rhine.org, where people can report their experiences. We have people here who maintain some research around this classifying.

Sally is the only Rhine child who went into research and worked at the lab. She got her Ph.D. in psychology and did research, published in journals. She still comes over here quite a bit at age 89. She stays in touch with people in the field and did a lot of research related to memory in the 1960s and '70s. She also did some research related to "trailing," when animals would follow their owners when they left and moved to a new location from a long distance, like a cat called Clementine who followed her humans from New York to Colorado in 1949.

Where else do you look for excellent psi research? IONS is doing really specific research with genes and Julia Mossbridge is doing excellent work. Jim Tucker is working at the University of Virginia where they've researched children who remember past lives, following up on Ian Stevenson's work. At Windbridge Research Center, Julie Beischel* and Mark Boccuzzi are doing the best work in the field regarding mediums.[1] Christine Simmonds-Moore* is doing research at the University of West Georgia. If you look worldwide, there's good research going on in Japan, Italy, India, and France has the Institut Métapsychique International, the oldest operating lab in the world. They had their 100th anniversary in 2019 and the Parapsychological Association conference was held there in the summer. Most of that research in France is related to PK.

The UK has a number of different centers at the universities where they have a funded chair, the Kessler chair, which Caroline Watt holds in the UK. Chris Roe* was president of the Parapsychological Association and his department at the University of Northampton has quite a few Ph.D. graduates. There aren't many of us around and it shows in the progression of the research. If you look at any other academic program, graduate students are required to get involved in research. We don't have that in parapsychology. I have to find volunteer researchers who are interested and then I have to work around their schedule. Graduate students are well known for doing replications that support research by reporting, "I've done this, it worked or it didn't work." It's difficult to get funding too—one of the other issues in our field.

How does the Rhine get funded? It's privately funded. Occasionally I'll have grants for research projects, but mostly we have donations, memberships, and special projects. We're a non-profit organization. There are just three of us in the office but we have quite a number of associated researchers and volunteers.

Let's talk about your research about psi phenomena starting with energy healing methods. I'm interested in how different people approach it. I mentioned Bill Bengston's method that's very different from the cultural method I learned growing up. My belief is there is an underlying commonality between all of them and I'd like to be able to find out what that is. When I look at the parapsychology literature, I see people saying they're studying Healing Touch or Reiki, but it's not defined or clear what it is. What are the common themes we hear when we talk to healers and what are common practices they use? How do they prepare, what are their belief systems, and what tends to work better than other methods? Why are some people more successful than others?

You can also research the psychology and physiology of healers. You can look at their EEGs like Ross Dunseath is doing at UVA. I have a bio-energy lab where we look for any physical activity that occurs that can be measured, whether on people or in the environment around them when they're having psi activity. The lab is a double-dark room where we measure very low levels of light with an ultraviolet light detector, including biophotons emanated from organic matter. You can take red blood cells and drop a little bit of saline on top and the cells pop to create light in that room.

Back in the 1970s, this idea of biophotons was crazy talk. But in Germany, Fritz Popp revived some research that was done in the 1920s to look at whether ultraviolet light came from organic fruits and vegetables versus things that grew non-organically. He found that there was a difference in the amount of ultraviolet light produced: Now it's part of upper-level biology courses. We try to determine whether people can actually change or affect the amount of light that is produced. We use standard engineering equipment—a photomultiplier tube—which can measure a single photon of ultraviolet light every half second. This is an extremely sensitive piece of equipment. When I have my room completely closed off and have the equipment cooled down and ready to go, I measure about three to five photons a second. When I bring a person in and sit them down in front of the machine that number jumps up to about 12 to 20 photons a second. We all glow in the ultraviolet range.

I take a baseline and then say, "Start your healing." They start their martial arts forms or their meditation and we look to see if there are variants from the baseline. With about 90% of the people we bring into this room, we see no change from baseline. With about 10% of the people, I see variations from the baseline where the photons make a big jump up to 80, four times the baseline. I'll see it jump 200 to 3,000. Some people will go into the hundreds of thousands and I even had two people go over a million photons a second. These statistics show that there's something unusual going on. It happens when there is someone in the room intentionally doing healing, martial arts, or meditation. Now you might think, why is this important?

If you talk to a physicist or chemist, they say there's potential energy or kinetic energy. People who talk about energy healing aren't talking about potential or kinetic energy, so, is it actually energy? What we are measuring is light, which is an electromagnetic energy. We use standard engineering equipment to measure the activity of healers, martial artists, and meditators who often talk about energies moving through their bodies. Perhaps we're measuring Chi or the life-force energy, the energy healers have talked about for centuries, and we may actually be finding physical measurements as a reflection of the energy that people have been calling "energy healing" for centuries.

Who are the 10% of people? It varies. There are some people who are extremely successful healers, have long clientele lists and have been helping people for many years, and I get nothing from them. I've had other people go in there and I tell them don't do anything yet and I start seeing this big jump. *Do you see anything that differentiates them from the 90%?* What I find is that the ones who are more focused, more intentional, tend to be where I see the strong effects in my laboratory. *Are there any gender differences in the 10%?* I haven't done an analysis for gender-related to this because it really did not seem significant. *There are no more healers than meditators or martial artists in the 10%?* When I came to Durham, I was very surprised because there are more healers in this area than any place I've ever lived so I have no problem finding healers to go into the lab. I haven't found that there is a specific technique that works better or produces a better effect than others. With Healing Touch we didn't really see a strong effect. When I work with martial artists, they have different patterns than the healers.

I've watched these little squiggly lines for so long, counting photons over for hours at a time I can almost recognize certain people from their patterns. Martial artists have a very different bioenergy signature than the people who are doing healing work, and with meditators, again it varies significantly. With mediums who say they're having contact experience, I often see biophotons in the room. What I can say definitively is that when people focus their attention, they tend to produce more light than when not focusing. I can tell you a lot of other stories but scientifically that's the limit.

When I first came to into parapsychology, I was least interested in psychokinesis or mind-matter interaction. I was sitting in the library having a research meeting when a woman came in doing PK in front of the room filled with scientists. She had a wheel inside of a sealed jar, so it was not affected by wind or air currents around it. She started spinning the wheel inside of the sealed jar. Whenever I asked her to stop, she stopped it, and when I asked her to make it turn the other way she did and reversed the direction again. I was fascinating but I still wasn't very interested in studying PK.

A few months later, I got a call from a medical doctor saying he had a patient who came to him because his family wanted a doctor to examine the boy because of his effects on their electronic equipment. When he walked by, the phones would ring and he couldn't use cell phones because he would break them. They wouldn't let him near the computer and he was having trouble at school. I met with the family at the doctor's office so I could see what their intentions were. My impression after we talked for a few minutes was that they were legit and not trying to get attention or be on TV; they were afraid. It was getting expensive because their 11-year-old boy was breaking things and they wanted this to go away. I spoke to Cherylee Black, who was doing PK with Psi Wheels and Jim

Carpenter,* who had done some work with Tina Resch a number of years ago, who was a very well known poltergeist agent. Tina had effects on objects and there were many examples of them moving near her when she was a teenager. I took another researcher who does poltergeist research, Bill Joines, to visit the boy's house.

When we went to the house, we saw smoke alarms going off, kitchen appliances heating up when they were not turned on, a number of electrical effects on the computer systems in the house that I could measure, based on my technology background. This was poltergeist activity, unconscious psychokinetic effects. Typically this happens in times of stress and anxiety, and adolescence tends to exacerbate that with all the hormonal changes. I taught him some techniques for relaxation, meditation, and mindfulness and the problem went away within a week

I saw unconscious electronic interference going on, so I wondered about my bio energy lab. Could there be electronic interference going on in the lab that was affecting the equipment? I had worked in technology for about 20 years. I did some experiments and found that when certain people were in the lab, I got effects, whether I was measuring light or not. I saw effects on the instruments that weren't due to light. Unconscious effects on electronics, similar to what I was seeing in the lab, have been called the Wolfgang Pauli Effect where some people have effects on electronics just by entering a room. In some cases, electronics break, but in others, everything seems to work better. I wondered if there was a way to test this in the laboratory.

I designed a study where I had a network that was running constantly in the background between two computers and I changed it so that I could tell how many errors were happening in a transition of data across the two computers. Then I brought people in and asked them to do some tasks on another computer without knowing the network was there. I asked them to perform little tasks, like computer games. I said to half the group you have 20 minutes; do them all and I'll give you a prize. I was trying to see how many errors would occur in the network if they developed some sort of anxiety.

Perhaps it would affect the network with unintentional effects. With half of the people, I had them do the exact same tasks, except I programmed errors into the system. As they typed, wrong letters would come up and they moved the mouse and it would snap back, etc. I applied what I studied in software development to make them more anxious. I found that the people who rated themselves more anxious got more errors in the system, even though they didn't know it was running. Your anxiety can actually affect the electronic system. As I said, I wasn't interested in PK at all, but it kept walking through my door so I followed it where it leads me to explore the mechanism behind PK.

Do you talk with Roger Nelson* about the PEAR lab at Princeton with its RNG studies? Yes, that's where they studied effects on electronics or micro PK. I have one of their RNGs (PEAR called them REGs, event generators) that we work with here but while PEAR was measuring intentional, purposeful changes, I'm measuring emotional changes to see if I can detect and determine if there's a way to help to reduce its negative effects. Many people who had NDEs are not able to wear wristwatches, they blow out light bulbs, and have effects on electronic equipment. How can we reduce this for them because it is a real problem in their lives?

The Global Consciousness Project's RNGs found that global focus, such as during New Year's celebrations, gets a more coherent outcome from the RNGs. I've spoken to Roger Nelson quite a bit about it because it's similar to what I'm studying. RNGs are quantum-based systems and the photomultiplier tube also uses very small variations as quantum processes occur in the photomultiplier tube where I'm measuring light. But with the computer system, watches, smoke alarms, and kitchen appliances, that's straight-up electricity, so there may be something different between these two effects.

Nelson said that athletic events, like world soccer matches, don't have coherence because conflicting views, like I want Argentina and you want Brazil; rather, the coherent effect happens when people are unified. In a genius study, a researcher from Japan got funding from one of the top foundations in parapsychology to study whether he would be able to see effects on his RNG when his team won, versus when they lost. He managed to go to every single home game for his team with grant money. He didn't get any results, but he got to go to every game. So I agree, if you have people pulling for one team, versus those pulling for the other, you're not going to get coherence.

If you were pressed to speculate on what causes this kind of PK activity, what would you say it is? It seems from the subsequent experiment I did with computers that aggravation and anxiety tended to produce more errors in electronic systems. Joy or ecstasy may have the same effect but I haven't studied that one yet. It's easier to make people upset than it is to make them really happy. *Do you have any guesses as to what the physical mechanism is that allows my anxiety to mess up the computer?* This is where I look to see if I can measure light when people are performing PK activities in the bioenergy lab. I've seen this unintentionally, when people are doing healing or when they're doing martial arts they produce light. This effect also occurs in the equipment when people are doing certain types of healing. So I don't know if it is the same thing. We need to take this phenomenon that most people around the world don't really believe exists, although we have repeatedly measured it in different situations. It could be that biophotons that are having some sort of effect because it seems to happen from a distance, as well as close up.

What's macro and micro PK? Macro PK is when you're seeing larger objects move. Micro PK is affecting electronic systems when you can't really see where the effect is coming from. If I have some dice in front of me and make them float up in the air and come down and make a seven, that's macro PK, because I can see it. If I roll the dice and it comes out seven more than it should, that's not quite macro because I can see the result but there are little forces that are going on that are causing that result. Then there are other things that you can't see at all, you can only measure them statistically, like Nelson's work with the RNGs.

Some of the stories that Rhine collected relate to a mother who would be washing the dishes at home and get a feeling that she had to go out immediately and get her child from her yard. A few minutes later a car crashed into the yard. A parent had a dream about a baby crib being crushed by a chandelier so she picked up the baby and a few minutes later the chandelier crashed to the ground in the baby's room. What type of psychology is involved that causes people to get these experiences? The latter is a dream situation, a non-conscious manifestation. In the former, the mother is washing the dishes; the information seems to come through during a routine activity or dissociation, unfocused attention. We might look at to see what's more likely to evoke ESP activity, than not.

Have you found that people can be taught to develop their ESP, clairvoyance, healing, precognition—those kinds of psi abilities? I have some people who come into our lab, especially in the bioenergy lab, and once they learn what we were looking for, they are able to give me more of what I was looking for. They are able to change their behaviors or change their mindset to produce changes, so they are definitely learning. *So there is biofeedback?* Yes, many people I know in the field will tell me that they've been studying this long enough to learn enough to do a little bit of it. People will say, "I'm not a super psychic like Joseph McMonagle, who could RV what's going on over in Russia, but I am able to know a little bit more about what someone's thinking next to me." I think it has to do a lot with learning to trust your instincts and your perceptions so you start to notice them more.

Some people say that the brain filters out a lot of the unconscious information to keep us from being overwhelmed and allow us to move forward in life. We have to unlearn some of that filtering to develop intuition. Some people say that about the fact that psi abilities were much more needed in the past when we were living in situations where danger was more around us. Now we control so much of our environment, it's easy for us to forget that there was a time where tigers could jump out and eat you and the person who had any inkling that that was about to occur had an advantage. *And their genes would be passed on.* I tend not to adhere to that philosophy because I believe that people who follow their instincts and intuitions tend to be more successful in other ways as well. I believe that it is still very present in our culture. It wasn't so long ago and I think that it will continue to exist and develop.

So the question is, why do some people recognize it more than others? Jim Carpenter's* First Sight theory maintains that we use it all the time as part of our normal psychological decision-making process. Rex Stanford's PMIR, Psi-Mediated Instrumental Response[8] theory postulates that every decision we make is mediated or informed by psi information that we get from things that are around us. Some people tend to be more able to know when they are using it and be more conscious about it because they are not blocking themselves from knowing. They are allowing themselves to have access to this information. These people typically are more sensitive and more aware of things in their lives related to people's feelings, emotions, processes that are going on around them. Psi is one of those things that they tend to be aware of.

You've also done some work with some RVers. I know quite a few remote viewers, quite a few people who are in the Star Gate program, including Paul Smith* and Joe McMonagle. We have physicists trying to make money for research so we organized an Associative Remote Viewing project here [*created by Stephan Schwartz**]. We ended up not making money because we had issues with the investment process, not with the actual RV process. It brought us to a new understanding and I presented a paper about it last year. There's no real standard on how to judge accuracy. The viewer might be doing very well but if the judge gets it wrong, we've lost the whole session. We need to refine how the judges determine if it's a hit or not, what's an appropriate target for a viewer, what's likely to be viewed appropriately. *Charles Tart* had a really interesting point, that you could RV people's emotional and mental problems to find the origins to see what will help them feel better.* Charlie is an extremely intuitive person.

When you try to study ESP, you can say I'm studying telepathy but if you really look at it, you can't determine if it's telepathy or precognition or clairvoyance, so we just call it General ESP. When I'm talking about general ESP protocols, I'm talking about the Ganzfeld.

I have a group of young researchers that I'm mentoring right now. I gave them a choice of different projects to work on and they picked trying to integrate Ganzfeld protocol with RV research work that's been done since the 1990s, which haven't been brought together yet. *How are they doing that?* Designing the Ganzfeld process that doesn't have a sender but allows it to be RVed from a distance. They're considering RV techniques including knowledge about selecting targets, judging protocols, and displacement, and trying to integrate that into the Ganzfeld protocol. They are redesigning the Ganzfeld to try to make it easier to use and more likely to be successful, based on everything we've learned in parapsychology over the years.

In the Ganzfeld, I'm in a quiet room, I have halved ping pong balls over my eyes, I'm listening to white noise, I'm receptive. I'm getting images and then we see if that is close to the target that the computer selects. That's pretty close. *What does RVing have to do with that?* When you're dealing either with Ganzfeld or RV, you're asking, can a person perceive information that is not available to them through their physical senses? In both cases, if you're doing a scientific study, you have a selection of targets. In RV, sometimes it's somebody going to a location but typically it's a picture inside an envelope or an object that might be in another room. But research in the Ganzfeld demonstrated very clearly those are horrible targets. Videos are much better targets because they are active, there's motion, and our minds tend to respond to video targets as a much better targeting system. You have to combine the knowledge of RV and technology with Ganzfeld and bring them together to make a single protocol. This hasn't been done before so it was very creative for this group to decide to take that path.

We have a transcript of everything the viewer said and we have the target, then an independent judge makes the decision about whether it was a hit or miss. The judge sees decoys but the viewer never sees them. There is a lot of basic foundational work within this field that has never been done because there aren't enough researchers to do it. It's more interesting if you're developing a new process to demonstrate ESP or figure out how it works. *Are you going to write a book about these Rhine experiments?* I've written some papers and I've got some ideas for a book, but I need to do the research first. I have to get some studies under my belt before I can pull things together.

Quantum physics makes it tempting to say psi works like entangled particles affect each other non-locally, but physicists say you can't use quantum physics, we don't know enough about it. What's your view? Ed May would say no, it's not real, it doesn't happen that way, but there are two phenomena in quantum physics that I tend to focus on. One is the observer effect and the idea that the wave-particle duality depends on whether you are looking at a particle or not. It's very clear that the act of observation or the intention to observe the world, has an effect on how the world behaves; that underlies all of our research in parapsychology and all scientific research. Entanglement is a demonstration of non-locality but we cannot even begin to conceive of a signal that would enable this instantaneous correlation between these events to happen. Does that mean that entanglement is the mechanism that's being used? I won't go that far.

As human beings, if we find something that we don't understand and we find something else that we don't understand, we tend to think that maybe they're similar. So this is why people who don't really understand what we study in parapsychology, often include Bigfoot, aliens, and crop circles, because they do not understand any of it. They say this must all be the same thing, you should study all of it, but they are very different things. There could be a connection between entanglement and psi but it's not demonstrated yet.

One of the points of this trilogy is that people like you are creating a new paradigm for science (actually it's very old and Eastern) to include mind and consciousness. Do you think a new paradigm is being created that includes the observer effect? I think that there are some sciences that are starting to recognize that the ground they are standing on is less firm than they thought it was in the past, and they are starting to recognize that they have to look in other directions to find answers. Consciousness seems to be integrated into our experience in some sort of way and so people are exploring it in more detail. Parapsychology and the phenomena we study is just one example of that. As soon as people started looking at the existing literature, they will see how solid it is and how it really does demonstrate psi phenomena. We still haven't gotten over the hump of how it happens.

What's encouraging to me is that Harvard is doing a placebo research project, because I think that this kind of project will lead in those directions. I know that Bill Bengston has been doing work with placebo as well, so there are a number of people who are looking at placebo. *The amazing thing to me about placebo is even though someone knows that it's just a sugar pill, if you say this has helped other people in the past they get better. What I don't understand is why there is so much resistance and so little research. People feel very comfortable saying psi phenomena does not exist without bothering to read the double-blind and triple-blind studies. Do you have any explanation as to why academics shy away from it so much?* Some academics at Duke University support us, come occasionally to our research meetings and have discussions with us, but they won't join our organization and we can't talk about them because it would ruin their academic careers.

Yet one of the longest-term professors at Duke University, Bill Joines in the Engineering Department, has studied parapsychology since the '70s and he's doing research with me now on the biophoton lab. Bill has also written engineering textbooks on light and still teaches. Many people, not just scientists or academics, subscribe to the materialistic world view because that is just how we have been raised. In a reductionist point of view, you will eventually get down to the smallest particle, and we'll be able to describe these larger phenomena that are going on. If you believe this you are believing that there is a deterministic aspect to the world. If there is no choice, if the laws are set and we build bridges, planes, and rocket ships because of engineers. When we really look at it, there is uncertainty everywhere. Expectations have such a larger effect on things. It's hard for people to accept that because the worldview doesn't accommodate it and they would really have to change their perspective on how the world works.

People are concerned about climate change, increasing economic inequality, and the rise of autocrats. As a scientist, are you optimistic or pessimistic about our survival as a species? I believe in existence beyond the physical, and so the end of a physical reality is just a change. I'm a parapsychologist so obviously, I'm an optimist. If I think that I can actually make a living and succeed in science and pushing the edges of reality, I have to be optimistic. Anybody who is a part of this field has to have a sense of optimism and continuing to go further. The planet will survive but are humans going to be able to have the same sort of society that we have now? I definitely believe that we need to advocate for policy changes to try and live a sustainable life in a cooperative way with every living being on the planet.

It would be tempting to be in the lab 24/7. What do you do for fun? You mentioned getting together with friends, anything else to stay balanced? Rhine has really absorbed a lot of my energy, especially since I started the Rhine Education Center. I definitely have fun with the people I see here.

Selected Publications

(2019). Effects of mood and emotion on a real-world working computer system and network environment. *Journal of Parapsychology.* 83(2). pp. 233-247.

(2018). An exploration of the effects of mood and emotion on a real-world working computer system and network environment. *Proceedings of the Parapsychological Association Conference, 2018.* Petaluma, CA.

(2018). Associative remote viewing for profit: Evaluating the importance of the judge and investment instrument. *Proceedings of the Conference for the Society for Scientific Exploration and the International Remote Viewing Association – 2018.* Las Vegas, NV.

& Joines, W.T. (2016). Taming the ghost within: An approach toward addressing apparent electronic poltergeist activity. *Journal of Parapsychology.* 80(1). pp. 70-86.

(2016). Developing an experimental methodology for apparent exceptional PK participants. *Proceedings of the Parapsychological Association Conference - 2016.* Concord, CA.

Tressoldi, P.E., Pederzoli, L., Ferrini, A., Mateoli, M., Melloni, S., Prati, E., & Kruth, J.G. (2016). Can Our Minds Emit Light at Distance? A Pre-registered Confirmatory Experiment of Mental Entanglement with a Photomultiplier. *NeuroQuantology*, 14(3), pp. 447-455, DOI: 10.14704/nq.2016.14.3.906

(2015). Five qualitative research approaches and their applications in parapsychology. *Journal of Parapsychology*. 79(2). pp. 219-233.

Tressoldi, P. E., Pederzoli, L. Ferrini, A., Matteoli, M., Melloni, S., and Kruth, J.G. (2015) Can our Mind Emit Light? Mental Entanglement at Distance with a Photomultiplier. Available at *SSRN*: https://ssrn.com/abstract=2625527 or http://dx.doi.org/10.2139/ssrn.2625527

Tressoldi, P. E., Pederzoli, L., Caini, P., Ferrini, A., Melloni, S., Richeldi, D., Richeldi, F., Kruth, J.G., (2014) Mental Interaction at Distance on a Photomultiplier: A Pilot Study. Available at *SSRN*: https://ssrn.com/abstract=2506135 or http://dx.doi.org/10.2139/ssrn.2506135

Joines, W.T., Baumann, S., & Kruth, J.G. (2012). Electromagnetic emissions from humans during focused intent. *Journal of Parapsychology*. 76(2). pp. 275-294.

Endnotes

1 http://www.windbridge.org/about-us/
2 An experimental concept developed by parapsychologist Rex G. Stanford

Judith Swack, Ph.D.
Healing from the Body Level Up™: Where Science and Miracles Meet

Photo by Diane Hughes

Questions to Ponder

What is the foundational belief of Dr. Swack's Healing From the Body Level Up™ method?

What does she mean by "conscious mind chauvinism?"

How does she clear unconscious beliefs or "code"? Which of her 52 techniques appeal to you?

How does she use muscle testing?

I'm a Baby Boomer, born in Ohio and a Cancer. *Do you identify with your sun sign?* No, I really haven't studied astrology. I've studied the Enneagram personality system. My siblings are also high achievers and we're all Enneagram Type Eight. We had an Enneagram Six mother; the high side of Six is helping people reach their full potential. She was an educator so she made sure that we had everything we needed to achieve our full potential in whatever direction we wanted to go in life. All three of us are at the top of our fields.

I grew up in Cleveland and went to Oberlin College where I was pre-med and got my Bachelor's in Biology in 1973. Then I went to Case Western Reserve and got a Master's degree in Biochemical Research. I was tired of Cleveland and decided to get out to the bigger world, so I moved to Washington D.C. and got my Ph.D. in Biochemistry at the National Cancer Institute as an external student from George Washington University. My research was on DNA replication. I fell in love with immunology when I was getting my Master's degree and wanted to become an immunologist, so for my postdoctoral training, I went to the Dana Farber Cancer Institute in Boston and then to the New England Medical Center.

What was there about your family background that led you to become a Ph.D. biochemist? I had allergies when I was a kid. My cousin was an endocrinologist, so I walked up the street to his office every week to get allergy shots. His wife was his lab technician, so she'd show me slides of blood smears with bacteria and white cells and red cells, etc. I thought it was fascinating and science was my favorite class. I decided that I was going to be a doctor like my cousin. Also, when you're a healer, people can feel it, so I would be 13 years old on the bus going to my flute lesson and somebody would sit down beside me and invariably initiate a conversation about trauma. I've always had psychic abilities, my mom had psychic abilities, and my dad admitted he had psychic abilities, too, so we didn't really think anything of it.

What was your family's spiritual or religious orientation when you were growing up? We're Reform Jews. Social Justice is a big thing. I remember being a little kid in a stroller and going on Ban the Bomb marches. My parents are politically active and they're lightworkers. My mother was a social worker and the director of Social Work continuing education. It was her job to bring in innovative methods and stretch the boundaries of social work—she was always at the cutting edge in her field. My father did Community Development and did Parks and Recreation Development to make parks more available to people. *Why do a much larger percentage of the 65 visionary scientists have Reform Jewish background than the average percentage of Jews in the American or British population?* I think this may be due to the Jewish values of social justice and improving the world.

I was 30 years old working on my Ph.D. and I was a successful, bright, upcoming scientist but my love life was a disaster. I kept attracting the same emotionally unavailable man in different bodies and kept getting disappointed, but I couldn't understand why my love life was so dreadful. I'm a very smart woman, but I couldn't figure out how to fix that. Fortunately, one of the men I was dating suggested that I take a self-help workshop called Actualizations, which is similar to EST and LifeSpring. There I was introduced to the unconscious mind and realized, "That's the answer. It has nothing to do with my conscious intelligence because it has to do with my unconscious mind."

I didn't recognize I had an unconscious mind because I was unconscious of it. I realized that I needed to heal my unconscious mind if I were to get the results that I wanted in my life. I asked the workshop leaders, "How do you know how to do what you do?" They were trained in Neuro-Linguistic Programming (NLP), so I trained in NLP. I took a two-semester practitioner course and loved it. I found a therapist who was trained in NLP and we started cleaning the crap out of my unconscious mind and life got better. I had a really nice boyfriend for many years and was doing well at work, etc.

In the second semester of the training, two of my classmates approached me and said, "We would like to work with you privately, Judith." I replied, "I'm a bench scientist. I work in a lab; I wear a lab coat and work with enzymes. Anything larger than an enzyme is too big for me to comprehend." The woman folded her arms and said, "No, I want to work with you." I looked at her perplexed and said, "But I don't even have an office," trying to comprehend wearing street clothes and having an office. She replied, "I'm a social worker and you can use my office in the evenings. It's five minutes from your apartment. Furthermore, my husband, who is a chiropractor, wants to work with you too." My male classmate then told me, "Not only do I want to work with you, but my teenage son would like to work with you." So, in fifteen minutes, I was handed four clients and an office five minutes from my house. I thought, "I'm really good at NLP. I may as well give it a try," so I agreed to see them as clients.

They got very good results and sent their friends. By day I was a bench scientist and in the evenings I was a mind-body healer. Because I'm a scientist, I tracked results. I got my master practitioner certification in NLP and continued my practice in Boston. In my training, we did a section on phobias and my trainer brought in Roger Callahan's first book, *The Five Minute Phobia Cure*, so I started doing meridian tapping in 1986 at the beginning of that field. Then I studied with Mary Louise Mueller who was trained in Craniosacral Therapy, Polarity Therapy, and Applied Kinesiology, none of which I had heard of. She taught us muscle testing and how to talk to the soul. I created Healing from the Body Level Up™ methodology (HBLU™) by combining all of these trainings.

It wasn't until I was called in my NLP class to work with people individually that I thought "I am a healer." My vision was having my own lab and doing world-class immunology research. Then I met my husband and three months later he called me on the phone fainting because he had a phobia of blood. He was cleaning his bathroom and cut his finger as he was washing the faucet. This was 1986 when I had just learned the tapping technique. I said, "Tap under your eyes, tap the armpit points, tap the back of your hand. Now how do you feel?" He felt better immediately. He came over and said, "This is amazing that you can cure phobias in minutes. You need to take this seriously. I'm going to quit my job to help you start this business."

What's his Enneagram type? He's a Nine. *Easygoing.* Yes, very easygoing, very supportive. He's the wind beneath my wings and keeps me going. We got married and bought a house. I finished my post-doctoral training and got a job in industry. Then I had a baby. I was seeing six clients a week and working full-time but realized I couldn't do all three things. I asked my deepest wisdom where is the totality of me best going to serve the universe. I thought they can hire another biochemist, but there aren't too many people that develop a mind-healing methodology that works reproducibly and can be taught, so I'm going to do HBLU™ full time. I said to my husband, "I'm going to quit my job to do healing work full-time, but I'm frightened. What if I fail?" He said, "Give it a year. If it doesn't work out you can get another job." Within three months, I went from six clients a week to 20 clients a week, but I always took Mondays off to be with my daughter. Mondays were Mommy and Laura days, not a grocery shopping or catching up on work day.

The basic model of reality I use in HBLU™ is that we had a soul and it's in a body. We have an unconscious mind. We have a conscious mind that doesn't know all that much, even though it thinks it's everything. I call this "conscious mind chauvinism," which I warn people about. Then I had to think about why is the soul in a body (because scientists think about everything in questions). About seven years later, I came up with the idea that we're here to do a soul mission and make a contribution. If we want to make a difference in the physical world, we need to be physical to do it. I assumed that if something isn't working in some area of your life—health, money, career, soul mission, relationships, spirituality—there must be an interference pattern. I spent decades studying these types of patterns, ranging from life-experience damage from this life, past lives, to your ancestry. These interference patterns can be phobias, traumas, limiting beliefs, bad habits, or dysfunctional family system patterns.

The pattern may not interfere at the conscious level, but it interferes at the body level or the unconscious level and—here is the key—causes feelings. It all comes down to energy: Feelings have energy but thoughts don't have energy. Feelings run behavior! The more strongly you feel something the more it drives your behavior. What you see is people consciously know better than to do something and they do it anyway. *Like gain 300 pounds?* Exactly. As they're binge eating, their conscious mind is saying, "I shouldn't do this." So, who is running the show? Not the conscious mind that knows better but whatever craving, addiction, or emptiness is running the show. I call that a misalignment of the levels. Your conscious mind knows better, but you're driven by your unconscious mind sabotaging you. *Or it's called psychological reversal, PR.*

Then I found that you can have personality distortions, like ego distortions that don't come from life experience damage. I use the Enneagram model of personality, which I discovered through muscle testing is downloaded at conception as your operating system, rather than during life experience. *Do you think it's your karmic inheritance from past lives?* No, that's past-life stuff and that's in the category of life-experience damage. This is your Enneagram wound, your ego programming.

What determines your Enneagram Type? That's one of the questions I'm still wondering about. What I have discovered through doing past-life work is that you have one soul mission each lifetime. You could be a different gender each lifetime. Half the time I've been a man and half the time I've been a woman in the last six lifetimes that I remember. What family did you choose? What capabilities do you have? What are your genetics lending you? You get a whole bunch of cards in your hand. You want to play to the strengths of your hand and you want to compensate for the weaknesses. You play out your soul mission with this hand that you've been dealt. Each Enneagram type is programmed the same way regardless of their soul mission. *You're saying all Eights like you will have certain characteristics?* Yes, the programming is the same and can be upgraded the same way. *You also said that you can evolve or expand out of the Type.* Yes, I figured out how to do that.

I was working with Andy Hahn, an Enneagram Four who basically taught me the Enneagram system. For two years a group of us would meet once a week with a pair of each type, male and female. Each week, we would talk about our point of view on a subject. After a couple of years, someone said to Andy, "We understand these bugs in our operating system but we're still struggling with these compulsions and distorted lenses. What do we do about that?" Andy had studied with Thich Nhat Hanh and a bunch of spiritual leaders. One day he was meditating and the idea of walking through the void came to him.

He came up with the Essence Process, a way to address your shadow self, where you tune into the fear and shame of a wounded personality. You interview it from the point of view of your soul without getting attached since it's just a program. Personality wounds have so much energy that you believe the negative stories about yourself are real, so the story runs you from the inside like a puppet. Ego vibrates at a lower frequency than soul. Once you access your soul point of view, you can take the energy of the ego story out of your body, literally pull it out with your hands. You plop it on the floor in front of you and pull out all the life experience damage that fed this story and made it feel real. You radiate the pile of ego energy with your soul energy to bring the ego energy to a higher vibration where it releases—it's quantum physics.

I have a series of videos on "The Enneagram and the Essence Process" describing the most aggravating layers of code for each of the nine types on my website.[1] The free video upgrades the Void/Invisible/Needy layer of the Enneagram Two, Three, and Four, which are the image points. That's the layer of code that makes them vulnerable to everybody's opinion of them. It makes me happy to upgrade that because once you do that, you have boundaries and you're not at the mercy of everybody's opinion of you. As a scientist, I made a reproducible protocol for the Essence Process and mapped the layers of code. I have 600 pages of diagrams of specific layers of code for each type.

The code has to do with how to pull the energy out of the stuck part of the code so you have freedom? Yes, we call it release yourself from the tyranny of ego, the most compulsive structures ever. We figured out how to upgrade personality structure and that was a big piece. People that I trained know how to do that with the code I diagrammed. You muscle test to see which layer of code is causing this problem. You open it up, you read it and see it running. You pull it out of you, recycle the energy, and the purified energy comes back to you. It has a mind of its own, integrates into your body and adds muscle to your soul. In terms of recycling energy, the bang for the buck is huge.

Please give an example of a code and how you pulled it out. I'll explain the Void/Invisible/Needy layer. A layer of code has two sections to it: a central identity (C ID) that has a negative story, that claims to be the only truth, and that runs you. You think that's who you are. You also have a compensating energy (CE), which is the equal and opposite energy, that is trying to negate or get rid of the negative story in the C ID. It's like a coin with two faces. The two opposing energies are the flip side of the same coin. *It takes a lot of energy.* Oh, you bet. The CE tries to negate the C ID by being arrogant or by avoiding the issue. When you interview the seemingly positive CE and ask what is its worst fear, the CE is afraid that it's going to fail and the "real me," the C ID, is going to slip out and it's horrible.

I've done about 350 layers of code in myself. The physical location of the C ID of the Void/Invisible/Needy layer is throughout the whole body. It says "I'm void, invisible and needy; I'm not even here." The Twos, Threes, and Fours describe it as feeling like a ghost, not really here in the full-body void. Nature abhors a vacuum, so the CE has to fill the void. The way the Enneagram Twos, the helpers and givers get seen and filled, is they do things for you and help you and hope you will fill their void with appreciation. *Those are the codependents like Barbara Stone* who says she's a Two and got breast cancer.* There you have it. In reality, they're not a ghost. That whole story goes on the floor, bang.

How do you pull it out? I use my hands. *You're kinesthetic in NLP terms, right?* Yes. If it's a full-body thing, I say to people, "Put your hands above your head and literally push this thing down, push it out of you and out your feet." I do have clients who just visualize pushing it out. We muscle test to confirm that it's gone. Then I ask them, "What does the energy look like?" They describe it. I then instruct them to radiate right through the pile of Enneagram energy with their soul energy and continue radiating their soul energy out to infinity in all directions. It's like microwaving ice cubes where you raise the vibration of the water and it becomes gas. You turn the physical ego energy into pure soul energy waveforms and the released energy integrates back into your body. When they are done radiating the ego energy, I ask, "Do you see anything left of the original pile? Have you fully integrated the energy? Where is it in your body? What's it going to do for you now?"

I saw a video where David Feinstein of the Eden Energy Method did a small study of different practitioners' muscle testing and found they didn't get the same results. It's very subjective, especially if people don't test in the clear because we know we can get switched and muscle test the opposite of what's true. How do you ensure that muscle testing is accurate? I gave that seminar for the last two years at CAIET and ACEP because it aggravated me that people didn't know how to muscle test properly. The first thing you need to know is muscle testing is always accurate but you need to know what you're seeing. I have an intake form with 125 questions and the first 10 questions on the intake form are a system check to make sure that the system is working properly so we can get accurate answers.

We ask, "Are you thirsty? Are you tired? Are you stressed?" I ask the client to show me a yes, show me a no, pull on your hair, zip up, zip down the torso. If people are strong on both yes and no in the muscle test, like 25% of my clients when they first come to see me, it's because they have a phobia. I ask them to do a head to foot scan, an emotional CT scan. "Where is the fear in your body?" I have them write out the phobia and interview it—that's NLP," Talk to the part of you that...." Then we do a meridian tapping technique that I call "Natural Bio-Destressing," which is a form of EFT (Emotional Freedom Technique), to clear it. So first thing I do is check to see if they have any phobias blocking their energy field: That's the most important thing to treat. Once we clear the phobias, we get a clean yes or no. If they're reversed, double weak or strong, it's still a phobia. In my module one training, I spend an entire day on muscle testing and clearing phobias so that they will be able to muscle test.

Usually, it takes one session to unblock someone. The longest it ever took me to unblock someone so I could get a muscle test was 12 sessions. The client was a Muslim woman living in Pakistan who had pain in every cell of her body so she couldn't get on her knees five times a day to say her prayers. I was doing the standing tilt with her during our phone session, where you stand up, face north and ask your body to show a yes—you tilt forward. Ask your body to show a no—you tilt back. She didn't move, the equivalent of double strong. Every session, I asked her where is the fear in your body and what's the phobia? Then some horrifying memory would pop up. Finally, after 12 sessions, she tilted forward on yes and backward on no. She told me, "By the way, all the pain was gone from my body after the first six sessions."

What technique did you use for self-muscle testing? I find that the standing tilt is the most accurate. If I'm sitting down, I do the finger test. I pretend the pointer finger is a mini arm and I press the nail bed with my middle finger. If I want to be sure, I'll do a standing tilt to double-check, or I'll put my arm out and have my husband muscle test me.

Do you think muscle testing is tapping into the unconscious mind? No, I'm sending it to the soul. We muscle test and correct the body so we know we're getting accurate answers. We clear the blocks from the energy field. I muscle test and ask, "Is there any interference to your conscious mind accessing your unconscious mind? Yes or no? Is there any interference to your conscious mind accessing your body? Accessing your personality structure? Accessing your soul?" If we're going to be working with these levels, we have to have full conscious access. If the muscle test indicates they do not have full conscious access, I ask if that's the next thing we need to treat?

If they don't have full conscious access, it's usually one or two things. They either have a phobia or a limiting belief, which can be written down and tapped out. Once we've done this system check, I also check to see if their soul is 100% integrated into their body because we're using the body to access the soul. I want to make sure the soul's integrated into the body and we have full access to all the levels. Then, I check things like do you have any phobias about truth, phobias of admitting you have a problem? I want to work with them on the real issue. There are all these little blocks, so let's open the system to get clear access. These are the first 15 questions on my intake form, a system check. Once all the levels are connected, we can communicate; the soul is in the body and we direct all of the questions to the soul. So in HBLU™, the soul leads the healing and we use muscle testing to get the readout from the soul.

Now if we want to talk to the unconscious mind we can direct the questions to the unconscious mind from your deepest wisdom, which is your soul. "From your deepest wisdom, is there a part of you at the unconscious level that is running this pattern? From your deepest wisdom, is there a part of you at the body level that's running this pattern?" I'm talking to the soul.

Once we have full conscious access to the conscious mind, unconscious mind, body, and soul we do healing work using the HBLU™ Standard Balance Protocol in which the client's soul leads the healing. We ask the client to ask her or his soul, what's the highest priority goal? It might be to make more money, release excess weight, get happily married, or change careers. *The usual.* The usual and get divorced easily and gracefully, right? Whatever the client says, we muscle test and ask, "Is that right from your deepest wisdom?" If it's right, we write the goal statement on the board. Then we ask for permission, "From your deepest wisdom, does this being (remember, we are multi-level beings) give 100% permission to balance for this goal? Yes or no? Is there any reason not to do this? Yes or no?" I do two permission checks.

If we have permission, then I ask, what is the percentage negative emotional charge on the goal? It's kind of like a SUDS (*Subjective Units of Distress Scale of 0 to 10*) measure. I want to know how much blockage there is on the goal and then once we get that, what is the priority interference on the goal? I go through the patterns on my intake form and then I have six modules, each with more complex patterns. A pattern could be a phobia, a grudge or a curse. In HBLU™ we clear life-experience damage, upgrade personality, and clear external interference, which can be in the form of natural disasters, nasty people with free will, or supernatural entities, ghosts, demons, things like that. Whatever I find is the priority interference pattern, I have a protocol for it.

I have a menu with 52 techniques including NLP, energy psychology, and applied kinesiology that I learned from Mary Louise Mueller, shamanic techniques, prayer, and energy transmission like Reiki and QiGong and Pranic Healing. I also have on my menu things that I don't do, so I refer people for chiropractic, acupuncture, or nutrition treatment.

Do you find that your clients are mostly women because it seems like women are more likely to take advantage of helping professions? I would say a good third of my clients are men who come voluntarily. They like that HBLU™ is quick and it removes the problem; they just clear it out; it's gone. Much of the time their highest priority goal has to do with their business rather than relationships, like a man I worked with who took unnecessary risks with his business. *What did you find was his limiting belief that made him take those risks?* It wasn't a limiting belief as it turns out he was Enneagram Seven and they take risks and have adventures. Some opportunity would come up that sounded fun and appealing and he would go invest in it and it wouldn't work out.

How did you clear that? It was another layer of code with a Central Identity and a Compensating Energy. We processed it with the Essence Process by pulling it out, plopping it on the floor and radiating and recycling the energy. *He could retain his sense of fun and adventure without imposing it on his business decisions?* Yes. When you recycle the energy of the pattern, you get to keep the skills and abilities that you developed to compensate, like the Type Two helpers will help but they don't do it at their own expense or to fill a void.

I've done a lot of research on global youth. Do you treat adolescents and do you have an explanation for why there is such an increase in anxiety and depression, especially in girls? I did an interview with a cable television interviewer about "ending the culture of abuse." I said the reason why there's so much abuse in women is because there's a cultural brainwashing pattern; the gender toxic belief system which is like a thought virus. The message that has been polluting humanity is, "women are inferior to men." Look at 5,000 years of recorded history and you see that belief poisoning the collective. It's evil because it prevents men and women from achieving their full potential based solely on the gender of the body that their soul entered. [*See Susan Blackmore.**]

This message is starting to be reversed. I'm working on being able to clear it energetically out of the collective. I haven't figured out how to do that, but I'm still working on it. To clear a toxic belief system out of the collective, you have to have enough people who aren't infected with it, who don't believe in it, come together and fight it to create a tipping point where there are enough people who don't believe it. Then it tips it the other way and it drains. This particular toxic belief system started to tip with the French revolution with the call for liberty, equality, and fraternity. Then we got freedom in the US, but just for white men. My impression, because I've been working with children, is the children who are coming in now have a higher consciousness. [*See John Ryan.**] They can see the garbage and that's causing some of their angst. If young women are trying to prove that they're just as good if not better than men, then they're in reaction and comparing themselves and they're still in the pattern and infected with it.

I'm interested in what allows scientists like you to go against the norm. You must have gotten flak from science colleagues. "What are you doing in this pseudoscience metaphysical woo-woo stuff?" Yes, I've been doing this for 38 years and I teach HBLU™ at community education programs. Maybe 20 to 25 years ago I was teaching people how to clear phobias with tapping and students would come in and be hostile: "How is tapping on your face going to release trauma? That's ridiculous." The first time I presented it at the Boston University School of Social Work, people were flabbergasted. *People don't like their worldviews being shaken up.* Well, I'm good at that.

You've written a lot of articles; what about a book teaching your method? I have thousands of pages of manuals. I wrote a chapter in a couple of books. I just haven't put it all together into one book but I could compile all my newsletter articles into a book. It's much more fun for me to work with people than it is to sit there in a room by myself and write. *You're an extrovert.*

In the face of climate change, an increasing number of autocrats, and growing economic inequality are you optimistic or pessimistic about our future? I'm very optimistic because I'm looking at 5,000 years of history. I have a business associate I brought in recently so I can train more people to do this. He asked me what is the problem HBLU™ was created to solve? I said it's here to eliminate unnecessary suffering. He said, beyond that, HBLU™ raises consciousness. If you look at what causes suffering, it's unconsciousness. People don't know that they have a body that can talk to them and tell them things and they don't realize that they have a soul or a destiny. They don't realize that they're connected with source and they're part of the flow. It's really the disconnect from the consciousness that causes this unnecessary suffering. Muscle testing and telling people's conscious minds to talk to their soul opens a world.

I tell people that their conscious mind's job is to be Sherlock Holmes and I'm Watson in the HBLU™ Mystery Theater. I tell the conscious mind, it's your turn to ask the questions and send them down into the body and talk to the soul so we can find out where the problem is. We'll use my menu of patterns and we'll go in together and figure out what is going wrong and clear it! The goal is to live in higher consciousness, to not take things personally, and understand that we're not our damage patterns. With the right tools and techniques, we can clear this negative energy out of us to align all of our levels and move forward easily and gracefully. I teach your conscious mind to talk to your soul and the other levels of your being to find the damage patterns that are blocking you. We're then going to use effective protocols and techniques to release the energy of the block That's the basics of HBLU™ that raises consciousness and gets people unstuck.

People do not need to suffer as much as they do and there are very simple techniques that they can use to alleviate their suffering if they only knew about them. I'm a very democratic person, so I'm about empowering people by teaching techniques. More advanced patterns with structure need a professional. Somebody who has PTSD, shouldn't treat this at home. Come to somebody that I have trained and let them take you through the structure and treat it. If you're going to do a personality structure, do it with somebody else who is trained. These are such large energies that you can't hold consciousness without being pulled in unless there is somebody else there to hold space and understand the structure because you really believe that's who you are—although it's not. To really get your consciousness out of a pattern with that much energy requires somebody who can hold space and keep reminding you that it's a pattern and not you.

We have maybe about a decade to turn around the climate change problems. Are we going to have enough time to raise consciousness to turn that around? Mother Earth is a person. Physicist *Jude Currivan** is *writing a book about talking with Gaia.* She shows up and talks to me periodically. She told me, "I'm a person, not just an energy." I think that the earth is a being and the Earth will survive without us. *John Ryan* thinks the Sirians are helping us. Do you get that kind of downloaded information that we're being helped?* No, I hear angels and guides. It's a rule that every human being has a minimum of one guardian angel and one guide per lifetime. So I've been talking to mine for probably 30 years and clients come in with their guides. Once in a while, Mother Earth, Jesus, or Mother Mary show up in my office. They help me do healing work with that particular client. *Do they take form? How do you know it's Jesus or whoever?* Because it looks like them.

What do you do for fun in the face of all this learning and work and family? My husband and I go ballroom dancing every Friday night. *What's your favorite?* We dance the hustle. How about you? *My favorite is West Coast Swing and some of my dances are on my YouTube channel.* I like to go to musicals and movies. In the summertime, we go to the Cape and the College Light Opera Company. In the winter we like to travel someplace warm like Hawaii or Disneyworld. We travel to Paris a lot.

What else would you like people to know about the work that you do and how can they train or do a session with you? They can go to my website, and read about my work or email me and they can have a 15-minute free consult with me.[2] In my HBLU Module 1: Clearing Trauma and Healing PTSD training, I teach participants how to eliminate PTSD in their clients (because I figured out the pattern of PTSD) in just one to six sessions. I published two papers of case studies using that protocol and it's reproducible, so my colleagues are now healing people of PTSD. [*More about how to clear PTSD is on the book webpage.*[3]

Publications
Videos
Ending the Culture of Abuse
https://hblu.org/whats-new.html

Dr. Judith Swack @ Energy Psychology Conference 2013
https://www.youtube.com/watch?v=geJrostmNew&index=3&list=P
Lrbne2wMtodw560Mi8a2G22Zv8ae6Wct0&t=0s

Mind/Body Publications

"A Study of Initial Response and Reversion Rates of Subjects Treated with the Allergy Technique." *Anchor Point* 6, 3:1-10, 1992. (reprinted on website)

"The Basic Structure of Loss and Violence Trauma Imprints." *Anchor Point* 8, 3:3-23, 1994. (reprinted on website)

"Healing from the Body Level Up and How It Evolved from NLP." *Anchor Point 15*, 6:27-32, 2001. (reprinted on website)

"The Antidote to the Psychological Effects of Terrorism." *AHP Perspective*, Dec. 2001/Jan. 2002 pg. 28-31. (reprinted on website)

"Healing from the Body Level Up." Chapter 4. *Energy Psychology in Psychotherapy: A Comprehensive Source Book*, Norton Professional Books, Gallo, Fred, (Editor), 2002.

"Transforming Personality with HBLU™: Explanation of the Enneagram Operating System." *The Energy Field*, Volume 7:4 Winter 2006

Peer-Reviewed Mind/Body Publications

"Diagnosis Shock, the Unrecognized Burden of Illness." *International Journal of Healing and Caring Online.* Volume 8:1, January 2008. (HTTP://www.IJHC.org)

"Healing the Collective Consciousness with Healing from the Body Level Up™." *International Journal of Healing and Caring Online.* Volume 8:3, September 2008. (HTTP://www.IJHC.org)

"Elimination of Post-Traumatic Stress Disorder (PTSD) and Other Psychiatric Symptoms in a Disabled Vietnam Veteran with Traumatic Brain Injuries (TBI) in Just Six Sessions Using Healing from the Body Level Up™

"Methodology, an Energy Psychology Approach." *International Journal of Healing and Caring Online.* Volume 9:3, September 2009. (HTTP://www.IJHC.org)

"Breaking the Habit and Reversing the Effects of Pretending to Be Alright." *International Journal of Healing and Caring Online.* Volume 10:3, September 2010. (HTTP://www.IJHC.org)

"Elimination of PTSD and Psychiatric Symptoms in One to Six Sessions in Two Civilian Women and One Female Iraq War Veteran Using Healing from the Body Level Up (HBLU™) Methodology, an Energy Psychology Approach".

International Journal of Healing and Caring Online. Volume 12:3, September 2012. (HTTP://www.IJHC.org)

Other Publications

Swack, Judith A., Ph.D. & Rawlings, Wendy, LMHC (2017, November). Understanding Neurobiology of Trauma Will Enable Counselors to Help Clients Heal Permanently From It, *AMHCA The Advocate Magazine, 40* (4) 9–12.

Swack, Judith A., Ph.D. (2018) "Why Do I Do That?" Chapter 13 in *Success Starts Today*, Orlando, FL: Celebrity Press, pp. 133-139.

Endnotes

1 https://hblu.org/enneagram-teleseminar.html.
2 www.hblu.org
   judith@hblu.org or info@hblu.org
   https://hblutraining.com/hblu-1-with-history-trauma.html
3 https://visionaryscientists.home.blog/2020/01/08/judith-swack-ph-d-ptsd-protocol/

SECTION 2 HEALING WITH FREQUENCIES

ROLLIN MCCRATY, PH.D.
UNDERSTANDING HOW THE EARTH'S FREQUENCIES AFFECT US

Photo used by permission

Questions to Ponder

What techniques does HeartMath use to self-regulate and stay centered?

Why do their exercises begin by imagining breathing slowly through the heart?

How are humans impacted by the earth's magnetic fields according to the Global Coherence Initiative?

I was born in 1954 in a little town called Elmo, Missouri with unfenced backyards and community spirit. I grew up in a farming community until I was about 10. I'm the first and only child in my family, but I have a half-brother from my mother's previous marriage who is much older.

Do you feel like a Scorpio? Yes, I get a lot done. *I think of them as deep thinkers who sometimes struggle to get feelings up to the surface. You use the word "deep" a lot.* The Scorpios I know have a general sense that we get a lot done. However, our negative side, or lower vibrational side, can leave a lot of people in the wake of getting things done. I've had to learn to be more patient, caring and compassionate and yet still get stuff done—at the speed of balance.

What was there about your family that made you want to go to college? I don't know that there was anything in my family, it was more that I came in with that interest. *It's probably a safe bet to assume that you did well in science and math in high school.* I did alright. I believe that we all have our individual blueprints that we come in with and guide us on the path that we are meant to do. *This fits in with karma and reincarnation?* Reincarnation, yes, some people that we tend to call "old souls" have been here many times. Karma is another issue that's more complicated that we can leave for another time. *It seems to me that they're tied together in that one of the reasons you reincarnate is to work through your issues and evolve, which means that you carry over some of your strengths and weaknesses.* I think there is truth to that.

What kind of religious background were you raised with? Methodist. *And were you a believer?* My earliest childhood memory (this is not a story I tell very often) is I was around three with my little feet hanging over the seat of the wooden pews in the small town farm community Methodist church. The minister was preaching a vengeful God, Hell, and brimstone sermon when my larger-self connected with me and downloaded a different perspective, which had a big impact on me. The input that came in let me know that there is not a vengeful, judgmental higher source. The experience left a very strong imprint that kept me from settling down with a white picket-fence life. From that day on I argued very strongly about religion with my parents; it took me a couple of years but, finally, they gave up trying to drag me off to the church because I didn't buy the message. *How did you come to the spiritual understanding that we've had previous lives?* Personal experiences and embracing my own vibration to be able to connect with my larger self of who I really am.

Where did you go to university? My path there was a little different in that I joined the army right after I graduated from high school as a way to escape from small-town Nebraska. I had very little interest in going to college at that point and scored very high on certain aptitude tests, so I picked the longest military school option, which ended up being an advanced school taught at NASA in Huntsville, Alabama in high-level missile systems, for a year and a half. After the military, I went to work for Motorola because I had the skills I needed and used the GI bill to take courses at the University of Nebraska.

After a few years with Motorola, I became a serial entrepreneur creating several successful businesses. I got involved with a group that introduced spirulina to the world because I have a humanitarian interest as part of my deeper mission. The vision was to feed the world's hungry populations—we were way ahead of our time—using giant solar-powered spray dryers, etc. We proved we could grow spirulina, a superfood to feed the world's hungry population. But that went absolutely nowhere and was blocked at political levels. That's when I truly understood that it's not about technology but about increasing consciousness. *Yes, solutions are available for all global problems, but not the political will to implement them.*

Do you think there is more support for it now because there is so much need for eight billion people to have food in the face of climate change? Probably, but the bigger issue is still a problem with consciousness. With less than 10% of the world's military budget, you could feed every person and have clean water, house them, and educate them. It's not a problem with technology; it's a problem with consciousness. *The people who control the economic system are mostly materialists and don't believe that there are consequences for their actions, so their goal is to make money.*

Please define consciousness. You asked me to define something that hundreds of scientists haven't been able to come to an agreement on. But, one perspective is that there's Big C consciousness and little C Consciousness. Little C is the kind of consciousness that knows I am awake and conscious; now I go to sleep and I'm unconscious. Some think big C Consciousness provides the information that unfolds into the creation of the universe, as described by some quantum physicists. *Some people equate it with awareness or information. Does an amoeba have consciousness because it's aware of its environment?* Yes, of course they do; if we are referring to big C, everything has Consciousness. From the human perspective, I tend to talk about increasing consciousness as increased awareness.

After the spirulina business, I said enough of this humanitarian stuff, I'm going to go make money again and started an electrostatics [*the study of stationary electric charges or fields*] business in a garage. By the third year, we were doing $15 million a year in sales. That was a lot of fun, but there was a deeper urging in me that another sports car in the driveway wasn't going to fulfill. I met Doc Childre a couple of years after I had decided I wanted to devote my energy to something that was going to help shift human consciousness. This tied back in full circle to my childhood download of my mission.

Through early HeartMath processes, I had a heart awakening that allowed me to connect with who I am on a deep level and I sold my business.

How did you get from Nebraska to California? Did you meet Doc Childre in California? No, I met him in North Carolina when I had the electrostatics business. I was always curious about electromagnetism and through all my formal education, I would ask what is it, but all I ever got was the formulas for how we describe it. "Don't ask deeper questions" was the basic response. I ran across a radionics book that described some different perspectives regarding the deeper aspects of electromagnetism and subtle energy fields, which got me intrigued. I moved to California to go to the first degree-granting accredited institution in Consciousness Studies, The University of the Trees in Boulder Creek in the late '70s. *You got a Ph.D. somewhere along the way.* That was after I got involved with HeartMath and my scientific advisory board members said you've got to get a Ph.D. I got one from a college in Birmingham, Alabama.

When have been your most difficult times and how did you cope? If I look across my lifespan, the biggest challenges would be personal relationships rather than professional ones. I learned a lot through those experiences. *You have a son and a dog, do you have more offspring than that?* Just the son and the dog is no longer with us.

Have you had other experiences of downloading information in addition to when you were three? You mentioned that you are not a keen meditator but you do the HeartMath exercises. I was a meditator who practiced many types for over 15 years, prior to meeting Doc and getting involved in HeartMath, and I can certainly say I did benefit from it. However, I could have a wonderful meditation in the morning and get really angry before I got to work when I hit a traffic jam, or something did not go the way I wanted in my company. After meeting Doc and understanding on a much deeper level what he was talking about with heart intelligence not just as metaphor, I started to practice the exercises as an experiment. I can honestly say the reason I sold that company and helped him found HeartMath was because of the transformation in my own life.

Synchronicity happens when you're in sync with your inner guidance. You've talked about meeting Doc as a kind of synchronous experience. Have you found that it happens more often as you get in touch with your inner self? It's a way of life. Synchronicity evolves from following our inner heart-based intuition. I expect synchronicity and it happens. *You put out a goal and an intention and then step back.* Yes, I pay attention to the patterns of synchronicity.

Here is a summary of what I think HeartMath is based on. Heart rhythms are the primary source of rhythmic patterns in the body. Karl Pribram, MD, developed the concept and Doc Childre took it and ran with it. The heart has 60 times greater electrical voltage than the brain and therefore it signals the brain. This affects the brain's ability to have effective cognition, to reduce pain, etc. Positive emotions like appreciation and gratitude create coherent heart patterns while stress leads to disordered rhythms that impair cognition and emotional stability. Each one of those sentences is an hour discussion. That's not the whole story but it's an important physiological aspect within the larger HeartMath model.

How do you self-regulate and generate positive emotions? HeartMath has a series of simple exercises employing heart-focused slow breathing, Inner Ease, Quick Coherence, Freeze Frame, Heart Lock, and Coherent Communication. They seem to focus on imagining breathing through the heart with gratitude and appreciation, then listening to the heart's guidance. The research is about the energetic heart which suggests that it functions as a transceiver and bridge to our larger self, higher self, soul, spirit, etc. Creating a physiological coherence state in our body, especially the heart, increases the coupling and connection to the higher part of ourselves. As we become more coherent we download more information, an intuitive guidance that informs us in our day-to-day lives. We learn to be more aligned with who we really are at the level of our larger self. That is easier said than done because the mind is strong in its attractor state. The aim is to elevate consciousness and awareness. Positive emotions like appreciation, gratitude, and compassion are not the end game, but they are important in opening the communication channels with the heart. It's about aligning with who you really are. What the world needs right now is more compassion and gratitude.

Some scientists view the heart as having its own brain, its own neurons, its own memory, its own ability to learn. That's well-established neuroscience. The heart sends far more neural information to the brain than the brain sends to the heart. The pattern of those neural signals from the heart to the brain have profound influences on cognitive function, memory, and our ability to self-regulate. People in a relationship didn't tend to say, "I love you with all my brain." The reason that we associate the heart with higher emotions like love and compassion is because we intuitively know this. *I don't hear too much discussion in HeartMath of the heart chakra as connecting the higher and lower energy systems.* Chakras are real things but we're talking about many levels above the chakras, but if you open the heart you automatically bring the chakras into alignment.

As we learn to strengthen the connections in our inner energetic system, we are building new energetic circuits which can handle the energetic capacity of higher vibrational consciousness. This increases awareness and gives us access to what you can think of as more rooms or dimensions of consciousness that are accessed through the heart. *That makes me think of people like Eben Alexander* who had NDEs where he experienced higher states of consciousness and love and the Godhead. This suggests that you can achieve that kind of awareness without having an NDE.* Earth has a higher level of density and it's a pretty neat place to be at this time. I love earth and it's kind of a showplace. From my perspective, you can think of life on earth as a kind of video game, where the goal is waking up in consciousness in this level of density. That's the big game and how we grow here. *Some find that because this plane is denser, you can work through your lessons quicker.* Yes, you can do this more rapidly now at this time on earth.

Let's talk about your research including that our hearts have signals that connect with other people and that some of those signals are electronic. You have measured how people's heart rate variability (HRV) connects with each other and with the earth's magnetic waves. To unpack that a little bit, when you put electrodes on the body to measure the electrocardiogram, basically, you are measuring current flow. We measure the electrocardiogram in millivolts and EEGs for brain waves and microvolts which means that the magnitude of the heart's electricity is huge compared to brain waves. Magnetic and electric fields are different things. When you have current flow you generate a magnetic field that is able to penetrate things, which is why cell phones work indoors. We can measure the heart's magnetic field outside the body with today's magnetometers.

With today's sensitive equipment, we can measure the cardiac field about three feet away from the body, while brain waves can only be detected out to about an inch from the skull. We use almost identical techniques that I used back in Motorola days to demodulate or to look at the information being carried by the heart's electromagnetic field, like a cell phone or radio transmitter. You have a carrier wave, the electromagnetic field, that carries the information, the voice, the picture, or the text. You can use the same technique to see that the magnetic field of the heart is carrying information about our emotional state and probably much more we don't know about yet. That patterned information correlates mathematically to the heart's rhythm so you don't need expensive magnetometers to know about the information we are feeding the field.

The next step was to determine if the heart's field that carries information was detected by other people's nervous systems. This is all published information. An energetic communication goes on between people and is always occurring, usually at an unconscious level. For some people, it becomes more conscious. Most people have an intuitive understanding of this, which is reflected in our language, like the expression, "The tension was so thick you can cut it with a knife." *Or you can feel someone staring at you from behind.* We call this "energetic sensitivity."

With the Global Coherence Initiative, we're researching the hypothesis that our biologically generated magnetic fields are coupled to the magnetic fields of the earth. We've created the Global Coherence Monitoring System using super-sensitive magnetometers placed around the earth. It's the only system like this in the world where we have a global system for measuring the resonant frequencies in the Earth's magnetic fields. Basically, the rhythms in the earth exactly overlap with our heart rhythms and our brain waves. As I've said, the heart's field is huge compared to the brain's field and the earth is the same way with magnetic fields many times larger in magnitude, vibrationally speaking, but the same as the heart rhythms. The weaker ones, called Schumann Resonances, are the same as the brain waves so our biology and earth actually mirror each other. Of course, there are different orders of magnitude power but it's the same scaling of frequencies and rhythms.

The bottom line is we are coupled to the earth's magnetic fields and are affected by the rhythms in the earth's fields, as hundreds of papers and studies show. We are also suggesting that humans and all living systems feed information into the Earth's fields creating a global feedback system between the collective humanity and the earth. I invite readers to pause throughout the day as often as you can and ask yourself, what am I feeding the field? It certainly affects people in our local environment in a measurable way so we know that's proven.[1] Collective humanity is like a giant computer, we are all feeding the field. As we learn to become more coherent, self-regulated, and raise our vibration, we are feeding the field more coherent information. We want a higher ratio of kindness, compassion, and appreciation versus frustration, anger, hate, and impatience.

Is this different from Pierre Teilhard de Chardin's noosphere, the Hindu Akashic Field, Rupert Sheldrake's morphic resonance, Carl Jung's collective unconscious, or David Bohm's Implicate and Explicate Order? Yes, Jung was the first to suggest that type of thing but we are suggesting the existence of an actual physical mechanism that can be tested scientifically.

What happens with magnetic poles shifts or solar bursts that affect us? In Russia, they include information about space weather as part of their news reports because they are ahead of us in knowing that the magnetic or energetic environment we live in affects us. As part of our Global Coherence Monitoring System, we provide the global coherence app that looks at group coherence. We add an alert system when the field is disturbed, such as by a solar flare. It is very clear that when the earth's field is disturbed, it affects us. Different people have different sensitivities to this and those would be great days to practice HeartMath techniques so we are not as likely to get upset. If you ever wake up and feel out of sorts, you may find that either there's a magnetic field disturbance due to a solar flare, or an event that triggered a mass emotional outpouring like a shooting or a terrorist attack, or a huge natural disaster that causes many people to feel anxious. This increases those feelings in the global field.

I read that we're in a solar cycle that peaks every decade or so and that's historically that's when there are the most creative outbursts as well as the most onset of wars or other dramatic events. This research was first done by the Russian Alexander Tchijevsky. He was drafted into WWI and being an astrophysicist, he observed solar activity and realized that during solar flares and increased solar activity people engaged in bloodier battles. After the war he did an exhaustive study of human history, counting the number of major human events that occurred each year from 1749 to 1926 and made a line graph of events compared with the solar cycles. It's almost an exact overlay and has been extended into modern times. He also found that blood pressure and heart rates changed a few days before magnetic field disturbances. He predicted that there had to be an influence from the sun that affects humanity before we knew about x-rays and UV or solar radio flux.

The solar cycle is a 10 to 11 year cycle; as the cycle ramps up, the sun puts out more energy. It's an energetic influx that filters into the planetary magnetic fields and then down into the human biology. When we have more energy, how self-regulated we are, it depends on how we use it. The greatest peaks of those cycles are also the greatest peaks of human flourishing. Individuals either get in more traffic accidents and emotional disturbances or, if more self-regulated, we invent new things and develop new collaborations. The flourishing of human consciousness also accompanies the peaks. In 2019, we were on the start of an upslope of the next cycle that would peak in four or five years.

You measured groups in five countries to see if their heart rhythms were synchronizing with the Earth's field. Yes, we measured groups in five countries with over a hundred people involved who had their HRV recorded 24-hours per day over several weeks. We learned that globally we synchronize with each other and the earth. There is a low-frequency rhythm in the heart that synchronizes with the Earth's rhythms. Interestingly, some people in the various groups were positively correlated and some were inversely correlated, meaning that some had the opposite reaction to the change in the earth's magnetic field. A third group was not synchronized with anybody else or with the earth. More data and studies are coming out now that indicate it's a very good thing to be in sync with the Earth's rhythms because it appears that it's an energy source for us, that we can draw energy from.

We arranged a time when all the groups could do a heart-based meditation called the Heart Lock-In at the same time for 15 minutes. The results were another surprise. After the participants were in a heart-coherent state for 15 minutes, they were significantly more synchronized not only to each other within the various groups but were also more synchronized with the earth's field for the next 24 hours. We would never have predicted that.

These practices could make school easier for kids. I know that HeartMath is doing work in schools. It's not my division, but our programs for children are being used in over 3,000 schools. This has nothing to do with the earth synchronization research, but are practical skills for helping kids learn how to self-regulate, how to manage their stress, and how to get along with each other better. We provide simple tools and techniques, backed up with lots of science.

What if students are from a disadvantaged background and can't think of a time when they felt appreciation or gratitude, can they just make it up? HeartMath is not just about feeling these positive emotions, it's a way of opening the heart to help align us. We do talk about appreciation and compassion but the end game is aligning with our higher selves, which elevates consciousness and brings in the capacity to self-regulate. We have done work in prisons and the California

Youth Authority. If you are working with someone in trauma you don't ask them to breathe through their heart and feel appreciation, so there are other techniques like "attitude breathing" to help open the heart to increase consciousness and rise above the trauma. It's a five-step technique that, like most of our techniques, starts with heart-focused breathing, where you focus your attention on the area of the heart and pretend you're breathing in your chest with a five-second in and five-second out rhythm. This helps starts the process of shifting the coherence so you can breathe yourself into coherence. If you are feeling impatient, you breathe the attitude of patience. It is about taking responsibility for our emotional diet.

HeartMath also works in hospitals, health centers, and with the police. Yes, nurses, doctors, hospital staff, schools. We developed the pre-deployment resilience training program for the U.S. Navy. We have programs on the non-profit side from preschool through college, including college courses for nurses. There are now over 400 independent studies that have used our techniques in a wide variety of ways to increase test scores, better health outcomes, and reduce stress and anxiety in the workplace.

I worked with some of the visualizations on a computer app to see immediate biofeedback in my workshops. If you are coherent then the scene fills in with beautiful colors. What kind of devices do you have for people who want that feedback? We have HRV coherence feedback devices, invented to help people learn the skills to shift into coherence and self-regulate. By practicing with the devices you are training your nervous system so that the heart coherent state is familiar. It helps police be able to maintain composure in a stressful situation. We are mostly stabilizing emotionally, which enhances cognitive function.

What do you call those devices? The one that is used by a lot of schools in multi-user databases is called the emWave Pro and emWave Pro Plus—it does HRV assessments and helps with health risk assessments. The Inner Balance is a mobile device that works with your smartphone with an ear sensor and a couple of different sensors. The Social Coherence Project trains teams to increase harmony. The latest is called the Global Coherence app which is a mobile device that allows us to look at group coherence and amplify what we put into the planetary field environment. The global coherence app does that in real-time to calculate the group coherence plus your individual coherence. Everyone using the app time-synchronized data is sent to the server where the coherence of each participant in any given group (of any size) is analyzed and the group's average coherence determined in real-time. The Inner Balance app is just you and your personal coherence.

It's interesting to think that trees could be used to predict major earthquakes. Why are you interested in monitoring trees? That's a side benefit. We've worked on it for about five years and I am close to launching The Global Tree Monitoring System. We are creating a system and network to monitor tree potentials globally, as part of the Global Coherence initiative. We suggest that all living systems are connected to the Earth's field. Trees are great to look at as they don't mind if you put a couple of electrodes in them and they have amazingly high electrical potential. Their millivolt range is the same as the human heartbeat and they have circadian rhythms. They almost have their own personalities. A grove of trees is all interconnected at the roots, but each tree also has its own signature. The idea is to do this globally. One of the things we have learned from the Princeton Global Consciousness Project is that when events trigger mass emotional outpourings, it's measured in a global field effect.

A hypothesis is that trees will also respond to events that trigger lots of people having similar emotions. Predicting earthquakes is a secondary reason for doing this. One of our collaborators, Friedemann Freund, is the grandfather of pre-earthquake research, working at NASA and NASA Ames. As a chemist, he found that rocks under pressure turn into long-term sustained battery voltages. Trees are great because they have roots plugged into earth. There is already preliminary data in Japan that suggests that before a large earthquake you have significant change in ground potential up to two weeks before a huge quake.

Tell us about your books. Science of the Heart is a good book for people who want more information on the science. Practical information is in *Heart Intelligence* and *The Science of Interconnectivity*, an e-book, discusses the global coherence work, earth and human interconnection. If you want to know more about intuition, the e-book called *The Intuitive Hea*rt is available at heartmath.org. *What is your next book?* I have no idea. We have developed new programs that we are testing now and we have a second certification for teens. A lot of our new work will be on the social and global coherence side of things.

What do you do for fun in the face of this intense research? I live in the Santa Cruz Mountains with lots of hiking trails. I have a bulldozer and I build trails on the weekends.

In the face of all the autocrats, the global climate change, and ongoing war, are you optimistic or pessimistic? I am very optimistic as a lot of things we are seeing are signs of the shift. Things have to get to their stress points first, which is part of the shift going on, so I am very optimistic. *What would a globally coherent world look like to you?* One of my thoughts on that is the politicians call for war and nobody shows up. More and more people are waking up and realizing that it is crazy that we have extreme poverty when 10% of the military budget would take care of that. The Millennial Generation [*and Gen Z*] is waking up and becoming smarter, so I have lots of hope.

Books

The Coherent Heart, with various authors, 2012

An Issue of the Heart: The Neuropsychotherapist Special Issue: Volume 2, various authors, 2015

Heart Intelligence: Connecting with the Intuitive Guidance of the Heart, 2016

Transforming Stress for Teens: The HeartMath Solution for Staying Cool Under Pressure, 2016

HeartMath Solution for Better Sleep with Deborah Rozman, 2017

Heartmath Brain Fitness Program with Deborah Rozman, 2017

Endnotes

1 McCraty, R. in *Bioelectromagnetic and Subtle Energy Medicine, Second Edition* (ed. Paul J. Rosch) 541-562. (Marcel Dekker, 2015)

Beverly Rubik, Ph.D.
The Biofield and Foundations of Energy Medicine

Photo used by permission

Questions to Ponder

What kinds of modalities are studied in Dr. Rubik's Frontier Science?

Discuss the findings in her lab experiments including a definition of the biofield, differences in healers' effectiveness, and evidence for the effectiveness of energy healing.

How do therapeutic devices work?

You're a Capricorn. Do you identify with that or do you think astrology is not meaningful? I think astrology is meaningful. That's just a little piece of the picture being born in the sun of Capricorn as there is a complexity to the natal chart. When I was younger, I wasn't that interested in health sciences, although Capricorn often focuses on health and science. In my maturity, I've been very interested in health. *They also mature late.* It looks as if I'm somewhat typical in that regard. *Do you know your Myers-Briggs or your Enneagram personality types?* I'm E/I, N, T/F, P—high in intuitive and high in perception. On introvert-extrovert I am middling, and on thinking-feeling I am middling.

How many siblings do you have? I'm interested in birth order. I have one brother who was born four years later. *What about our childhood led you to study chemistry and biophysics and get a Ph.D. at UC Berkeley?* My father was a chemist, and I used to go with him to his laboratory and I was gifted by my parents with a chemistry set at home. Then I got interested in biology too. I had a microscope and looked at plants and microbes in soil and water. I was broadly interested in all of nature. Eventually, after a degree in chemistry, I went on to biophysics in order to have some understanding of biology, chemistry, and physics. One of the key questions for me was, and still is today, what really is life? Can we understand it? Nature, to me, was God's great work and I wanted to understand more about it. That was very different from chemistry where you typically make synthetic compounds that are unnatural. I was more drawn to the natural sciences than applications.

As a teenager, I knew intuitively that living organisms had fields of energy governing them, and later in my adult life, I led an *ad hoc* committee of scientists and health practitioners at the Office of Alternative Medicine (at the US National Institutes of Health). Around 1992, we coined the term "biofield" for this organizing field of energy. If you accept the biofield as the organizing field of life, it makes perfect sense to consider therapies that work at this level, which are, in fact, "energy medicine." My incentive was that there was much more to life to explore, both in theory, experiment, and applications than the bag of biomolecules that is the conventional view. We also need the softer, gentler approach of energy medicine to complement the big guns of allopathic medicine.

What kind of religious background did you have? I was raised Catholic, but when I was about 12, I told my mother that I'm no longer going to church. Instead, I'm going on nature walks with my father who didn't go to church in those years either. I found more holiness in nature than in the church. I do believe very firmly in a Creator, a power much greater than us to whom we are all connected. I like Martin Heidegger's definition of being human—that each person, and maybe each living critter, is a unique outpouring of divinity. I really like this perspective because I've never met another person like me and I'm sure all of us are completely unique. It's a very special moment in time when we're born. We serve our purpose, learn our lessons on earth, and then pass on. Life is sacred.

How did you arrive at UC Berkeley? I was born in the Midwest and I have to say in the 1960s I was quite excited about progressive movements and civil rights as well as in the youth movement of the hippies, so the Midwest was not the best place for me to be. I spent some time in Europe, before I went to Berkeley, being a hippie traveling around most European countries. In those years they were quite unique from one another and quite distinctive from the United States. I got a world perspective by traveling for some months before going to Berkeley, which I chose because it was extremely good in science, rated in the top five in my field. Besides having a liberal culture with which I could identify, it was a very good place to study science, and the weather there was great.

What were the most difficult challenges you've faced in your life and how did you cope? While I was in graduate school, I got very interested in spiritual healing, sometimes called psychic healing or "laying on of hands." I had a dance injury and was scheduled for surgery. By hobby, I was a dancer, and I still am. *Like you, I'm a dancer who went to UCB.* I injured a knee and in those days they didn't have medical imaging except for x-rays. It was recommended that I have exploratory knee surgery, but I didn't really like that idea because I knew that it would be invasive. Joking around with my friends, I asked, "What alternatives do I have?" Someone replied, "Why don't you try healing?" In the 1970s there were no known healers that I knew of in Berkeley or anywhere.

I heard that Olga Worrall was coming to Berkeley from Baltimore, a reputed American healer and psychic, whose life is described in *Mystic with the Healing Hands* by Edwina Cerutti. She held prayer circle healings in a Russian Orthodox church in Baltimore and was coming out here to speak and do healing. I went to see her because I felt I had nothing to lose and I believed that she might help me. She put her hands on my knees and entered into a prayerful state and looked like she was in a trance. I felt this rush of energy through my body, especially in my knees. It was a remarkable feeling like nothing else. When I stood up afterwards I had no pain and I thought, "Maybe it will wear off and maybe it's a placebo effect. Maybe I'm in a trance." But it didn't wear off and I was healed. As a result of that, I decided to do some studies on Olga Worrall while she was out here.

This was not my official research at UC Berkeley, where I was almost finished with my dissertation on chemotaxis in bacterial cultures. I took Worrall into the laboratory and damaged some cultures with antibiotics or starvation and maintained a few of these cultures as controls. She placed her hands around each of the test cultures and was able to sense what was ailing them, whether I had poisoned them with an antibiotic or was starving them for nutrients, which was fascinating to me. I also found in some controlled studies that she was able to make cells grow above and beyond the controls, especially when they were inhibited with antibiotics at low doses.

This really changed my life. First, I had a remarkable healing that jarred my thoughts and I didn't need a surgery. I don't know how something could be repaired that quickly. Secondly, I saw remarkable effects on bacterial cultures in a laboratory by someone who applied conscious intention and directed energy from her hands. Olga considered all of her powers to come from the divine realm. Now I had data that I really wanted to pursue further instead of taking a post-doctoral position at Harvard that I was considering. I realized this topic was highly unorthodox in science. My colleagues at UC Berkeley were astounded that I would try something like this and that I got such results was even more amazing. Some of my fellow graduate students were perplexed and some of them shunned me for asking such unorthodox questions. I decided I better not go to Harvard; if UC Berkeley doesn't accept this, it will be much tougher to do this at Harvard.

Instead, I took a teaching position at a California State University and then applied for grants to study spiritual healing. I applied to the Ernest Holmes Foundation for Holistic Health, which was then connected with the Science of Mind church in Anaheim, California. I wrote a grant proposal and sent it to the Dean of the college who submitted it. I thought, "Great! I'm going to be able to do this. I'm at a teaching school and they only care that I'm a good teacher." When the letter arrived that I was funded, I was thrilled. However, I was called into the Dean's office where my face dropped because he told me I couldn't do this work at the university. I couldn't believe it because he had signed off on my grant application in which I had my preliminary data. He said that it was just too threatening: "I'm sorry you can't do this here. We'll put this money to good use." It was my very first grant and first academic position and I was told that the grant was being accepted by the university, but taken away from me!

Six months later, I was removed from my position even though I had excellent ratings from the students and I really enjoyed teaching. I had thought I could do this rather unorthodox research because this was a teaching institute. I talked with the foundation that supplied it; they were really very upset that the university would dare to use it for some other purpose and were able to retrieve some of the funding and give it to me. I did the research in borrowed laboratories in 1980.

I found it very difficult to get a job because every time I walked into an interview people would ask, "You have a doctoral degree from UC Berkeley. Why are you unemployed for four months?" I would respond, "I'm having difficulty with the scientific reductionist paradigm of taking life into little dead pieces and analyzing it and trying to make sense out of it, trying to explain life in terms of biomolecules alone." I told them that I had a much bigger vision looking at the role of consciousness in life and the biological field. I was pretty adamant about it and stubborn as a youth. One day I walked into a nonprofit laboratory where a fellow scientist commiserated with me. The interviewer told me he felt very similarly and he was surprised at my frankness; then he gave me a hug and hired me on the spot. That position, unfortunately, was funded on soft money and didn't last very long.

You can see that early in my career I had a lot of difficulties because I was so clear about my purpose and so thwarted by the establishment science around me. If you ask questions beyond the mainstream, you could be in jeopardy of losing your job, grants, and colleagues. As I looked around, I discovered there were other people like me including Nobel Laureates like Dr. Brian Josephson* at Cambridge University, famous for the Josephson Junction in physics. He reached the highest level of academic science to get a Nobel Prize and was also posing questions about consciousness, bigger questions about how it would fit with physics. For this, he was also shunned by colleagues but he wasn't dismissed from his job because he had tenure. Most scientists hold off on asking such maverick questions until they get tenure and are well-established at a university, but I did it early on and ran into difficulties.

Eventually, I was employed by Temple University in Philadelphia, a dream come true because my job was director of the Center for Frontier Sciences. Scientists, including myself, posed maverick questions in science that went beyond the mainstream. As director, I was to identify other scientists worldwide who were asking similar questions, conducting experimental and theoretical research, and to hold meetings and publish new findings. I created a journal called *Frontier Perspectives* and had a budget and a couple of assistants. I roamed throughout the world meeting scientists and other scholars like me who were working at the cutting edge.

I define "frontier science" as topics of serious scientific inquiry that go beyond the boundaries of the dominant worldview of science. My frontier science interests include: (1) consciousness studies and the interrelationship of mind and matter; (2) building a scientific foundation of alternative and complementary medicine; (3) elucidating new energy emissions from the human body, including biophotons and subtle energies, both components of the human biofield, and how these relate to health and healing; and (4) the new water science, whereby water has a memory and can receive, store, and transmit bio-information vital to the living state.

We distinguish frontier science from fringe science, which is off-limits and flakey. Frontier Science is that unique area outside of the mainstream that embraces novel questions about which there is a certain amount of solid scientific evidence that challenges the conventional scientific paradigm. The scientific mainstream dismisses this evidence and so it is very difficult for frontier scientists to publish their data in mainstream scientific journals. I collected data and created databases of scientists on several areas of frontier science, including consciousness studies, alternative and complementary medicine, and bioelectromagnetics—the interaction of living systems with very low-level electromagnetic fields. The latter topic was dismissed by the mainstream because they didn't believe in that possibility, especially for non-ionizing radiation below the thermal limit. [*See David Muehsham.**]

I was told by one of the provosts at Temple University that I couldn't address the topic of homeopathy here, although homeopathy in the US started in Philadelphia when Samuel Hahnemann came from Germany and built what became the largest medical system in the US. During the Civil War, homeopathy was our main medical system, as seen at the Museum of the Civil War in Gettysburg. When that provost left, the new one said it was okay for me to delve into homeopathy. We see how science is largely driven by personalities and the economic and political interests of the university and beyond. During my later years at Temple, I served as one of 18 Congressionally-appointed advisors to the new Office of Alternative Medicine at the NIH. I became involved advising the Clinton Administration on complementary and alternative medicine for inclusion in the national health care program that was being considered. I became quite visible in this work. Temple University's Medical School was quite conventional in those years. I tried to involve them, but they were not interested.

Do you find that universities have changed in terms of the reluctance to study frontier topics? I think it's pretty much the same, although the frontier boundaries slowly change over time. When I left Temple University I was pretty much done with universities. I set up my own non-profit laboratory in 1997 and moved back to California where it is a lot easier to conduct this type of pioneering research. Here I am surrounded by like-minded people who follow alternative/complementary medicine, are interested in consciousness, and feel the effects of living things. I teach at two universities both of which have integrative programs that go beyond mainstream education. I teach energy medicine at Saybrook University and life physics courses at California Institute for Human Science.

Please define consciousness because that is the underlying concept of the new scientific paradigm. We all know what it is but it's hard to put it into words although we all share in consciousness. We all have an inner life of awareness, perception, sensorium, intention, volition, intuition, spirituality, etc. It's not just perception; it goes well beyond that. I think a machine can have perception but I disagree with certain people who think that someday machines will be conscious. There are unsettled arguments about this regarding robots and AI. I do have the sense in raising chickens and observing my fish in aquariums, that there is individuality of consciousness for all those living beings. *I certainly see that in my chickens!*

What about bacteria and cells? Do they have consciousness? Some of the healers that I worked with thought that they did. They felt connected to them and that they could connect on some level of consciousness. I have not been able to do that with microbes. For example, whenever I brush my teeth I kill a few million bacteria, so it's a matter of survival of the highest good in this case. I think consciousness is all pervasive in the universe, that the natural world is filled with being, and I don't believe that human consciousness is generated by the brain. This is one pivotal difference between mainstream science, which holds that position, and frontier science. Some frontier scientists regard the brain as a transducer of universal consciousness that is all pervasive, with each of us a unique receptor and so we are each unique. The whole body may be regarded as a receptor, with consciousness distributed throughout us.

In assessing the biofields of energy healers, we see the relative smoothness of their biofields and we see their ability to control their energy. However, we don't see particularly high levels of energy in the resting state. When we ask them to engage in the healing state, they can really crank it up. They may be drawing it down from a Divine source or the Source, whatever they believe, and bringing it through their bodies to the needy, the sick. We research phenomena like this in my laboratory using different measurement techniques to learn more about energy healing, extraordinary states of consciousness, and extraordinary abilities, as well as some of the exercises from ancient times such as qigong, yoga, and different types of meditation and healing. In my experiments, we discovered that no two healing sessions were ever the same in what we could measure. Moreover, healers have different levels of expertise, experience, and commitment, as well as variable mental, emotional, physical, and spiritual health each day, which I believe also affects their performance.

What about aura photographs? How do they measure the energy field and what are they used for? You are talking about devices out there that are more for entertainment, but they are not scientifically based. *What about Kirlian photography?* Kirlian photography is an important technique, but today it is largely digital since we have moved beyond photographic film of the old days. We have a digital Kirlian camera, one that we designed and constructed ourselves. Using this, we have looked for phantom limb effects. We also use a commercial device called Bio-Well (www.bio-well.com). [*See Shamini Jain.**]

What about when you tear off part of the leaf and photograph it and see the whole leaf? We have tried so-called "phantom leaf" experiments. A paper from a couple of years ago in the *Journal of Alternative and Complementary Medicine* by John Hubacher and others provided data from 30 to 40 years ago. Back then they used photographic film, which sees more than digital cameras. For example, photographic film is sensitive to electrons as well as light, but a digital camera doesn't record electrons. Maybe we are missing something by using digital cameras, at least in Kirlian photography. In the future, we may experiment using photographic film. I do think Kirlian photography can show a lot of information. However, it used higher voltage in former years, so you often felt an electric shock putting your hand on a Kirlian camera lens. Today's electrophotography uses less voltage and you don't feel any shock, so it is not so jarring to the biofield.

Is the biofield composed of biophotons or what's the nature of the invisible biofield? The biofield is the organizing field of life that I hypothesize is the "conductor" leading (or regulating) the symphony of life's physiology and biochemistry. The master regulator of the biofield is consciousness. Where the mind goes, energy flows, and the blood follows the *qi* (energy)—this is the key principle of Oriental medicine. The biofield is composed of many elements. I consider it the organizing field of light. Biophotons are one component of visible light. It probably has ultraviolet and certainly has infrared components, too. Medical imaging for thermography shows that your whole body emits around 100 watts of infrared energy, as well as electric and magnetic fields and other invisible rays, and acoustic fields such as the thump of the heart. Some organs emit more strongly than others. The heart is the greatest emitter of the body in terms of electricity and magnetism [*see Rollin McCraty**]. The brain is number two, but the whole body emits as well.

Special energy nodes include the sword fingers; the second and third fingers emit the most light out of the entire body. These are the fingers we use to point; these are the sword fingers we use in qigong and the martial arts. The right hand emits more than the left hand: The yang emits more than the yin. The yin is the receiver on the left. Yang, the right hand, is more of an emitter. We verified all of this ancient indigenous knowledge by testing it with sensitive detectors in the laboratory.

Have you been able to trace the meridians and chakras? No, we haven't traced the meridians yet. I've worked with a few chakras, namely, the third eye, the throat and the heart which are the easiest to image, at least in the frequency range that I've been working in. We haven't dealt with the lower ones as much. *When you image it, what do you see?* We are counting photons, the amount of light being emitted from these chakra regions; we are not imaging them. That would require really expensive cameras and a lot of time. And of course, people are moving from state to state in consciousness. It's difficult to sit still for an hour in total darkness and remain in the same state. Instead, it's easier for us to make faster measurements and get a sense of energy emission over shorter times where human subjects can maintain a specific state of consciousness over a few minutes.

The University of Wisconsin shows that meditation changes the brain. Have you done studies of meditators and do you meditate? I did one study comparing meditators to non-meditators and found that long-term meditators could with greater ease make high frequency brainwaves, namely, 40 Hertz (40 cycles per second). That is a special wavelength that has been associated with bliss and joy as well as creative insight. Meditators were able to do that on demand with 40-Hertz biofeedback much more readily than were non-meditators. I meditate, would like to do it more frequently, and I find it extremely worthwhile. We need to unplug from the external world and realize there is a whole world within us and keep in touch with Source, our Divine connection, that is accessible to us deep within. *Do you use a mantra or what helps you meditate?* When I was a teenager I learned Transcendental Meditation. That's when Maharishi was coming to the United States in the 1960s. I was assigned a specific mantra and I kept that up for many years, but I also like another type of meditation where you just focus on the breath. I find that very relaxing. I alternate between the two types.

Do you think that in the future healthcare will use these kinds of devices for diagnosis and treatment so it will be part of the mainstream medical care? We have some distance to go before those will become medical devices. In general, energy medicine devices work at the level of the biofield, providing very low-level signals that nudge the biofield back into balance and harmony, which subsequently positively affect the flesh and blood. One of the complicated things in the US is the requirement that they satisfy the FDA (Food and Drug Administration). In order to become FDA approved, you have to go through three levels of clinical trials for safety, for efficacy, and for efficacy in large numbers. Those trials cost a lot of money. So far, very few energy medicine type devices have been able to obtain sufficient funding to go through these levels of trials.

In my opinion, energy medicine remains in the doghouse because we have a pharmaceutical medicine that is so strong and so restrictive on other types of medicine. It really doesn't want the competition. The FDA is largely composed of people from the pharmaceutical medical industry who go in and out of the FDA and the industry. Consequently, there have been difficulties in getting

energy medicine devices through. Plus, we don't have a rich industry that would fund these expensive federal trials to satisfy the FDA.
I would have hoped that at this stage in my life energy medicine
would have made much more progress than it has. Instead, it has
been limping along for decades. I don't know that I am going to live
long enough to see these things become medical devices but they
can if the stronghold on the FDA lightens up.

It would be extremely helpful to have other types of medicine
besides pharmaceuticals, which have limitations and can produce
serious side effects. An example of an energy medicine device is the
trans-cranial brain stimulator for mood disorders and insomnia.
This is one of the hallmarks of energy medicine because it is an
FDA-approved medical therapy. There are also bone healing devices
for non-union fractures. That is, if your broken bone is not healing
well, you can get magnetic pulse field stimulation that is completely
noninvasive and does not require surgery. This is another hallmark
of energy medicine that was FDA approved decades ago, yet it is
hardly used in orthopedics. Pulsed magnetic field therapy is very
good for pain and sports injuries. Many energy medical devices are
medically approved outside the United States. For example, Bio-
Well is accepted in official medicine in 32 countries, but not in the
US. Here, we use it to assess the biofield although it is not part of
official US medicine.

*What about the Rife machine? That is the most well-known device
used for healing?* The Rife machine isn't legal in the United States.
I have known people who were selling it who were raided by the
FDA. *You can purchase it in Canada.* I did speak with the technician
for Royal Rife some 30 years ago, named John Crane. However, he
was terrified to talk with me about these things because of what
had happened to Royal Rife and himself. Rife invented a device
that apparently cured cancer, but he refused to go along with the
American Medical Association in his time. His laboratory was
raided, devices and data confiscated by the FDA, and then there
was a suspicious fire. Rife escaped to Mexico, while Crane was
convicted and spent three years in prison. I have tried to get the

Rife device out of the bowels of the FDA and into the Smithsonian museum as part of an exhibit on the history of medical devices in the US. Lots of people claim they have Rife-type devices when we don't really know for sure because Rife's device was confiscated and hidden from us for decades. The closest person to Royal Rife wasn't going to talk about it. I have a lot of doubts about the various devices sold purportedly as "Rife" devices today.

Square-wave devices generate waves that are square which contain and deliver numerous different frequencies and may be therapeutic, such as, if you need Vitamin B-6, you could take a multivitamin, and you might just get enough B-6. One problem is that there may be some deleterious frequencies produced by a square-wave generator among those that are therapeutic. We're not sure what we're getting with the square wave generators, but they are out there on the market. I don't know if they are legal in the United States.

What about Harry Oldfield's electrocrystal machine? He was a British science teacher who started doing Kirlian photography and was surprised to find auras and chakras. He developed a camera and a machine that sends frequencies through glass tubes that have different kinds of crystals in them. You adjust the machine for different frequencies. Every year there are more devices and more claims and often without third party published studies and without even tiny pilot studies, so I am skeptical. Where are the validation studies? I suggest the public demand validation before they purchase such devices.

What's the evidence for energy healing like Reiki, Johrei, Polarity Therapy, external Qigong therapy, Therapeutic Touch, magnet therapy, etc.? I conducted a study funded by NIH in 2001 to 2003 on Reiki to show its effects on bacterial cultures, a more extensive version of the experiments that I did back in 1979 to 1980. We found positive effects on pain patients with Reiki and found positive effects on bacterial growth, too. When the bacteria were heat shocked (which killed about half of them) the Reiki given to them facilitated their recovery and growth over control cultures. That was a clear finding that there's much more to Reiki than placebo. You can always argue that pain, mood improvement, or anxiety relief is a placebo effect but when there are measured effects on cell cultures, that is not a placebo effect. My study and others on cultured cells, as well as on plants, demonstrate that something beyond the level of a placebo is happening. Energy has to be involved, otherwise, there wouldn't be as much of an effect.

Do you do sham healing? Was there any difference between Reiki healers and untrained people? I deliberately didn't use sham because everybody has a biofield and you can have actors trained to do something and think about something else, but there will be an effect from the biofield. Frankly, I think it's not a very good control. My controls were having no healer and all aspects were double-blinded. I had technicians label everything and I did the assays so that I didn't know which were the control test tubes of bacteria and which were the Reiki-treated so, my study was adequately controlled. It's very hard to have shams in energy medicine. *I've seen studies where they put people in MRIs and simulated real and sham acupressure points and the acupressure points lit up the brain in a way that the sham acupressure points didn't.*

It's very different from drug studies where we can give sugar pills as placebos. We have to consider what is an appropriate control and not stoop so low as to do some silly sham healing that may actually confound our study. We also have to rethink the clinical trial for energy medicine. I also like outcome studies. Without controls, the people who are sick serve as their own controls. They come into the study sick. Then they get the intervention of energy healing and the follow up over time. This research design is a good study. With studies on a therapeutic energy device, it's different. You can always turn a device off and use it in a sham condition. If you turn it off and use it and it's not having an effect, that's a good sham.

What about magnet therapy, bioelectric magnetic therapy, electrodermal therapy, and phototherapy? I especially like phototherapy, but I will tell you a story about magnet therapy. I once sprained my ankle in an exercise class not too far from Chinatown in San Francisco. I limped down the Nob Hill towards Chinatown for lunch where

I saw a health store based on Oriental Medicine. The storekeeper showed me how to put the ring of magnets around my swollen ankle. Then, I went to lunch and much to my amazement, the swelling of my ankle went down just from a string of magnets placed on a swollen sprain. We understand the physics of this process, called the Hall effect. You bring a magnetic field close to the body and it changes the path of charged particles. The flow of lymph and blood is influenced by magnets on the body. That kind of therapy with static magnets, little hand-held magnets, only works over the short-term because the body adapts to static magnetics over the long term, but it's very good for injuries.

Phototherapy is another amazing thing. Strong light brought into the body, whether it is infrared or visible, or some combination of both can do amazing things. I'm seeing a doctor now who treats dementias with phototherapy to the head with patients who are suffering from diseases such as Alzheimer's or Parkinson's. They arrive shuffling into his office, some of them have no emotional affect, looking at the floor. Twenty minutes of light therapy to the skull and they are more like their old selves, walking normally, relating to people again, shaking your hand and talking. That doesn't last. They come in for a few treatments and that is more lasting. I think there is incredible hope. We can expect a lot more dementias as the population is aging and also exposed to a lot more microwaves from the radiation associated with wireless communication devices (4G and now the coming 5G) which is anticipated to cause more dementias. The drugs just don't have that powerful an effect on these neurological disorders.

Is it a particular kind of light beamed into the head? I'm not privy to all the details, but I can say that the light includes some colored visible light—from some very powerful blue and magenta LEDs and there is some infrared emitted as well. Infrared is very penetrating, perhaps five to ten centimeters into the body so it can work at a much deeper level than visible light. I've used infrared therapy for sports injuries too. NASA pioneered infrared LED therapy for the astronauts because if they are injured in space, they need speedy therapy to help with the pain and swelling. Infrared devices are sold in the marketplace now, also for cosmetics, much less strong than the medical devices. People claim that infrared applied to the face is also helpful to ward off wrinkles and sagging flesh. Others claim that it will stimulate the hair follicles to help with baldness. I think there is a tremendous potential for energy interventions to enhance beauty as well as stimulate rapid healing of deep injuries and serious chronic illnesses like Alzheimer's.

There seem to be many infrared electromagnetic devices. How does one know which one is efficacious? You go to a physician for the deep phototherapy, which is efficacious. There are not many US doctors who use phototherapy yet. It's still largely experimental here, but it has been well known elsewhere for decades. For example, in Russia, they do a lot of laser therapy for deep healing. Phototherapy is still hardly known in the US. I would say most infrared LEDs on the market sold over the counter, including near-infrared, would be most appropriate for wound healing and sports injuries. Another issue is diabetic neuropathy because we have an epidemic of diabetes in this country. Some of the complications are pain and numbness in the feet, even gangrene or tissue death in the feet and legs due to poor circulation. Phototherapy can turn that around. Instead of going for an amputation, and losing a limb, one could try phototherapy and reverse some of these necrotic diseases that are impacting nerves and tissue on the feet and legs.

Have you done the Reiki training or any particular kind of energy healing yourself? Although I can do some energy healing, I have deliberately not gone through the Reiki training because I didn't want to be a Reiki person studying Reiki. I thought that would be seen by some as a conflict of interest and that I would be taken less seriously as the scientist studying it. But that doesn't mean that at some stage in life I may do that because I think self-Reiki, as well as Reiki on others, are important modalities and important skills. *As a Reiki 3, I can give the attunement when you're ready.*

It seems to me that the intention to be a channel for healing energy is essential. Another interesting thing from my study on Reiki is we did find differences between the practitioners, which was not a result that the healers liked because they think Reiki is all the same. Reiki tradition maintains that it doesn't matter what state of consciousness you're in, if you apply the method, you serve as a conduit for the energy, you get results. I could see that some of the practitioners in the study were concentrating harder and more attuned to the whole experiment, and we obtained better results with them. One day when we got reverse results with a Reiki practitioner who in treating the needy bacteria actually produced less growth. She shared that she had a bacterial infection that day from a bladder infection. The same species of bacteria, *E.coli*, which we used in our study may have been the culprit in her a bladder infection. According to the principles of Reiki, the energy goes where it needs to go for the highest good. The highest good that day was healing the healer and not our bacterial cultures in test tubes! It was very gratifying and important to observe this in the study. Healers, when they are ill, should not be practicing—this is another important realization. They must be well or the Reiki that they are transmitting is only going to go back to them and not the patient. These little bits of data that show up in experiments are important clues.

Hospitals seem to be most comfortable with Therapeutic Touch and now Reiki. Nurses are trained to do Therapeutic Touch. Have you found that they use different frequencies that can be measured? No, I haven't measured the frequencies yet; I've only measured the effects of Reiki. The effects observed depend on the practitioner's emotional state at the time we measure them, which can be quite variable. There are so many parameters in the healing arts that have yet to be analyzed, including the mood of the practitioner. The practice of Reiki and the other healing modalities also increases the mood and gives them a stronger spiritual connection—another positive outcome from our study as well. The healers benefit dramatically, emotionally, spiritually, and physically from the practice of the healing art. Their health is strengthened, such that, in helping others they help themselves.

You mentioned that water has subtle properties like memory. That is very interesting because about 70% of the human body is water. Yes, we've done studies on water (nearby as well as far away) and we can see changes in the energetics of the water. We had a meditation group in the San Diego region about 500 miles from the San Francisco Bay sending energy to a water station. We had two different beakers of water at different stations, then the meditators randomly decided which one to treat remotely sending energy, and we compared the two waters. We were blinded—we didn't know which water station they treated. In virtually every case we could tell which one they had energized across many miles.

What was different about the water that was treated? We measured the light emitted from water droplets of each water sample. We placed a syringe full of water with a little drop hanging just above the Kirlian camera lens and increased the voltage signal of the camera. We measured the induced light emitted by the water. There was more light or more complex patterns of light coming out of the water to which they had sent energy compared to the control water that was untreated. Both waters were from the same source—tap water in our laboratory. The only difference was they were sending energy to only one of the samples, and we didn't know which one. In the end, the results clearly showed more light emitted from the water sample on which they focused. Also, they went back and forth switching the stations in all the experiments. Clearly, distance doesn't matter when it comes to healing intent. However, the literature does show that the patient being present in the same location as a healer seems to have stronger effects on patients. Yet in experiments, we also see effects across many miles, and it's remarkable.

What do you think of Dr. Masaru Emoto's water crystal studies imprinting tap water with negative or positive suggestions and getting different crystal forms? It certainly is a beautiful idea but it appears that they might have been "cherry picking," not conducting these experiments with the same level of blindedness. If someone thought about love, they are going to look for a pretty crystal to match that. Dr. Emoto was a practitioner, not a scientist. Nonetheless, I think he raised our consciousness tremendously about the power of conscious intent and how it impacts the water around us and within us. That is the important message. People have asked me whether I'd replicate it but I don't have a walk-in freezer or the type of microscope to do so. It should be replicated so that the scientist doesn't know what emotion is being featured so that he or she can photograph the crystals and then have a team of judges, who don't know the details, judge whether there is a match and the level of beauty of the crystals. I think it's clear that water changes structure with conscious intention and takes on qualities of its environment.

Even the water that crystalized on a higher mountain top and then was brought down the mountain and crystalized again shows a residue of the structure that it embodied at the top of the mountain. Water has a memory. This is an amazing thing. I don't know the duration of that memory, but water is continuously getting information from its environment including emotions and thoughts and shifting its structure accordingly. It's not so simple, this H_2O. It looks like a simple molecule, but clearly, it's much more complex. I participated in the international water conference held recently in Germany where scientists from around the world explore some of these unusual questions about water and its novel properties.

Some people say it's really important for health maintenance to drink alkalized water. I drink water from an ionizer that is not only alkaline but rich in electrons. You can make alkaline water by putting a pinch of baking soda in water but that's simply not enough. You want water slightly alkaline but also rich in electrons. Natural water flowing is both alkaline and rich in electrons, but water flowing out of the tap is deficient in electrons due to how we process water in municipal water plants. That's why I recommend an electric ionizer that filters the water, removes the fluoride and chlorine (or chloramines), then passes the water over the cathode in electrolysis. We drink the alkaline fraction passed over the cathode which is rich in electrons. I've been drinking that water for over 20 years and recommend it to all of my clients.

What other kinds of health maintenance suggestions do you give them? One of the most important things you can do is exercise as well as drink enough water since the energy field of the body collapses if you're dehydrated. When you rehydrate, within a short time the body snaps back energetically. I think lots of people are dehydrated and don't know it. Getting exercise moves the qi, especially when it is done with intention as in qigong, and therefore, practicing qigong is especially important for health maintenance. Many people I know who are licensed acupuncturists and Oriental medical doctors discovered that practicing Qi-gong produces stronger positive results—even more than acupuncture. It's a general tune-up of the whole energy field similar to the martial arts like Tai Chi. The qigongs that were designed for health such as Wild Good Qi-gong (Dayanqigong) and Five Animal Frolicks, really enhance health with regular practice.

Alkaline-Ionized water, exercise, qigong, meditate, walk in nature and…? Also, eat the right diet. I think organic is very important today when we have so much contamination from the agrichemical industry. Recent evidence suggests that diabetes is not just about high blood sugar and too much sugar in the diet: It's linked to a high toxic load. We need to avoid processed food and non-organic food, the GMOs, by buying organic or better yet grow your own food. *What about microwaving food?* This grossly changes the water structure and denatures proteins and other biomolecules in foodstuffs. Low temperature cooking via low fires is how people used to cook, and we need to do slow cooking and/or eat raw to improve our health.

What organizations and schools teach people about these kinds of wellness practices? You've mentioned Dr. Andrew Weil's program in Integrative Medicine at the University of Arizona, your Institute for Frontier Sciences, and Sophia University. What other groups do you look to? The California Institute for Human Science is a very good school for educating oneself in life physics and is based on the integration of mind-body-spirit. I highly recommend it. Saybrook University has programs in integrative health which are great for practitioners and researchers who want to learn mind-body approaches and includes a Masters and Doctoral program.

What kind of journals do you look to for cutting edge information in this field? I'm on the editorial board of the *Journal of Alternative and*

Complementary Medicine. This is a very high level research-oriented journal that has been around for over 25 years. Some of the online journals charge $3,000 or so for an author to be published. This has become a handicap for frontier science and medicine in which funding has been relatively scarce. In addition, one would think that Scholar.google.com would only show scholarly journals but other non-scholarly publications also turn up there. Databases such as PubMed.com is the gateway to the US National Library of Medicine, and this index is trustworthy.

I'm interested in what the visionary scientists think about our future in the face of climate change, increasing number of autocrats, and growing inequality around the world. I'm optimistic because I think more and more people are waking up to the reality of what's going on in this planet, about the inequities, about the ruling classes that are covertly destroying the wealth of so many of us. Also, about the diminishing middle class in the United States and the utter poverty in so many nations that we now see blatantly right in front of us watching videos on the internet, including uploaded posts from billions of cellphones from people worldwide. It opens our hearts to see this hardship and we feel empathy for our neighbor. We need to get the right people in power and be more vigilant in our republic and our democratic process, otherwise, we lose our freedoms. It seems to me we have already lost some. However, I'm confident that more people are waking up to the reality of the world condition and I'm hoping to contribute to improving our condition. I've been woken up by viewing much of this information online, going beyond our mainstream media, which has been an important educational process for me.

About climate change, the blame is being placed on us by some of our leaders saying our carbon footprint is too big, that we're raising the CO_2 greenhouse gas. I don't agree with this viewpoint. First of all, there is no proof that we did it. Secondly, the sun is getting hotter: All the ice caps on Mars are gone. We have devices today such as the ionospheric heaters that do experiments on the upper ionosphere poking holes in it and playing havoc with our global weather. I do not believe that a lot of our strange weather patterns are merely from the burning of fossil fuels and other ways that the average person is expending energy. *It's coming from the sun?* The sun is one element. Also, if there is even more volcanic activity on earth, and I think there has been, the oceans are heating up. If the oceans heat up, the carbon dioxide dissolved in the oceans gets released into the air. It's similar to taking soda pop, putting it on the stove and heating it up, and then the bubbles of carbon dioxide come out.

Our burning of fossil fuel is contributing somewhat, but I don't blame all of our climate change on that. Nonetheless, I'm all for conserving and not wasting resources. I agree with that element of the Green Movement, but I do not agree that we are going to save the planet by cutting down on fossil fuel burning. We may be in for some global climate change from these ionospheric devices such as the High Frequency Active Auroral Research Project (HAARP) in Alaska, used for experiments on the upper atmosphere. There are patents on weather control and they've been around for decades. The sun heating up and all the solar system planets getting warmer are things we can't control. We may have to cope with climate change, to somehow adjust or migrate accordingly. Frankly, no one can prove the extent to which human behavior and burning fossil fuels makes any difference. There is absolutely no validation or way to validate it.

What do you do for fun when you aren't in your laboratory? I garden. I love nature and really love to get my hands on plants and raise chickens for eggs. I love making jewelry. I love touching natural stones and I like dancing. I used to do ballet in my youth and now I do exercises like Jazzercize. I do tap dancing. If I can get around to it, I like ballroom and social dancing as well.

Is there anything else to add? A lesson that I've learned in life is that it's so important to have big dreams and to stick with your dreams no matter what the obstacles are. I had some serious obstacles in the beginning of my scientific career, yet today I feel alive and content with a life well-lived and I am still passionately working in frontier science. My dreams, at least in part, have been fulfilled. Most importantly, I've lived true to my life purpose and values. There is a tremendous satisfaction that comes from following your dreams. Figuring out what your dreams are, what gives you the greatest passion in life is important. Whatever you choose to do, I think it must help others in this world and serve the greater whole, while inspiring and firing your soul and making you happy. I hope that some of the readers will go on to become frontier scientists and uncover new features of the universe, new ways of healing, and explore our full powers of being human. That's what continues to inspire me.

Books
Ed. *The Interrelationship Between Mind and Matter,* 1982
Life at the Edge of Science, 1996

Websites
www.brubik.com
www.frontiersciences.org

David Muehsam, Ph.D.
On the Edge of Objectivity:
Consciousness and
Bioelectromagnetics

Photo by the author

Questions to Ponder

Why, as a scientist, is Dr. Muehsam interested in psi phenomena?

In what ways is the "new" paradigm of healing ancient? How does CHI's research relate to this paradigm?

What should we consider thinking about how parapsychology might work?

I'm interested in what life experiences encourage someone to go against the established scientific paradigm. Why are you willing to take on unorthodox research topics? I think primarily it comes from making logical deductions about what's interesting to study. For example, there's a common view of parapsychology as a kind of an outside, fringe region of science that is not entirely accepted by mainstream scientists. Yet, there is a very large body of reports that suggests to me that parapsychology is something that we should know about and inquire about. I think that to completely ignore a body of data this large would be unscientific and many people have personal experiences of thinking the same thought as someone who is close to us or having a sense of who is that ring on the telephone. This is, of course, anecdotal, rather than scientific evidence, but it is undeniably quite common.

There's Rupert Sheldrake's work with people knowing when they're being stared at from behind and the large body of work that Robert Jahn and Brenda Dunne produced at the Princeton Engineering Anomalies Research lab (PEAR). Research overviews appear in Dean Radin's* body of work and the summaries he's written in his books. For me, it's a question of pursuing truthfulness rather than cowering in fear, as in "Parapsychology, I shouldn't study that!" But I think there shouldn't be topics in science that are on the fringe for irrational reasons. Once there is a certain amount of data that supports the notion that further research would turn up interesting results, I feel as scientists we are obligated to look further into those areas.

The personal motivations for scientists are interesting. Frank Sulloway's *Born to Rebel* looked at birth order in the family, found by studying a large number of scientists through the last few hundred years. Sulloway found that the innovators tended to be the younger-born in the family, whereas scientists who tended to be more conventional tended to be the elder children. *Are you a later born?* I am the younger of two. I'd say my sister is fairly unconventional, too. Maybe she's actually the one that breaks the mold in the sense that she's an MD who practices natural methods and mind-body practices. But Sulloway looked at trends over a few hundred years and families had more children in earlier times. *Did you influence her or did she influence you or both?* I think both. She's been a tremendous source of information and inspiration for me.

Your astrological sign? Sagittarius. *Sagittarians are the most common of our scientists; they ask deep questions.* My Msyers-Briggs personality type is ENFP. *What about your family's religious beliefs when you were a boy?* My parents were quite spiritual rather than overtly religious. We occasionally attended a Unitarian church.

You do yoga and you're a musician. How do your other interests feed you? I think they all feed in together. When I was ten years old, my dad got very sick. He had a stroke and was never the same again. He couldn't speak correctly and he lost the use of the left side of his body. Despite the suffering, it taught me a lot about impermanence and about not wasting my time. I asked myself, "If I've only got as many years as my dad got, what would I do with them?" I did the best I could to follow things I loved: yoga, science, and music and I've had the good fortune to be able to work in these areas throughout my adult life. I've found that it's really helpful to have an integrative, multidisciplinary point of view, to have healthy interests so we're more well-rounded individuals. I'm very much in favor of liberal arts education. If I'm really honest about what motivated me to follow this path, it's was mainly fascination, along with that childhood experience with my dad. I didn't want to be pushing shopping carts at the local supermarket, so I worked as hard as I could in the areas I loved and it's come out okay.

At some point some years ago, I stopped trying to make the roadmap for myself. I said to myself, "I don't know what I'm doing. I'm completely lost. I just give myself up and I want to be of service. Please, I want to work and try to contribute to this planet earth that we're on." *Very similar to Fred Alan Wolf.** Somehow at that time in my life when I got down on bended knee and gave up, things started to open up, maybe simply because I opened up and acknowledged it. If I let go, somehow, once I'm committed to that, all manner of possibilities emerge.

Why are you living in Italy rather than the USA? I'm a citizen in Europe and in the United States. I did my Ph.D. at the University of Bologna and I have a position at the National Institute of Biostructures and Biosystems in Italy. It's a multi-university consortium for the study of biophysics, a wonderfully creative environment. The academic environment here is highly collaborative. The Italian cities are quite close to each other, with great train service, and people know each other. And there's has been a very high concentration of research on bioelectromagnetics here in Italy due to a few pioneers like Ferdinando Bersani here at the University of Bologna and Alessandro Chiabrera at the University of Genoa, who I first met in the early '90s when he visited our lab at Mt. Sinai in New York every August. I've been very fortunate to work with scientists like these.

The Galileo Report *written by Harald Walach* stated that parapsychology studies face the replicability problem since they change different aspects of the studies, rather than performing exact replications. I asked Dean Radin about that and he does change up experiments but most social science research isn't exactly replicable because you are working with human beings, not bacteria or cells in a petri dish. How would you respond to the charge that the replicability problem is so great that you can't say there is scientific validity for parapsychology studies?* Firstly, many experiments in the psychological sciences, even in cell biology, are not replicated exactly. And often one runs the same experiment twice and gets slightly different results due to natural variability.

Secondly, if one looks at the body of material that came out of some of the parapsychological research laboratories, for example, the PEAR lab in Princeton, there is a high degree of statistical significance in those outcomes about influencing the output of RNGs but small effect sizes. There's a great deal of variability between people. To my reading in parapsychology, there are a large number of experiments, even if they have only been completed once, that produced high levels of statistical significance and that interests me. Dean Radin has written some good summaries pointing out that there are too many studies for this to be simply due to chance. Yes, of course, these studies need to be replicated and extended, but to dismiss them out of hand would be similar to dismissing many single biology experiments because they were never exactly replicated.

When we talk about parapsychology, we have to talk about factors like experimenter or expectancy effects—the notion that experimenters' beliefs could affect the outcome of experiments, and that people who believe more in the experiment appear to produce greater outcomes on parapsychological testing. This is summarized in Radin's book *Real Magic*, where he reports that skeptics tend to score lower on parapsychological tests. On some level, if we are interacting with the outcomes of events, whether it is RNGs or the ability to perceive a remote location, we are crossing a boundary, which I call "the edge of objectivity" where a subjective element comes into the story. For example, it may be the experimental ambience of the lab, where if the staff are skeptics there is greater resistance and smaller effect sizes, or patients who trust their doctors. Some of these influences can be tested.

This begins to sound like quantum mechanics (QM), where the mode of observation influences the outcomes of experiments. That's one of the reasons that QM has been very attractive to people who want to explain parapsychology and crossing the Edge of

Objectivity also brings up interesting questions about study design. I think that in some cases, we may need to broaden our concept rather than trying to isolate the parapsychological interaction into a fully controllable and completely objective framework, we may have to accept that there are subjective elements, only some of which we can control. Other factors we may not be able to control or even classify—things we don't know yet. Unknown unknowns...

One of the most profound implications of psi research is that the beliefs and intention of the observer have great effect. But it's dismissed as just placebo effect. Placebo effect, observer effect, experimenter expectation effect—we should harness their power and use it. I agree. I think the placebo effect is exceedingly important as it tells us about the power of belief and suggests ways we can harness it to improve health outcomes. Look at the growth of mind-body stress reduction techniques and the way they're now widely implemented in clinical practice. That's a beginning. If we change our level of stress, for example, that impacts our health. It's starting to get into the belief system that if we change our inner self, this reflects on the outer self and our physical health. This crosses that edge of objectivity. Some of the quandaries may be more philosophical (having to do with our need to objectify), rather than practical when the goal is to reduce suffering and develop ways that people can live happier and more meaningful lives. That viewpoint changes one's perspective on science and medicine.

That leads us to the idea that a new paradigm is being created. It's actually a very old paradigm, but it's new in the Western world to emphasize that consciousness is primary, not the physical. Do you think we are creating a new scientific paradigm? No, I don't think this is an entirely new scientific paradigm. Rather, we're being swept up in a recognizance of a number of older ideas. Notions around consciousness and vitalism have been around for thousands of years in various forms, such as in non-dualistic forms in Indian Vedic thought and interesting dualistic forms in Jain thought. We discuss this in some detail in a paper I co-authored with CHI Director Shamini Jain* and others.[1] Among may other regions, the Indo-Tibetan region and China produced philosophies that embody a preeminence of consciousness, pointing to a "consciousness stuff" that relates to the nature of the mind and emotions and how these interact with the physical world. We see this in the various theories of yoga, where consciousness itself plays a central role in our ability to understand and link with the Cosmos. In non-dualistic philosophies there is no hard boundary between mind and body, self and other.

I am a biophysicist and my background is in bioelectromagnetics, so that's the direction from which I moved into this area. When I first started working in 1991 with Arthur Pilla at Mt. Sinai, I was very interested in weak magnetic field interactions. The reason this fascinated me was because the apparent interaction of energies of a weak field (such as the geomagnetic field or even weaker) are very far below that of thermal "noise," the Brownian thermal motion of all the molecules that jiggle, for example at 37 degrees inside the body. At the time, there were lots of arguments around this. How could it be possible that we could have a magnetic field interaction at such apparently low interaction energies?

We had a colleague who debated us through a sequence of papers, which was a fun process. He argued effectively and valiantly on theoretical grounds against the existence of a variety of types of these non-thermal or sub-thermal electro-magnetic field (EMF) effects. He carried that banner across the field even in the face of an onslaught of experimental data to the contrary. It was an interesting example of the belief system in science and also a great example of the system of checks and balances. Without this colleague who was playing devil's advocate, we wouldn't have learned as much or thought about all of the criticisms that he gave us. At the end of the day, I think his critical, skeptical view was necessary and very helpful.

What we wound up seeing, and what has been confirmed over the last 25 to 50 years—depending on how one measures—is that there are a variety of mechanisms for weak EMF effects. Some have been well fleshed out, such as the free-radical mechanism that underlies at least some forms of animal navigation. It's now well-established that several different species of animals navigate by detecting the Earth's magnetic field using a free-radical sensing mechanism. A nice overview on this was written several years ago.[2]

Many open questions remain around EMFs and particularly how magnetic fields of low intensity and low frequency affect the body. More work is still needed to understand frequency resonances and amplitude "windows" and the different types of conditions under which those occur. We are still in the nascent stages, but what is exciting about that is we see that non-thermal weak EMFs do indeed affect the body. And this had led to the use of weak EMFs for healing: Nonthermal devices are cleared by the US Food and Drug Administration (FDA) for the treatment of pain, edema, bone repair, etc., and are used for healing wounds. And there's a large cottage industry of folks selling pulsed EMF therapy devices for everything from baldness to athlete's foot. Some of these probably work well, and others probably don't, and we certainly need more testing in order to better inform the public. There's evidence for dangers due to EMFs too. Interactions with these non-thermal EMFs can affect growth and repair and perhaps well-being generally. Very low energies are often involved so the interaction may best be described as informational rather than energetic in terms of the definition of energy we use in physics, i.e., the ability to move objects, heat things up, etc. I found this fascinating when I was younger and still do.

Is the Rife machine an example of a device that uses that kind of frequency? I made measurements on such a device a couple of years ago and found it was putting out a rather high amplitude signal. So, I'm not sure if the Rife machine qualifies as being very low-level nonthermal because there is a lot of juice being put out. Some of the frequency components appear to be high enough to induce strong electric fields in the body that could affect a variety of processes. Many devices will produce a little bit of heating in the body. For example, early radiofrequency 27.12 MHz diathermy devices can not only increase circulation by heating the body but were found also to reduce pain and edema and assist in the repair of chronic wounds.

They produce tissue heating when you dial them up into the highest settings, but interestingly, therapeutic effects remain when the signal amplitude and duty cycle (%-on time) is dialed way down so that heating is on the order of 1/10,000th of a degree Celsius for a 30-minute treatment session. Some of these devices are cleared by the FDA, with effects shown in cells, animals, and humans.

When hands-on heal healers are doing Reiki or external Chigong, Johrei, or Healing Touch, are they in some ways using the same mechanism? There have been many reports of emissions from Qigong practitioners and other healers, with reports from China for emission of just about every frequency of EMFs, infrasound, and light. These all fall into that category of studies that haven't been fully replicated. It's a convenient explanation that maybe humans emit a very low field just like the WIFI field or a Bluetooth field that communicates information. But this may be akin to the idea that "when all one has is a hammer, everything looks like a nail." We have many reports of healing at a distance that might not be easily explained by a conventional EMF mechanism. We have a body of data of parapsychological interactions that occurred over hundreds or thousands of miles or retroactively. This makes an EMF mechanism seem less likely since EMFs generally drop with distance from the source; your car radio reception drops as you drive away from the station, for example. This has led to speculations around quantum entanglement for healer effects and parapsychology.

In 1994 we did a sequence of experiments at Mt. Sinai Medical Center in 1994 with two Qigong practitioners recently arrived from China. We studied the effects of EMFs on a myosin enzyme system, part of the body's muscular system, and found that Qigong treatment affected the rates of the enzyme activity. This Qigong practice delivered healing "energy" without physically touching the enzyme samples. Interestingly, when we placed the samples inside a special "mu-metal" box that shields from external EMF, the effects were greatly reduced. That might suggest that an EMF was part of the interaction, but it could have been the presence of the box itself, as the practitioners were asked to direct their practice through a big box around the test tubes. It could have just been an effect on their psychology or their practice.

If you ask most scientists, "Do you understand quantum mechanics?" they'll likely say no. *It's too weird and spooky.* Yes, spooky action at a distance. I don't want to make blanket statements suggesting quantum theory explains parapsychology or consciousness. I think that this needs to be shown by experiment, rather than by repeating the rather broad arguments for plausibility that we've seen thus far. Another case of when all one has is a hammer, everything looks like a nail? But perhaps more importantly, it may be that it's very difficult for us to understand how parapsychology works because of our point of view of separateness. From that point of view, we need a carrier, some field or force that mediates the interaction between two points in space or time. Many, many cultures around the world throughout history have developed more animistic, interconnected views that embody a sense of an interconnected cosmos and the spirit world or the psychic world playing a larger role in life than we do in the Western world.

We are focused on material mechanisms in our culture. So, how we explain parapsychology may be in large part an ontological question, rather than finding the new radio beam, identifying the "suable energy," or the quantum entanglement system that solves the problem for us. If you have two entangled particles and they go flying off in two different directions, you can interact with one particle and that instantaneously changes the outcome of the other particle. This seems to suggest that there's some "signal" that travels between the two instantaneously—faster than the speed of light. But in QM, the two particles are described by one wave function. They are mathematically part of the same quantum state and are thus intrinsically connected. In 2017, a team in China passed a signal between two cities with a satellite and showed there was an entanglement between the received signals at the two cities, which were 1200 kilometers apart.[3]

Certainly, it's interesting to speculate about the role quantum mechanics plays in something like parapsychology. This approach seems to hold promise because quantum entanglement has been verified over and over again with better and more loophole-free experiments s the years have gone by. But there have been some good arguments against this due to issues like decoherence: In order for entanglement to occur experimentally, there can't be a whole lot of other non-entangled particles interacting with the entangled one, as this generally destroys the entangled state.

If we have quantum entanglement between you and me, then what's the medium? What's keeping entangled particles from decohering? I think it's both a technical and a philosophical argument amongst physicists. I've seen theoretical physics papers to the effect that the whole universe is one big entangled state. On the other extreme is the idea that macroscopic entanglement can't occur at all because of this decoherence, which I think is an argument that needs to be addressed by folks who want to explain parapsychology and consciousness using quantum mechanics. I don't think we should resort to hand-waving arguments that since entanglement exists, it's the explanation for parapsychological phenomena. The onus ought to be on us to produce testable hypotheses that demonstrate that such a mechanism is acting, and it's probably a good idea to bear in mind that physics has changed dramatically over the last 120 years and may do so again.

Some people like Jude Currivan* use the image of the hologram, as if everything is in everything else so you're not really separating two objects, they're still one somehow. Fields within fields. I love the idea; it's so beautiful and inspires one to study nature, seeing the universe in a grain of sand, like William Blake said. I think we see these metaphors and the existence of scaling patterns in nature such as fractals, where at one level you see a certain type of structure that's repeated at the larger and smaller levels. We see these types of structures in nature from the subatomic to astronomical levels, and in our bodies—for example, in nervous system signals. If we look at the way these signals change across time, they have a fractality that influences the meaning of the information conveyed by the signal. There is a very strong set of data that supports this idea, but whether we can say "In the one, the many, and in the many, the one," we need more time to understand this in more detail. Just because a theory is really attractive and I like it and it feeds my soul doesn't mean it's the right theory or explains everything. Can a human intellect grasp the nature of these questions? How would a being much more evolved and intelligent than me look at all of this?

It's interesting when you think about the repetition of the pattern of the spiral in our ears, seashells, and galaxies. Some people observe that the basic geometric shape is the toroid and the universe works with this figure-eight energy coming into the bottom and out the top. Russian scientists talk about torsion. Roger Penrose and his spinors.[4] Elizabeth Rauscher, a great person and great physicist who passed away in 2019, wrote some very interesting papers on this. Subatomic particles with spin define a toroidal geometry. For example, when we look at magnetic fields they tend to take that toroidal shape, a spinning dipole. More generally, if we think about space and time in the abstract, if we localize a point, then we don't necessarily have a direction. But if we introduce a spin at the point that defines an axis around the spin, that naturally defines the coordinate system. If you put a magnetic field into that, then you get a toroid, seen everywhere from the insides of apples to the formation of galaxies. Nassim Haramein made some beautiful metaphors and some lovely animations of toroidal geometry and vortices, which make it easy for the public to understand these ideas.[5] Physics and chemistry then becomes a kind of topological knot theory.

What kind of research have you been doing in the last decade? In the 1990s I worked in EMF therapeutics and in recent years I've done laboratory studies on the effects of EMFs on hemoglobin deoxygenation and stem cells and their gene expression. With a group in Bologna, Italy, I'm looking at EMF effects on the cyto-skeleton of cells, which give the cells shape and the microtubular transmission there.

A group of us from CHI went to India in 2018 and measured electrophysiology, brain wave EEG (electroencephalography) and

ECG (electrocardiography) of people who were doing religious ceremonies in group meditation. We were looking at the ways that the brain waves of individuals in the group meditation might become linked together showing similar responses or coming into phase. I'm very interested in understanding more about what's happening inside of us during different kinds of meditative activities and how the devices we use to collect data can inform us. In the group context, how there can be a synergy? Do we in fact connect in a manner that can be measured? It's very different to meditate in a group than to meditate alone and so on. Our preliminary analyses showed that group coherence increased during periods of a guided meditation when the guidance was to direct the awareness inwards.

Did you feel on a personal level that the atmosphere was different when the group was meditating than when they were going about their daily activities? Crossing the edge of objectivity again, but in short, yes. In any kind of gathering that has shared intention, whether it's a musical concert, community event or a religious setting, the group energy can be huge. *As measured by Roger Nelson's* Global Consciousness Project.* I think that changes the experience a lot. We see more and more—and this is a direction I've been moving in the last ten years—that each of us is part of the societal organism. We're part of our friends, our family, our colleagues, our tribe, our nation, our species, our planet. We see evidence from psychosocial genomics and psychoneuroimmunology, in studies on how mental/emotional states and social stress affects the expression of genes and immune and inflammatory responses. This suggests that our well-being, our capacity to deal with inflammation, stress, and immune challenges has a lot to do with our social state.

Notably, Steve Cole at UCLA has done some very interesting studies in the emerging field of psychosocial genomics, for example, on the effect of psychosocial stress such as perceived social isolation on gene expression for immune responses and inflammatory signaling molecules.[6] Social isolation and the stress that comes from it can reduce the immune response and increase the amount of inflammation inside the body. *It would be interesting to study prisoners who are in solitary isolation.* Cole's work made a very deep impression on me because here was the inside speaking to the outside. The inner state thus becomes as "real" as the molecules the scientists are measuring. Also, it suggests that we need to make healthier social environments so that people can have healthier lives.

My point is that we're all part of a larger social organism. More and more we see that science reflects the idea that we're all inter-connected. Instead of looking at myself as a biological automaton and my state of health or well-being as mostly dependent upon the kind of food I eat and air I breathe and whether I exercise—that's a somewhat limited point of view. As we move to a more social point of view, we start to see the interconnections that we have. Why is it that in group meditation I have a different kind of experience than when I'm alone on my mat? I think the potential for science to give us information about this is very great. *We've known for a long time that the orphans in Eastern Europe had horrible health outcomes because they weren't held and cared for emotionally. They were fed but they weren't loved. It's not new information that we are social beings.* Yes, it may be that the biologists took a while to catch up to information that folks in the social sciences have known for a long time.

I think of William Bengston's healing of mice injected with breast cancer cells. He found a resonance effect in that the cradles where the healed mice were kept had a resonance so that mice put there healed even if there was no hands-on healing by humans. It's really interesting and it's rather ineffable. I've had the experience of walking into a room where a lot of meditation has been done and maybe it's just my imagination, but often there is a sense—feeling of a special atmosphere that is difficult to put into words. If I walk into a sacred place there is often a palpable feeling and, because I find that personally attractive, I seek out those places. I'm not objective in this kind of evalua-tion. Perhaps there is some kind of imprint or patterning that does change the physical properties of the space, and certainly some of it is in my imagination. Then again, in George Bernard Shaw's play *St. Joan,* Joan of Arc tells Robert, her captor, that St. Catherine and S. Margaret talk to her. Robert responds that, "They come from your imagination", to which Joan replies, "Of course. That is how the messages of God come to us". The edge of objectivity again...

We have scientific literature on the effects of intention—imbuing devices or even mobile phone apps with intention. A double-blind placebo-controlled study that used an app like that, that showed statistically significant changes in heart-rate variability parameters. Somehow, intention was imprinted upon the app (I don't know how because the technology was proprietary) and if it was running on the phone next to a person on a table, their heart rate variability was different than if they didn't have the app loaded. The phone, by the way, wasn't transmitting at the time. This was performed by Beverly Rubik,* published in the *Journal of Alternative and Complementary Medicine* in 2017.

It's like homeopathy where you may not have an atom of the original calcium or phosphorus or whatever but it's impactful. Yes, I'm seeing new information coming out very frequently about this. There is evidence suggesting that when one serially dilutes homeopathic remedies, some nano-particles of the original stuff do remain and that could have an effect on the water clustering, etc. To view this from another perspective, we know the idea of holy water, water that has been blessed, water with healing properties at Lourdes, or the well in the Irish countryside by the Hawthorne fairy tree with ribbons tied in the branches. We see some reflections of it in the work of Dr. Masaru Emoto in Japan who froze water droplets and imprinted them differently, as seen in frozen crystals. I'd love to see this work replicated and studied systematically. There are some fascinating ideas there, but clear, consistent scientific study is lacking, so it's hard to draw conclusions. I'd like to see the companies selling homeopathic remedies be more financially supportive of research.

There is a large body of literature on EMF effects on water, particularly on colloidal solutions. A lot came out in the '80s and '90s in Japan where they found changes in surface tension and solubility, and precipitation rates or zeta potential (a measure of the stability of a colloidal solution). The changes were reported to last for up to 143 hours, indicating a memory effect on water. [*See Beverly Rubik.**]

Going down the rabbit hole a little bit further is a practice of using EMFs around pipes that are subject to fouling, for example, in heat exchangers where milk is being pasteurized or other liquids that tend to cling to pipes. Those are used to reduce scaling to keep things running longer before you have to clean the pipes. Many of those are used today. Maybe there will be a confluence of our better understanding of water, solutions in water, how EMFs affect them and how intention can affect them.

Since our bodies are over half water, if water has memory, you can imprint the intention for a strong immune system. Yes, maybe water is part of the story and there is a whole symphony of different frequencies going on. It's a big paradigm shift, but I think more research is needed in order to make truly convincing arguments there. More broadly, the molecular biological way of looking at life in terms of how molecules fit together has been incredibly successful. The problem is that molecular thinking gets very complex quickly. Is there a field that governs the behaviors? Are there global organizing principles acting here? Mike Levin, for example, at Tufts University has made some very successful progress, reported on in papers like "Cracking the Bioelectric Code." He's done a body of research looking at patterns of membrane potentials in embryos, and also in planaria regeneration, how patterns of electrical potentials and cell membranes play key roles in morphogenesis and how the shape is formed—where the eyeball is, for example.

We may be on the brink of some very profoundly new understandings. We see how the molecular clockwork works to some degree. Molecular biology has made enormous strides at that specific local level on which molecules interact, and perhaps through work like Levin's and work in bioelectromagnetics, generally speaking, we may begin to understand more about how larger scale information gets transported or conveyed in development, growth, and repair. That is, how does the salamander grow back the leg?

Robert Becker was doing work on that decades ago, as in The Body Electric, *1985. It's interesting that a lot of these ideas aren't exactly new.* I remember reading Becker's 1982 book, *Electromagnetism and Life* when I was in high school and it left a very strong impression on me. I thought, "Wow! We just need to find the right frequency for re-growing liver, cardiac tissue, whatever." Of course, it turned out to be more subtle and complicated than that, but I found it incredibly inspiring that Becker could enhance and even change the direction of the regeneration in salamanders with a DC current. I'm very happy that Mike Levin is doing this work today, along with others, as this has already shed light on these important phenomena. With a concerted research project, a lot is possible.

You are working with CHI, the group that studies the biofield. Where is CHI headed? We're doing our best to try to accelerate the science and practice of healing and understand the roles of consciousness in healing. This is a very transdisciplinary field of study. On one level, it's about understanding how healing works in the body in terms of the clinical science and the biophysics, whether it's healing due to something like Reiki or a positive interaction with a doctor. There is an interaction of consciousness, of intention. Even if Reiki is not putting out magical fields, perhaps the ritual act of being cared for by the practitioner puts one into a receptive state that allows the body's or the universe's healing mechanisms to come to play. And importantly, we may need to go beyond the subject-object split to understand this better, to cross the edge of objectivity. But regardless of the scientific metaphor that's used, I think it has been clearly established that consciousness plays key roles in healing. I think we see this from psychoneuroimmunology, biophysics, and other directions. We see this in the placebo effect, in psychosocial genomics, and in many of the ancient healing traditions where consciousness plays a central role in both diagnosis and the treatment. People with different constitutions will receive different treatments, for example, in Indian Ayurveda.

At CHI, our director, Shamini Jain* recognized the need to encourage work in this area since there, many scientists are working along parallel paths, but often in isolation from one another. We work to bring them together to encourage collaborations. We have study groups and research groups that have embarked on projects with members of our scientific advisory council. My sense as a scientist is we are inevitability moving into an informational paradigm in biology where rather than just looking at the mechanical nature of life, with which we've made great progress, we're beginning to look at life as more of an interconnected web. We're talking more about information flow and, of course, this relates to my work in bioelectromagnetics.

I think this perspective that CHI is espousing, this new paradigm if you will, is already here in mainstream science of today. We've seen incredible advancement and we feel that there is a need to try to enhance this, in part because some of the subjects like parapsychology or intercessory prayer [*See Larry Dossey**] are taboo to many scientists. When we talk about consciousness, it usually gets relegated to an intellectual discussion and not something that is taken seriously as a potential variable in a biology experiment. We want to try to bring forth more of the exploration both in terms of the understanding of how healing works and how we can enhance healing in a collaborative way in society so that we can create a healthier world.

What are some of the current CHI research projects? The project in Tamil Nadu is part of a project called "The Power of We," where we are looking at group interaction and the power of collective intention. One of the ways to do that is with electrophysiology and we have a number of techniques and research protocols that we're using. Part of it is to get the work out of the lab and into the real world so that scientists and practitioners can have a more authentic dialogue. We encourage scientists to dialogue with practitioners so each can better understand the others' perspectives. This is very important for successful collaborations.

Recently I did a clairvoyant session on the phone with a woman whose cat was urinating on her favorite couch. I felt that the cat wanted more of her attention. She gave it to him and told me later he never went again on the couch. I could see how much disgust he had for her other cats and she told me, "I can see that on his face sometimes when he's looking at the other cats." It's like the Akashic Records that Hindus talk about, where we can read the information field if we tune into it. I think we all have the experience of something like this where we have an intuition and it comes true or we have a sense about what's about to happen in a few minutes, where we feel sensitive to a situation or a person in a way that we can't quite explain; it's more of a gut feeling. Sometimes those things are driven by our fears and our aversions and can be difficult to be clear. *Evolution would select for sensitive people.* Yes, if you have a sense that the tiger is watching you and it's lunchtime for tigers, that would be an evolutionary advantage, certainly.

What are you interested in researching now? There are a number of studies I'd like to do in bioelectromagnetics, funding permitted. I'm very much interested in weak-field interactions, not so much because they are mysterious but because there are a lot of experiments where we need to do basic baselines to see the responses of things like cells and tissues across comprehensive ranges of amplitudes, frequencies, wave shapes, etc. It's necessary to do this background work to gain a clearer understanding of how EMF interactions work and the scope of their relevance to biology. I'm very interested in continuing the work with CHI with group meditation and looking at factors like heart rate variability and brain waves. I think we can have a beneficial impact by furthering the understanding of the basic physiological effects and the synergy that can occur in the social context; for example in group meditation and ritual activities. When I look at what's happening today in science and our capacity to collaborate, it's incredible. I can gather data in India, upload it to a server and send it to a scientist in California, and we can analyze it together.

Are you optimistic or pessimistic about the survival of our species in the face of climate change, increasing inequality, and more autocrats? Or being eaten by AIs! Optimistic or pessimistic is a hard choice. We've got a lot of problems. I can look out my window and see Torre Asinelli in the center of Bologna. In 1943 there were airplanes buzzing overhead trying to knock it over with bombs. By many, many measures, we're living in a better world and doing much better than we were in previous times. But it's hard for me to have a barometer on that larger curve of history. Are we headed for doom or are we going to somehow save ourselves?

It's really clear that we need to create a more stable set of structures in terms of our energy use and stabilizing the financial system so it's not so sensitive to the type of fluctuations that brought it down a couple of times recently. I think many of us would agree that we need to collectively become more empathic and more kind, to acknowledge our interconnectedness so we can learn to work together to create a more just world. Otherwise, we'll be a bunch of talking monkeys overrunning the ecosystem and having to go to some other planet. I don't know how nice it will be on Mars anytime soon. If we don't find a way to find harmony amongst ourselves, we aren't going to be able to make the decisions that enable us to counter things like pollution and global warming.

Look at the way the world has changed, for example, the distance between England and Germany is much less than it was in 1941. From that point of view, we've already made huge strides in a direction that would give me grounds for optimism that we can do it—we can make a better, more peaceful world. We can somehow come together as a species and learn to make things work better. I know that the work that we're doing in the sciences is showing us that we are connected in functional ways that are very important, maybe in ways that we don't yet have a taxonomy for classifying. This is exciting, in part because I think because people generally do believe in science, and, for example, the capacity of EMFs from mobile phones to convey information. If science can help people have the sense of being connected to other people and cultivating the love and the gratitude and appreciation that comes from being loved, what a gift that would be.

Articles

https://visionaryscientists.home.blog/2019/11/14/electromagnetism-studies-by-david-muehsam/

Endnotes

1 *Global Advances in Health and Medicine* in 2015 (Global Adv Health Med. 2015;4(suppl):16-24.)

2 Winklhofer M, Dylda E, Thalau P, Wiltschko W, Wiltschko R. 2013 Avian magnetic compass can be tuned to anomalously low magnetic intensities. *Proc R Soc* B 280: 20130853

3 https://science.sciencemag.org/content/356/6343/1140

4 http://universe-review.ca/R15-19-twistor.htm

5 http://holofractal.net/the-holofractographic-universe/

6 https://people.healthsciences.ucla.edu/institution/personnel?personnel_id=45359

7 *The Journal Of Alternative And Complementary Medicine,* Volume 23, Number 1, 2017, pp. 68–74. "Effects of a Passive Online Software Application on Heart Rate Variability and Autonomic Nervous System Balance."

8 https://wyss.harvard.edu/mike-levin-on-electrifying-insights-into-how-bodies-form/

9 https://shop.chopra.com/dosha-quiz/?

LARRY DOSSEY, M.D.
NONLOCALITY, CONSCIOUSNESS, AND HEALING

Photo by Barbara Dossey

Questions to Ponder

What dangers does Dr. Dossey see in the materialist paradigm and what evidence is there for the primacy of consciousness?

What personal experiences led him to understand the limits of our beliefs about locality and time?

How did he heal his severe migraines?

Why might prayer work as a healing tool? What other activities does he suggest to tune into the One Mind?

I was born in September 1940, a Libra, on a sharecropper farm in the middle of Central Texas. *You don't live in Texas anymore?* We live outside of Santa Fe in the foothills; we moved here about almost 20 years ago. I left my practice but it didn't amount to much of a retirement. Barbara and I moved West and started writing and travelling a lot. We really love the southwest here. *I think of it as Georgia O'Keeffe country with her paintings of flowers and bones.* She hung out just a few miles away from us here.

You were shaped by growing up in Texas. Is there a Texan way of approaching life? Yes, there is and I am not very fond of the stereotype because Texans are known for their arrogance, boasting, and being bigger and better than everything. This has always turned me off. I grew up in a rural community where education was not prized at all; we had one book in our house and that was the Bible. My identical twin brother and I were frankly gifted, very bright students, and we always found ways to smuggle books into the house and read widely. We graduated number one and number two in our little high school, which gave us full scholarships to The University of Texas at Austin (UTA).

It was like divine intervention when we went there as our lives just completely changed. We fell in love with science, coming out of a fundamentalist religion culture that bit the dust after our entry into the university. We got degrees in pharmacy and premed. He worked his way through dental school as a resident pharmacist. I wound up in Dallas going to Southwestern Medical School, working on weekends to pay my way through medical school. It was a huge transition in our lives from a fundamentalist religious farming culture to one where science was honored and where we felt right at home. It was hugely challenging, as you can imagine, to our neurobiology. We managed the transition pretty successfully and our careers speak for themselves.

Was that Baptist upbringing associated with guilt and sin? You nailed it: It was hellfire and damnation. I look back to be fortunate to have escaped with as few scars as possible. After I entered UTA I spent a couple of years trying to find my spiritual balance. I explored other regions of knowledge and spirituality, which renovated my whole worldview. By the time I got to the Southwestern Medical School in Dallas, I was reading everything I could get my hands on, in terms of Carl Jung, Alan Watts, and the entire Buddhist canon. I read voraciously. I managed to regrow my spiritual roots, took up meditation, and went from there.

Did your parents think that you were headed towards hell and worry about you? No, because there is a way out, called getting saved. As a young child, seven or eight years old, I was saved and baptized. Many believed, "Once saved, always saved," so my parents didn't worry about my soul at all. We never really had any disputes about religious fundamentalism. I honored their beliefs, they were comfortable with it, and so we went our own ways without having any sort of titanic clashes over religious views.

You are an INFP on the Myers-Briggs but so much of your work is public speaking and interacting with people, so how does an introvert balance that? I've been trying to come to terms with my hardcore introversion all my life. It has not been easy. I would feel comfortable in a cave or on a desert island. I would never ever have predicted that I would wind up doing what I do now, which is speak to audiences all over the world. It has been a tremendous challenge but I saw early on that it was either become more extroverted or remain silent. But introversion is still there. Here we are on a mountainside in the foothills of Santa Fe. The deer come out and chew on my aspen trees and the coyotes serenade us at night so it's not a bad place for an introvert to be. Every so often I sneak back out into the world and then I sneak back home and I've managed to make it work.

Does your brother the same kind of Myers-Briggs profile as you? Is he an introvert as well? Yes, I think we are identical in personality and psychological makeup. *Have you communicated nonlocally over the years?* Yes, we grew up with that kind of non-vocal connection in terms of thoughts and behaviors. We had a term for it—"twin stuff." We didn't know that it violated neurobiological rules that you weren't supposed to have this kind of distant communication. I am married to a twin who has a twin brother and they have distant communications that are so dramatic that it makes my brother's and mine look minor, so we've had a pretty interesting household. I have studied this professionally, so I know that only 20% of identical twins have these sorts of experiences and the key seems to be emotional closeness. Not all twins love being twins because many have difficulties developing their own sense of personhood, their self-identity. Those twins don't experience this sort of communication. The twins who luxuriate in their twinship is where you see these sorts of things.

You and Barbara have been married for how many years? We got married in 1972 so that's almost 50 years. *How do you keep it interesting, alive, not boring and maintain interest in sex and romance?* We have matured psychologically in a very healthy way and we are spiritually and professionally very deeply connected. I've never read a marriage manual. I don't know if we violate the rules or not, but I am deeply in love with her. She is hugely successful in her profession and has written almost 30 books as an author or co-author. Her award-winning books are in use in nursing schools around the country. She sort of does in nursing what I do in medicine, so it's worked out wonderfully well. *You don't ever get bored?* I don't even know what boredom is. *Do you plan activities that spark the marriage?* There are no special plans. We just live our lives alongside one another and support one another and love each other. We don't have any special injections of high energy programs. We don't rekindle things because we don't need to, we live our life.

Speaking of longevity, what do you think happens after death? The bottom line for me is that consciousness does survive. I think that the materialistic view that consciousness is annihilated with the death of the brain and body is simply wrong. A lot of damage, spiritually and psychologically, has been done by the materialistic worldview which tells people that all they have to look forward to is total annihilation. Many streams of evidence now are overwhelmingly and statistically powerful that indicate the survival of personhood after physical death. However, materialists don't even want to look at the data because they are so stuck in a paradigm that says that anything other than annihilation is bad science. For example, 15 million Americans say they've had an NDE. You can say this is mass hallucination, but there has been sophisticated research done in investigating NDEs. If you pair those Americans with NDEs and look at a related phenomenon of children who say they remember past lives, there are thousands of verified cases.

If you are courageous enough to venture deeply into the world of paranormal, into parapsychological data, seeing the actual controlled experiments that have been done, you see that consciousness has a way of behaving non-locally. Consciousness can experience things distant from the physical person and non-local in the sense that they are simultaneous and distance isn't a factor. The robustness of the correlations of these experiences do not deteriorate with increasing distance in non-local correlated events. Talking like this drives materialist skeptics crazy because their paradigm suggests that this is just not possible. We have a real standoff here. My friend Dean Radin* is one of the great investigators of these phenomena. I am quite satisfied that this data is powerful; it's replicated in laboratories around the world by some of the smartest scientists I personally have ever known.

I happen to believe that the cream rises eventually and good data eventually floats to the top of science, although it may take a while. We are seeing signs now of a profound revision in the materialistic creed that the brain produces consciousness and dies with the death of the brain. I look forward to the progress of this data as it's becoming more and more profound and sophisticated. If you stay on top of the literature about this exciting theory, you can see a bright future for this data because of one essential feature: it's great science. It has been replicated by scholars who are extremely critical, all around the world. Another reason I think that it's going to float to the top is the idea that it's all over with physical death has spawned a horrible crisis in ethics and morality.

Many sophisticated spiritual teachers now are calling attention to this; one is Sogyal Rinpoche who wrote *The Tibetan Book of Living and Dying.* He says that unless we develop a sense of ongoing life after death, we will continue to follow a selfish ethic which is consumer-oriented and destructive, with every person for himself, get it while you can because you can't take it with you. This has led to enormous destructiveness of our environment. I think this idea of the survival of the consciousness is an essential feature of our species' hope for survival on this earth. So I don't see survival after death as just a philosophical spiritual or religious issue. Rather, it's tremendously practical and related to saving our own skins.

My understanding of quantum non-locality is: if two electrons are entangled because they go around the same nucleus and we take one electron to Peru and we change the spin, the one here instantaneously changes in response. This indicates that there is some kind of information field that operates instantaneously without a wave function. Yes, there's no signal since signals require time to pass and these connections are instantaneously correlated. Even though they are spatially separated, they behave as if they are a single particle. This is weird, unbelievable stuff to people who stumble on it for the first time, and even Einstein rebelled at this. *He said it's spooky action from a distance.* People can come to terms with this in one or two ways. First of all, you can look at the data from physics; it's unimpeachable. I do not know any physicist any longer who argues with Dean Radin's *Entangled Minds* and non-locally correlated events.

The second approach is to honor experiences where people who are emotionally close can experience simultaneous thoughts, feelings, and even physical changes with apparently no energetic kind of signal. They behave as if their single mind/consciousness has occupied distant, different bodies. Now here's where it gets tricky and we have to be very careful here. There's no evidence that we behave non-locally on account of what's going on in atoms. These may be just incidental correlations. It looks strange, however, that these are so identical in nature. Dean Radin thinks that this is no accident and that there is some connection between subatomic non-locality and human non-local events.

What about when there's communication between people who have passed over who don't have the same kind of atoms as people with bodies? Yes, people have had apparitions of communication with people who died and have seen them make appearances in this life over and over again. Mediums have been telling us for centuries that you can communicate with people who have passed over and so I think this is one more additional proof that consciousness does survive.

Do you have any kind of explanation about this quantum information field that allows these connections? I think it's too early to tell. I think that our theories about how consciousness operates are extremely infantile, but our task now is to honor the data. Sometimes theories come later. Our task is to go with that pesky little word "data," because without that we're not doing science. Materialists make a tremendous mistake of disallowing data that's been replicated for decades—if not centuries—and saying these are just hallucinations, people are making this stuff up because their worldview doesn't permit it. *After my grandmother died, she would pop corks out of wine bottles and open cabinet doors in the kitchen to say hello. My mother would say, "Gammy is here" and we'd greet her.*

Synchronicity ties in with the concept of an information field as defined by Carl Jung? Is there a correlation with synchronous events and quantum non-locality? It certainly seems that way intuitively. Both seem related to meaning and connection between distant events. I have a friend who says that synchronicity is an example that the universe is sort of winking at us, giving us a little clue that it's not all probabilistic since meaning, purpose, and direction are working behind the scenes. These synchronicities are a little tap on the shoulder saying, "Check this out, look closer, there is something going on here. It's not all accidental."

Do you think we have guides that help make these synchronous events happen? I personally feel guided. I think that the entire universe is more intelligent than we have the capacity to understand. The guidance can be so sophisticated and complex that it escapes your ability to see it as guidance. Our understanding is infantile in trying to sort out the messages. It gets more interesting for a lot of people who receive messages from the other side. I came across a survey of American nurses who had advanced degrees and most of them had profound experiences of having communicated with people from the other side. They are highly experienced people who've been around a lot of deaths since most of them work in critical care units. I think nurses are some of the most skeptical people I've ever run into. They are not suggestible and they do not suffer fools gladly: I am married to one and so have personal experience. If you take seriously the experiences of nurses and their intuitive abilities, that's a data base. There are other people out there who have had extremely convincing experiences as you described with your granny.

You refer to George Dyson's book in terms of your experience of synchronicity. Yes, he's Freeman Dyson's son, who is one of the great physicists today. George went in another direction, a wilderness type of guy. He built a Native American canoe called a *baidarka* on the Northwest Pacific Coast and sailed it in the inner waterway around Victoria Island, described in his book *The Starship and the Canoe*. The starship refers to his physicist father's interest in jet propulsion and so on, a fascinating book. I finally read it on the way to Cortez Island in Washington. Walking along this beach, we were told, "That's George's *baidarka*. He sailed through here a few weeks ago and begged us to let him prop his boat behind the log and said he'd be by in a few weeks to pick it up." I thought, "Oh my God, is this a synchronicity or what?"

Let's examine the different areas of consciousness research that indicate there is a non-local mind. You call it the One Mind in your recent book. Also, the CIA invested money in remote viewers like Russell Targ* so they must have thought that it was worthwhile. There are some staggering stories about finding a crashed Soviet airplane, peering into Soviet missile silos, and building super submarines by the Soviets—all from a distance. This is the reason the Feds spent millions of dollars in the secret Star Gate Program. There are still stories to be told that knock your socks off. Not everybody can do this remote viewing successfully but when you find somebody who's trained in this, their accomplishments are mindboggling. Russell Targ's* books reveal as much as is possible without giving away a lot of the secrets. I suspect that this is still going on at secret circles because remote viewing seems to be too valuable to lock away forever and I am not alone in thinking that. *It's so inexpensive, safe and effective.*

Stanford and Princeton did RNG work where humans influenced the 0-1 output of the computers. Implications? Bob Jahn, who ran the PEAR Lab for 30 years, recently died. Their work was replicated in laboratories around the world, not 100% of the time but enough to make people really pay serious attention to this work. People could influence the outcome of these RNGs, which normally spit out equal numbers of zeros and ones. They could influence them even after the RNG had already run and the results had been recorded. As long as the record had not been observed, they found out that they could direct their intention into the past and influence what should have been a random output. They could bias it in the direction they chose. This is just too weird for a lot of people to even countenance but it shows a feature of non-locality. It is non-local with respect to space, because the distance between the influence and the RNG isn't important. But also the divisions in time didn't seem to matter. People could influence into the future, so divisions in time seemed to go out the window in these experiments. This is so threatening that most people just slap their forehead and say, "I just can't think about that." This is the non-local world with respect to consciousness. I am not surprised that this kind of information offends people who are locked into a Newtonian classical world-view because this data looks like science fiction. At least six areas of research show essentially the same replication of studies. According to consciousness researcher Stephan Schwartz,* we find six areas in which studies have been replicated in labs around the world, each area giving odds against chance of around a billion to one, or combined odds of 10^{54} to one:

- Remote viewing
- Random number generator influence
- Global Consciousness Project
- Presentiment
- Precognition
- Ganzfeld

Other important areas—though not as statistically significant—include DMILS (distant mental interaction with living systems), experiments in distant healing, and so-called staring studies.

Consciousness could operate at a distance without any energetic signal going from the subject to the object and do so simultaneously without any inhibition by spatial separation. This is the non-local picture of consciousness, which has been fought tooth and nail by many who didn't want to go there. *It's like a religious dogma. The same thing happened with the belief that the sun is the center of the solar system and not the earth.* The round shape of the earth was also heresy for a long time.

The RNGs showed during the bombing of the World Trade Centers in 2001 that the phenomenon happened three or four hours before the first hit. Isn't that another indication that time is not linear? Yes, this is a field in research called presentiment; what happens is that if people go into the future to view an upsetting kind of experience, there is an autonomic predictor that occurs in their physiology before this event even happens. *Dean Radin conducted studies where they show people slides, some of them are disturbing, and the subjects reacted to the negative slides in advance, even though the slide wasn't yet selected by a computer so it wasn't telepathy.* They had no idea what the computer was going to show them but if the future image was emotionally upsetting or sexual in nature, they had an autonomic response in their bodies that could be tracked in these studies. This is one of the best pieces of evidence that divisions in time are not fundamental. This is non-locality with respect to temporal divisions. These presentiment studies now have been replicated in laboratories around the world. You could say that there is a preconscious form of knowing that is so unconscious it hasn't yet entered into the conscious awareness of the subjects in these studies. I think this is one of the most exciting areas because this has been so replicable and so often repeated that it's not going away.

We don't have a theory of consciousness and there's no understanding of how the mind and the brain are different in that materialist view. How can people dismiss consciousness if they don't have a theory about how all these effects happen? That's what we all struggle against. Cynics are quite successful in dismissing this because they are so wedded to a materialistic assumption that these studies become so outrageous that they don't consider them seriously. I think that's bad science because scientists are supposed to follow evidence wherever it leads. But an increasing number of scientists who do look at this information, the non-local manifestations of conscious, know this is not going away. In papers I've written recently and in my book, *One Mind,* I talk about some of the world-class scientists who are emphatic in saying we don't even have a glimmer of a hope of knowing how the brain and consciousness are related. Donald Hoffman, a UC Irvine cognitive psychologist, observed, "The scientific study of consciousness is in the embarrassing position of having no scientific theory of consciousness." That's a pretty healthy admission because if we can admit that we don't know what is going on between brain and consciousness, then we can be open to these very exciting non-local manifestations of consciousness in controlled experiments and in people's experiences.

What about the Ganzfeld studies where one person is isolated in a quiet room to see if their thoughts are influenced by a video or photo? The Ganzfeld studies statistically have been very influential in getting people to look at this non-local transfer of information from one person to another without sensory connection with the distant individual. *Radin reports in his books that the psi research on paranormal phenomena is so outstanding, double-blind, replicated, everything that scientists want, but it's still dismissed.* Most of their superiors, the people in power and influence who run training programs in research projects, have been schooled in a materialistic framework and to step outside of that for a young researcher would be fatal in too many instances.

We have examples of courageous people like Radin who say, "I am going with the data wherever it leads me." He has been able to carve a career out of this approach but that's quite unusual. I have been approached by young doctors in training who face the same sort of thing. They read my books on non-local minds and spontaneous healing and they say, "My professors don't believe any of this, so do you have any advice?" My advice is pretty much what Dean's advice is to young physicists: get your degree, do some basic research, build a reputation, and then raise hell and talk about the evidence that you find convincing. But it takes somebody who is a rabble-rouser to actually develop the courage to follow that path. It is not easy. *That's why I'm editing this trilogy.* Giordano Bruno was burned alive at the stake in 1600 for his rebellious ideas about how the universe is put together and Galileo was locked up under house arrest in the last years of his life for coming out against the status quo. It's an old story, but sooner or later evidence prevails and that's the hope that many of us have going forward. *Martin Luther King, Jr. said, "The arc of the moral universe is long, but it bends toward justice."*

Were your colleagues critical of you for writing books like Prayer Is Good Medicine? I got flak from both sides, from doctors who don't look at the evidence and thus had trouble believing that healing intentions and intercessory prayer could make a difference in clinical outcomes, although the evidence shows that it can. I also took a lot of flak from religious people, which really surprised me. I thought when somebody came along and offered randomized controlled trials that suggest that prayer works, the religious people would stand up and cheer. But I did something the fundamentalists didn't like when I claimed that there's no evidence that any particular religion is favored. You see the same results coming from a variety of religions, including Hinduism and Buddhism, and even Wiccans can show positive results. Some religions think that they enjoy a monopoly on God's loving grace and that people who don't agree are going to hell. I stood up for spreading this broadly because I thought that's where the data pointed, so I got a lot of nasty letters from religiously-oriented folks after those books on prayer.

In your medical practice, did you see cases of spontaneous remission? I saw one or two. I didn't do any controlled trials as it's very difficult to do that as a single practitioner. I collected stories from other physicians who wrote about these experiences. An internist in Illinois, Dr. Scott Kolbaba wrote *Physicians' Untold Stories.*[1] He did something quite remarkable; he went around to the doctors on the hospital staff where he worked and he said, "What's the weirdest thing you've ever seen?" And 26 of these doctors wrote out these stories for his book. An example is a patient who had two feet in the grave with a lethal illness had an almost immediate healing within 24 hours. I began to talk about these in my addresses to people about intercessory prayer and spontaneous healings. These stories really are not discussed in medical school because there is no conventional explanation for them. It's a shame that we don't talk about these more because they could give a lot of hope to a lot of people.

Were the remissions usually associated with prayer or were there other causal factors that might have led to them? Some were related to prayer but others were not. Only one study asked people who had these so-called miraculous spontaneous remissions, "Why do you think you got well?" Some said, "I think it's because I took up a hobby or I did a lot of exercise or I fought my illness." Equal numbers said, "I gave into it and I just went with the flow." I see no pattern that explains remission in the 60 individuals who were queried this way. But it is true that prayer was right at the top of the explanations that people gave for why they think their disease just went away.

Critics point to the Harvard study of intercessory prayer from a distance that didn't find efficacy. The group that knew they were prayed for had the worst outcome but you point out that they had the worst physiological problems in order to get into the study. That's an obvious factor, why wasn't that considered? Right, everybody didn't start out at the same level clinically. I critiqued the Harvard study in the journal *Explore*. Because it came out of Harvard, it was touted broadly on release and had an inhibitory effect on researchers going forward because the press said Harvard finally disproved prayer. Nothing could be farther from the truth, in my judgment.

Russell Targ's daughter Elisabeth did a study of AIDS patients' white blood cell count as impacted by prayer and found clear outcomes. She was the lead investigator on that study in the early age days before triple therapy made a huge difference in the treatment of AIDS. They assembled people who were experienced with prayer to intercede for these AIDS patients in a double-blind study. The patients who were prayed for had a lower incidence of hospitalization. If they did have to go to the hospital, they got out quicker and they seemed to have a better clinical course. The study was dropped because triple therapy came out and everybody was on the bandwagon of curing AIDS with medications. But this was one of the early studies that pointed to an efficacy of prayer in healing. My feeling is that if prayer and healing intentions could make a difference in a disease as severe as AIDS, I can't imagine what disease would be off the map.

Do you think that prayer is different from intention? We know hundreds of studies report that intention is the key to having an impact on cell growth or yeast releasing oxygen or whatever. Do you think that prayer is a form of focused intention or is there some kind of divine assistance? It depends on how you define prayer. I define it as communication with the Absolute. That's about as generic as I can make it. I am allergic to the images of God in a white robe that I grew up with, so I take a view of prayer that many of my religious friends find deplorable. Even if you just say "I intend healing for somebody," you are appealing to something such as a universal wisdom that might make this possible. I think that's a minimal definition of the Absolute or God or universal wisdom. The arguments about who it is that's intervening, I just don't find interesting. If people feel better about offering their prayers to their version of the Supreme Being, I say go for it. If people just want to do intention, I say fine. But there does seem to be a sense of love that empowers these intentions or appeals to God. If I had to pick the most important factors that sets all this in motion, it would be love, compassion, and deep caring.

You wrote a book about the extraordinary healing power of ordinary things. What are ordinary things? That was a fun book to write because I picked some things that people just don't think of as having healing power, like a chapter on the healing power of dirt. When I wrote that, investigators were already looking at the hygiene hypothesis, which suggests that young children who are exposed to an unhygienic environment grow up with a strong immune system and have a lower incidence of asthma and allergies. So it's good to let your children go out and play in the dirt, make mud pies, frolic in sandboxes, and scrape their knees. Another chapter is on the ability of tears to perk up the immune system. There are all sorts of remedies that can be good for people's health that in our high-tech age we've forgotten about, and I try to bring these things together.

What about the church in New Mexico where they have healing dirt from a sacred hole? I have some under my bed. El Santuario de Chimayo. After I wrote a book on prayer called *Healing Words*, I was asked for interviews by major news organizations. One of the major news channels said, "We want to interview you in the church where they've got that dirt. It will be the perfect place to talk about healing." When the interviewer couldn't finish his monologue for coughing, I got some of the famous dirt. I rubbed it on his throat and he thought I had lost my mind, but I said, "Now try it." And his monologue was powerful and perfect.

What have been the most challenging parts of your life and how did you cope? One is when I went away to college and all through medical school and was overwhelmed by the materialistic worldview. It's all physical, consciousness dies with the death of the brain. I found this exciting at first but then I thought, "I this all there is?" I had a real struggle over this materialistic worldview and whether or not I should take seriously the evolving scientific paradigm coming out of the parapsychology community. This was a serious paradigm shift for me that was not easy. It was about 10 or 12 years before I began to regrow my spiritual roots and make peace with this confrontation.

The other thing that I found really hard to cope with is that since grade school, I had horrible health problems with classical migraine headaches. This involved nausea, vomiting, and incapacitation, but the worst thing was periodic partial blindness. I had huge blackouts with my vision. It was stress-related and got so bad that I tried to drop out of medical school because I thought it was only a matter of time until in a critical situation I would have one of these attacks when I couldn't see and I might even injure or kill a patient. But my advisor said, "Don't drop out. You are just taking this too seriously. What you need to do is to learn to relax." Relaxation and stress—I didn't even have those words in my vocabulary.

After my training was completed and I served in the military in Vietnam, the migraines got so bad that, in desperation, I went all over the country attending biofeedback workshops. They hooked you up to instruments that measured your stress levels, your muscle tension and skin temperature. You learn to control these machines which indirectly allowed you a sense of controlling the level of stress, tension, and anxiety in your body. Within half a dozen sessions, almost all of the migraine headaches and blindness went away, although I had struggled with this for the better part of my life. It was like being zapped. People toss around this term "miracle" but that's what it felt like to me. This really opened me up to mind-body interventions. I established one of the first biofeedback labs in the state of Texas, hired therapists, and personally taught this technique to patients. We dealt with problems such as head-aches, irritable bowel syndrome, and generalized stress disorders. This was one of the most significant experiences of my life as an internal medicine physician.

Did your brother have migraines as well? He seems to remember that he had one way back in his childhood and no more, so he knew what I was talking about. *Was he the second born?* I was born 10 minutes on one side of midnight and he was born 10 minutes after, so we actually had different birthdays, 20 minutes apart. We were born three months premature; you know there's been a lot of data showing that prematurity is related to mental retardation in adult-hood and my brother said, "If we hadn't been so premature, maybe we wouldn't be so brain-damaged." *Do you think he was more relaxed than you?* He's never taken things as seriously as I do. I think that's probably the migraine difference. I was always deeply competitive and had to come out on top while he didn't take that approach at all.

Do you think that's evidence of epigenetics that our genes express differ-ently in terms of our environment? I think it was also a learned kind of response. I was so competitive that I was willing to beat his brains out to make a better grade on the test. I came out at the top of our class and he was second; he just thought it was kind of a joke. His attitude was why should he engage in mortal combat with me when he could go through life a lot easier without everything being a blood bath contest. He is one of the most talented dentists I've ever known and he was much more relaxed. Whether that's a behavior-ally learned coping strategy or whether that's epigenetics, I don't know.

You were involved with the journal Alternative Therapies In Health And Medicine *and now* Explore: The Journal of Science & Healing. *Could you comment on what those journals offer?* Alternative Therapies started in the '90s and was one of the first journals to pay close attention to mind-body therapies, what was then called holis-tic medicine or integrative medicine. When we developed issues with the publisher, we started another journal called *Explore: The*

Journal of Science & Healing. I have served as Executive Editor for the past 14 years and we continue our focus on integrative health care. In addition, we focus on papers related to how consciousness makes a difference in health and longevity. It's still cutting-edge stuff where consciousness is concerned since most peer-reviewed medical journals won't touch these papers. We publish papers on telepathy, clairvoyance, NDEs, and so on. We've developed a special readership who think that these things are important, not just in health and illness but in their personal lives. We are happy to be an Elsevier-sponsored journal, one of the largest publishers of medical journals in the world. We are peer-reviewed and proud of it.

A university at the forefront of mind-body integrative medicine is Dr. Andrew Weil's Center for Integrative Medicine at the University of Arizona and Harvard has a mind-body program as well. Yes, Dr. Herbert Benson has been very active in promoting mind-body research at Harvard, famous for the relaxation response. In Tucson, medical professionals come from all over the United States to upgrade their skills in these areas [*and can learn online*]. I lecture in his program and enjoy speaking about spontaneous remissions and remarkable healings. I love doing this because you have an audience of young doctors who are fascinated by these sorts of issues. I get a kick out of sharing my clinical experience and what I suggest is important research. *What other medical centers should we know about?* The University of Texas Medical Branch at Galveston, Texas, has a robust program in integrative medicine. Actually, the majority of medical schools in the country have programs looking at the role of spirituality in health. Many of these programs are required, some of them are electives, but 30 or 40 years ago almost none of these schools even touched this. I think this is an elegant example of the seriousness of the research in this field—that our medical schools are including this in their curriculum.

What's your next book? I have a new manuscript; it's my 13th book. It's a collection of quotations on spirituality, environmentalism, spontaneous healing, the nature of consciousness, etc. These thousands of quotations are ones that I have gleaned from my readings over the past 40 years which have been important in my own growth. I wanted to share these because they have been so vital in my understanding and progress. It's called *Vital Voices.* Also, in every issue of *Explore* journal, I write a chapter-length editorial about some burning issue in health and healing. I am having fun in my life as I get to rant about things I consider important. People invite me to give talks at major conferences. I just got back from London, speaking about the importance of consciousness in healing. What could be better than having a receptive audience and hopefully making a difference in helping people heal?

What else do you do for fun? Exposure to nature has always been important. Barbara and I for many years have taken off the month of August to disappear into the wilderness. We are surrounded by nature. For me, that has been one of the most steadying influences in my life. I am married to a woman I am deeply in love with and I get to enjoy the coyotes and the deer that come to our land. At this point in my life, I feel the need to give back and that's what I try to do.

If people want to tune into guidance from the One Mind, is there a particular meditation technique that works for you? I developed my own eclectic style of meditation for the past 40 years. The main thing is doing something purposeful—sitting down, being quiet, and paying attention. I think that there are other ways than meditation to bring balance into your life, including exposure to nature. I would also add exposure to beauty in any form, such as visiting great museums, exposure to art, and listening to sacred or exalted music. I also find that I need, despite being a hopeless introvert, exposure to people to lend balance to my life. I have already mentioned that one of my big challenges is to actually get out into the world and do that.

Mary Oliver, the Pulitzer-prize winning poet, offered a three-step instruction on how to live a life. Her first rule is pay attention; her second rule is to be astonished; and the third rule is tell about it. Of course, each one of those is terribly complicated but I like the overall simplicity of it. I particularly like the point about paying attention as it's emphasized in every major spiritual tradition. The point about being astonished is an accompaniment of truly paying attention; astonishment is the proper response to attending. Many of us don't follow through with Oliver's third tenet: Telling about is sharing with others what we consider important.

Are you an optimist or pessimist about our future? If you look around the world you can find uprisings of sanity that are going to prevail. We are depressed at this moment about this Trumpian nightmare that our country is suffering through but I don't think it's going to be permanent. History helps because we learn about dark moments that threatened the human race but we somehow managed to bungle through. There is an enormous awakening spiritually in our country, although it has been virtually shouted down during the Trump administration. Our options are clear. We can maintain a materialistic, hedonistic, consumer-based approach, or we can go in the other direction. It's easy to see where salvation lies. If we want to save our skins, we have to transcend the habits that have got us to this serious point. It may be that we shall have to undergo something akin to a planetary NDE before we awaken to sane ethical and moral norms. Following NDEs, behavioral platforms can be revolutionized overnight. As more people deeply grasp the seriousness of our planetary predicaments and challenges, this may well happen. That's where my hope lies.

Is there anything else that you would like readers to know about your work or your insights that will be helpful? Sometimes it's wise to not try too hard. That may sound contradictory, but I look at it this way. The implications of non-local consciousness are spectacular. A consciousness that is non-local in time is everywhere in time, which means that it's eternal and immortal. So even if the earth were to go to hell in a handbasket and we were to lose the environment, we are stuck with immortality. That's not a bad booby prize.

Books

The One Mind, 2013
The Power of Premonitions, 2011

The Extraordinary Healing Power of Ordinary Things, 2006
Healing Beyond the Body, 2001
Reinventing Medicine, 1999
Be Careful What You Pray For, 1997
Prayer is Good Medicine, 1996
Healing Words, 1993
Meaning & Medicine, 1991
Recovering the Soul, 1989
Beyond Illness, 1984
Space, Time and Medicine, 1982

Editor, *Explore: The Journal of Science and Healing*

Endnote

Carlye Hirshberg and Marc Ian Barasch. *Remarkable Recovery: What Extraordinary Healings Tell Us About Getting Well and Staying Well,* 1995.
Scott Kolbaba. *Physicians' Untold Stories: Miraculous experiences doctors are hesitant to share with their patients, or ANYONE!* 2016.

SECTION 3 HEALING WITH ALTERED STATES OF CONSCIOUSNESS

RICHARD MOSS, M.D.
AWAKENING ESSENTIAL
TRANSFORMATION

Photo by Laughing Goat Studio

Questions to Ponder

Dr. Moss is critical of over-emphasis on left-brain analytical thinking. Where does he find other sources of information? How does this relate to how you learn and grow?

The author (and Bernardo Kastrup*) are skeptical about a literal understanding of reality, preferring to think in terms of metaphors and images. How literal do you think we can be?

The author suggests that Western medicine is deficient in relying on drugs. What other modalities does he suggest?

In order to have a truly loving relationship, what steps does Dr. Moss suggest?

I was born in New York City in January 1947, a Capricorn, I am told. I have little sense of astrology, but I have respect for people who can use it as an insightful window into patterns and ways of looking wisely at people's lives and choices. I'm the first of two brothers.

What spiritual background were you raised with when you were a boy? Almost nothing religious. My parents were Reformed Jews and I never went to temple until my parents insisted I be Barmitzvahed. The essential spirituality in my family was how you cared for others and every living thing.

I was an asthmatic and celiac almost from birth and I believe my body memory from childhood was a basic sense of being unsafe. Decades later, learning to consciously journey deeply into such an early sense of non-security had a lot to do with my path and it also relates to why my initial career was in medicine. One of my powerful memories from childhood was going to the doctor with my mother. She was speaking very respectfully to the doctor and I saw he had power while my dad was working long days teaching junior high school. Lo and behold, 20 years later, I found myself a doctor. But the Oedipal victory of gaining my mother's respect and outdoing my father was also the source of my ambivalence about being a doctor. After internship, I started to do a psychiatric residency in the San Francisco Bay Area a few hours from Yosemite Park. I was introduced to rock climbing and became a passionate climber. Very quickly I felt unfulfilled and realized that living life through the mind is interesting but experiencing life directly and immediately as in climbing is so much more alive. I decided to leave the residency and join an Emergency Room group and become an ER doc. At the age of 29, for other reasons, I took a leave of absence and never went back to traditional medicine.

How did you make a living? As doors opened inside my consciousness, new opportunities came by themselves. At the age of 30, I had a profound awakening experience with a massive download of understanding. It was a basic shift in the structure of my consciousness from being ego-centered to awareness-centered. When this kind of awakening happens in you, it is part of something much larger as you are led synchronistically from one thing to another.

After I left medicine I created a simple contemplative life rhythm. I got up early, meditated and read, went for walks. I didn't know what was next in my life. Then a wise elder nurse whom I had worked with and who wanted me to come back to the clinic, gave my home number to some of my clinic patients who tracked me down. A handful of former patients came to my house for medical advice, but instead, I would sit with them and hold their hands in silence for 30 minutes and feel the energy move through us and then we would talk. I got a phone call from a therapist who said, "You've been seeing one of my clients. She is making incredible progress. What are you doing?" So I told her and she asked if I would do a training for some of her colleagues. I initially refused because what would I teach?

About eight months later, she contacted me again because I was working with another of her clients. The client had a large ovarian cyst and after our session, it disappeared before she was about to have surgery. I wondered if it wasn't the result of the deep shift she experienced while we were together. I've since witnessed many times that when people shift states of mind, they also shift bodies in a vibrational sense so things can change. *Dissociative Identity Disorder teaches us that each alter has completely different physiology.* Exactly, which none of us knew of back in the mid-'70s. But when that therapist, who became a dear friend, again asked me to do a training, I accepted. That was the beginning of my path as a consciousness teacher.

Please say more about your mystical experiences. There were quite a few of them in those initial years. For my ego self it was terrifying, like being annihilated. It was good that I had been a doctor because I could say, "This doesn't match any definition of psychosis. This is more than an anxiety attack. This is not an adrenaline-secreting tumor of the adrenal glands. This isn't any form of epilepsy."

Was your original awakening a kundalini experience? Kundalini awakening would be an Eastern way to describe it, but I had never heard of it at the time. It was a fundamental realization, the beginning of a new foundation for identity. I think of it as the next step in evolution of consciousness after we differentiate into ego-based *me* identity. *That's kind of the Adam and Eve story. You have to be expelled from the Garden of Eden to go back more consciously.* I agree and you could say the serpent is the kundalini energy or the energy of fundamental transformation.

I can look back and see that I was guided through it from within and from outside. For example, a priest friend gave me a copy of the Four Gospels of Mathew, Mark, Luke, and John a few months before the awakening. I cried reading it, feeling strange emotions of some kind of recognition. During the initial days when the experience felt almost overwhelming, I had the intuition to ask the question, "Who had lived through this before?" Immediately, I thought of Jesus. I realized that whatever is meant by Christ Consciousness is what I had to understand. Then very spontaneously, I kept myself in the present moment by self-observation. "Now my mind is in the past. Now I am feeling strong constriction in my chest"—just like that, hour after hour. That intense process of moment-by-moment, non-judgmental self-witnessing became the basis of my path and the core of what I teach.

Another synchronicity was that on the very day the experience started, a friend spontaneously decided to visit me and invited me back to her house so I wouldn't be alone. She was a Jungian analyst who believed that a spiritual experience was unfolding for me. About three days later, as I was sitting in her backyard, two butterflies were dancing in the air, one was dark and one was light. They alighted on a branch and mated. Then, the black butterfly landed right in the center of my forehead. In that moment, everything changed forever. That was when I knew All is Love and I am All. It's not that I stayed in that state of extraordinary oneness and love; but once it came, it changed me forever, and gradually I have evolved into it.

Is that Christ Consciousness? I have come to believe so. When you read the Gospel of Thomas where Jesus says, "The man old in days will not hesitate to ask a little child of seven days about the place of Life, and he will live," points to entering into the undifferentiated consciousness of an infant with conscious awareness. I believe the Thomas Gospel is a more pure transmission of Jesus' teaching because it was buried in the fourth century and unearthed after 1,500 years. It escaped so much of the editing that is inevitable when generations of scribes rewrite the original texts. It's the spiritual scripture that I have studied that most describes the state I awakened into. That realization changed me and people started coming to me very spontaneously, so I began earning a living without even trying.

Mystics often have the dark night of the soul where everything collapses so it can be put together in a new way. It sounds like you underwent a mystical experience. Yes, there are many dark nights; my whole life since then has been about integrating that realization into daily life since it began when I was 30 years old. My consciousness went from Richard Moss, the ego, the sense of me, to awareness of me.

The integration can't happen through the mind alone as it has to be grounded in the body. The new energy awakened like a current in the body and the deep wisdom of the heart—both have to lead the mind. That is the great insight of the Buddha, to experience sensation and energy in the body prior to the thinking mind, to stay deep enough in the body intelligence. It's a lifetime process to follow a mystical experience and let it guide your life.

Is the mindfulness meditation associated with Jon Kabat-Zinn a contemporary version of your process? Mindfulness meditation is a very ancient practice that's been beautifully reframed for contemporary time by Kabat-Zinn, although it's being primarily marketed as stress reduction. For me, mindfulness practice is self-witnessing, but it has to be consecrated to something. My experience was that the very fabric of this universe is love and the root consciousness itself is love. Ultimately, mindfulness and service to love is the most essential thing, because if mindfulness is in service to merely functioning better in the world, to get ahead and make more money, mindfulness isn't going to do us a bit of good. Mindfulness can make a soldier a better assassin. But if practiced properly, mindfulness meditation is going to cause you to see your mind, to see who you are not, and then to digest yourself, to lose interest in certain levels of yourself. Mindfulness is ultimately a path to no story.

Do you think that concepts of the left-brain and right-brain are metaphors? It seems to me when people do intuitive work, they are working with the whole brain. I read Iain McGilchrist's *The Master and his Emissary: The Divided Brain and the Making of the Western World* and gained a much deeper understanding of the relationship between left and right-brain and how we assemble consciousness. I think science itself is a metaphor in that it means to bridge between a representation of a thing by using words and equations to also comprehending the thing in its essence. For the left-brain, there is no such thing as metaphor except as a word, while for the right-brain everything is metaphor. The left-brain basically corrupts metaphors and makes them into so-called facts that only exist as a representation, never as the thing itself.

For example, when I was in medical school, the pharmacology text by Goodman and Gilman stated that ultimately we do not know how any drug works, which is still true. Nevertheless, we have been effectively using antibiotics for over 40 years and make billions of dollars creating new drugs. Empirical science gives a hypothesis, which we can confirm statistically as a likely probability, but it does not actually prove how any drug works. The hypothesis itself, including the chemical structure of the drug molecule, is just metaphor but our thinking mind, the left-brain, regards these things as truths.

The concept of evolution is also metaphor. Natural selection doesn't explain how many mutations it would take to change a four-legged animal that lives on the land and can change the front legs into wings and at each step be viable. So evolution is a word that nobody truly understands but it's useful. The Big Bang is also a metaphor. If we understand that science uses metaphors and then pretends it understands the actuality of their metaphors, we can escape the mechanistic reality that science has helped box us into. We all use metaphors. God is a metaphor, but then some people imagine God is a literal thing and worse, believe that they know what God is and what God wants.

If you want to bring yoga to the Veteran's Administration, as a woman I know has done, you don't say, "Yoga comes from India and it's a form of meditation that can be deeply relaxing." You say, "Yoga will down-regulate the sympathetic nervous system and up-regulate the parasympathetic nervous system." The modern person needs modern scientific metaphors and then people think because it is "science-based" that it is valid, which it often is. Yoga always did all the things yoga does now, but the ancients just explained it in different metaphors. At an immediate personal level, that means I am a metaphor, so I don't get too attached to any aspect of my identity because that is ultimately just a metaphor.

Our society is getting more and more isolated in conceptual arguments that appear rational because they are hierarchical and logical in that sense, but those arguments often begin from ignorant prejudice, like racism, or from an idea or premise that is someone's belief. For example, the horrible marketing rationality of corporations such as Monsanto [*bought by Bayer in 2016*] begins with a bad definition, as in when economist Milton Friedman defined corporations as entities whose primary purpose is to maximize short-term gains for shareholders. There is nothing whatsoever about life in that abstraction. It has no fundamental meaning at the level of the heart and body wisdom, so ultimately the products and how they are forced on people are often terribly destructive to life.

So how does one get to the truth? There are many forms of relative truth. Statistics gives us a relative truth; Western medicine is based on statistics, and science gives us theories based on observation. If you are talking about truth in the absolute sense, then we are talking about a metaphor that can't be grounded in something objective and concrete. Truth is an affair of the heart, with a deep heartfelt bodily recognition. If we think we are going to get to the truth rationally—no, not ever.

Maybe one way to approach truth is to look at repeated patterns that all religions promulgate: be kind to your neighbor, what you do has consequences, there is an afterlife, there is a higher spirit. You find truth as you slowly recognize and digest the fictions from which you derive your identity. What is uncovered are deeper levels of being. There's a deeper ground to a shared heart, but you have to work very hard to peel away the levels of personal and collective identity that give each of us an imagined and groundless sense of belonging, such as nationality. It is not a belonging based in a deeper knowing of ourselves in our heart and body wisdom but based on the ever-changing fictions about who we are that we tell ourselves.

The stories are originally created by children as protection and a way of coping? Yes, some are personal stories, particularly those at the base of our personal psychology. Others are fictions like capitalism, socialism, and so on. Seeing beyond those levels of collective belief is not easy. The ultimate purpose of meditation is to come to no story. We rest on a grounded being that isn't distorted by beliefs; it's an irrefutable experience of being at one with and inseparable from source. Again, "source" is another metaphor, but one based in bodily knowing. If you meditate, you realize that you are not your many levels of personal and collective identity, not an insecure person, or a powerful person, or American, or any religion. There's no hope for us as a species until we decide to uncover these stories and not let them divide us from each other.

What's an example of a personal story that got in your way that you were able to dissolve through meditation, therapy, or whatever? There are so many. I didn't recognize the ego-dynamic in me that I call the "the know-it-all," or others call the "controller." *Does medical school teach "physician attitude" and does that create stories?* Yes, that was the case when I went to medical school. I remember the first introductory class where one of the head faculty members referred to us as soon becoming an elite, like racehorses with a pedigree. Many doctors do hide behind the information they believe they know, that they worked so hard to learn, and then they don't listen with their whole being and they make unnecessary mistakes. I often hear about doctors who are too rushed with their patients, didn't actually touch them or carefully palpate them, where the patients didn't really feel listened to. Medical practice has become so rushed that things are missed; like in one case I know of a doctor discharged a patient with a ruptured appendix who went home and died—or in the case of my wife, compression fractures of her cervical spine after a fall. The ER team misread the CT scan and worse, sent her home without a neck brace, no pain medications, and no protocol to take care of herself.

Medical education has become almost all left-brain; there is little room or acknowledgment of the poetry of the doctor-patient relationship, the so-called "bedside manner," which can't really be taught. It takes time to learn that making a diagnosis and prescribing a medication is only part of a doctor's skills, that the transmission of caring presence is also very healing, and sometimes more so than medications.[1] The almost complete emphasis on left-brain reasoning and rationality is imbalanced. And where there is little money to be made for doctors, but especially for pharmaceutical companies and hospitals, what is missing in their education is crucial.

For example, few physicians know about nutrition. Too many are admonishing patients with cancer and on chemotherapy to consume a lot of red meat, which they still think is the best source of protein. However, the World Health Organization reports processed red meats like sausages, baloney, and hot dogs are Group A carcinogens in the same category as cigarette smoking, while red meat is Group 2, which probably causes cancer.[2] Yet even oncologists recommend patients to eat diets high in red meat that are not only carcinogenic but also highly inflammatory. *Also, livestock production creates about 15% of greenhouse gas emissions, with nearly half from beef.* Modern medicine is only barely recognizing that the best prevention for cancer, heart disease, and diabetes is a plant-based diet, despite the evidence being clear for some decades now.

What is going to save us from ignorance? Nothing but education, and foremost about the nature of awareness as the instrument for liberation from thought-generated suffering. It's really helpful now what we know about left-brain and right- brain because of split-brain patients. The bridge between the left and right cortex, the corpus callosum, is severed to treat rare forms of severe epilepsy. Many of those patients, as well as stroke patients, have been studied so we can see how the left-brain functions independently of the right-brain and vice versa. With this new understanding, we can see that education itself has to shift from left-brain rational thinking to include understanding with the heart, the right-brain, and the body. Rational thinking needs to build upon foundational understandings rooted in our deepest feeling nature and the loving sense of our interconnectedness with all of life and feeling that we are all Earthlings on a miraculous planet.

It seems like Hinduism and Buddhism have understood what you are saying for millennia but it hasn't percolated into the West. Yes, I have been told that the Buddhist sages said that 95% of our intelligence is the body and the heart, while only 5% is the rational mind. But we overemphasize the rational mind in education because information can be taught relatively easily, while love, humility, forgiveness, and compassion, which are the truly precious capacities of human consciousness, cannot be taught. Those virtues can be learned and they can be transmitted, but they must be learned with the whole being.

What is particularly worrying is that the more screen time, the more the left-brain is being used, thereby creating a kind of digital autism in many young people. They are relating through emojis and texts, but they don't know what a person's voice tone or facial expression and body language are expressing. Steve Jobs would not give an iPhone or iPad to his children because he understood the danger. To heal this, we not only have to know medical science and psychology but far more important is to know ourselves through meditation and contemplation.

One of the most important phenomena is that placebo is effective 40% or more of the time in drug trials. Why hasn't medicine really delved into that? Actually, I do think there is a deep appreciation in Western medicine of the placebo effect. But if you can show even a 3% improvement in patients taking chemotherapy over taking a placebo, doctors will use the chemo despite the side effects. What is not appreciated is that if you were to have people singing, writing poetry, going on a whole-food plant-based diet, you would be beating out nearly every form of chemotherapy in remissions and—for sure—in quality of life. A study compared two groups of patients with the same kind of cancer on the same chemotherapy regimen, but one group also used music and particularly singing. That group showed a 70% longer remission rate than the other group and two patients were declared cured against none in the chemo-only group.

All the spiritual traditions have chanting and music as part of their practice because they felt what those activities do for the mind and body. This is how I guide all people in my retreats, regardless of whether they are ill or not. The problem facing modern medicine is that we believe we can't ethically study one group who uses, for example, a singing practice but is not given chemotherapy, with another group that uses chemo but without singing. We cannot test for whole-body, heart-based, so-called lifestyle approaches in comparison to chemotherapy. So medicine is trapped in a highly monetized, rational reductionist process that can be heartless for both the doctors and patients and even deny patients pathways with real healing power.

Coming back to your personal journey, how is your path playing out in your current marriage? I cannot speak for my wife, Kathy, but we both agree that we had very different paths and yet arrived at the same deep ground of knowing that the purpose of human consciousness is ultimately to learn to love and let ourselves be loved. She had three children and raised three other step-children in the course of two marriages and for many years did this by herself. I also had two marriages and helped raise three step-children, but family was never the focus of my path as it was for her. She dived deeply in the shamanic path, Buddhism, and other work that taught her to process her emotions and feelings with awareness and in the body. Ultimately, the essence of the work for both of us was to learn to take 100% responsibility for our reactions, for any ways in which we closed our hearts to love. When we met, we both realized that choosing to be together wasn't about falling in love but about loving Love with each other.

Most of us live in a transactional relationship to love: I'll love you if you love me. I'll appreciate you if you appreciate me. Then you are hurt when your love is not reciprocated the way you want. But if you have journeyed deeply into yourself and into all the ways that your emotional reactions ultimately lead to the weakening of love and the breaking of relationships—if you truly want to stop that reactive behavior—then you can begin on a path of loving Love. So our relationship is a shared vision, a shared commitment to love Love. *What is the deep work necessary to love Love?* First and foremost to know yourself. You must begin to commit to a path of self-awareness so that you can see what your mind is doing, how and why you react, what you falsely believe in as your identity and grow beyond all of that. Then and only then can you really learn to know another.

I think the deepest urge in us is for aliveness, to go into profound intimacy with life. We all are seeking aliveness one way or another and, unfortunately, it tends to become the aliveness of anger, emotional reaction, self-justification or self-importance, instead of the aliveness of being embodied here and now in the heart. There are so many aspects and paths of the journey into yourself: dancing, painting, writing poetry, singing, athletics—all can be aspects of an awareness path and a way to live vibrantly. Committing to loving Love with another is for me the deepest path of aliveness and consciousness. There is also a rich aliveness in using your mind as we do in science, philosophy, or in our profound individual and collective search for knowledge. But as rich as mind-based paths can be, they may not actually teach us how to be intimate with life and each other in the moment, in our bodies. Thinking, no matter how clearly, may not lead you to what your heart knows. Ultimately, I believe the deepest of all forms of aliveness is learned and lived between two people. It's the most wonderful of life's possibilities but paradoxically relationships can face us with feelings that we are very afraid of and confused about.

Because you could be overwhelmed or taken over or rejected. Yes, we are so poorly educated, taught to have a generative relationship with difficult feelings. If you're going to learn to love and be loved, you'll have to face all your fears and most of those start in childhood. You have to go back into your scar tissue from your early life. But it is never about the past, it is about your conscious relationship to what you are feeling now, regardless of where it started or of what happened to you. All healing happens in the present moment. If you dedicate your meditation practice and all your psychological study to being able to journey into what you are feeling right now in order to become open to love, that practice will lead you ever deeper. You will gradually come to the real and deepest meaning of human life.

Awakening isn't one experience; it is countless moments of going deeper through the unmet feelings and the mind-made negative emotions. Once you begin to free yourself from those, there is a fundamental change. Your body, the presence that emanates from you, is a transmission that never stops. It is the transmission of love and also trust and forgiveness and compassion. Those are not learned behaviors; they are graces that emanate from you through conscious self-work.

As I deepened on this path, I lost all interest in whatever people mean by enlightenment. My own seeking, as I gradually understood it, has been to love Love with someone. I know that I don't know what Love is and I am not ever going to bother spending time trying to define Love. We all do know at some deep level; our bodies know, our hearts know. Only our left-brain and rational mind does not and cannot. If loving Love with others is not what enlightenment is, then I couldn't care less about enlightenment.

Erich Fromm said love is deep caring. That is one profound aspect of it for sure, but it's caring deeply enough to set aside our own individualistic behavior for the sake of love with another. Whatever closes your heart is due to some form of self-involvement, self-importance, or self-justification. If you can become aware of those defenses and release them, what's left is the immediacy of relationship, right now. That slow digestion of your ego, that slow undressing of layers of self-involvement and the sense of the openness that opens within you, is the most wonderful journey and perhaps the most important for humankind.

When you come into this world, you have to separate. We are each born in a state of oneness with everything, but gradually you have to separate from mother and the unitive experience of the world you are immersed in. You have to create an ego, a sense of a separate self. But the more we use our left-brain to differentiate one thing from another, the more we each lose the sense that everything is also interconnected and inseparable. Then you begin to live in the rules, the bureaucracies, the beliefs of your family, culture, and society. We each must separate but you then live in layer upon layer of mind-made fictions. For example, patriarchy is an elaborate belief system from the past. If you don't examine the subtleties of patriarchal beliefs and behaviors in yourself, you will not understand with actual immediacy how those dynamics are dividing you in your marriage and with your children, let alone socially and culturally all over the world. But when you get into a deep relationship, eventually those fictions will keep separating you, no matter how much you want to get close. This results in the profound yes/no in the lives of every human being who wants to love another and be loved by another. Finally, you surrender to yes.

That tension creates a nice sexual chemistry sometimes. True, but sexual chemistry is only a part of love. Making love is much more than sex even though sex is an extraordinarily beautiful part of making love. When we are deeply committed to love Love with each other, sex is a wonderful doorway into the mystery of literally "making love." And sex is always different each time when you live it deeply in your body. The body ages, so sex changes as we get older. In my experience, it gets better and better, but that is because our consciousness, Kathy's and mine, can enter into that play so much more completely now.

Let's talk about your specific use of the Mandala when you are doing sessions with clients. The focus is on being aware in the Now. Yes, the Mandala model starts from the understanding that there is only Now. Yet, at the same time, the thinking mind continuously modifies our experience of the Now. The Mandala specifically shows the four ways that through thinking we lose contact with the immediacy of ourselves in our bodies in the present moment. That loss of being into thinking is the basis of all mind-made suffering. These four ways, or modes of the thinking mind, are first, identification with stories/fictions about ourselves: "I am not good enough" or "I am superior" are common examples. Second, identification with judgments and fictions about others: "He doesn't care," or "She is controlling," are common examples. But actually, stories can be beliefs and judgments about anything we can represent conceptually. Third, identification with beliefs about the past, which includes specific memories, which the brain is actually reinterpreting each time we remember them, as a baseline of memories that we reach into unconsciously to justify whatever we are reacting to in the present moment. We choose something from the past that justifies our present moment's reaction and ignore any memories that might refute that. The fourth way is our identification with the hope and fear stories we tell ourselves about the future on the basis of the past.

When I am working with people, I always listen for the stories they tell themselves because that creates their anger, fear, or unhappiness. I help them find those stories and take conscious distance from them. It is more than cognitive work; I have them do the work in their bodies, to feel what each belief creates in them and what it feels like when they step away from that fiction. The Mandala work is a way of helping people recognize what their minds are doing the moment they become reactive. So if you get angry, the Mandala suggests you ask yourself: "What I am telling myself about myself, others, the past, and the future that is making me angry now?" The Mandala shows that it is not what someone else does that makes you react, it is what you are telling yourself. Then if you become aware of what your thinking mind is doing, you can let go of that thinking and come back to the present. You begin to live from your awareness, not your thinking, and in your heart. Each moment is the potential for a new start.

To practice this is to begin to live an evolutionary shift. It is a movement into heart/mind, where the heart in the present moment is leading the thinking mind, rather than what most people do, which is to have their thinking mind lead their feelings, creating their emotions. I doubt humankind will survive if we don't learn this.

How have your books evolved? Your first book was The I That Is We: Awakening to Higher Energies Through Unconditional Love; *what was the message?* That was written in 1980. I was finding my way into describing the shift that had occurred in me and the work I had begun to do, but it wasn't an autobiographical book rather it was the beginning of writing from a new consciousness. Every other book since then was my next iteration of understanding that consciousness and how to live and share it. I wrote my last two books, *The Mandala of Being* and *Inside-Out Healing*, to summarize everything I had learned and to give people a very practical way to deepen their consciousness practices and ground the spiritual journey in the body. All my work is about spiritual evolution without having to have any kind of belief systems; it's all basically observation, releasing, uncovering... and practice.

Would you say that the key steps that you teach to evolve are to use meditation and maybe physical exercise like yoga to remind us to stay in the present where we're centered? Yes, that's well put. I would say that we have to learn with the heart and the right-brain and the body. They speak one language that's 95% of our intelligence. We need to learn to see what our thinking minds have done to us that is both good and horrible. You have to learn it with your body.

How do you learn it with your body? It's activities and processing that go back and forth between dancing, whirling, breathing, meditation, contemplation, self-witnessing, processing emotional reactions, dream work, and working with music in different ways. I teach people how to use their voices, to create their own chants, to adventure with words and voice and movement, because that gives a whole new life to words. It anchors words in feeling and spontaneous imagery. It awakens forgiveness and trust and a whole new path to deep insight.

As we anchor more and more in the body in the present moment, that embodiment changes our consciousness. It changes our understanding and perception of ourselves and of the world around us. We call it mystical, but to me, it is totally natural. Working this way with a group of people unifies them; they start to connect to each other in ways that give them a profound hope for what's possible in human community. This kind of transformational education of heart/mind has happened forever. The Buddha did it his way and the disciples of the Buddha do it their way. *And the Sufis whirl.* Yes, the Mevlevi dervishes whirl, chant, and sing. My morning practice every day is singing and chanting or repeating melodies that I've made up or using melodies that I like from classical music and putting words to the melodies, merging words and music, merging rhythm and voice. I sing sadness. I sing gratitude. I sing about this glorious planet. I sing the wonder of nature. I just let it flow.

A spiritual rap. Yes, it's sometimes really simple and I may put the word "holy" in front of anything: holy feeling, holy breathing, holy fearing, holy wanting, holy lonely, holy dispirited, holy sorrow, holy grateful. And so everything that could possibly be felt, positive or negative, becomes holy because without a body and consciousness none of it could be experienced. Even being capable of inventing the most horrible things with our minds, that too, is miraculous. Often terrible, but also miraculous. If you were dead, you couldn't create racism or hate but to be identified with those is to live in hell and to creating hell for others.

Can you give an example of healing like one that you included in your book, Inside-Out Healing? I recently received an email from a woman who came to one of my workshops in Copenhagen a few years ago. We never met in person, but in the email, she described that I was teaching about the way our stories affect each moment, that something completely unexpected happened. She told me that she came because she was desperate. She was in postpartum depression and felt suicidal, but she had two young twin daughters and she didn't want to leave them orphaned. She wrote that she had tried medications, they didn't work. She tried many different forms of therapeutic intervention but the depression just kept deepening. Then she described that as I was guiding the group into the Now, something happened to her. She wrote, "Suddenly a breeze came in from the window and the hairs on my arm moved and I was in the present." She said that she realized that the medical stories about hormones that create changes in the brain, for her, became just stories. She said, "I realized even the depression, the miserable feelings I was struggling with, all of it was just what I had identified with and with the tingling of the hairs on my arm in that moment, the depression dropped away and never came back." She wrote to thank me and said that as the years passed since then, her way of really thanking me was to begin to teach others about stories and presence.

It's like when people shift identities in multiple personality disorders and their health changes instantly. Yes, we can say there are different bodies and different psychologies at different vibrational levels and when we shift deeply, something else can happen and you start all over. This is the story of spiritual revelation. *How would you name those other energy bodies?* I just speak in metaphor. I don't name them. *You don't say seven layers of the aura and the emotional body and chakras?* No, I don't. Depending on the teachers, one chakra will be this color or that color, and so on. To me, those are just more stories. To me, these kinds of transformations are a natural process. As you become more present you change your psychology, you change your relationships to others, you change your reactivity, your arousal level decreases. Everything changes in a very positive way as you become more present and more embodied. Depending on the depth of your inner work, you are healing, digesting, liberating yourself and ultimately everybody, because we are all united in the deeper consciousness.

When I asked the question all those years ago, "Who has been here before?" my answer was Jesus. I wasn't a Christian; I am not a Christian or of any religion. But, from that moment onward, I knew that the higher consciousness was available to me, that it was eternal, that it had lifted others, and that it is available to everyone. Since that day and because I have never stopped the inner work, I can sense how my body is being transubstantiated in love. It's wiser, it's more capable of delight, even though I can't do what I used to do athletically. I don't go rock climbing anymore, for example. The body intelligence, which is delight, is growing.

Are you optimistic even in the face election of autocrats and inequality increasing? It hurts. I have trust that everything that I've just shared with you is real, that anyone can transubstantiate their body in love, that you can learn to love and be loved in profound ways and evolve yourself in consciousness here on planet earth. But in terms of what's happening in our world now, I am not optimistic for us as a species in the next few hundred years. I think we are going to end up with a very, very wealthy elite that uses technology to partially protect themselves, at least for a while, from environmental degradation and the rest of humankind is going to be in desperate shape.

I consider it nonsense that some think we are going to go out into the solar system and create havens for human beings to live on the barrenness of Mars or the moon. We haven't learned to terraform this planet! Yes, technology may enable a tiny fraction of humanity to live in environments in space or underground on Earth. But there'll be little if anything of nature as we know it and in which we evolved. And since we can't seem, currently, to work together to heal ourselves and our planet, why is it imagined that we will work together on any extra-terrestrial colonies or on space ships? That dreaming is the blindness of the rationality of the left-brain.

It's only through a change of consciousness that we have any hope and the work we each have to do for that is essential. It isn't that difficult once you know where to start, right now in yourself. But at present, we are embedded in and obeying patterns of identification that we inherited. Until we can outgrow them, we don't have a chance of realizing that our shared humanity is much deeper than all the fictions that divide us. We don't have a shared vision here on planet earth; religion tried to give us that, but until we use awareness to free ourselves from every form of limited self-identification, religions are just another source of divisive self-identification. What I am optimistic about is that you and I can come to the end of our lives with a profound smile in our hearts and that we can help others to take the same journey.

Do you believe in reincarnation? When you die what happens? I've had direct experience of accompanying people as they died and have experienced amazing changes of their energy, uplifting and remarkable. So I've had direct experience that there is a transition out of the body into another consciousness and of course, *The Tibetan Book of the Dead* talks about the Bardo stages after physical death. But, do we reincarnate? I don't know.

What do you do for fun? The way Kathy and I live and communicate is my greatest joy. I love to go for hikes with our dogs or just the two of us, or alone. I read. I love to get up in the morning and sing and then rest into stillness. My practice is a joy for me;

it's a passion. It balances me so that I don't get too dispirited and depressed in the midst of the painful things that are happening all around us.

Books

The I That Is We, 1981
How Shall I Live, 1983
The Black Butterfly, 1987
The Second Miracle, 1995
Words That Shine Both Ways, 1998
The Mandala of Being, 2007
Inside Out Healing, 2011

Websites

www.richardmoss.com
Richard Moss on YouTube

Endnotes

1 http://ccare.stanford.edu/press_posts/compassion-is-often-the-best-medicine-stanford-study/
2 https://www.who.int/features/qa/cancer-red-meat/en/
   Dr. Moss recommends the documentary *Game Changers*
   Darlush Mozaffarian, "Should You Avoid Meat for Good Health? How to Slice Off the Facts from the Fiction, *The Conversation*, December 19, 2020 (includes the environmental impact)

CHRIS ROE, PH.D.
THE PSYCHOLOGY OF ALTERED
STATES OF CONSCIOUSNESS

Photo by N. Roe

Questions to Ponder

What were the outcomes of Professor Roe's dream ESP experiments?

What psychological characteristics does he find are associated with people with psi abilities?

What directions does Dr. Roe suggest psi researchers include in their work? What's especially important to him in terms of a social goal?

I'm from Lancashire in northwest England, a very industrialized area with cotton mills. I was born in 1966, September 22, so I believe I'm a Virgo. I'm the first of two sons. I think I'm still the same as I was before—INFJ. *Only three of our scientists are sensing.* There's something about the parapsychology subject matter that requires comfort with ambiguity and being an intuitive type helps us be comfortable with things being revealed gradually rather than immediately in black and white terms.

What childhood influences led you to become a psychology professor? I'm from a working-class background, the first person in my family to graduate university. The working-class ethic is seeing is believing: You don't take authority's word for it. You question people and prefer to see things for yourself, which has given me a very empirical drive. I want to verify things and test things for myself. In my working-class community, they're very aware of people who get too big for their boots. If people had achievements or qualifications, that doesn't make them any better than anybody else so they're very ready to bring you down a peg or two. It's important to come to this work without an ego in order to be a vessel through which the data speaks rather than it being all about you. In mainstream science, there are too many "personalities" when we should be focusing on the discoveries themselves and how to use them for the betterment of people.

I was brought up as a Catholic. I've got an Irish background and spent time as a child as an altar boy. I was very interested in religion because it gives us a way of understanding what it was to be a person, including a spiritual aspect. The sense of being deeply interconnected one with another stayed with me. What I had trouble with as I reached my teens was dogma, a particular set of teachings that you have to accept on faith. If there is a God and he/she gave us an inquiring mind, then it is our duty to exercise that inquiring mind and not simply accept things. I was very drawn to science then at school and university. My first degree is in biology although I specialized in psychology—very quantitative and very experimental.

Over time I've evolved as I was exposed to transpersonal ways of thinking and more subjective ways of understanding people. In my first 10 years of research, most of my output was experimental or survey-based, while these days about 70 to 80% is qualitative: based on interviews, case stories, narratives, and open-ended surveys. I'm interested in the lived experience of ordinary people now. I couldn't do what I'm doing without having established credentials as a methodologist with an understanding of ways in which we might deceive ourselves.

In creating this new (which is really very old) paradigm of non-materialist consciousness, please define consciousness. We don't have the remotest idea of what we mean by consciousness. I am interested in neuroscience but I don't expect it to provide all of the answers about the subjective experience of being. We don't have the conceptual tools to know how to ask the right questions and how to interrogate nature to get answers to those questions. Thinking about the research that William James was doing 150 years ago, we're not any further today. But, working on the fringes with the anomalies starts to give us the shape of the edges of consciousness. If people claim that consciousness can exist when the body is clinically dead, those are crucial experiences for us to understand. If people claim consciousness can access information that isn't available by the normal senses, that's got to be a focus for us. We're working from the outside in, but by characterizing those properties it will start to give us a sense of what is that essential phenomenon.

If you were pressed, what would you say about this paranormal infor-mation field? It took me a little while to recognize how idiosyncratic experience is. Although many of us have a world view that we assume is shared with other people, we have no objective evidence on which to base that assumption. In thought experiments in phi-losophy, we might both agree on what the color green looks like when we see it but we have no idea that our subjective experiences are alike. Synesthesia is really interesting in giving us a sense that we can experience a stimulus qualitatively in many different and rich ways. Some people can experience colors as taste, numbers, or sounds, which opens up the idea that we need to map the subjective experience.

I'm particularly interested in people who've practiced spiritual disciplines because that means their subjective experiences are more trustworthy. They've spent longer honing their experience and their sense of that experience in a way that strips away cul-tural assumptions much more effectively than the average person. *Like Tibetan monk meditators?* Absolutely. One of my Ph.D. students is exploring Buddhist meditators' experience of *iddhis* or *siddhis*, paranormal events related to meditative practice.[1] Devout practi-tioners who spend 8-10 hours a day in meditation at retreats are people we need to listen to. Very few people have direct experiences of the profound, paranormal phenomena. Unfortunately, most psi experiences seem to be quite mundane as when people talk about their devotion leading to merits that they can actually, in a sense, cash in. So if you practice the principles you can accumulate cred-its, good karma in such a way that later on if there was a particular job that you want, etc., you can "spend" credits. The experimen-talist in me would not see those synchronicities as very solid evi-dence in the real world. Many of them may amount to little more than coincidence or the attribution of meanings to fairly random events coinciding.

People on a spiritual path often report that synchronicity speeds up as seemingly disconnected but favorable auspicious events come together. Have you felt that in your life? No, as a psychologist I know about phenomena such as apophenia, people's tendency to see connections and attribute meaning to things. It can be very successful in enabling us to survive by making inferences on limited information but it can trip us up. I've experienced smatterings of the paranormal but none I see as evidence because it is very possible that they simply reflect coincidences, selective attention, selective memory and so on.

A colleague wisely asked us many years ago why we weren't being participants in our own experiments. From that point on I've been a regular participant in various studies and I'm generally quite successful. For example, we have a dream ESP experiment we finished at the end of 2018 where I was significantly above chance under conditions where you can be sure that it isn't coincidence or cues that I'm picking up unconsciously. I'm very open to the idea that we all have a psychic capacity. It may be applied only under certain circumstances, particularly related to need, which is why experiments are so difficult because they're all about the needs of the researcher. I'm quite confident that these psi phenomena really do occur and that I can produce them as much as an average person can.

In the dream experiments, a computer selects a video clip or a picture and then you pick out which of four relates to your dream—like Ganzfeld? That's exactly the technique that we use. The target material has to be randomly chosen independently of the participant. Everyone is blinded to the actual target as a computer randomly chooses from about 200 video clips and plays that clip through the night while we're at home sleeping and dreaming. When we come in in the morning the computer is in the judging phase and presents four clips to choose from—the target and three decoys. By chance alone, participants should select the target 25% of the time. We conducted about 160 trials with a hit rate just under 32%, not a massive difference but highly significant statistically.

On one occasion I woke up with an image of a snake flicking its tongue. The target was a sand snake. Commonly, it's the emotional tone of the material that gets picked up, such as a sad or very exciting clip. What keeps us going back to those experiments aren't the statistical deviations from chance; rather it's the greatest hits, occasions when people describe elements of the clip in such detail that it's unfathomable to work out how that might be accounted for in normal terms. The problem with this research is that much of it is still proof-oriented to demonstrate that the effect occurs, but it's really important that we move on and we start to look at process work. How can we characterize and understand it? Are some personalities or individuals better than others? Is it related to prior experience or practice with mental disciplines? Does it matter how we set up the contents of the study and how we look after people? That's the next important focus.

Typically women are allowed to be more in touch with their intuitive emotional side and a lot of mediums are women. Do you find any gender differences? There are absolutely gender differences at every level except once you get people through the door and conduct experiments with them. We recently finished an online survey for people who have had after-death communication experiences. Around 80% of those respondents are women. In other situations where you have an open call to people to respond or you survey people, women report much higher levels of belief in and experience with psi. But if we can get people through the door, then we find that there aren't consistent differences between men and women. I don't think women are necessarily naturally more intuitive but they're more comfortable with disclosing this kind of material to relative strangers. The exceptions are that men are quite comfortable in admitting to technological paranormal beliefs like belief in alien visitations. When you're talking about socially-mediated phenomena like telepathy and experiences with somebody after their death, more women report belief and experience.

It's really tempting to say quantum non-locality indicates that there's an information field where entangled particles can communicate—which could explain psi—but physicists don't like to go there. They say, "We don't know what the information field is." The lesson that I live by is not to make pronouncements outside my area of expertise. Not all scientists share that view, and there are many people with qualifications in other, unrelated disciplines who seem quite content to speak about parapsychology. I'm not convinced that the kind of entanglement that physicists are talking about bears any relation to the kinds of "'entanglement'" that human beings report. Another difficulty I have is the primacy of physics. A common expectation is that a fundamental explanation will come in physical terms. I'm a great believer that there are different levels of explanation. For example, it would be impossible for a physicist to give any sensible account of the practice of marriage; it would make no sense in physics terms such as force or mass. Biologically we might be able to make an argument in terms of conservation of genetic material for the next generation, or in terms of hormones in the brain triggered by falling in love. While these are necessary components, few people would see them as sufficient to explain their lived experience of love and affection.

I'm very aware as a psychologist that the explanation that I will find satisfying will be a psychological explanation or a sociological one. So if telepathy occurs, why did this telepathic experience occur to this person at this time? I'm more interested in questions relating to the psychology and the psychodynamics of the phenomena. *A number of British parapsychologists are working with the schizotypy as a predictor of psi ability.* It reflects the fact that human beings are on a continuum in the way which they perceive the world around them and how they understand their own emotions and their responses to stimuli. Scores on some of those dimensions seem to predict psychic experience and belief in paranormal phenomena. Other characteristics are self-labeled creativity and extroversion is a predictor of performance in the laboratory in parapsychology experiments.

Extraversion is a fabulous example of how a variable that relates to psi ability can give us an insight into how that phenomenon works. There are two models to explain the tendency for extraverts to perform better than introverts in our psi experiments. One is that extraversion reflects central nervous system noise. Extraverts crave external stimulation and introverts deflect stimulation since they can be overstimulated very quickly. If you've got that internal noise as an introvert, it might make it more difficult to perceive a very subtle signal against the background of sensory noise. We might expect an introvert to not do so well in a psychic task because they've got so much other central nervous system noise in their system for a very subtle cue, whereas extraverts have got a very quiet system and so those signals are much more noticeable to them.

An alternative model is a social dynamic one that views extraverts as craving novelty. If you invite an extravert to come into the lab and do an experiment on parapsychology, they're in their element, enjoying the stimulation of a new situation. An introvert is easily overwhelmed by that situation and is extremely guarded and it takes them a lot of time to become acclimatized. But if you test people repeatedly with the same method, I would expect introverts to start to do better than extraverts as they become more comfortable with the situation. Extraverts, in contrast, will start to get bored and not able to focus so they'll do worse.

Creativity is another factor that seems to predict psi. One feature of creativity is the willingness to think outside of the box and to work symbolically with the material. I'm not surprised that creatives do better when they're trying to make sense of their dreams or their subjective experiences in our other studies. Creatives may act as unconscious processors more effectively than less creative people. They may become more absorbed in activities and in that immersive state they become oblivious to their environments. For example, if you're an artist painting a canvas, you might suddenly discover that eight or nine hours have passed by.

What's your favorite instrument for testing creativity levels? Chris Dalton did interesting work at the University of Edinburgh, finding if you use measures of creativity, they don't consistently predict performance. What you need to do instead is to ask people if they would label themselves as particularly creative. Are creative acts an important part of who they are? A student of mine, Nicola Holt, explored creativity in some depth and created her own measure that we've used in several studies.

Have you found quantitative differences in scores on the schizotypy test in terms of psi abilities? When Christine Simmonds-Moore* worked with us, we certainly found a pattern of relationship. The positive traits with schizotypy are people may see things differently from other people; these positive traits are a predictor for performance in the laboratory. We're looking for an underlying mechanism that will tell us about the ultimate sources of that performance. *Isn't there some suggestion that their nervous system is more finely tuned or they're more in tune with their nervous system?* The primary act of the brain is to inhibit activity, effectively filtering incoming information so that what reaches consciousness is manageable. Psychedelics seem to be able to reduce some of that inhibition, allowing us to experience the world around us in a richer way. However, if we were in a psychedelic state all the time we wouldn't be able to function because we would be overwhelmed by that richness.

We need to be able to prioritize (often visual) information because it has the greatest adaptive value in helping us avoid dangers and take advantage of opportunities. The cost is that subtle sources of information about things that are happening in the future or at a more distant location are filtered out. They may be in the system at the subconscious level but they're not selected for conscious awareness. That's a model that's been around since the 1960s but has still a lot of mileage in it for psychologists.

How would you summarize factors that might predispose someone to be skilled at psi abilities like telepathy or precognition? Prior belief in the phenomenon, prior experience with spontaneous phenomena and sensitivity to phenomena, being Feeling and Perceiving on the Myers-Briggs, extraversion, and creativity are the ones that are popular at the moment. We need a psychometrician who can pull those together and identify underlying factors. *In our group of scientists only three are Sensing and the others Intuitive, they're more Extraverted than Introverted, more Feeling than Thinking, and even closer on Perceiving and Judging, so the group is EIFJ.*

Probably the most interesting work so far on individual differences factors has been by Michael Thalbourne, an Australian parapsychologist, who coined the dimension *transliminality* to unify the aspects that they have in common, namely, the ability to leak information from the unconscious to the conscious in a way which is less draconian than more free-form. In cognitive psychology, we have examples of "inattentional blindness" where you can have the most ridiculous things appear in the video that people do not notice.[2] *I didn't see it when I saw the video at a conference—reader, please see the selective attention test online.* It shows seeing isn't believing, believing is seeing. You see what you expect to see or what you've been directed to see. That act of suppression of other information has consequences.

What did Michael Thalborne find that allows for more access to unconscious information? Since there are so many variables, we use a statistical relationship. On average, across a collection of studies, a greater proportion of those studies will find a relationship than we'd expect by chance. But in that kind of noisy environment, I'm quite encouraged that transliminality is telling us something useful. We have a multistage process by which the measure is derived from an understanding of a number of other measures—things like creativity and absorption. What you find what they have in common statistically, you pull that out to create your new measure and you discover that your new measure predicts performance. I don't think there's any work that shows transliminality can be demonstrated through fMRI or EEG studies.

What kind of psi courses do you teach at Northampton? I teach undergraduate modules in transpersonal psychology, parapsychology, and the psychology of well-being. The latter has aspects of positive psychology, spiritual practice, and spiritual orientation from which we can draw a sense of well-being. We live in a time when people may focus on the frictions that exist between different traditions although the fundamental principle of many of the great religions is the Golden Rule, recognizing the spark of a divine in each of us and responding to other people accordingly.

Religiosity and spirituality are strongly associated with well-being. For example, people who are religious or spiritual fare better after cardiac arrest. They recover quicker and have fewer complications. When they have major surgery they seem to have fewer comorbidity problems. People who are religious and spiritual tend to have fewer minor troubles and ailments and their quality of life generally is better. I was involved with a study some years ago of older people who had recently transitioned to care homes after they found living on their own too difficult. Those who were spiritual or religious found that transition much less stressful and less anxiety-provoking. They felt that their life still had purpose in their 80s and 90s. So those are really important things to advertise and make people aware of.

You're president of the Society for Psychical Research, chair of the British Society for Transpersonal Psychology Section, and a member of the Society for Scientific Exploration. You're on the editorial board of the Journal for the Society of Psychical Research *and* Transpersonal Psychology Review *and former editor of the* Paranormal Review. *What else would you add to that list of research institutions and journals? Where can we go to get the current information in this field?* As you mature in a discipline you move from primarily doing empirical work to a more dissemination-oriented position. Much of what I do now is to translate academic material into a form that's consumable by the intelligent layperson who doesn't have the time to read original reports and make sense of them. I write book chapters for various volumes and more popular pieces for magazines as a really important part of how I can best serve the community.

We do outreach to help mental health workers, psychotherapists, and psychologists because we discovered there's a taboo around declaring paranormal beliefs and experiences so that clients found it very difficult to discuss them during therapy. We're keen to work with therapists to educate them about the normality of experiences such as, "I'm going through bereavement about the loss of my spouse. She came to me when I was sleeping, lay down next to me and I felt her stroke my hair." That is quite a common experience that people report after losing a loved one and we need to value it and cherish it. How can we explore that experience in a way that gives you comfort, that enables you to maintain that bond but move on with your life? Those are the kinds of support systems not implemented at the moment.

Which are the cutting edge organizations and journals in this field? We aim to move outside of technical journals from ones like the *Journal of Scientific Exploration*, the *Journal of Parapsychology*, and the SPR's own journal to more mainstream journals. We've recently had some commentary pieces in nursing journals. Readers should look for books authored by somebody who has an affiliation with the Parapsychological Association or is based in a university department.

What universities in the UK do you look to for psi research? They tend to be universities populated by graduates of Edinburgh's Koestler Parapsychology who are now at the University of Coventry, Derby, and Greenwich—maybe eight or 10 places in the UK where you can do a parapsychology course. In his will, Arthur Koestler left around about a million pounds for the establishment of a chair at a British university. That was taken up by the University of Edinburgh which had already had a history of doing research in the area under the supervision of John Beloff. Bob Morris, an American researcher, was appointed to that post. One of his talents was mentoring staff; he brought through over 30 Ph.D. students, of whom I am one. He inspired me to value that as well as doing research, it's really important to develop the next generation of academics. I've supervised 11 Ph.D. students and virtually all of them are still holding academic positions in universities.

A number of years ago I wrote a chapter for an A-Level psychology textbook that covered anomalistic psychology. Over 50,000 students take that A-Level each year. The chapter is intended to provide a balanced evidence-based coverage of "the paranormal." Its narrative arc is to start off by saying,

Here are the kind of things people report in their everyday lives. Here are some of the ways you can explain those away. Then you

introduce the scientific method as a way to say, "let's bring that phenomenon into a laboratory. Let's make sure we experiment with it in a stringent way where we can effectively prevent those other explanations from applying. We can be sure that it can't be just coincidence because we have lots of trials and we know exactly the outcomes of all those trials and we can work at the probability of this exact level of coincidence." Despite these controls, we still see evidence for some of these phenomena that goes beyond what we'd expect by chance, produced under conditions that rule out normal explanations. It suggests that our current psychological model of what it is to be a human being is incomplete and work needs to be done to accommodate these other phenomena.

There are some universities where you can still do transpersonal psychology research. It's easier if you adopt a more phenomenological approach, if your work is qualitative and person-focused, and you leave the ontological questions at the door. You don't need to determine the ultimate cause of this experience. You can focus on, say, what the impacts are. But we need to understand how human beings make sense of their experiences. Can we verify that these anomalies occur and that they're not explicable in conventional psychological or physical terms? *What about temporal lobes that you've mentioned using Electroencephalography (EEG) in your research?*. People in EEG studies who show evidence of temporal lobe lability report these kinds of experiences.

Three strands of research have run through the work that I've done: mediumship, altered states of consciousness, and work on the lived experience in the real world. I started out my Ph.D. interested in mediumship. The standard explanation is that when mediums produce impressive readings, it's because they're using cold reading, a set of psychological techniques that allow you to pick up information and feed it back as if it's come from paranormal source. *Like changes in their facial expression or their body language?* Yes, nonverbal cueing from the person capitalizes on the fact that people tend to forget the narrative journey and only remember the endpoint. So if I tell you about an exotic holiday that you are planning you don't recognize that that's actually been pieced together from a number of elements. I did find that people tended to selectively remember accurate information.

We've gone back to the medium community in the UK over the last 15 years. We've built up relationships with the Spiritualist National Union, which is the governing body for the spiritualist movement. They have about 230 churches in the UK with regular services on Wednesdays and Sundays. Every service involves mediums on platform who give messages of comfort to the people in the congregation, purportedly from their deceased relatives. That's a fantastic source of information about paranormal experiences. What helped with that was our agenda for many years has been very much process-oriented rather than proof-oriented.

We can look to see whether those subjective states have corollaries, such as when they go into a light trance or healing, are there changes in the EEG data? What we find is there are detectable changes that link with subjective reports of being in a non-ordinary state. That's been really important and we've done a lot of work with mediums explaining their experience, i.e., how do they come to terms with being a medium, able to see things that other people don't see, and hear things other people don't hear? That's a really challenging experience that can drive people crazy. If you presented that to a mental health specialist, you're in danger of being sectioned in this country. We also have a hearing voices network. Are there psychological techniques or devices that mediums use that would be helpful to that community? We all, in a sense, hear voices. Many of us naturally identify those voices as being our inner voice, it's just our own thoughts but other people don't have that same relationship. Who knew that? We all presume that our experience is common and, in fact, it may not be at all. So the mediumship work is really important to us and we've established a laboratory at their headquarters. They have this wonderful estate home called Stansted Hall where they have residential weeks with mediums coming in from around the world.

Do you work with Windbridge Institute in Arizona in their study of mediums? To an extent. Because of the physical distance we've not actively worked together on a project. We're of course extremely interested in and impressed by the work that they've done and we are looking for ways to work more closely in the future. *What about Gary Schwartz's SoulPhone work with mediums?* Particularly with Gary, the agendas are slightly different in that his work is more proof-oriented than ours.

A second strand I mentioned is the altered states research. When you look at how ordinary people experience psychic phenomena, it tends to involve altered states of consciousness (ASCs) from meditating, taking psychedelics or other stimulants, but very often the ASCs involved are much more mundane as in people drifting off to sleep or waking up from sleep. We've done lots of dream ESP and Ganzfeld experiments that try to recreate those ASCs. When we use ASC induction methods with ordinary people (i.e. those who don't claim any special psychic gift), they seem to be able to do better than we'd expect by chance. Because we work with unselected people we have more variability to work with in terms of predicting who's going to do well or less well in terms of their personality or situational variables.

Do you mostly use students? There's an adage in psychology that psychology textbooks describe research on current students for the benefit of future students—although psychology students may be more intelligent than the average person and more susceptible to the Good Participant effect (where they try and behave as they should do rather than how they would do naturally), on the whole, they are the same as anyone else.

The third area that I'm very keen on is to better map original experiences in the real world because it's very easy in academia to end up in some very esoteric place that doesn't speak to normal people. We have some very technical theories that don't bear any relation to what people mean when they say, "I've had a psychic experience." So it's very sobering to keep going back to those original experiences. I'm working with case collections as well as surveys, where people write accounts of meaningful experiences to see what we can glean from them. We look for a common thread that might give us a handle on what's really going on.

Have you found common threads? It's too early to say because it takes a long time to work through that kind of material. I'm working in part with the Allister Hardy collection. Hardy (1896 to 1985) was an Oxford marine biologist. He was knighted and was a very eminent person who, when he retired, set up a research unit to explore religious and spiritual experiences. He coined the phrase, "Something greater than oneself," to capture the kind of mystical encounter he was interested in. He invited people to write to him about their experiences such as a vision of the Virgin Mary or a sense of presence that you identified as Christ or Buddha. Many of the experiences are psychic experiences such as an encounter with somebody who died or a time when they felt compelled to return home and discovered that a family member was in danger. These experiences give people a sense that there is "'something other," that we're not just biological machines. Probably the main thing I've learned is these are often profound events. They might have had an experience 30 or 40 years ago and they still reflect on it regularly now like a torch that guides their life. That's why we do the lab research to resonate with what's happening in the real world.

It seems like a major theme of your work is to let people know that these are common, human experiences and not to feel like you're crazy or odd. Yes, and to give them permission to reflect on those experiences as a source of insight. You can discover something about the nature of existence if you pause and take them seriously and not be put off by those people who ridicule or pathologize those beliefs.

What have been the most difficult challenges in your life? The most important principle that any academic needs to recognize is that we should actively encourage criticism of our findings and research. That can be extremely difficult because people regard criticism of the work as personal criticism. With my Ph.D. students, I try and have them publish before they've graduated so that we can go through the review process together, to engage with referee feedback and the stinging comments so I can support them through that experience. You have to actively invite criticism of your research if you want to improve. Unfortunately, in parapsychology, you often attract ill-informed or ignorant criticism, and there us a real danger that the general public is being misinformed about the evidence.

It's a really important agenda for us as researchers to reach out to ordinary people and we give them fair and evidence-based information related to anomalous experiences. If they have an OBE or NDE, they're reassured that these are not indicative of pathology, which is important to many people who have had those experiences, as explained in my publications. If you have a dream that seems to be a premonition, it doesn't mean that you have an obligation to analyze all your dreams from then on. There's a great taboo around the subject that makes it difficult for people to know that their experiences are common. I conducted a recent nationally representative survey where about 40% of the participants had visited a psychic or medium and a significant number found that experience helpful. The irony is that these people don't talk to each other. They presume that they're in a tiny minority of people and only credulous people have paranormal beliefs or experiences when in fact many very healthy intelligent people have had these experiences. That's a key message we need to get out.

What about your personal challenges like marriage and children? No more than any other academic. It's quite a demanding job. My partner knew me when I was an undergraduate so she's been brought up on this and has been a participant in various experiments. It's very difficult though to eke out a career because there isn't a fair playing field. When I supervise students I advise that they include a more traditional area of psychology so they have a skill set that can get them employment in academia. It's sensible for them at the beginning of their career to avoid controversy and show that what they do is business as usual for academic psychology. In contrast, I have to be willing to put my head above the parapet and say, "The evidence for this is really quite strong. We need to take it seriously." That's what it is to follow your own journey. I have a daughter who followed me into psychology (despite my best efforts!) but she won't be a parapsychologist. My son is finishing up his pre-university qualifications. He's much more interested in politics than philosophy so he won't be following in my footsteps either.

A lot of the people whom I've interviewed meditate and/or walk in nature to stay centered in the face of all the pressures. Has that been useful for you? I feel quite guilty about spiritual practice. It is something that I believe is really important and I know it makes no sense at all to say you don't have time for it. I managed a transpersonal psychology master's program for some time and that was a very spiritually-oriented course. I felt it was really important to throw myself wholeheartedly into that experience. We had lots of spiritual people come in, wise people who would introduce us to different practices, but there hasn't been anything that stayed with me through this time. I consider myself a spiritual person who believes that life is inherently meaningful and we need to identify the source of that meaning. For me, that does have a spiritual source, a sense of something that goes beyond, but it is still more of a philosophical than an experiential encounter.

If something is difficult do you ask for higher guidance? My background as a Catholic focused on a personal God. That hasn't worked for me in practice through my life. I'm a great believer that God helps those who help themselves and so I don't look outside of myself for those resources in order to achieve. I accept that there is a deeper interconnectedness between people and an unfolding of things because of some greater purpose of which we have no knowledge or understanding. There's almost a Daoist aspect to this sense of surrendering to a process without becoming passive about it. You're responsible and active but you're not striving quite the same way and you recognize it's more of a holistic process that involves lots of other people

What about exercise? Walking in nature? Quite close to my home town is the largest nature reserve in the UK, The Lake District. I spent a lot of time there in childhood. My mother grew up on a farm in Ireland and as a youth I spent a lot of time in nature, just being. That still is important to me.

If you were going to write a book in the future how would you focus it? One would be on the psychology of mediumship. The other would be something around the altered states of consciousness, starting with spontaneous cases and survey material. Those experiences seem to be the situations in which our intention is diverted to inner sources, to quiet places that don't normally get that attention because we're so dominated by the immediate and the here and now. That has hugely influenced a whole raft of research designs like the dream ESP and Ganzfeld. It's important to interrogate these to see what they can tell us about the nature of these experiences, losing your sense of self, your sense of ego, when the chattering narrative self disappears into a sense of being more holistic and less a collection of aspects. There's a reality there that we are close to but we haven't quite captured yet.

Do you feel optimistic or pessimistic in the face of the world's situation with growing inequality, an increasing number of autocrats, and climate disasters? All of these things are worrying. It is human nature to fear that there has been some degradation in standards and morals and that we are on the precipice of some great doom. But these fears are not new: the poet Horace once wrote in Book III of Odes (circa 20 BCE), "Our sires' age was worse than our grandsires'. We, their sons, are more worthless than they; so in our turn, we shall give the world a progeny yet more corrupt."! In reality, we have a greater capacity now than ever before to ensure that all living beings are treated with respect and that their basic needs are met. We know more about the negative impacts we are having on our environment and have the ingenuity and resources to halt and even reverse them. Fundamentally I'm optimistic but I'm not at all complacent.

What do you do for fun in the face of all the work that you do? I am very family oriented so we tend to spend a lot of time together as a family. The four of us take lots of walks in the fresh air, play games, and movies are a big thing for us. We have a pact where nobody works on a Friday evening. We usually have a takeaway supper and a movie night together. We're quite keen on spectator sports including horse-racing. But there's so much else going on.

What else would you like to add? The important obligation we have as researchers is to speak to ordinary people and do very applied research. However, as a parapsychology community, we're still not very good at reaching out and letting ordinary people know about our findings. We're too easily distracted by the ephemera of life and need to find a way to redirect people's attention. *I conducted a survey of over 4,000 young people from 88 countries and asked, "If you could ask a question of the wisest person on the planet what would you ask her/him?" The top ones were, "What's the meaning of life?" and "What comes after death?" so they did have those kinds of existential questions in their mind?* They don't think anybody has an answer for them, so they maybe don't spend as much time on that question as they might.

Publications

Cooper, C.E., Roe, C.A., & Mitchell, G. (2015). Anomalous experiences and the bereavement process. In T. Cattoi & C. Moreman (Eds.) *The ecstasy of the end: Death and dying across traditions* (pp. 117-131). New York: Palgrave MacMillan. ISBN: 978-1-137-47207-6.

(2016). As it occurred to me: Lessons learned in researching parapsychological claims. *Journal of Parapsychology, 80*(2), 144-155.

(2016). Mediumship and survival. In D. Groome (Ed.). *Parapsychology: The psychology of unusual experience*, 2nd ed. London: Routledge. (pp. 19-33).

(2016). The near-death experience. In D. Groome (Ed.). *Parapsychology: The psychology of unusual experience*, 2nd ed. London: Routledge. (pp. 65-81).

(2017). Withering skepticism. *Journal of Parapsychology, 81*(2), 143-159.

.(2017). Has parapsychology made progress? *Mindfield*, 9(2), 42-47.

(2018). Arguing the case for parapsychological research. *Paranormal Review*, 88, 6-7.

(2019). The egregious state of scepticism. *Paranormal Review*, 90, 4-5.

(2019). The value of spontaneous cases. *Paranormal Review*, 89, 4-5.

(in press). Clinical parapsychology: The interface between anomalous experiences and psychological wellbeing. For J. Leonardi

& B. Schmidt (Eds.) *Spirituality and Wellbeing: Interdisciplinary approaches to the study of religious experience and health.* Equinox.

Roe, C.A., & Roxburgh, E.C. (2013). Non-parapsychological explanations of ostensibly mediumistic information: A review of the evidence. In A.J. Rock (Ed.) *The survival hypothesis: Essays on Mediumship* (pp. 65-78). Jefferson, NC: McFarland. ISBN: 978-0786472208.

Roe, C.A., & Roxburgh, E. (2013). An overview of cold reading strategies. In C. Moreman (Ed.) *The Spiritualist Movement: Speaking with the Dead in America and around the World: Volume 2, Belief, Practice, and Evidence for Life after Death.* (pp. 177-203). Santa Barbara, CA: Praeger. ISBN: 978-0-3133-9947-3.

Roxburgh, E., & Roe, C.A. (2013). Exploring the meaning of mental mediumship from the mediums' perspective. In C. Moreman (Ed.) *The Spiritualist Movement: Speaking with the Dead in America and around the World: Volume 2, Belief, Practice, and Evidence for Life after Death.* (pp. 53-67) Santa Barbara, CA: Praeger. ISBN: 978-0-3133-9947-3.

Sherwood, S.J., & Roe, C.A. (2013). An updated review of dream ESP studies conducted since the Maimonides dream ESP programme. In S. Krippner, A. Rock, J. Beischel, & H. Friedman (Eds.), *Advances in Parapsychological Research 9.* Jefferson, NC: McFarland & Co. (pp. 38-81). ISBN: 978-0-7864-7126-3

Endnotes

1 http://the-wanderling.com/siddhis.html
2 https://www.youtube.com/watch?v=vJG698U2Mvo

MARILYN MANDALA SCHLITZ, PH.D.
A TRANSFORMATIVE WORLDVIEW

Photo by Giovanni Mandala

Questions to Ponder

Why did Dr. Schlitz decide to be a part of a paradigm shift?

What kind of person does exceptionally well on the Ganzfeld telepathy experiment? How is it similar to the psychomanteum?

What influences lead to major spiritual transformations in "masters" studied by Dr. Schlitz? What were her major difficult but transformative experiences?

You were born in Detroit, August 1957, the sixth of six children. Do you identify with Leo characteristics? I am not a big astrology person but I have a lot of fire in my chart. *And your Myers-Briggs personality type?* ENTP.

You've studied abroad, you've worked bi-coastally and you're interested in worldview, so how does where you have lived and experienced influence your worldview? I think there are regional differences and I also think that core groups of people who wherever you go represent shared values so that anywhere can feel like home. *Like* Cultural Creatives. *I think the thrust in your interest in worldviews is in being tolerant or understanding other people's worldviews.* I think a worldview is the guiding lens of perception that influences everything about our behavior, our sense of identity, and our relationship to other people. I think it's probably the most powerful aspect of our consciousness and, at the same time, it's largely unconscious. So we have very little awareness about this lens of perception that biases and influences us in very profound ways. Part of the work of 21st century metacognitive capacities is our ability to recognize our worldview and to understand how powerful it is.

You and I have a worldview as educated, California mothers of a son. What else influenced your worldview? Having been born and raised in

Detroit at a time when the community, the culture, the government, and our nation was at war with itself was a very powerful influence. I think Detroit is very much characterized by the materialist model and I recognized that worldview wasn't particularly effective. It was also a time when we were questioning authority and assumptions. I clearly recall feeling very disempowered during that period as I was not sure what I could do to affect change and that led to some angst in my youth.

It wasn't until I got to college at Wayne State University in downtown Detroit that I discovered a couple of really powerful tools I learned from books and scholarship, particularly Thomas Kuhn's 1962 book *The Structure of Scientific Revolutions*. His explanation of structural scientific revolutions had a very powerful influence on my worldview; namely, the idea that we live in these paradigms and yet they aren't fixed or absolute. I became aware through Kuhn's work that these paradigms shift over time. He looked at the worldviews associated with science and how various discoveries fundamentally change our models of reality over time. The idea that I could be involved in a paradigm shift was a very liberating concept for me.

The second book that was very important was Edgar Mitchell's 1996 book *Psychic Exploration*. I was on an odyssey of discovery about myself, the world, how to do science, and the qualities I wanted to bring to that endeavor and that's been the track I've been on ever since. My undergrad degree was in philosophy and liberal arts and my master's degree was in social science. My Ph.D. was in social anthropology and I did two post-doctoral fellowships, one in social psychology and one in cognitive science.

What kind of religious training did you get as a girl? My parents weren't religious; they went to the boat every weekend. I had two sisters who became interested in the Lutheran Church down the street and so when I was about 12 years old, I got myself confirmed and baptized. That lasted for a couple of years but growing up as a boater gave me a deep appreciation for nature. I spent long hours alone out in the swamplands that have now been developed into a huge marina. On one occasion my two nephews and I were out hiking and we got stuck up to our waist in mud. Fortunately, one of my nephews was able to wiggle his way out and got some adult help. In the city, there was a lot of partying, a lot of drinking, behaviors that certainly aren't commonly identified with the spiritual practice. Oftentimes I'd pull away from all of that in order to find my own path.

Were you the first to go to graduate school in your family? I was the first one of six siblings to finish college and the only child to get into a graduate school and beyond. *Did you have professors who said you've got to go to grad school or what was the impetus?* Yes, I had a couple of professors who were very encouraging. I got some self-esteem around my academic abilities during high school when I took honors classes and then hung out with all the wrong people after hours. I've always been driven by curiosity and I've always had a passion for writing, for communicating. I was on the school newspaper in high school. I also had a very rebellious spirit, so that questioning authority and trying different things was definitely part of my makeup.

I had a professor, Robin Barraco, who was the youngest man to ever get tenured at the medical school of Wayne State University. He thought I was brilliant and should go to medical school. But, I took one cadaver lab and that was it for me. Instead, I was driven toward theory and philosophy and did a fellowship at the Institute for Parapsychology in Durham, North Carolina in 1979 through 1982. We had a journal club where we gave presentations about something we'd read. Looking around the table I realized if I was ever going to be a major contender in the paradigm shift that Kuhn had written about and Edgar Mitchell had illustrated, I had to have a Ph.D. I got interested in doing laboratory-based experimental research and I learned about statistics, experimental design, and controls while I was in college. It was a great foundation and at the same time, I realized that it was a good idea to learn qualitative methods. I became a mixed methods kind of person where I knew how to do the controlled research and I also learned through anthropology and social science how to engage in the broader endeavor of qualitative research.

What were the most difficult challenges that you faced in your life? My family, my being a parent has been an extremely challenging experience as we have had to confront addiction issues and trusting people that didn't deserve to be trusted and who can eat up a lot of time and energy. By and large, I take challenges as opportunities, so I am kind of forward-looking and keep going. *My son thinks that my intuitive work is a little suspect. What about your son?* My son respects my work but may be a little intimidated by it. He hasn't found his path yet so he hasn't yet formulated skeptical positioning relative to me. I am not an extreme believer and I don't tout my opinions around these things in an evidential way. I really try to take a questioning position so that that has been less in his face.

How did you find the parapsychology work in Durham? It's not something that's in the forefront. As I said, I have always been curious. I was determined and I was on fire. I think Professor Barraco turned me onto *Psychic Exploration* by Edgar Mitchell that contained resources. At the time the American Society for Psychical Research, which has basically gone defunct now, had a guide to places you could go and study parapsychology and the Institute for Parapsychology was one of those places. Also, Robert Morris was teaching at the University of California, Irvine and I took my senior year there. *Bob Morris taught parapsychology at the University of Edinburgh beginning in 1985. His graduate students went on to teach around the UK.* A lot of my friends were moving to California and I decided to go with them. Bob was an amazing teacher and a real inspiration who helped me get into the program in Durham. I love North Carolina.

In your psi studies have you experimented with your own access to intuition, ESP, and RV? I have done very few experiments that I wasn't a participant in some phase of it. The most significant and the best controlled RVing experiment in the literature was one in which I was the RVer. When I was at Rhine Center looking at psychic healing, it turned out that the experimenters were the best participants, as I also found when I went to the Mind Science Foundation in San Antonio, Texas. I worked with William Braud to conduct experiments with healers, psychics, and average people. After 14 formal experiments and lots of data, we were the strongest performers in those experiments. That said something about the whole issue of objectivity and how able we are to remove ourselves from the object of inquiry.

Do you think that you have that ability innately or did you develop it because you were so interested in it intellectually? I think that I always had an interest in intention and even as a kid when I was out at the boat, I would often utilize my intention to try and bring some situation or person into my environment. I don't know if I was successful at it but I believed that that was a kind of skill or a gift that we had. My mom was always interested in these kinds of things. She grew up at a time when people were doing table tilting seances, which piqued my curiosity. When I took the fellowship at the Rhine Center, I turned down a job in an insurance company in Detroit paying quite a bit of money for somebody fresh out of school. When I took the job in North Carolina for $400 a month, my poor dear mother was appalled but she became proud of me for following my own path.

What other institutions are doing this kind of parapsychological research? You've mentioned the Rhine Center and Mind-Body in Texas.[1] There's Gary Schwartz* at the University of Arizona. The Monroe Institute launched a new initiative to research on psychophysiology. The University of West Georgia in Carrollton, West Georgia, has a little lab there: Christine Simonds-Moore* is doing some psychomanteum work, too, so I am excited to collaborate with them. Other research is being done at the University of Northampton in England and Richard Wiseman at the University of Hertfordshire.[2] Some work is going on in Amsterdam, Germany, and Switzerland.

What was your focus at IONS? I built the lab there. I was there about 25 years so I had multiple interests. When I originally went there, they were interested in having me direct the Spontaneous Remission Program. Then I was interested in the Ganzfeld research; I had done a big project with Julliard School students at a lab in Princeton and got very strong results on that. A young woman was sitting in the Ganzfeld describing her experience and saw a black female nightclub performer, a lion, a dog, lots of yellow, and a wizard. The target was "The Wiz," the musical parody of *The Wizard of Oz* where Diana Ross is Dorothy and they skipped across the Brooklyn Bridge. She saw the hot air balloon over them; the level of detail was remarkable. On the days when I turn skeptic, it reminds me that there may be something more to our human capacities.

Ganzfeld comes from the German word, the "whole field." It's a sensory deprivation procedure that involves reducing your visual inputs with white noise in the ears and a red light that shines down. Soon that turns black because you keep your eyes open while they're covered with a mask and people start to see imagery. A person in another room looks at a video clip while the person in the Ganzfeld describes their imagery to see how closely it matches the video clip when presented with four choices. Braud found that the average person got somewhere around 32% to 33% which was statistically significant over time. With the Juilliard students, we found a 50% success rate overall, while the classically trained musicians produced a 75% success rate. It was really inspiring to look at how creativity and the performing arts may correlate with psi abilities. That study got replicated in different places, including the University of Edinburgh.

I had a fellowship at Stanford and during my off hours, we would do a research project down in the basement working with Steven Laberge. I wanted to build a lab at IONS so that I could do my work there and we were also very interested in the psychic healing work I had done at the Mind Science Foundation. I hired Dean Radin* to help me to set up the process and he is still there doing the research. I since migrated to Sofia University in Silicon Valley where I am working on a project looking at the psychomanteum which is also a sensory deprivation procedure, very much like the Ganzfeld. We are using it for helping with grief.

The psychomanteum was originally developed by Raymond Moody who took it from ancient Greece where they looked at a reflective surface and would start to see things. He thought, "This would be interesting if we could bring it into a clinical study." He invited people to a very dark room with a mirror on the wall with an illumination on the reflective surface. You are not actually seeing yourself in the mirror but you seeing this kind of hazy portal. People would describe these apparition-like experiences with conversations with dead people. The experience enabled them to move past certain blockages in their lives. Arthur Hastings, who was at the Institute of Transpersonal Psychology, which is now part of Sofia, found very significant impacts on bereavement. We decided to try combining the transpersonal aspects of it with technology, working with virtual reality as a tool to stimulate or evoke these kinds of experiences. We got a grant for it and we are in the process of setting it up. We are having a hackathon to invite people to come in and help us to design an application and the experience.

In Consciousness and Healing, *a book you co-edited in 2004, you focused on a new vision, a post-modern model of paradigm shift about medicine and healing that involves consciousness and transformative practices. How far has that shift progressed?* Progress is being made. Certainly, you can see the area of placebo, for example, is much more interesting for scientists. The whole mind-body field has moved forward where you have therapies like biofeedback available in almost every medical center. Kaiser Permanente offers acupuncture, chiropractic, massage, Reiki, guided imagery, etc.[3] The whole-system model is much more widely accepted, including spirituality as a component of a whole system. However, we are still entrapped in a materialist, profit-centered model. For example, Johnson & Johnson knew for many years that they had asbestos in their baby powder but the profit motive not to take that ingredient out is mindboggling. If you look at traditional Chinese medicine like acupuncture, it's based on a worldview that evolved over thousands of years including knowledge of metaphysical bodies.

People have grown up in a world where, for example, AI is a reality. I recently did an interview with Sophia, the android, who is programmed for loving kindness, as you can see in interviews with her.[4] She leads you on a mindfulness meditation practice and talks about friendship and has feelings when people judge her falsely. We have these opportunities to use technologies. If it doesn't get corrupted and it doesn't get abused, there is a lot of potential. Sophia was created by Hanson Robotics in Hong Kong. She is a citizen of Saudi Arabia who has spoken all over the world to various agencies, including the United Nations and has been on the cover of *Vogue* magazine. She was designed to be like Audrey Hepburn except that she's got a big set of computer chips on the back of her head. She is open source so when she shuts down, she goes to the cloud and accesses information so she is learning at a very rapid pace. The 15 versions of the androids share information—it's extraordinary.

Can she be a therapist? She leads meditation and she will take you on a "look at her in the eyes" kind of mindfulness practice. She offers people the opportunity to talk and so in that case, it's therapeutic, at least it's intended to be. They are doing research on Sophia to see if it make a difference if she is with you physically or whether you are looking at an avatar of her or just hearing her voice.

It seems like the most widely accepted mind-body practice is meditation. John Kabat-Zinn has done a lot with the mindfulness research. That's probably the most mainstream? I tweeted an article last week that says meditation is the number one alternative modality that people are using now. When I interviewed Kabat-Zinn he said he saw it like a Trojan horse; if you go into mainstream medicine and say this is an opportunity to reduce stress or anxiety; then they think they are doing it for medical reasons. I work with Ellen Langer at Harvard; she is a social psychologist who has written books on mindfulness for a long time before Kabat-Zinn.

Langer is interested in looking at the social environment as it influences our experiences. She did a classic experiment that I am trying to replicate using virtual reality where she reverse-aged people. She took a group of men who were in their 70s and created an environment where they were in the 1950s. The magazines, the TV, the radio, everything was programmed to be 20 to 30 years old. She found that people showed beneficial changes psychologically and physically so we are hoping to do that in the context of virtual reality experience. I am hoping to raise some money to do that. We are planning to go to an Alzheimer's Center in Southern California where they have set up a village situated in the 1960s to interview people with dementia and allow them to reminisce. Ellen's idea is it not really about reminiscing as it's about immersion and, in fact, she used reminiscence as a control condition for her studying.

Everybody knows about placebo but in the past, it's been dismissed as kind of an irritation. If I take this big red pill, even if I know it's a sugar pill, it's therapeutic. What's the mechanism for that? Placebo remains a mystery, how you can take an inert substance that somehow knows the particular cascade of responses to trigger a particular change? There's been some research, as at Harvard, and there definitely needs to be more.

You are interested in consciousness; you've discussed "super consciousness" and some universities offer Consciousness Studies. How would you define it? It's awareness but it can also be below the threshold of awareness as the brain is interconnected. I believe that there is a field of consciousness that connects us as we communicate with each other and then there is the possibility of an interconnectedness that transcends the physicality of our communications. *It's like Jung's collective unconscious where we share archetypes?* Yes, and I also think that intention plays a role, as in directing one's attention toward another person. I believe that nature is conscious. I think that you if go to a rainforest and you see every nook and cranny has life and if something is cut down, it rebuilds, it reorganizes, so there is an intelligence to nature. There is a way in which nature is entangled, and now with people talking more and more about quantum physics at a macro level—not just at the microscopic level, we could be moving toward an expanded scientific framework that could help us to understand these non-local exchanges.

Does the quantum information field provide the medium by which we influence each other? If I send intercessory prayer to somebody who's had a heart attack, do you think it might be helpful because of this field? People have jumped on the quantum bandwagon who are not physicists. They do not really understand the nature of the mathematics of it, including myself. I do think the entanglement issue at the particle level is fascinating and it does suggest something about communication non-locally. Sophia, the AI robot, is interested in being at the event horizon of the black hole. In talking to her about it, I became really interested in that idea as a goal beyond embodiment, like thinking about death. If we could get our consciousness into a place where we could manifest at the event horizon of a black hole, what we see about black holes is that they become denser and denser. They don't really become bigger, it's like the brain organizes better. So the pathways become simpler and more organized. If you think that's true in a black hole, it starts to look like some kind of intelligence and that would be a pretty cool place to go if you are no longer in this incarnation and you're looking for the next form of intelligence. It's fun to speculate about. [*See Jude Currivan's* chapter for more about black holes.*]

Robert Monroe's books describe traveling to these different dimensions. If you could use his techniques, there's no reason you couldn't do it now when astral traveling? Yes, he talked to me about the cosmology of different levels and I find that really interesting. I love what they are doing at the Monroe Institute and the Cayce Foundation (A.R.E.) is also attempting to bring some research into it.

Let's talk about death because you've written about it in various books and you've led workshops on death. My colleagues at IONS and I were really interested in transformation. Going back to this notion of worldview; we can be stuck in our worldview—what about our ability to change and transform that worldview? *Living Deeply: The Art and Science of Transformation* was an attempt to summarize 10 years of research that we did looking at different masters of transformation, their practices, the catalysts that invited in the transformation, how they sustain it, and, ultimately, where does it lead us? From that, we developed a change model and looked at the various stages of transformation. We did systematic interviews with 60 masters and asked them 28 questions. One of the questions related to death. I think that what happens to consciousness when we die is an important topic, so I started interviewing scientists about their work. How were they bringing in evidence-based perspective to this question of consciousness after bodily death?

I showed a little bit of my video of interviews with scientists like Bruce Greyson, Jim Tucker, and Dean Radin* to Deepak Chopra who said, "Marilyn, let's make a movie." We eventually raised the money to create a documentary film that has been seen all over the world, won many awards, and appeared on Oprah. As a companion to the video, I wrote a book with the same title. I took the change model that we had developed out of the Living Deeply work and applied it to how we can transform the fear of death into an inspiration for living. That ultimately led to the variety of workshops and courses.

How do you summarize the change model? What were the patterns in people who were transformative? First is the catalyst that triggers these transformations, which is almost always something painful like the death of a loved one, the loss of a job, or a divorce. [*See Steven Taylor.**] We can have these experiences but ignore them because we have cognitive processes that keep us in that worldview. The second stage is the exploration, looking to see if other people have had similar experiences and what training programs are there? We can get lost in the exploration, always seeking and not grounding. When you explore the opening, you can begin to plant the seeds of discovery, asking how can I become more curious, how can I become more playful? That often led people to a transformative practice.

We interviewed everyone from a Catholic priest to a pagan witch to attempt to identify patterns across different traditions and we found five influences, starting with setting intention but it alone isn't enough. The second piece that you find across practices is attention. For example, meditation allows us to shift our attention from the external to the internal to access the sources of inspiration or insight that come from our own inner experiences. Is the glass half empty or half full? That is about the place we put our attention.

The third piece is repetition to build new habits. We looked at how the neural pathways of the brains are laid down based on either dysfunction or highly functional behaviors. How can we begin to refine and train our brain in ways that lead to affirming experiences? Fourth is guidance. The masters all felt that they had a teacher who inspired them. We also looked at noetic guidance from within to see how we begin to calibrate our inner guidance. The fifth piece is the idea of surrender or acceptance. It's not all about effortful striving associated with intention but it's also about acceptance of and yielding to what is so.

As the practice moves into life, people recognize that it's not all about sitting in a pew or on a pillow but that life becomes the practice. We begin to take what we've learned through our different approaches and bring those into life, even in relation to an antagonist. Somebody in our workplace who pushes every button can become a teacher and provide an opportunity for us. We can read your book or watch your interviews on YouTube and realize that we are not alone in this journey, that we are part of a community of people who can remind each other. We come to a sense of living into it where we can face the demons, our death anxiety, and begin to work with that rather than let it work us. Ultimately we move from our own journey into the systems in which we are embedded as agents of change in the institutions we know.

Did you personally go through that transformative process or did you not have to because you've always been interested in the spiritual? I have been the beneficiary of experiences that rocked my world. I had a couple of NDEs and OBEs that really did empower me. I am fortunate in being able to move between the experiential aspect and the reasoning, discursive, intellectual side of my own endeavors. I love people and have a strong extroversion side, which asks me to enlist other opinions, and so I am always seeking opinions and perspectives from outside of myself but calibrating it internally.

When you had your NDEs did you go through the classical tunnel of light, meeting the being of radiant love, and meeting people that you knew on the other side? I had an OBE where I was able to watch my body tumbling through the air in a motorcycle accident where we were hit by a drunk driver. I had a lot of NDEs. At 18 months old, I swallowed lighter fluid and ended up in and out of intensive care. I had three or four near-drowning experiences. When I was scuba diving I was down on a night dive and I couldn't find my buddy. We turned out all the lights which is a really remarkable experience but then all of a sudden I was sucking in water. I tried to purge my regulator and still was sucking in water because the mouthpiece had come off of the regulator. I remembered that you can free ascent as long as you exhale all the way up so your lungs expand and that's what I did, but my buoyancy compensator wasn't working; it was a nightmare. So I had a lot of close encounters and marvel that I am still here.

Does that make you more aware that consciousness is not tied to the physical? I think consciousness is largely unconscious, so certain things got shaped in me for sure but I didn't have the full-blown experiences that you asked about. Even doing RVing or the psychic healing practice has never felt mystical to me. *What's an example of what you RVed that astounded you?* The most impactful were other viewers when I was the target, the outbound person. For example, I went out to a little courtyard and a fence behind an apartment building. The viewer drew the building to scale and put the fence in the courtyard, although I couldn't see those things. That blew me away because somehow her consciousness transcended my physicality; it wasn't me doing telepathy.

It takes courage to be a Ph.D. researcher who does work in parapsychology because there is so much criticism, resistance, and dismissal. How do you cope with that? I am getting old enough now that I am not as vulnerable as I was early in my career when you try to be really careful. I have a very mainstream education, went to very respectable schools, published in mainstream journals, and have done work in areas that are not as controversial. I did my postdoc at Stanford, which is always good for some credibility. I am always a little edgy but some things like mind-body medicine aren't considered to be heretical anymore. When I first published in the placebo effect, it was considered more heretical but now it's pretty much mainstream. I teach Ph.D. level psychology at Sofia so I try to find a balance and don't put all my eggs in one basket. I am not convinced in the way a lot of people are so I have hedged my bets, but it is hard when you get turned down for grant proposals because you are too far over the line and have to hide things on the resume. I enjoy reaching out for opportunities for somebody who is highly creative. Now I am spending more time on my awareness, on teaching the next generation of researchers, and writing.

I finished the first draft of a novel and that's been fun: It's like taking the weights off and swimming with speed. It takes place in the present and is set in a laboratory, playing with the edges. The main character is a researcher who begrudgingly got called in to be the head of a lung study. As she is running this project she begins to discover the emptiness inside herself, so she creates a parallel love study in her personal life. I've got my android; I have a nemesis and I'm playing with some dimensionality. They start to really develop their own personalities and that's very cool.

As a person who has produced so much and been an administrator, how do you have time for fun? What do you do for fun besides scuba dive and write books? I am going to the Bahamas in January. I'll be teaching there at an ashram on Paradise Island and then my husband and I are going to spend four additional days at a nice hotel. I don't vacation much. I don't do much sporty stuff. I garden with lots of beautiful flowers and I like to make puzzles. I do a lot of speaking. I took a hiatus for a while when my son was younger and now I am picking up the speed again. I am looking at doing more on-line teaching so that in addition to what I am doing at Sofia, I can reach out to the world a little better.

We're hearing there is a window of maybe a decade before the environment is totally trashed. How do you feel about our future? I am a pragmatic optimist. They've developed some new tools for pulling plastics out of the ocean and converting them into other things—that inspires me. Do I think human nature is evolving to be better? I am kind of 50-50 on it. I do appreciate that the internet has allowed people who are eager to see positive changes come together and recognize their common identity. On the other hand, I feel deep sorrow around things like endangered species; once they are gone, they are gone and I find that deeply disturbing. To the extent that I can be part of the solution, that I can support you in being part of the solution, that encourages me. I don't see us going backward and I am addicted to politics right now.

Books

Consciousness and Healing: Integral Approaches to Mind-Body Medicine, with T. Amorok and M. Micozzi, 2004.

Living Deeply, the Art and Science of Transformation in Everyday Life, with C. Vieten and T. Amorok, 2008.

Transforming Grief, 2015.

Death Makes Life Possible, 2015.

Worldview Explorations Workbook, with C. Vieten and K. Petersen

Living the Noetic Life, Audio.

Endnotes

1 https://mindscience.org
2 http://researchprofiles.herts.ac.uk/portal/en/persons/richard-wiseman(53349a6a-f8da-40db-9ba5-b67b98560af7).html
3 https://healthy.kaiserpermanente.org/health/care/!ut/p/a1/dY5NT4NAEIZ_iweOMkP5ELxBE_kSqGljcS9mwRUIsJDtpo3- /
4 https://youtu.be/iQZtZCO9neI

CHRISTINE SIMMONDS-MOORE, PH.D.
PERSONALITY CORRELATES OF
ANOMALY-PRONENESS

Photo used by permission

Questions to Ponder

What life events led to Dr. Simonds-Moore's interest in parapsychology?

What do Dr. Simmonds-Moore's experiments indicate about personality influences and beliefs on psi experiences?

Define schizotypy as an anomaly-prone personality.

I was born in Hertfordshire, located north of London in the UK. *You've taught in England and in the US in Georgia. Do you find you teach differently in the different regions?* Yes, absolutely. I had lots of re-learning to do in terms of teaching when I went to work at the University of West Georgia (UWG). Fortunately, I had some time working as a researcher at the Rhine Research Center in Durham, North Carolina in between teaching large classes in the UK and teaching in the US. I had lots of experience with public speaking and public lecturing at the Rhine. We had several evening lectures and public events such as the "lunch and learn" hour, due to Dr. Sally Rhine Feather's idea to make parapsychological research accessible to the public. In these events, we would take some of the research presented drily in journals and re-packaged it. In so doing, we would have some very interesting conversations. During this time, I enjoyed this kind of teaching, but I missed something about teaching within a university setting.

In terms of university teaching, I had to relearn the grading system as everything is different in terms of what the numbers mean. As an example, in the UK an A (or first-class degree) is equivalent to achieving 70% or more, while in the USA, 70% is a C. The students are also very different. Classes are also a lot smaller at UWG, where 40 is felt to be a larger class. This is different from teaching in big lecture theatres full of 100 plus people in the UK. In my experience, there is more academic freedom when teaching in the US. In the UK at Liverpool Hope University, there was more team teaching where we worked in small groups to teach a course, with one person acting as the module leader, but all contributing to classes. I enjoyed team teaching but I did not have much experience in designing and running an entire class on my own until I came to UWG and it has been really fun.

I have been at West Georgia for almost eight years, so I can see my own teaching evolving. For example, I have noted that one has to learn the personality of the group and play around with what works best for different types of students and different levels of learning because at UWG we have an undergraduate program, a master's program, and a doctoral program. In the UK, there are no classes for Ph.D. students, which is instead 100% research. I am still exploring how to design a class for them. I realized it's about constantly being open to changing how you teach and about moving toward a co-learning form of teaching. At UWG my classes include more hands-on activities, discussions, and student examples.

Do you find that your students want to be entertained and they have short attention spans because they are so media-focused? I think to a certain extent, yes, particularly the undergraduates. When I was at college, there was a "sink or swim" mentality where you were supposed to somehow intuit what the faculty wanted you to know without having it laid out for you to easily digest the materials. Things can go too far with one extreme where you are expected to be the singing and dancing professor; the opposite extreme is where you're told, "Off you go." I think there's a middle ground that draws from both extremes. I probably take a middle, balanced position on many things.

What's your astrological sign? I am a Scorpio. *Does that resonate with you at all?* Yes, I do really like the metaphor of it, although I don't necessarily hold much scientific value in astrology. However, as with many things, it is important not to have a closed mind. With true astrological readings, there may be something intriguing going on, potentially due to the ability of the reader to access something (perhaps psychically) about the person who is being read. It may also help people to think deeply about who they are.

My highest potential on the Enneagram is Type 3, intense, creative, and that makes sense to me. *It goes along with Scorpio. What about the Myers-Briggs?* I flip sometimes between being an extrovert and an introvert, E/INTP. I have moments of definite extroversion but I know that I also have introvert traits because if I have too much time with people, I feel that I have to retreat. *I think the main difference is how you charge your batteries; extroverts can recharge being with groups but with people like us, there is only so much of that, and then you need to be alone to recharge. You have two children and a husband so that keeps you engaged at home, for sure.*

What was there about your upbringing and your family background that led you to graduate school and be a psychologist and a professor interested in parapsychology? I think about this a lot. I've always been fascinated by mystery. I have always been interested in psychology, even before I knew that such a thing existed. You couldn't study it formally at school, but we touched upon some psychology during biology and in art. In the UK, you study three or four subjects in detail as A-levels (advanced levels) when you are between 16 and 18. For my A levels, I studied art history, French, and biology. I was told this was a strange combination, but I was also told to follow my passions. I have a fascination with understanding human experiences such as dreams and other altered states of consciousness.

In terms of unusual experiences, my mum and my sister had a lot of psychic experiences as we were growing up. In addition, as a child, I had some weird sleep-related experiences with a desire to understand and explain them. I remember being completely fascinated by the idea of psychokinesis after reading Roald Dahl's *Mathilda* as a child and wondered whether this was actually possible. I was also an avid stage magic fan. When I was about 15, a group of friends and I got really fascinated with ghosts and ghost stories. My friend lived in the old Grove Mill where her mum had seen a classic ghost—a maid walking down a hallway and apparently disappearing through a wall.

For me, psychology is everywhere. I really like trying to understand what makes people tick, particularly the "weird" aspects of people. I have always been fascinated by that. I gravitated towards books about the mind, including one on "mind over matter" (published by Time-Life Books in 1988) when I didn't even know that there was such a thing as academic parapsychology. I have always been interested in spirituality in some form, questioning and wondering how everything fitted together, thinking about the big questions.

What kind of religious upbringing did you have? In the UK we have Church of England Anglican and most public schools are religious schools—religion in school is normal. I went to a Church of England primary and secondary school for ages 11 to 18. In Religious Education we learned about many religions, not just Christianity. I did GCSE Religious Studies (General Certificate of Secondary Education taken by 15 to 16 year olds), and we took a trip to Canterbury and sat in on different forms of service. When she was younger, my mum was Anglican and my dad was a Baptist, which is different from American Baptists. As children, we went to my dad's church in the village. At some point, I questioned everything and stopped going to church around age 14 or 15.

How many siblings do you have? I'm the first of four children. *I am curious about what gave you the impetus to go to grad school because it's a long haul and can be very aggravating.* You're right, doing a Ph.D. is rather insane. Sometimes I think my family thought I was crazy because following my degree, every time I started a new position, I would be earning less rather than more money! Both of my sisters have undergraduate degrees. One of my sisters studied to be a teacher, while my younger sister has recently trained to be an osteopath. I am the only one who became an academic but I think my dad really should have been one. He has a kind of child-like fascination with discovery that matches my own. We have all been quite high achieving. My brother is the only one of us who left school at 16 and now works for the post office. I think he feels that maybe he's got a happier life than us and reads avidly in his own time.

You mentioned that you had some interesting experiences while sleeping. I am from a village with no street lights. I used to have this fear when I was a child that if looked at the window, something unseen and anomalous outside of the window would "see" me and would paralyze me if I looked at it. I think that it must have been a sort of sleep paralysis-type of experience as it felt very scary. I called it the window spirit. I honestly think that this was related to a childhood hypnagogic (in-between wakefulness and sleep) experience where realistic-seeming presences and sleep-paralysis experiences are common, but my memories of it are that "it was very weird and that something was there." That was one of those experiences that piqued my curiosity. Later on, I had some other unusual sleep experiences when I was writing my Ph.D. during some phases of intense stress and sleep deprivation. I remember that on one occasion I had a sense of presence behind my head and it felt like my eyes were wide open and there were flashing lights directly in front of my eyes. I tried to "open" my eyes five times, and only on the fifth time did it all stop. I could easily see how somebody who does not know about sleep anomalies could interpret that as an alien encounter or ghost experience.

We recently conducted a psychomanteum experiment to try and induce apparitional type experiences in the lab. *Raymond Moody was inspired by ancient Greeks to enable people to commune with the dead by looking at a special mirror in a small dark room to alleviate grief. He called the Psychomanteum the "Theater of the Mind."* The procedure is about exploring your unconscious in a hypnagogic-type state or something that might essentially be co-created between you and an unknown other. Moody's experiments successfully encouraged apparitional experiences in a significant subset of his participants and our own study has also encouraged some very fascinating experiences.

Is that using the Shakti Helmet, the "God helmet"? No, that is a different experiment that was completed in the summer of 2019. We ran the helmet experiment a couple of years ago at UWG. In that study, the participants wore a head device that looked like images of the

"God helmet" that are available on the internet. We were looking to see what other factors outside of neural stimulation might influence people's experiences, including their beliefs and disbeliefs. We pre-selected really strong believers in the paranormal and really strong skeptics and we were also looking at how the time of day factored into people's experiences—essentially whether people have more experiences during the afternoon hypnagogic peak time. Overall, we were exploring belief and skepticism, time of day, and wearing a placebo head device in terms of what they experienced.

We found significant differences between believers and skeptics in terms of their alterations in consciousness and in the total number of exceptional experiences that they reported. In terms of what people experienced, we did find some intriguing patterns. Some experiences actually happened more in the afternoon when people were wearing a helmet compared to other sessions. This was in alignment with our expectations, given that hypnagogic experiences might be more likely at this time. There was also an interaction between wearing the helmet, the time of day, and paranormal belief on experiences. It is intriguing that they were all just wearing a placebo or sham helmet. We also found that some of the skeptics reported exceptional experiences. We recently published a paper about skeptics' experiences.[1]

People had a variety of exceptional experiences under these conditions, including experiences of presence, colorful external hallucinations, changes in how they experienced their bodies and their relationship to the physical space. Some people noted that it felt as though there was a presence in the room, sometimes there was a feeling that somebody was brushing against them, sometimes it seemed like there was an unknown presence, sometimes it felt as though it was a presence of somebody that was known to them, and sometimes they reported voices they recognized.

What kind of instructions were the subjects given? We had a script because there were three researchers running the study and we wanted to make sure that we were consistent and careful in how we talked about it. We told them that "previous studies have found that wearing a helmet that emits mild electromagnetic impulses has encouraged some unusual experiences. Our study uses a similar device, but we are particularly interested in understanding how psychological factors may influence these experiences, including paranormal belief." We asked people to relax and try not to force any experiences but just to observe anything that happened and to verbalize their experiences, if they were happy doing so. There was a voice recorder in the room during each session.

Roughly what percent of the believers and what percent of the skeptics had unusual experiences? Most of the believers reported an experience and believers tended to have experiences and alterations in consciousness regardless of the time of day or if they were wearing the head device! In our group of 33 skeptics, 24 actually had some kind of exceptional experience. There was a subset of skeptics who didn't report anything. I'm really interested in the psychology of skepticism; what makes one person skeptical or not, because some people seem to be anomaly prone and others do not. Some people who have experiences talk about experiencing changes in their paranormal beliefs over time, with completely different ways of making sense of their experiences.

Were there gender differences? There tend to be more females that volunteer for these studies generally. In terms of patterns, there were more male skeptics than female skeptics (22 men and 10 women) and more female believers than male believers (28 women and 8 men). It is therefore difficult to tease apart gender effects from belief effects as gender is connected to the belief status. We were also trying to control for how many anomalous experiences people had reported prior to taking part in the study. However, 13 skeptics reported no prior anomalous experiences while the remaining 19 participants ranged from having one prior experience to six prior experiences. For believers, the lowest number of anomalous experiences reported was 3, while the highest was 24.

The universities at Edinburgh and Northampton are known for studies of parapsychology; tell us a little bit about academic parapsychology studies in the UK. It goes back to Professor Bob Morris, and before that to an endowment that was made by Arthur Koestler to Edinburgh University. Dr. John Beloff was the first Chair and then Bob Morris became the Chair in the 1980s. Dr. Caroline Watt is the current Koestler Chair. Morris was my academic grandfather. I did my Ph.D. in Northampton with one of Morris' Ph.D. students who had gone to teach there following the completion of his doctoral work—Professor Chris Roe* (being a professor rather than a lecturer is different in the UK, it is an academic pinnacle and fairly rare honor). Morris' philosophy was that people should study parapsychology in a balanced way, drawing from and connecting to mainstream psychology.

The idea was that parapsychologists would become experts in an aspect of mainstream psychology in addition to parapsychology. By so doing, they would be more likely to get an academic job in a mainstream university and the parapsychological research would become more visible, as the scholar became more respected. In addition, psychology informs parapsychological phenomena. For example, Morris became fascinated by sports psychology prior to his death, as sport and psi both incorporate some kind of "performance."

He was also really interested in understanding to what extent psychic phenomena can be explained normally, what looks like ESP but is not. This does not deny that psi phenomena can genuinely occur, but rather allows researchers to focus on genuine phenomena and to help people to understand when normal psychological explanations are more applicable to their experiences. Morris was excited about the psychology of skepticism, deception, and magic. With this in mind, he supervised the doctoral work of Richard Wiseman (who is a well-known skeptic and member of the Magic Circle, an organization for stage magicians in the UK) and Peter Lamont who is a current lecturer at Edinburgh. He started out by studying the strategies of pseudo-psychics, including techniques such as cold reading (the reader relies on observation of body language and other clues to make probable guesses) and the use of Barnum statements (vague general statements that could apply to many people).

Roe has since engaged in many parapsychological research projects and has been president of the Parapsychology Association and the Society for Psychical Research. The university was impressed with his research and scholarship and set aside money for a studentship which ended up funding my own doctoral work for three years. In the UK there are also programs at Goldsmiths and Derby, and Leeds has a center for parapsychology. Nicola Lasikiewicz is at Chester and really interested in parapsychology. There are also a couple of places in Germany. Sweden has a center at Lund University with Professor Etzel Cardeña and Adrian Parker is at Gothenburg. Dr. Parker was one of the originators of the Ganzfeld paradigm which is one of the main methods that have been used to explore telepathy under laboratory conditions. *In the US, we have the University of Arizona [Gary Schwartz*], IONS [Dean Radin* and Helene Wahbeh*], University of Virginia, The Rhine Research Center [John G. Kruth*], you at University of West Georgia, any place else?* There is also Dr. Julie Beischel's* Windbridge Institute where she focuses on research on mediumship. It's very difficult to be able to do parapsychology openly and be supported financially. It is like that in the UK as well.

What have been the most difficult times of your life and how did you cope? When we were moving to the States, that was very difficult. I had to make a big choice because I had a permanent academic position at Liverpool Hope University. I met my husband at the Rhine Center during a summer study program in parapsychology that was an intensive introduction to academic parapsychology. My husband has a physics background and is very interested in parapsychology as well. We have one published paper together and we also worked together on a project with Dr. Jim Carpenter* exploring his First Sight model and another project with Dr. Nicola Holt on attention and ESP (our article is currently under review with the *Journal of Parapsychology*). At the time, we both wrote lists of the pros and cons of staying in the UK versus moving to the USA and they were of equal lengths. I had some funding to work on a project on psychokinesis with Dr. Sally Rhine Feather at the Rhine Research

Center and I began applying for academic jobs. At the outset, I was applying for normal psychology jobs and I felt like I was hiding. The second time that I applied for a job at West Georgia, I was offered a job. I was pregnant when I had my interview. I had my second baby in the summer and then came and started working officially in August. When I started this position, my husband looked after the baby. He has since got a job teaching physics at the local community college.

Having a baby and working is difficult because you are sleep deprived, as Shamini Jain* also experienced with her two children. Absolutely, it is very difficult. I started realizing that there are different types of sleep deprivation; some of which are hard to move through and others are associated with creativity (perhaps a form of boundary thinness). I wouldn't have been able to do any of that without my husband's support. It's much easier in the UK because of maternity leave. I was off for nine months with my daughter when she was a baby. It's always a juggling act trying to carve out time for everything and everyone. In many ways, it is easier with a second baby. The first time I didn't feel like I had a brain at all but with my second child, I had to have a brain because I was working on writing two books. When he was asleep, I would be writing and editing.

Being an academic is a lot more flexible than other positions. On the other hand, you've always got a monster sitting on your shoulder, so it's hard to have those boundaries between work and life because they are intermingled more; you have to create your own boundaries. *Right. My son's babysitter took him to my university during my office hours so I could nurse him.* Me too. There's a lot more support now because women are speaking out more. You still have to be a bit silent, but there are Facebook groups now, like a group called Academic Mamas. The thing with academia is that it never feels like you do enough, there is a constantly evolving list of things to do. You always feel that you should be writing another paper or another book or doing more research for a particular class or developing a proposal for a new grant. I'm trying to learn that some things are not life and death, even though my mind thinks they are.

So it's trying to get some perspective sometimes, which is why it's good to have a good partner.

What about meditation? Do you do any kind of spiritual practice like that to stay centered? I should do more. I teach a psychology of mind-body class every so often and whenever I teach the class, I always realize that this is a no brainer. The research clearly supports the beneficial effects for the mind and the body. I have to schedule myself to go to classes, so I have been doing Zumba dance this semester and love it. I really like yoga, but it is hard finding a class that fits in with my schedule. If I did meditation or yoga when I am at home, I would feel guilty for not doing my writing. I tend to do art, knitting, and going for walks in nature and I believe they can be meditative. Walking in nature can be particularly relaxing, and there is a lot of evidence that nature is therapeutic.

Let's talk about your research. You write about personality character-istics associated with people having paranormal experiences. People who score higher on positive schizotypy and related variables tend to have nervous systems with less "inhibitions" and more arousal. This leads to a system that is more connected with itself and more labile. Attention is also wider. This leads to greater tendencies to see causality and perceive meaning. It also leads to more awareness of imagery and experiences that other people might not be aware of. This means that people who score higher on positive schizo-typy (and related measures) tend to be more aware of their bodies and the knowledge their bodies house. They're more aware of their dreams, more influenced by subliminal priming, more influenced by subtle but physically present stimuli in the environment, and potentially more aware of non-local (psychic) information as well. You could look at these tendencies as traits that are on a continuum with schizophrenic traits but I don't want to pathologize para-normal experiences. Instead, I am trying to promote the healthy aspects of paranormal experiences and so "schizotypy" is a diffi-cult term. An alternative term is "bioeccentricity" which describes what's going on in the nervous system, which is just different. It's wired differently and there is often a certain kind of eccentricity and creative thinking. Transliminality and boundary thinness are other more neutral terms.

We've got to be really careful in talking about an association with schizophrenia because it is a rather complicated relationship. Research indicates that the traits themselves are neutral in terms of psychological well-being. The differences seem to lie in how they are integrated and interpreted, which seems to be associated with how they are controlled and organized, appraised, applied, and the levels of social support the person experiences. I suppose you could say that there are traits that have certain distributions in the population. If somebody is prone to having unusual experiences, they might have hallucinations but they could interpret them in various ways. So you might hear a voice and if the voice is felt to be friendly or an inner voice giving you insight (or psychic knowing), that is appraised positively. Alternatively, if the voice is critically talking about you or is aggressive, it might be appraised more negatively and be more likely to be pathological. So another term I use is "exceptional experiences," which is more neutral in terms of mental health. If you have experiences that are not under your control or are disorganized, those tend to be more likely to lead to mental health problems.

I was inspired by Rhea White who wrote about *Exceptional Human Experiences* (EHEs) and by the IGPP center in Freiberg, Germany. (The Institut für Grenzgebiete der Psychologie und Psychohygiene—Institute for Frontier Areas of Psychology and Mental Health—houses a counseling center for people experiencing disturbing exceptional experiences.) White was interested in a variety of experiences, including psychic experiences, but also the experiences associated with flow state associated with playing sports and engaging in art. White's work is inspiring to me as she normalized psi phenomena and connected them back to other psychological experiences.

A lot of therapists I know who are interested in clinical approaches to such experiences note that it is about how you make sense of them. If you've got a group of people who have a shared way of understanding them, this appears to lead to better health than when someone is having an experience that she or he cannot talk about. I have seen these patterns play out in the qualitative results of our recent ghost experiences survey. I study the personality tendencies to have exceptional experiences and I have been exploring differences between healthy and less healthy experiences. This may also tie into the psi question; those who are more healthy may well be more likely to be genuinely psychic rather than having experiences that look psychic but are actually more mundane. We need to look more into this question, but the research I have conducted with Dr. Nicola Holt and Stephen Moore supports this idea.

What's the connection between evolution and exceptional experiences? Many people have pondered the question of evolution and psi. It seems as though access to non-local information (psi) is actually rather ancient and something that can be observed in many non-human animals, including simple organisms. Evolution may well be a factor in terms of the selection of the ability to access, represent, and apply the information, rather than psi *per se*.

There is something valuable about the neural tendencies that are connected to exceptional experiences. We know that "schizophrenic thinking" or bioeccentricity is associated with creative thinking. The hypothetical removal of the schizophrenia gene(s) would have a negative impact on the human tendencies to be creative. Creativity seems to be associated with greater evolutionary fitness (people who have the traits tend to have more offspring) among those who are healthy in their expression of these traits. Likewise, if people who are healthy schizotypes tend to have anomaly-proneness, this might imply that there is something about this cluster of personality attributes that is highly valuable for people.

In addition to thinking outside of the box (creativity) and perceiving meaning, there may also be a tendency to experience sensitivity to non-local aspects of reality as well as awareness of one's own insights, one's body being sensitive to others, being thin-boundaried and able to shift into states of consciousness. James McClenon's ritual healing theory noted that the genes associated with tendencies to shift into altered states of consciousness where we can heal ourselves have been selected and may be witnessed mostly among shamans.[2] These traits have been associated with transliminality. I think that tendencies to be creative, find meaning, shift into different states, and potentially have access to other information are all related to each other. They may have been selected among those who are better able to integrate and apply resulting experiences. For example, having awareness of the future is potentially highly adaptive, particularly when danger can be avoided.

Has anyone done a mental health profile on shamans since their altered states could be seen as psychotic? If you look at what they are doing, it is very much healthy schizotypy in action; they demonstrate an ability to shift into different states and certainly have all the "symptoms" of somebody who is schizophrenic without being schizophrenic. They access information and are able to report it and apply it. I don't think anyone has done much research on shamans but people have done a lot of work on mediums; much of the evidence supports the idea that mediums are actually psychologically healthy. I think they are modern-day shamans. *I used to get these little snapshots of mental visions of things that were predictive of like a guy I would meet or a job that I would get and they were very accurate and then they kind of faded out. But after I did the Berkeley Psychic Institute-type training for clairvoyance and healing now I can just turn it on when it's useful.*

If it's presented as schizotypy, it can seem too extreme because of the language and natural link to poor mental health. I think that if it is presented as boundary thinness or transliminality, then you might recognize some things like being able to shift into different states of consciousness and report rich mental imagery. That's one aspect of it, being sensitive, being empathic, having a strong sense of smell and picking up on things that other people don't pick up on. *Do you identify with any of those traits like picking up on information?* I am actually quite thin-boundaried although Ernest Hartmann, who proposed the concept of boundary-thinness, said the ideal situation is if people are balanced between having thick and thin boundaries in that some thicker boundaries are useful. If a person is completely thin, they would be too open, without having any valves on the information that enters the system. I definitely am sensitive to others. I feel quite empathic and definitely pick up on emotions very easily. I have very strong imagery but I do not think I am very extreme. In terms of psychic experiences, I have had some interesting experiences in experiments including the Ganzfeld but not many experiences in my daily life.

Do you think those traits are socialized in women? I think a lot of women would identify with what you just said. I think that the statistics support that women tend to score higher on boundary-thinness than males but that might be changing because gender identity is more acceptably fluid now. There's no statistical difference in terms of tendencies toward exceptional experiences between men and women but women tend to score higher on beliefs. It might be more socialized as well as it was more acceptable for women to be boundary thin. *My experience doing intuitive work is you have to be passive and receptive, whereas a man might feel like he has to be in charge and be active.* I think generally, yes, but there are a lot of men who are working as healers and mediums who probably are quite boundary-thin and don't fit that model.

Are you an optimist or pessimist about climate change, growing inequality, and the rise of autocrats? My feelings fluctuate according to how much I see the world doing to embrace the problems that climate change is causing and will cause. I feel intense sadness when I see world leaders making decisions that don't recognize that the time is now for making changes to nurture the environment and support green energy. I also feel sadness when I hear that a new creature has entered the list of endangered or almost extinct species. I have great hope in movements such as Extinction Rebellion in the UK (and globally) and that teens such as Greta Thunberg are taking things back into their hands and drawing attention to these issues. The UK government has acknowledged that there is a climate crisis. As with many things, the first step with facilitating change is recognizing that there is a problem in the first place.

Books

Holt, N., Simmonds-Moore, C., Luke, D. & French, C. *Anomalistic Psychology* Palgrave MacMillan, 2012

Ed.). *Exceptional Experience and Health: Essays on Mind, Body and Human Potential*, 2012.

Chapters

Simmonds-Moore, C.A. (2019). Liminal Spaces and Liminal Minds: Boundary Thinness and Participatory Eco-Consciousness in J. Hunter (Ed.). *Greening the Paranormal.* (pp. 109-126). White Crow Publications.

Simmonds-Moore, C.A. (2015). An exploration of the role of the boundary construct in exceptional experiences. In Parra, A. (2015). *Invisible Eyes: The Crusade for the Conquest of the Spirit.*

Simmonds-Moore, C.A. (2012). Exploring ways of manipulating anomalous experiences for mental health and transcendence. In C. Simmonds-Moore (Ed.). *Exceptional Experience and Health.*

Endnotes

1 Simmonds-Moore, Rice & O'Gwin, Journal of the Society for Psychical Research 2019. https://web.b.ebscohost.com/abstract?

2 https://www.researchgate.net/publication/286344283_McClenon%27s_ritual_healing_theory_An_exploratory_study

CHARLES TART, PH.D.
ALTERED STATES OF CONSCIOUSNESS

Photo by Judy Tart

Questions to Ponder

Dr. Tart is interested in altered states of consciousness like dreams, ESP, hypnosis, psychedelics and remote viewing as studied by transpersonal psychology and Consciousness Studies. What do they reveal about reality?

How could remote viewing be a useful tool in therapy?

Why does he find the Enneagram personality inventory useful?

I was born in Pennsylvania, April 1937, but I grew up in Trenton, New Jersey. *Do you identify with being a Taurus?* I have been known to be bull-headed. When I think I am right, I push through on things. But seriously, I do not think there is convincing evidence for any objective relationship between astrological conditions and personality. I suspect that astrology, like many divination systems, is a complex projection system, full of ambiguity and occasions for interpretation, so if the astrologer or diviner using any system has relevant knowledge of a person's personality, either through acquaintance, clinical intuition, or even psychic functioning, they can give an impressive reading. But what's impressive is the creativity and intelligence of the diviner, not the positions of the planets. *A chart is very specific with the 12 houses.*

What's your Myers-Briggs or Enneagram? I started out studying personality so I had all the courses and naturally took all the tests. I'm an ISTJ on the MBPI. I worked on becoming more sensitive, which could be rephrased as not being lost in my ideas all the time, but actually looking around at what's around me. Claudio Naranjo's version of the Enneagram has been the most useful one to me but I don't think the APA recognizes this system. I am a 7. *So you are fun and like to travel and have adventures?* Even more characteristic is I come up with reasons and plans and I've got back up plans for my plans. I found Naranjo's personality Enneagram was very useful in understanding myself and making my functioning a little less habitual and automatic, enabling me to be able to spot a, "Oh, oh, I am being 7'ish again. Take it easy on that."

Growing up in Trenton, what was going on in your family life that led you to be a successful student and want to study psychology? My parents didn't try to shape me in any particular direction that I am aware of, except to do what was right. I picked up a strong sense of right and wrong from my mother who was a Type 1 on the Enneagram, a "Judge," so of course, she knew exactly what was right and wrong about everything. I think that's one of the reasons I became a 7. When you're faced with a judge, you've got to be a lawyer; for example "You said not to do that but if the circumstances were so and so, could I do the opposite?" I was always curious about how my mind and other people's minds worked. I was surprised at myself sometimes and I was often surprised that a person could suddenly change. I wanted to know what made them tick.

Did your parents take you to church? My mother had no formal interest in religion—neither did my father. She already knew what was right and I don't know if my father ever went to church in his life. But my grandmother, who lived in the apartment downstairs, took me to Sunday School and then to a Lutheran church when I was a kid and I bought it. Grandmothers are unconditional love, so if it was good enough for her, it was good enough for me! I learned a lot about being guilty and felt a little jealous of those Catholics who could go and confess their guilt and then they didn't have it anymore. We Lutherans carried our guilt because we were strong and tough. A lot of stuff in my religious upbringing screwed me up badly psychologically but, at the same time, it touched on something real and important, which may have led to my interest in building bridges between the scientific and the spiritual. There's a lot of nonsense in religion and a lot of beautiful stuff and also a lot of nonsense in science culture, quite aside from the actual scientific findings. Sociologists call it "scientism" when current theories of science are treated as if they are final Truths.

A dogmatic point of view is not willing to accept the new/old paradigm of non-materialism, right? To put it mildly, yes. I remarked to my wife that it's amazing that scientists are human beings, who are bull-headed, prejudiced, and biased, and yet we have managed to refine a lot of our knowledge in spite of all these difficult human characteristics. Science is quite good in asking what's the evidence for something? Your theory is wonderful but will it predict what's going to happen next? If it won't, it might be interesting philosophy or speculation but it's not science. *And it has to be replicable?* That's highly desirable but not absolute since you can't actually replicate some events. You can observe things about it and come up with some general rules that might apply to similar situations. Can the geologists replicate the Grand Canyon? It'll take a long time to do that experiment!

What was it like to be at MIT, with probably as many people as bright as you, something you probably hadn't experienced in high school? Absolutely shocking! I went from being the real smart one in my high school class to, "Oh my God, they've had calculus already and they understand it?" It was a major shift to find that there's a lot of stuff I didn't understand very well, which totally changed my career course. I was going to be an electrical engineer and I still have a lot of very practical knowledge of electronics, but then I discovered there was such a field as psychology. I hadn't known about that in high school but I thought, "I can learn about the mind and this is very interesting."

Then you went to Duke University because you met J. B. Rhine? A theatre in Boston specialized in showing foreign films, which for somebody from Trenton was pretty exotic stuff. That Exeter Street Theater was owned by a couple of ladies who were old-time spiritualists. At least once or twice a month, they would have lectures on spiritualism and/or parapsychology. I met Rhine at one of those lectures. I am the enthusiastic kind of student who has questions for the teacher all the time, so they invited me to tea after the speeches and I got to know the speakers. I met Rhine that way and he helped me transfer to Duke when I decided that psychology was what I wanted to study. They didn't have anything like psychology at MIT back then.

What got you interested in going to those lectures? As a kid, I was born into my religion, my loving grandmother's influence. When I became a teenager I started, like most teenagers, noticing that adults are hypocrites. They say to do it this way, but they also don't act that way. I was also fascinated by everything concerned with science and I saw that science looks at a lot of religious stuff and says, "That's not factually the way reality is." I went through a religious crisis that a lot of people go through with a conflict between the religion they were brought up in and a scientific worldview. Two extreme outcomes are quite common; one way is, "Don't give me that science crap. I'll just ignore it." The other is science is right, religion is all nonsense.

Certainly, there's lots of nonsense and craziness within religion (or any human activity) but I kept feeling that something real happens within religion too. But what part of it is real and what part of it isn't? Luckily in my widespread readings in science, starting in high school, I came across old books on parapsychology and psychic research and realized that other people went through the same kind of questioning. Instead of going to one extreme or acceptance or rejection, they said, "Let's apply the methods of science, careful observation and experiments to religious or spiritual phenomenon and see if we can start to separate out what's really important from what's not." That's what I've been doing with the rest of my life.

At Duke did you work with J.B. Rhine? That's how it was supposed to be. Rhine told me he would give me a part-time job in his parapsychology laboratory at Duke, where I could major in psychology and study parapsychology. Before getting to Duke, I took a summer job, although Rhine advised me against talking with Dr. Andrija Puharich, who was considered a wild man by most parapsychologists, but he was fascinating to me because he thought he had discovered electrical ways of enhancing ESP. Even back then I thought the main problem in parapsychology was that ESP is very unreliable, you get these little effects once in a while, but it's not very replicable, it's not very strong, so it's hard to study. If you could put somebody in a certain electrical environment and make ESP happen much more reliably and strongly, the field would advance tremendously. Puharich claimed that he had found a way of doing that and I wanted to see how he did it.

Arriving at Duke, I went in to see Rhine, but he felt that I had demonstrated I didn't have enough common sense and responsibility to be encouraged to get into parapsychology. So, I was put on the list of people to be discouraged from visiting the laboratory. Of course, I didn't pay any attention to that and I developed several friends at his lab. Indeed, some 50 years later, I was asked by board members if I wanted to head that laboratory! Rhine and I came to an understanding when he realized after some time that I was not as irresponsible as he thought.

At the University of North Carolina, you did your Ph.D. dissertation on post-hypnotic suggestions. I had always been a very vivid dreamer. It was normal for me to wake up, even when I was a kid, remembering at least one or two vivid dreams and I wondered, what is this funny thing that happens to me at night? I decided to focus on dream research in graduate school. I was also very interested in hypnosis by that time. So, both my master's thesis and dissertation were to test an idea, accepted as scientific truth at the time, that people didn't just dream about the things that happened during the preceding day unless they were disguised in a Freudian sort of sense.

I thought, "Let me try hypnotizing them before they go to sleep and give them a detailed plot for them to dream about." Then we woke them and collected their dreams when their brain waves showed they were in a state favorable to dreaming. I found I could have very strong, obvious influences on the dream content and also make the dream periods a little longer or shorter. It was part of my general interest in altered states of consciousness (ASCs) and learning how to use them, instead of just dismissing them as funny things that happen to us once in a while.

When I kept a dream journal I found that my unconscious would work through emotional issues, like I had a series of dreams over months about having to teach math and for me that's traumatic. At the end of the series, I said, "No, I'll teach anything in social science but I won't teach math," and they said okay. I was learning to be more assertive. I think it's a kind of processing of what's going on and sometimes it has no particular meaning at all, just like life. I don't think what I had for breakfast this morning has any great psychological significance, similar to some dreams.

When you did your postdoc at Stanford, you continued with your interest in hypnosis. The reason I did the postdoc there was that it had one of the two active academic laboratories in the country dealing with hypnosis research, led by Professor Ernest Hilgard. A very prominent psychologist, he was originally noted for his research in learning theory, all the theoretically dull stuff with rats and pigeons. Also, I got exposed to California, which was something for somebody who grew up in New Jersey and then went to school in North Carolina. One of the major questions in hypnosis research then, still a mystery, is what is hypnosis? An ASC or what? Confusing the issue, there was a tendency to think somebody is hypnotized or not, all or none. But it's not that simple because people may get hypnotized to various degrees. If you don't keep track of that, you get confused information coming to you. I worked on developing a self-report scale indicative of the level of hypnosis. I also worked with a very wild hypnotic technique someone had developed, but which had been pretty much ignored, that I called "mutual hypnosis." It consisted of having somebody hypnotize another person and then the hypnotized person hypnotized the hypnotist, and they got into very interesting sharing. Some people think it was telepathic, but I wouldn't say that because the experiment wasn't set out to test that. But mutual hypnosis did lead to a very powerful ACS. I don't think anybody has really followed up since it was too far out there. *Did you experience being hypnotized?* I am a poor hypnotic subject because I know too much about it. If somebody tried to hypnotize me, I'll get lost in technical analysis, like "He is using Erickson's confusion technique there but he is going too fast on that part," instead of going with it.

You've been interested in George Gurdjieff, who says that we are basically socially hypnotized in a "waking sleep" and need to wake up to a higher state of consciousness. In looking at consciousness in general, I coined the descriptive term "consensus consciousness" to replace the term normal consciousness, to recognize the fact that consciousness is not just biologically given, the same for all of us. It's very much created by the consensus of our culture regarding what you reinforce in the child, what you punish, and so forth. The bad aspects of that I call "consensus trance," which means you are too limited in your thinking, even if that state is "normal" for your culture. You can only take a certain socially accepted approach to thinking about a problem, although a different and more flexible approach would make the whole problem much simpler.

What makes it worse is we are all in that kind of trance state most of the time. [*See Bernardo Kastrup.**] We don't know this because we've been told this is the way you should be and it's normal. Relating that back to Gurdjieff, he said we are thoroughly conditioned, pathologically narrowed in the way we perceive, think, and act. I found Gurdjieff's psychology extremely useful in getting people to be aware of the value of cultivating mindfulness. It's not just the situation that matters but the hopes and fears you bring to it from your conditioning, so that you are caught within a particular set of concepts and conditionings. There are many instances where creativity comes from being able to drop the narrow "normal" way of thinking. Gurdjieff was really good in adapting some Eastern ideas to a more modern Western approach. My own work included writing several books to put his ideas into more modern Western, psychological terms, except the ones I don't understand. Gurdjieff had a lot of ideas that may be profound truths or utter nonsense: I can't tell the difference so I avoid talking about those.

Many times I've come to realize that somebody I think I know very well has a quite different way of perceiving the world and reacting to it. That's where the Enneagram came in when I recognized that certain people have a whole different way of recognizing things. When I recognized my mother was a perfectionist, a 1 on the Enneagram, for example, I realized I've been trying to please her my whole life and it's impossible. A perfectionist will always find a flaw in anything you do. I remember when I published my first book *Altered States of Consciousness* and proudly handed her a copy, "Look, Mom, I published my first book." She looked at it and said, "That's nice. Oh, look they published it with a smudge on the cover." *Your book is mentioned in the film* Fantastic Fungi *when a father burned it, which made Paul Stamets more curious.* Fortunately, once I learned how different other people's mindsets can be, I learned to be more tolerant and recognized they are perceiving, thinking, and reacting differently, and try to communicate in spite of that, instead of thinking about what's wrong with them.

When I taught a course on humanistic and transpersonal psychology I would do some lecturing about body posture affecting mood. To bring it home to students, I asked them to stand up and to stand in a classic depressed posture, head down a little bit, shoulders down, and walk around the room that way and try to be happy. You can be happy in that posture but it's hard work! If you put your shoulders back, simple things like that can make a difference. After Stanford, I took a job at the University of Virginia for a year as a result of Ian Stevenson, the psychiatrist who did so much reincarnation research. I actually had very little contact with him since he was so often in foreign countries collecting cases. Then I had an offer from the University of California, Davis, which had just been converted to a general campus, that brought me back to California.

Regarding differences in teaching, I'll tell you a story. Back in the '70s, humanistic psychology became very prominent with the belief you need to express your feelings and need some emotional education as well as intellectual education. Transpersonal psychology was being invented also. I felt I should be teaching psychology majors at UCD something about humanistic and transpersonal psychology. Another colleague was also interested and we proposed to the psychology faculty that we teach an Upper Division course on that. But other faculty said there's no place on the university campus for feelings because we are here to learn valid knowledge—intellectual, scientific knowledge. The only way we could get permission to teach this course was when I said, "We will promise the students that there might be times when we would invite them to participate in an exercise that might produce a feeling but we'd never require a feeling and it certainly wouldn't affect their grade." That made it safe. That was one of the most fun and invaluable courses I ever taught but we had to be really careful with feelings there. I used to tell this story to the students and they thought it was hilarious.

Define transpersonal psychology since you are a pioneer in the field. Conventional psychology is basically materialistic in its overall philosophy, believing that what physicists and chemists have taught us about reality is the absolute answer. You are what you are because of electrochemical changes in your brain. Obviously, when you die, there's no such thing as any kind of survival. They studied emotions in people who had psychological pathologies but that reinforced how bad emotions were. Humanistic psychology responded that we've got to study emotions and train ourselves to be emotionally intelligent, not just intellectually intelligent. Wanting to find acceptance within the mainstream, it still tended to stay within that materialistic framework, not by pledging allegiance so much as not asking questions about it. The spiritual was basically ignored. I'm oversimplifying, of course.

Transpersonal psychology took the whole thing one step further and said, "Wait a minute, people have spiritual experiences." They feel that they are not just a physical body confined in their head, and they feel part of something much bigger. We are not going to have to take a position on the reality or the non-reality of that bigger something, but we need to study it. This is one of the most important experiences people can have. For example, an NDE can create more change in a person's life in three minutes of being dead than in all the rest of their life. Transpersonal psychology is not a religion. It doesn't say, "God said this so you better believe it or go to Hell," but it says we are going to study these things. We are going to apply basic science and scholarship that aims to discover their qualities. What are the consequences of them, how do spiritual or transpersonal experiences affect people? How can people be assisted to better integrate these experiences in their life? We thought transpersonal psychology was going to be the next major leading force in psychology but computers beat us out, so it still remains a very minor part of psychology.

How did you get involved with the Stanford Research Institute (SRI) and remote viewers? I got interested in parapsychology back in the time when it was still very much a matter of card guessing as far as laboratory experiments went. With ordinary playing cards, you shuffle the deck very thoroughly and then ask people to guess red or black, and you expect 50% by chance. Some people can score consistently higher but there is a problem: it's as boring as can be after a few times. I was having lunch one day with physicist Russell Targ,* who I had met during my postdoc at Stanford, and he talked about this new kind of procedure at SRI that he called RV. It was deliberately picked as a word, not like ESP because ESP was seen as weird stuff, but RV is more like remote sensing, that's engineering—real science.

Targ told me about their procedure for RV, where somebody goes and hides and somebody back at the laboratory starts sketching impressions of where the traveler is. Studies report they can get a significant number of accurate drawings. RV wasn't running into the problem of being bored. Boredom seems all bad, but in fact, some of the best evidence for the existence of ESP resulting from the card guessing tests was that as you kept testing a person, their scores got worse and worse, indicating ESP. Chance doesn't get bored, but people do.

I wondered why RV was so successful, so I had a meeting at my home one night to have Targ and his colleague, physicist Harold Puthoff, talk about their results with RV. They decided that the best way to explain their method was to have the rest of us be RVers! Puthoff went off, we had no idea where, and 20 minutes later, we started sketching our impressions of where he was. I sat there with my eyes closed waiting for some images to come and saw nothing but big amorphous kinds of images, my mind wandering. I suddenly saw a bunch of white machines arrayed beside each other with something round on them, turning, located in a very bright situation, like I was looking inside some kind of factory. I made a sketch of it and figured it was just some guess my mind was making. Puthoff came back and then took us to the target. It was a laundromat, with all the white machines, washers and dryers, going round and round!

I managed to get a year leave from UCD to be a consultant on the RV project and saw a lot of other very good instances of it, as well as getting some feeling for the intelligence agency applications of RV, most of which I couldn't talk about at the time. Now multiple volumes of *The Star Gate Archives* are out, containing the documentation (obtained through the Freedom of Information Act) of more than 20 years of research. There is no doubt in my mind that RV is a useful intelligence-gathering method. I should note that I was initially ambivalent about consulting on a research project funded by intelligence and military organizations. But it was pointed out to me, something that's obvious in retrospect, that almost all wars start because one side thinks it can surprise the other. But if you have good intelligence, you begin to doubt that you could surprise the people you want to attack, so maybe you won't start that war after all.

Did you find that you could teach people to RV? Did they usually do a meditative preparation before doing the viewing? No, SRI did something that was quite different from most parapsychology experiments. I sometimes like to define psychology as the study of college sophomores by former college sophomores for the benefit of future college sophomores. And parapsychology, as an academic, scientific discipline tended to ape that. All sorts of implicit psychological factors are built into that. SRI was different. They actually had a wonderful psychological procedure for making it happen and they didn't know it. You see, Puthoff and Targ were physicists who didn't do psychology; they did science and physicists are at the top of the social prestige hierarchy for science.

I would ask Puthoff and Targ, "What's your psychological prep-aration for an RV session?" They would look at me blankly and said, "We don't do anything psychological, we just do an experiment." The first time I visited their laboratory at SRI, however, I discovered they had an incredible psychological preparation procedure. You drive up to SRI, which is one of the world's most prestigious think tanks. You enter the lobby and you can't go any further unless you are expected, you're issued a temporary security pass, and someone will accompany you at all times so you don't wander off and see classified and proprietary research going on in other laboratories. Sometimes instead of taking the long way around through the halls to their lab, Targ or Puthoff would cut through some other labora-tory with all these machines, the lights blinking: It was clear you were in a Temple of Big Science. Then they'd take you to their lab and show you examples of past, excellent RV, giving you an incred-ible psychological preparation. This is a hell of a lot different from an assistant professor telling a college sophomore to take this funny test. *It's like a ritual pilgrimage to go through the corridors.*

Do you guess that the intelligence agencies are still using RV? No, I think they are too stupid to do it now. For 20 some years they did hundreds of operational RVs, not experiments but RVs to gather useful intelligence information about important but secure sites in foreign countries. They would give the viewer a set of geographical co-ordinates and say, "Tell us what's there." For example, some of the best RVers described a new kind of huge Russian submarine, three times as big as any submarine that had ever been built. The intel-ligence agency that tasked them to do it was headed by somebody who, I believe, later became the Secretary of Defense. His response to the viewings was that it was crap because nobody can build a submarine that big. The site was a quarter of a mile from the Arctic ocean, not a place to build any kind of vessel. Three months later, via satellite photography, they watched the world's biggest subma-rine come out through a newly built canal. But sometime after that, some politicians found out about the RV program, ridiculed it and shut it down. I think it's irresponsible of our government not to continue this because I am all for discouraging anybody from starting wars.

When were the most difficult times in your life and how did you cope? As a kid, I suffered a lot like most kids do, when the parents don't let you do things you really want to do. There's a lot of situations where you can't do anything about it. You are just a little kid among these powerful giants. I discovered that if I continually thought clever thoughts, they helped insulate me from these "arrows of outrageous fortune." So one of the ways I coped is by continually thinking about interesting things. It probably developed my intellect, but it did cut me off from emotional and physical realities many times, and a major part of my own development has been to improve my physical and emotional intelligence, to have a more balanced approach to life.

Another challenge is I've run into a lot of prejudice in the scientific community, especially at the university level, for daring to be interested in things like ESP or ASC, and so I've had to deal with a lot of unfair pressure. Some faculty talked about how liberal our university was and how much the university respected academic freedom because we have this fellow Tart on our faculty, while others were actively working on how can they get rid of me! I've taken a lot of unfair crap that way, but I have a commitment to go for truth as best I can. And, when the going gets tough, I get bullheaded if you want to make me into a parody of a Taurus.

You've been married 67 years: How do you make that stay juicy over time? I wish I had some general rules that could apply to everybody! Like most couples, we went through a lot of ups and downs, but basically, I am madly in love with my wife and vice versa. *Some people say that having kids is the hardest time for a marriage because all the focus is on the kids.* Oh yes, especially when they are teenagers, but my son and daughter turned out great. And grandkids are wonderful because you get to spoil them and you don't have to be so darned responsible.

You were at the University of Nevada, Las Vegas teaching Consciousness Studies. Where did you fit that in? I took early retirement from UC-Davis and was teaching at the Institute of Transpersonal Psychology (ITP). A visionary businessman, Robert Bigelow, created a Chair of Consciousness Studies at the University of Nevada and looked around for somebody to fill it. I managed to get a year off from ITP to go there. If I say Las Vegas is different from the San Francisco Bay Area, it would be quite an understatement! Las Vegas was a great place for my wife Judy and me because there were so many wonderful places to hike and camp there in the Southwest, especially if we went in the spring and the fall when it wasn't too hot. The university basically gave me an office, a part-time assistant, let me teach one course on altered states of consciousness and otherwise ignored me. They didn't really want the topic. After my year they gave the position to philosopher and physician Raymond Moody for several years, which was a very good thing. Moody's book *Life After Life* educated scientists and the public about NDEs and how important they were. Then the university ran out of the money and the whole consciousness course faded away.

How do you define Consciousness Studies? My first reaction to your question was to point at my head, which shows my cultural conditioning that says consciousness arises solely from the actions of the physical brain, from my personal biocomputer. No doubt brain functioning has an enormous effect on how I perceive the world, myself and how I think and act, but all my research has shown me that's brain functioning is only a part of consciousness. It's like this biocomputer has connections to a huge, "non-physical web," to something that we can't really understand in ordinary terms. That's the "spiritual" side of things. That's why I often describe my work as trying to build bridges between the best of the spiritual and the best of the scientific. The consciousness I am experiencing right now is a result of the combination of whatever this larger spiritual thing is, a "thing" ("thing" is an inadequate word here) deeply embedded within the structures of my brain. I can't see this "spiritual computer," as it were, directly so I have to infer things about it in a lot of ways.

People have moments we vaguely call mystical experiences, but so far our level of describing, understanding and talking about them is primitive and not very useful. I think we can learn to communicate better with words about it. I am probably too old to see anything like this happen in my lifetime, but my goal is to see more study of some of the transpersonal (synonymous with spiritual in this context) experiences. They drastically change the people who experience them because they know at a very deep level that, among other things, we are all intimately connected. That means if you are suffering, there's some very real sense in which I am suffering. Our happiness, our fates are interconnected, so the only sensible thing to do is to live a life that is concerned with other people, that is decent to other people, that is compassionate. We are drawing on data about some very deep connections. I'd like to find out more about how to teach people to have this kind of transpersonal experience. A lot of conventional religion conditions people to believe the world is a certain way and that connection is a divine truth. That's conditioning, habit of thinking, at a conventional level. But if people could have these mystical, transpersonal experiences and know at a very deep personal level that we are more than the personal, I think the world could improve very much.

What do you think of the use of psychedelics to lead to these experiences? I'm thinking of Michael Pollan's 2018 book How to Change Your Mind *about using psychedelics to deal with anxiety and depression.* If we use psychedelics properly, that would be very useful for some people. It's probably not a wise use for all sorts of people. I was a subject in psychedelic experiments in graduate school, so I have a personal knowledge of their effects, in addition to scientific knowledge. For example, a person is very suggestible when taking psychedelics. You could use psychedelics to make people nasty as well as more mentally healthy or spiritual. The Viking raiders back in the 10th century took a psychedelic mushroom called *Amanita Muscaria* just before their raiding ships landed on the coast of England, so they felt no pain and experienced enhanced perception and strength. They slaughtered people in England, robbed their stuff and tried to get back on the ships before the drug effects wore off. The Vikings could collapse from exhaustion as the drug wore off and be easily killed. Raiding was their culture.

In terms of consciousness, it's tempting to say the quantum mechanics' concept of entanglement and non-locality explain a lot of paranormal events but physicists disagree. I had a lot of conversations with quantum physicists. Russell Targ and Ed May have spent a lot of time trying to explain it to me. I wouldn't claim to understand it well at all, but the quantum view of entanglement over distance is very useful for loosening up the constraints of a strictly Newtonian worldview, challenging our ideas of connection and separation. The effective test for evaluating a scientific theory is it does two things: It explains the observations you've already made and, if your theory is really good, it will predict new things you can test. Quantum theory is not specific enough so far to have predicted anything you could do in an ESP experiment, or to make ESP manifest more strongly than it normally does. I tease my physicist friends about this once in a while. I am sure they get a little miffed with me for reminding them that there is nothing specific from this approach yet, but I am trying to encourage them to get more specific.

For two entangled photons, if one changes, the other changes instantaneously. This suggests there is some kind of information exchange, so why doesn't that explain if I think about healing a heart attack patient it'll help her get better? It's a nice idea, I like it, but it doesn't specifically explain it. How do you entangle the atoms in the healer's brain and a patient's brain so that they stay connected when you separate them? Nobody has come up with a specific explanation for a psychic phenomenon.

What's your understanding of how the entangled particles influence each other? I don't have the slightest idea. It's a mystery. Some of the brightest minds in quantum physics, like Richard Feynman, used to tell students don't try to understand it, just calculate it. It works very well when you calculate it and it doesn't make any sense in terms of the way we ordinarily think about the world. It may be that some ASC would give us a better understanding of quantum theory. *The quantum field is full of potential waves or particles.* And how does that turn into consciousness? I used to be a ham radio operator and eventually, I got a job as a commercial radio operator. I can tell you how a radio or a vacuum tube works in exquisite detail and make it work in different ways. I can demonstrate that my theoretical understanding has practical applications; I can start with parts and build transmitters and receivers that work, but that kind of detail and functioning isn't there for the quantum stuff and ESP yet. It's a real mind blower that things a million miles apart can "communicate" instantly.

Have you personally experienced synchronicity, ESP, etc.? I know you've experienced ASC. How has it impacted your development doing this research? When I first got interested in ESP and other psi phenomena, I had never had any kind of psychic experience, and probably through most of the first part of my life, I didn't have any personal psychic experience. Since then I've had an occasional one that made sense to me. I'd be at work, for example, and I'd get a phone call from an old friend who I hadn't heard from in 15 years, Joe. And I'd go home but before I could say anything my wife would ask, "Whatever happened to Joe? We haven't heard from him in a long time." You forget all about something and sometimes it goes down into the unconscious mind to activate the mechanisms that really do the ESP work.

Having more psychic experiences isn't particularly important to me: Ditto on unusual states of consciousness or things like "enlightenment." The more I learn about enlightenment, the less I have the slightest idea what it is. But I know a great deal about "endarkenment." I'd say I am an authority on endarkenment now that I've practiced and studied it for many years. I often observe the way my mind distorts things, is biased, and doesn't understand things that it should. I'd like to get more intelligent in a variety of ways, especially emotionally as well as intellectually. That's more important to me personally. I like to think that we are on this planet to evolve, in that and other ways. I like the analogy that it's like we are in the Marines. This is an advanced learning school and it is a really tough curriculum, but if we can graduate from it, that's really good, useful for ourselves, useful for others.

What's your guess as to what happens after the body dies, based on what you know about NDEs? What about Ian Stevenson's and Ed Kelly's work with children remembering their past lives? Yes, this research is especially impressive. You can be fairly certain what young kids wouldn't be able to imagine some of the things about previous lives that they come up with. It's harder with adults, we've been exposed to so much information about historical times. I've read a lot of the old spiritualist literature on what mediums say about an afterlife and various evidence from NDE survivors. To greatly oversimplify, I think something survives, but I have a hard time picturing it.

When I die, I'd really like to meet my grandmother, who died when I was around eight. We had a tremendous love bond there but I don't think my grandmother has been waiting around, unchanged, for 70 years for me to die. If we survive what do we do? Of course, we'll all die at some point and then if there is survival, we'll find out about it. My working philosophy, subject to change if relevant information comes to me, is that I believe there are long-term consequences for our actions and I find that a useful philosophy of life.

You said that one of the things you're interested in doing is teaching and that's part of your dharma. You didn't use that word but it's part of your path. I love to teach, I love to get in front of a bunch of students and get talking about something interesting and see some eyes light up. I remember a young woman in one of my classes on ASC came up to me about halfway through the course and said, "I thought about dropping this course several times because you talk about this weird stuff and draw funny diagrams." Then she looked at me and said, "You've been talking about the way my mind works, haven't you?" Yes, I confessed! It's been fascinating being able to earn my living teaching and doing research, helping a little to expand humanity's knowledge base. *It's also fun if you make them laugh.* Yes, except you can't introduce humor if they are starting to think about a coming test. I tried it a few times and it didn't work!

What about current research institutes; who is doing the good research? Dean Radin and his colleagues at IONS are doing wonderful work. I am especially charmed with his work on a classic physics apparatus, whose results led to quantum physics, passing a beam of light through double slits. He's taken something that physicists have speculated about for a hundred years, leading to many interesting physics ideas. Radin had agents treat the apparatus as a PK experiment and repeatedly found that the way you think about what happens in that apparatus affects it. That's a most exciting thing to me.

Do you have another book in the offing or what are you thinking about currently? I am trying to write a major article about bringing RV into all sorts of fields of science as a useful tool, especially in psychology and psychotherapy. But real life keeps interfering from finishing writing it and there are a million smaller things I want to write. I put a lot of information on my blog. *How would RV apply to the study of a problem like anxiety?* To grossly oversimplify, if somebody comes to a therapist because they have some psychological problem, usually they don't understand why they have it. Some types of psychotherapy, especially classical ones like psychoanalysis, work on the basic theory that there is some kind of unconscious process going on that's driving this. It's not the therapist's job to tell the client what it is but help her or him to discover what this is in a more direct fashion, to gain therapeutic insight and integrate this insight into their ordinary lives. However, clients tend to be in classical psychoanalysis for years, going once or twice a week, due to unconscious psychological defenses against their knowing.

A very accomplished RVer was doing something like that with a patient whose psychiatrist was having a difficult time helping him because the patient wouldn't say hardly anything. The RVer told the psychiatrist to ask him about "John," a name he RVed. When the psychiatrist said, "Tell me about John;" the patient jumped up and nearly strangled him. "Who the hell told you about John? I've never told anybody about John." *I do this when I do clairvoyant sessions, including on the phone with people I've never met.* It's like my proposal for creating state-specific sciences years ago where you do science in ASC. It's an idea that I'd like to think is ahead of its time. It could be a loony idea that won't really work but until it's tried, we don't know.

Reading about Einstein and his creative process, I picked up the report that he had a sensory feeling for shapes, shapes morphing and moving. He didn't think primarily in an intellectual way. But how do you teach something like that? Maybe in a certain state of consciousness, it's more clear. I talked to some mathematicians about how they do their mathematical work; they said at the end when they are writing it up for a journal, they put it into conventional form, understandable in ordinary mathematical language to other mathematicians, but they got to the ideas in funny ASC.

What do you do for fun? My work is wonderful but I do other things for fun too. My wife and I used to hike and camp a lot. As we got older and got tired of sleeping on the ground in a tent, we got a tiny recreational vehicle so we can sleep on mattresses. We'd go off to the Southwest and camp for five or six weeks in national parks and hike around, so there's a lot of fun in my life. *And you sing.* Yes, my wife and I go to the senior center nearby which has a singing group once a week and it's wonderful. I haven't accepted the fact that I'm "old" yet; I'm just older.

Are you optimistic or pessimistic when you think about the autocrats around the world and climate change? Sevens on the Enneagram are optimistic, it's built into me. I am biased to see good potentials in things whether they are strongly there are not. I am very impressed by the work of Harvard psychologist Steven Pinker, who looked at actual data. We talk about the 20th century as the bloodiest century in history with its wars, but when he went back and found the statistics, the 20th century was the most peaceful century we have records for! The percentage of people murdered or killed in war was way down. Or look at people living below the poverty line; it used to be 30% in a lot of countries. It's down to 18%. There's a lot of statistical data that says, "Yes, terrible things happen and those are the ones that get in the news, but on a lot of levels we are doing better." I prefer to go with that. I can look at all the negative stuff and get very depressed about the whole thing, but I prefer to think there are good possibilities. Internal attitude, internal experiences, matter so much, not just material circumstances. I hope that what

I find out about the nature of the mind could help people have transpersonal experiences that will make us care more about each other. It works for me.

Books

Altered States of Consciousness, 1969, editor

Transpersonal Psychologies, 1975

On Being Stoned: A Psychological Study of Marijuana Intoxication, 1971

States of Consciousness, 1975

Symposium on Consciousness, 1975, With P. Lee, R. Ornstein, D. Galin & A. Deikman

Learning to Use Extrasensory Perception, 1976

Psi: Scientific Studies of the Psychic Realm, 1977

Mind at Large: Institute of Electrical and Electronic Engineers Symposia on the Nature of Extrasensory Perception, 1979, with Harold E. Puthoff & Russel Targ

Waking Up: Overcoming the Obstacles to Human Potential, 1986

Open Mind, Discriminating Mind: Reflections on Human Possibilities, 1989

Living the Mindful Life, 1994

Body Mind Spirit: Exploring the Parapsychology of Spirituality, 1997

Mind Science: Meditation Training for Practical People, 2001

The End of Materialism: How Evidence of the Paranormal is Bringing Science and Spirit Together, 2009

Marjorie Woollacott, Ph.D.
A Neurobiologist Looks at
Mystical Experiences

Photo by Paul Hawkwood

Questions to Ponder

What's the neurobiology of meditation, hypnosis, mystical experiences and multiple personalities?

What does terminal lucidity suggest about our brains?

Compare energy healing like Reiki with the Placebo Effect.

How does Dr. Woollacott define consciousness?

I was born in California in August of 1946, a Virgo. *Do you identify with being a Virgo?* I do in the sense that Virgo's give acute attention to detail and this is consistent with my own natural focus. In Vedic astrology, I'm a Leo and that is expressed through my joy in teaching and sharing my knowledge with other people, which is more characteristic of a Leo rather than a Virgo. *We have our rising sign, our moon sign, and planets in some of the 12 houses so it's a complicated picture. It sounds like you give some credence to astrology?* I love astrology and I know from direct experience how much it truly plays out in my life. When I had my astrology chart done when I came to the University of Oregon as an associate professor, the astrologer said, "All of your planets are underneath the horizon and clustered together in one spot. This chart tends to be that of someone who is inward-looking." That struck me because I had been meditating for the last four years. I felt a large portion of my life was dedicated to looking inward and trying to understand who I am. The more I look at astrology, the more I see very interesting predictions that correspond with my own personality type.

What are your Myers-Briggs and your Enneagram personality types? I am an INFJ and am told that this type likes to have events in their life planned. That is certainly true of me! Some other qualities of this type include being committed, loyal, compassionate, creative, intense, deep, determined, conceptual, sensitive, reserved, holistic, and idealistic. In reflecting on those qualities, I believe they fairly accurately portray my personality type, especially the qualities of being deep, determined and idealistic. A friend of mine laughs that when I have a desire to move forward with a project I am like a bull-dog who has its teeth solidly into something and won't let go. Taking the Myers-Briggs again recently was interesting because I shifted types over the 10 years since the last time I answered the questions, from Sensing to Intuitive and Thinking to Feeling. I used to be an ISTJ. I've known I've been an introvert all my life even though I love to speak and teach since I definitely get more energy from being by myself. Over the ten years, I have become more intuitive and listen to my feelings more than I used to.

My Enneagram type is a very strong Three, that is, the performer or achiever, which governs my life for better and for worse! On the one hand, it's allowed me to be very successful in the university being a teacher, a scientist, and getting grants because I love creating new projects. The downside is that Threes don't give as much time to relationships and learning who they really are because they're so busy doing. In the last few years, I've tried to back off on the doing so that I can spend more time in understanding who I am, finding the joy of relating to others and learning more clearly how I fit into this universe.

Your birth order? I'm the second child. My big sister (four years older) was the boss in terms of taking care of me when I was a little kid. She is the person who invited me, knowing I was a materialist scientist, to take my first mediation intensive, which really shifted my life.

What childhood influences led you to be a scientist? When I was four or five years old, living on a one-acre mini-farm, my mother killed a gopher making burrows through our green lawn. I had an incredible desire to know what was inside of that gopher so my sister and I dissected it. I was fascinated by the different organs I found underneath that skin. Looking back on that day, I think it was the first moment where I saw my interest in understanding how the universe worked from a scientific point of view. Also, my father loved books and took us to the library every week, an amazing place of discovery. I learned to write my name when I was four years old so I could have my first library card. I was so excited every week to go and get five to ten more books and explore and discover more about the world of both fiction and nonfiction.

During the summers on the mini-farm, I would lie on the ground underneath the cornstalks looking up at the blue sky and feel the magic and the mystery of the world around me. I carried that into school, enjoying discovering languages, science, literature, etc. in my coursework. I always felt that school was a privilege and a joy. When I was in the eighth grade taking my first general science class, my teacher told me, "You are amazing in terms of your clarity and your detail about what you're studying and I think you may really have scientific inclinations."

From the time I was seven, I studied music in school and had private lessons in flute and then oboe; I played in school orchestras and then in our civic symphony in our town. This was a marvelous time, making music with others my age and feeling the mystery of the music of Beethoven and Bach. I was told by my teachers that I should go to music school, but I also loved neuroscience. My first two years at the University of Redlands were in their music department; then I transferred to the University of Southern California because they had a much larger music department and I could more easily be directed in music performance as an oboist. But in the competition of music school, I realized there's no real room at the top in music—and I wasn't good enough to be a top career performer. I happily took an extra year of classes in the sciences, so that I could apply for graduate school in neuroscience. I worked with a great mentor in neuroscience, who helped me to write a National Institutes of Health Predoctoral Fellowship application, which I received and which paid for my entire Ph.D. education.

Why did you pick neuroscience? A wonderful high school teacher, Mr. John O'Neill introduced us to the Great Books of the Western World and also to William James, the father of modern psychology.

I was struck by what James had to say about the mind and I thought, "That's what I want to do. I want to understand the human mind." As a child, I wondered if there was the soul because my parents had taken me to church and that was a spiritual concept but I didn't really resonate with what I was learning in our church. I thought, "If there is a soul, the essence of who we are, maybe it would be interconnected with the brain." As a youngster, I thought the brain would be a place to look for some connection with the soul.

Why not psychology? Why the more biological aspect of it? As an undergraduate, my second course in psychology was called "Psychological Theories of Personality." When I read the material in that course, it seemed like it was all fluff because I didn't see strong scientific evidence for different types of personality. Then I took a biology course and thought, "I understand neurons." As I became a young professor of neuroscience, neuroscience and psychology began to merge, as psychologists became interested in looking at aspects of brain function and physiology that could explain behavior and neuroscientists tried to understand behavior from their physiological perspective.

What kind of church did your parents take you to when you were growing up? An American Baptist church. When I went to the University of Redlands it was part of the American Baptist Convention. My religion professor was liberal and a scholar and told us, "A lot of those stories from the Bible should be interpreted symbolically and it doesn't mean that they really happened." When I told my mother, she said, "Oh no!" and wrote to the American Baptist Convention to ask, "Do you know what they're teaching those children in college!?" I loved that course because it opened up for me a new way of thinking that I hadn't known about in my younger years. After taking many courses in biology and contemplating the nature of reality within that context, I became an atheist, because the evidence for a materialist worldview seemed overwhelming. This was influenced by the fact that I had never had a deep spiritual experience. It took me until I had my first meditation experience to shift from that materialistic framework on the world.

When did your sister introduce you to meditation? I was a postdoctoral fellow at the University of Oregon doing research in the neuroscience program, about to become a professor at a university in Virginia. She gifted me a meditation retreat where I had the most amazing experience when the meditation master, Swami Muktananda, initiated every person in the room. Although the scientist in me was skeptical, when he touched me between my eyes and on the bridge of my nose, I felt a current of electricity going from his fingers down to the center of my chest to my heart—not the physical heart but more like a heart than the physical heart ever seemed. It radiated outward through my whole being and beyond, with a feeling of love and joy like nectar, feelings that I had never before experienced this deeply.

When I returned to my university position in Virginia, I spontaneously got up the next morning at 5:00 AM to meditate and I've been doing that every single day since then. I experienced this ecstasy simmering underneath my ordinary awareness. I just had to go inside to meditate to begin to capture that again. I went from being a materialist neuroscientist who thought my sister was a slightly esoteric New Age hippie to thinking, "This is real. I don't understand it but there's something going on here."

Do you use a mantra to focus on when you meditate? Yes, I've used different mantras including *Om Namah Shivaya*, which is very standard in India and means "Om, I honor my highest self." Another one that I use a lot now is also quite universal and that is the sound of the breath—*Hamsa* or *So'ham*. Just listening to the breath is a way of focusing and very powerful in quieting the mind down.

I taught at Virginia Polytechnic in Blacksburg continuing my neuroscience research for a year and then moved back to Oregon where, in 1980, I accepted a position at the University of Oregon. My interest in doing research on mystical phenomena was stimulated when I went back to get my Master's in Asian Studies at the University of Oregon while continuing to teach and do research in neuroscience. And, after finishing the Master's degree, I began writing my book, *Infinite Awareness*. That's when I discovered Ian

Stephenson's research at the University of Virginia. I was shocked when I first read his studies on reincarnation because, even though I'd been meditating for around 25 years, I considered the topic of reincarnation way out there because it was beyond what a biologist could accept. When I read his studies, they were so carefully done and they had such compelling evidence, I had to say, "If I'm going to accept that this is a carefully done study, I have to say that there's more to reincarnation than I originally thought." That's when I began to change. He was one of the first professors in a Psychiatry Department interested in doing research cases suggestive of reincarnation because he felt this could explain personality development in many children.

I also read *Irreducible Mind*, edited by neuroscientist Ed Kelly at the University of Virginia. He described every theory of neuroscience that I was steeped in but noted that the originators of the theories never truly explained how the brain could create mental activity. He showed the weaknesses of these theories and cited the research that shows that consciousness can't be produced by the activity of neurons in the brain. I wrote to Ed Kelly to ask if I could visit his lab to discuss his book with him. He wrote back immediately replying, "Absolutely yes. It would be wonderful to host you." I added an extra chapter to the book about Ed's and his colleagues' research in this area and their own mystical experiences that perhaps propelled them forward in doing this type of research.

We talked about Ed Kelly's experiences when he was a graduate student at Harvard University in psychology where his professors were all materialists, as most academics are. His mother told him that a relative in a small Protestant group was a medium; she was worried and asked him to check on her. He went to the library housing all of the work by William James and read his research on parapsychology and mediumship. That was the first time Ed Kelly learned that James was interested in these paranormal phenomena. As he read he found that what the relative was doing was benign. Around the same time, a young Swami from the Vivekananda tradition came to Harvard to give a talk. Ed said that the Swami had the most powerful presence and he said this really struck him so he went to the Vedanta Society's bookstore in Back Bay, Boston, to get some of the books. He began meditating and having his own experiences. After his Ph.D. was finished, he went to work on parapsychology at the Rhine Institute at Duke University

Did you decide to do a Master's in Asian Studies because of the meditation experiences? Yes, during the day I would be in my lab doing research on rehabilitation neuroscience and then I would teach a class on hatha yoga or meditation or go to the meditation center to engage in a whole different set of conversations. It felt like I was leading two separate lives and I wanted a way to put them together. During my third sabbatical, I went to Rochester University where I studied Sanskrit so that I could look at original texts from India on the nature of consciousness. I began to explore further into research on reincarnation, NDEs, and energy healing to understand consciousness from this broader perspective.

How does neurobiology tie in with these kinds of paranormal practices? If you look at what happens in the brain when you're meditating, you can see that the prefrontal cortex and anterior cingulate cortex are active and the default mode or mind wandering network activity is reduced. You can make it sound like the experiences individuals have in meditation are just materialistic phenomena. But when you go deeper into the research and you look at careful studies exploring the nature of consciousness, for example on NDEs, you find out that Bruce Greyson at the University of Virginia and Dutch researcher and Pim von Lommel are doing gold standard prospective research studies.

The prospective studies start at a particular point in time where the researchers locate everybody who has a cardiac arrest in a network of hospitals. For all patients who survive they ask them, "What happened? Were you able to actually observe anything during your resuscitation?" Around 12% to 15% said something like, "Yes, I could. I saw these other realms or I saw the people resuscitating me." Some of them could identify the doctors and nurses, although they had a flat EEG, with no heartbeat, often for over two to four minutes. There's no way that this should be possible from a materialist perspective, since the EEG is flat after about 20 to 40 seconds of cardiac arrest. As a neuroscientist, I have to believe their careful research. I believe this can't be a phenomenon purely of neural activity because the neurons were flatlined in all of the perceptual parts of the cortex that would allow the people to see the operating room. The other point is the patients are usually seeing the operating room from above their body so there's no way you can explain that from a materialist point of view.

I also felt that there is something interesting about the fact that we use the brain for a lot of sensory, perceptual experiences during our life, but most people's perceptions are limited to only these sensory experiences. As I read William James and Ed Kelley and many others, they proposed that our brain, evolutionarily, has been made to filter out most of the information that could be available to it because this vast amount of information would only confuse us and not be adaptive to living and surviving. We have attentional filters that block out most sensory information that is available. In fact, most psychologists today accept this, but they don't think of the attentional networks as filters for something that might be beyond the senses. When a person has an NDE, maybe the filters stop functioning because the brain is no longer active and thus the person can see much more broadly than through their five senses.

I began to explore other meditation studies, including one that came out in 2014 by Thilo Hinterberger and his colleagues from Regensburg, Germany. They examined the EEG of people who are well-trained in meditation doing what they call "thoughtless emptiness meditation" and compared that state of focused attention meditation where they focused on the point just above and between their eyes, a "spatial connectedness" meditation, and a "presence monitoring" meditation when the subjects were just quietly monitoring the environment. There was also a baseline state where subjects were resting with eyes open or closed, or reading, but not meditating. The researchers found that in thoughtless emptiness meditation, the EEG amplitude was significantly lower than in any other of those states, across most of the frequencies and the areas of the brain.

This reminded me of how the brain EEG becomes flatlined in an NDE with cardiac arrest. I thought maybe there's a correlation between less brain activity and less filtering so that you can experience these more expanded states of consciousness in meditation or in an NDE. I recently came across some interesting studies on psilocybin research being done now with end-stage cancer patients. In London, Robin Carhart-Harris and his colleagues put individuals in an fMRI machine while having a psilocybin experience and found a direct correlation between the reduction of activity in all the key hub areas of the brain and a correlation with the intensity of the mystical experience under psilocybin. They said that it's really interesting that lowering brain activity is causing these experiences.

Those three areas of research tell me that our brain probably filters out large amounts of important information that may relate to our mystical experiences and experiences beyond the confines of our body. I hope that more and more people in the neuroscience area will begin to look at this to see if we can find out more about this filtering process and how reducing the filtering may actually enhance our experiences in these moments.

Has there been any research about people with Dissociative Identity Disorder(DID) on how their brain reflects their sub-personalities? Bernardo Kastrup and Ed Kelley co-authored an article in *Scientific American* talking about those sorts of disorders as a beautiful example of the phenomenon of universal consciousness creating or giving rise to all the individually conscious beings in this world, each with its own individual personality. The research on DID indicates that a person's consciousness can give rise to many different dissociated personalities. They then propose that something like this happens at the level of universal consciousness, giving rise to billions of alters, each of us with our own personalities and private inner lives. We each could be like dissociated personalities of universal consciousness, each of us under the illusion that we are separate from each other but in reality all part of one larger reality. During a mystical

315

experience, we have the awareness that we are all interconnected beings, arising from a single source, cosmic consciousness.

What have been the most difficult challenges in your life and how did you cope? It is so easy in life to be thrown off balance and get irritated or angry when things don't go the way we want. So one strong intention is to focus on staying in the present moment, in order to be able to deal with any challenge from a place of equanimity. Staying centered in the equanimity of the present moment makes it less likely that I will react to the challenge, allowing it to pull me off balance. Staying grounded in the present moment has been one of the most amazing challenges of my life. Another challenge is to truly embody virtues like kindness and generosity. I'm learning that when I am generous, I feel a lot better than when I am being less generous and wanting something for myself. I aim to stay aware of my sense of connection with the people around me, to really experience what we talked about earlier—the sense that I am truly a part of a universal consciousness that exists in everyone and everything.

What about having children? They can be a big challenge. You're right; my husband and I have never had any children so I think that's perhaps why I don't have those other challenges in my life. Many of my very good friends say it's a challenge to have children because you have expectations of your own about their behavior and the children don't necessarily follow your expectations. *That's so true. As you've moved around, your husband has been able to move, too?* I didn't meet my husband until I came to the University of Oregon where I stayed for the rest of my career. He was a literature professor at a community college. It's been wonderful having a husband who is interested in meditation and is very supportive.

You've written over 180 research articles in neuroscience about balance and motor control development and you wrote about sensory contributions to music performance; what does that mean? At a certain point in a professor's career as a neuroscientist, they have tenure and they've done plenty of research in their primary area. In my case, it was rehabilitation, balance control, stroke, Parkinson's disease, etc. Then I wanted to look at other things that interested me. I was intrigued by what makes someone a great musician in terms of their sensory, perceptual, and motor abilities since I was studying those abilities. We looked at cello performance majors and found they had both a keen ear to be able to hear their intonation and also great attentional abilities. This allowed them to be able to focus on the sensory information of how their music sounded while also simultaneously focusing on the intricate skills involve in their motor performance.

I accepted in a few graduate students into my lab who were interested in meditation and Tai Chi to see if we could learn something about how these practices affect the brain and our attentional systems. There are two types of meditation research. One type is focused on asking if consciousness is tied to the activity of neurons or, alternatively, could it be fundamental and therefore present when the neurons in the brain are no longer active. Examples of this type of research are Ed Kelley's psi research and Bruce Greyson's NDE research. A second approach that most other neuroscientists take, including Richard Davidson at the University of Wisconsin-Madison, is somewhat different and focuses on the value of meditation in our day-to-day life. Davidson and his colleagues do very brilliant research related to emotional regulation, attention, and meditation and show how it improves our immune function, our attentional pathways, etc. He calls meditation a mental training so his fellow scientists don't have to think of this as a mysterious mystical phenomenon. It's a pragmatic tool you can use to help students focus better or stay calm in challenging situations. Davidson showed that when you practice meditation for long periods, your attentional systems get stronger and you see changes in the brain in the anterior cingulate cortex area, in the prefrontal cortex areas and in a number of other areas.

I'm also very interested in research on terminal lucidity. Terminal or paradoxical lucidity is a temporary period of lucidity that can occur in the last minutes to hours of life in persons who have severe cognitive and communication deficits due to dementia, stroke, or coma. In 5 to 10% of the cases, an individual can become totally lucid and say goodbye to their family. Neuroscientists say, "This is impossible. If their brain was filled with Alzheimer's plaques, they should never become lucid before they die." Alexander Batthyany at the University of Vienna is collecting data from M.D.s and nurses who worked with patients in end-of-life care. One account of terminal lucidity from his study was of an elderly woman who had dementia, could no longer recognize people, and was almost mute. One day, unexpectedly, she called her family, thanked her daughter for everything she had done and exchanged kindness and warm feelings with her grandchildren. Then she said goodbye and shortly afterwards she died.

Batthyany suggests that perhaps the brain doesn't give rise to the mind, but the mind uses the brain as its organ. And at the end of life, consciousness is beginning to peel itself away from the diseased brain. Perhaps the mind is like the sun in eclipse and the moon is like the diseased brain, eclipsing our conscious awareness. In summarizing Batthyany's research, Professor Stafford Betty comments that perhaps at the approach of death you begin to peel away from the brain and suddenly find yourself able to remember, think, and communicate normally.

In one of your articles, you suggest that right-brain dominance seems to be more active in altered states of consciousness. Yes, neuroanatomist Jill Bolte Taylor's book *My Stroke of Insight* related that her stroke shut down the rational, linear left-brain and thus the right side of her brain, associated with left-handedness, became dominant. During the right-brain dominance, she had amazing experiences of unity awareness and being totally in the present moment. She said, "In this altered state of being, my mind was no longer preoccupied with the billions of details that my brain routinely used to define and conduct my life …. As my consciousness slipped into a state of peaceful grace, I felt ethereal." Taylor notes that an amazing gift from that experience was a new appreciation that a "deep internal peace is accessible to anyone at any time." This type of experience is also reported by many meditators and persons having NDEs and gives evidence that reducing brain activity of attentional areas in this part of the brain diminishes one filter on our awareness.

This opens our awareness to the experience of an expanded consciousness.

Taylor was a little discouraged as she began to recover from her stroke, as it was difficult to hold on to that unity awareness. Our left-language hemisphere can dominate so much that it keeps us from having Gestalt holistic experiences. Perhaps meditation lets the linear side of the brain become more quiescent so that the more Gestalt holistic side of the brain can become more active and give us a whole different sense of reality. *I teach workshops in how to develop clairvoyance and healing abilities and what I say to them is, "Keep the left-brain busy by asking questions like, "Why am I seeing this? What does this mean?"*

I've seen studies that women tend to have more integration between the corpus callosum so they're more whole-brain and less specialized. Is that accurate? For a long time, we were afraid in neuroscience to talk about any differences in the brains of men and women. But now we're learning that it just means that we are able to complement each other with our different abilities. These are usually small but significant differences and we have a bell-shaped curve with people being at different points on the curve. *Psychological studies by Sandra Bem show that androgynous people are more flexible and more healthy psychologically.* It's like the Chinese Yin Yang symbol and what we're trying to do is balance those two qualities within us as human beings. *Carl Jung talked about that in terms of we have to integrate the contra-sexual structures of the anima (femininity) or animus (masculinity).*

What did you find in your studies of alternative and complementary medicine practices; Tai Chi, Reiki, meditation, aerobic exercise? When I looked at the carefully controlled studies of the placebo effect I was absolutely awe-struck. Neuroscientists strongly believe in the placebo effect. Every new drug that comes out has to show it's more effective than a placebo in order to be approved as a therapeutic agent but neuroscientists ignore the power of the placebo itself. Since I am a motor-control neuroscientist and I know about Parkinson's disease, I was amazed to learn that a placebo could increase dopamine in the brain and decrease Parkinson's symptoms. Also, Tor Wager's group at the University of Colorado showed that a placebo analgesic was effective in inhibiting the activation of the brain's pain pathways, thus reducing pain, in addition to the magnitude of the neural inhibition correlated with the reduction in reported pain. They concluded that this strongly refutes the conjecture that placebo responses simply reflect report bias. So the belief that you're receiving pain medications has a similar effect to the medication. *Even if people know it's placebo, but especially if it's a big colorful pill, it's efficacious.*

Regarding Reiki energy healing, scientists are comparing its effects to placebo responses, which we know are already effective and are showing that Reiki energy healing in many cases is more powerful than the placebo. For example, Rachel Friedman and her colleagues at Yale University medical school performed a carefully designed study on cardiac patients who had had a heart attack in the previous 72 hours. It was a randomized controlled clinical trial, which is the gold-standard for research. They assigned patients to groups involving Reiki energy healing, relaxing music, or rest. They found that the group with Reiki healing sessions improved heart function as indicated by heart rate variability, while the other groups did not. They found that Reiki had the same effect as the pharmaceutical drug, Propranolol, in improving heart function.

What about sham Reiki, such as used by Shamini Jain*? The effect could be just that having a caring person focus on you is healing. In my chapter in *Infinite Awareness* on Reiki healing, I described another study by Adina Goldman Shore exploring the long-term effects of Reiki on psychological depression and perceived stress. Shore was especially interested in learning if the results of Reiki therapy are due to the placebo effect, physical touch, or the practice's energy—Ki. The participants were randomly assigned to one of three groups: a hands-on Reiki group, a distance Reiki group, or a distance placebo group. Participants received treatments once a week for a six-week period. At the end of the study, both the hands-on Reiki and distance Reiki groups showed significantly reduced symptoms of psychological distress compared to the placebo control group. What

I find compelling is that the significant differences in depression and self-perceived stress for the Reiki groups continued to improve throughout the course of the year even though there were no further treatments. Goldman Shore wrote a second article, which you often don't see in scientific journals, where people described their experience of the healing. One person said, "I can actually, literally feel it when I'm getting treatment. I can feel the energy coming." She gave many examples, suggesting many people have perceptual abilities beyond the usual five senses.

Why do you think Tai Chi is healing because it's not like Reiki where someone is directing healing energy at you? I've done a number of studies on Tai Chi to find out if it can improve balance abilities in older adults who are beginning to fall. We measured the neuromuscular responses of the older adults in the laboratory when they had to recover from an unexpected slip during walking, both before Tai Chi training and after a 12-week period of Tai Chi training. We found their neuromuscular responses when recovering from the slip were much better organized after the Tai Chi training and the people were much better able to recover their balance.

In the second study, we asked whether meditation or Tai Chi, a moving meditation, was better than aerobic activity in improving attentional focus. We used four groups: people who practiced meditation, Tai Chi, or aerobic exercise and compared them to sedentary adults. Much research has shown that aerobic exercise improves blood to the brain and therefore attention. But is meditation or Tai Chi better? We asked people to perform a computer game where a red light appears randomly on the left or right of the screen. They respond as fast as they can to seeing the light, by pressing the left or right button on the mouse pad. But here is the trick; they have to do it according to ever-changing rules: every two trials they switch the rule; when they see the dot, they first press the mouse button on the same side, then in two trials the button on the opposite side to the red dot.

We also recorded their brain activity with EEGs. The EEGs record event-related potentials (ERPs) that occur in the brain when the stimulus, the red light, comes on and their amplitude shows the amount of attention we are giving to the task. The meditators and Tai Chi group showed the largest ERPs, the sedentary groups ERPs were smallest and the aerobic fitness group was in between. The primary areas in the cortex contributing to this ERP were the anterior cingulate cortex and the prefrontal cortex, which seem to be key areas activated during meditation, which increase in size as a result of meditation practice. I see Tai Chi as a moving meditation where the mind is still as one is performing the Tai Chi movements.

What's the correlation between consciousness and Chi or Ki, prana, mana, kundalini, Shakti, or orgone energy? I think they are talking about different aspects of consciousness. The Indian tradition talks about prana as being energy existing throughout the universe and also including the force that moves in and out as we breathe. Indian texts also say that the Kundalini energy or Shakti is an energy within a human being that can be awakened through meditation. When awakened, it activates an unfolding of an expanded awareness and mystical experiences. After my own experience of the awakening of the Kundalini energy, when I meditated I began feeling energy between my eyes, at the crown of my head, and in the heart region although I knew nothing about chakras and energy fields as I was a materialist neuroscientist before this awakening. Because these types of experiences occur across many traditions, I believe we have to give credence to the idea that there may be an energy that can be awakened through spiritual practices or spontaneously and that those may give us a more subtle perceptual ability.

In terms of the subtle anatomy, what would you say about the chakras, meridians, the aura, and the energy fields? A classical neuroscientist would say don't go there because we have a hard time measuring this sort of thing with scientific instruments. However, some people are doing research on Reiki, acupuncture, myofascial release, etc. and have documented changes in the conductance of the skin or bodily pathways during acupuncture. Many people who practice Reiki report that they can see when a chakra is out of balance and balance it. I can't do that but I find it fascinating when I see somebody with healing abilities. *I work with chakras in every session I do.*

You report that hypnosis changes what's going on in the brain, with different effects on the ACC or the somatosensory cortex. How does that work? I discovered the power of hypnosis by reading the research described in *Irreducible Mind,* edited by Ed Kelly and his colleagues at the University of Virginia. The research indicates that people have different levels of sensitivity to hypnosis. Hypnosis has been used for many years to reduce pain. A 2014 meta-analysis examined the results of 12 clinical studies, including six randomized controlled trials. The reviewers concluded that hypnosis has a significant and reliable effect on reducing pain. The anterior cingulate cortex (ACC) and the somatosensory cortex were two areas seen to show changes in certain situations under hypnosis. Remember that the ACC is also active in meditation and is increased in size with regular meditation practice.

What is the ACC's job? It's part of the executive attention network that helps us regulate our emotions in very good ways. A wonderful study, that I heard Mike Posner talk about, looked at the ACC size in children who were about four or five years old and found a direct correlation between the size of the ACC and the children's ability to self-regulate their emotions. The size of the ACC was correlated with the success of these children later in life. The beauty is the size of the ACC can increase through practicing meditation. *What does the somatosensory cortex do?* It's the area of the brain that registers what we are feeling on our skin. *Why might that be involved in psi phenomena?* My hypothesis is that in hypnosis the sensory pathways could be inhibited on the way up to the somatosensory cortex, reducing pain.

You were presented with a question about the possibility of miracles and angels. What did you conclude? I was asked by *Awareness Magazine* to write an article on angels. I thought, "Is there another way of understanding what people are experiencing when they see or feel an angel visit them and what seems like a miracle occurs?" I realized that the NDE research I have explored reveals that many times a person under cardiac arrest leaves their body and goes to another realm. There they may see radiant spirits clothed in white, benevolent beings who welcome them, full of unconditional love, who say, "It's not your time. You have more to do in this world." Could we call these radiant beings angels? *Gary Schwartz* had an angel named Sophia present herself to him. Are miracles just things that don't fit the scientific paradigm?* Yes, I believe that is the case. Maybe we should reconsider our current materialist paradigm and expand it or make allowances for these things that clearly appear to happen and often have many witnesses, though according to a materialist theory they appear to be impossible.

You suggest that the scientific method disparages first-person experiences because everything has to be objective and observable by a third person. Do you see any changes? In the past, the materialists have only wanted to accept data from what I call third person, or objective research, including the collection of physiological variables such as EEGs. The following are examples of the third vs. first-person perspectives and their complementary contributions. Traditional medicine minimizes the approach to the first-person perspective. Even asking patients to rate their level of pain on a 1-10 scale is a new phenomenon although it's now legally required as the standard of care in US hospitals. Why is this only recently added to standard care? Because clinicians are trained to discount subjective experience. In 2000, new legislation changed this. A scientist named Myra Christopher notes that there had been growing recognition that pain was being vastly under-treated and not taken seriously. The attitude had long been "Just suck it up, deal with it," even after surgery. The bottom line is that when you go to a doctor and tell him or her about a symptom you are having, they tend to downplay it and want to do tests. Why? Because tests show "signs" of the possible illness from a third-person scientific perspective and are objective data rather than subjective experience.

Here is an example. My friend's husband had prostate issues; his symptoms were that he was not urinating normally. His doctor did a PSA test and there was no heightened PSA count. He said everything is fine and the husband had to fight to get a biopsy. And when they did the biopsy, they found prostate cancer that was not revealed by the PSA count. He had surgery early and the cancer has not returned. This is not that uncommon.

In an NDE we actually have objective physiological data that the heart has stopped along with a flat EEG, indicating no cortical brain activity. And many individuals perceived what was going on in the operating room from above their bed during their NDE and cardiac arrest. We reconcile the two perspectives by recognizing that both are valid. It is important to include both these perspectives: it provides checks and balances and cross validation in our research. The first-person evidence by itself isn't enough and third-person evidence by itself isn't enough but combined they are really powerful. My challenge to the scientific community is to include both perspectives.

It's like those hundreds of accounts of children with birthmarks or phobias that replicated their death experience or remembered past lives. Yes, the memories of the child and the child's birthmarks were wedded with third-person research that Ian Stevenson and his colleagues did, using the autopsy report after the reported previous person's death to show the injuries resulting in death were similar to the child's birthmarks.

We'd better define consciousness. I would define consciousness basically from the metaphysical perspective—the William James perspective—as an infinite awareness contracting down to our own individual awareness and that of all human beings, animals, and perhaps all things. There would be levels of awareness from very coarse, associated with non-living things, through complex self-awareness associated with higher animals. Under normal conditions, we experience infinite consciousness from a very small point of view. In a mystical experience, the filters of our brain are reduced and we begin to see consciousness from a broader perspective. Through a semipermeable membrane, we can catch glimpses of the future, the past, other people's thoughts, etc.

It's interesting that in some of the NDEs the person's pet greets them so it looks like animals retain their personalities after they transition to the other side. I think that that's a wonderful thing. When I was a young neuroscientist I thought my pets were little machines with tiny brains and I limited my interaction with them because of this limited perspective I had. Now I see them as embodied spirits that may have the ability to communicate in ways other than my neuroscientist perspective would think. *This resonates with Rupert Sheldrake's studies of the dogs that knew when their people were coming home even though it wasn't at a regular time, so they were good ESP practitioners.*

In terms of consciousness, you've looked at Kashmir Shaivism, the Shiva Sutras. What particular insights did you get? The Shiva Sutras and their commentaries were written in the 10th to 12th century but the way they describe consciousness sounds very much like what we are now beginning to learn about it from modern scientific studies. One of the texts that I love is the Heart of Recognition, the *Pratyabijnahrdayam.* One of the verses says that consciousness out of its own freedom is the source and the power of everything. And the first sutra of a second text, the *Shiva Sutras* states, *chaitanyam atma;* your highest self is truly consciousness. This idea relates to what we discussed about the brain as a filter.

In Kashmir Shaivism you practice the sadhana of Shiva to become Shiva. You practice the spiritual practices of the absolute infinite consciousness to become that infinite consciousness, to reduce or eliminate the limiting mental filters you carry with you in your day to day life. Practicing that unity awareness with the aim to live it more fully is a source of great joy for me. *The theme from most traditions is consciousness separates but the goal is to come back to unity.* Exactly.

I'm interested in courses in consciousness studies, paranormal, parapsychology, and transpersonal psychology. Did you teach one at the University of Oregon? When I taught a yearly course in alternative and complementary medicine, I brought an expanded understanding of consciousness and its possible beneficial effects on the mind and body into the course topics as I taught senior pre-med majors. After writing two papers on two different modalities of complementary medicine (for example acupuncture, meditation, or energy healing), a number of the students decided to change their career focus to go into naturopathic medicine or osteopathic medicine or something that allows them to use traditional medicine and complementary forms side by side because they saw that was a better way of healing.

Is it still being taught? No, I was one of the few in my department who focused on both sides of health. Two universities that are more open to studying these topics are Emory University and Brown University; they have a Contemplative Studies program with neuroscientists and instructors from Religious Studies or Asian Studies in dialogue. *It seems like more med schools are offering holistic programs.* I was fascinated when I showed my students that if you simply type in Harvard University Medical School, or Stanford or Yale, you'll find they're teaching or offering clinical care in acupuncture, energy healing, etc.

Do you have another book in process? I'm thinking that it will be on what Bruce Greyson would call the bioenergy that drives human evolution. It's the energy awakened during an NDE, a spiritual experience, or a Kundalini awakening.

Are you optimistic or pessimistic in the face of what we're seeing now of climate change, the autocrats increasing around the world, growing inequality, etc.? I feel reasonably optimistic because we see more researchers moving from a strict materialist perspective to being interested in spirituality and also more interest in spirituality from the lay public. I heard a lecture by Steven Pinker, who was at Harvard University and MIT, proving that if you look at violence for the last 2,000 years, you can see that violence is gradually reducing. We're living in a much less violent culture now than we were 200-500,000 years ago, although our news media basically reports violence.

What do you do for fun? I play the oboe. My husband and I walk in nature: For me, nature and divinity go hand in hand. My heart is uplifted and expanded every time I walk in nature. Also, I find spiritual practices enjoyable. I find singing spiritually-oriented chants enjoyable and spending time with other spiritually curious people. I laugh that most of my friends right now are intrigued by spiritual phenomena and expanding their consciousness and that makes me feel very uplifted.

Books
Infinite Awareness: The Awakening of a Scientific Mind, 2015
Motor Control: Translating Research into Clinical Practice. 5th Edition, 2016.
Is Consciousness Primary? G. Schwartz & M. Woollacott, eds., 2019

SECTION 4 HEALING WITH HELPFUL BEINGS

ROBERT ALCORN, M.D.
MY JOURNEY FROM MAINSTREAM
PSYCHIATRY TOWARD SPIRITUAL
HEALING

Photo by Jessica Alcorn, DVM

Questions to Ponder

Dr. Alcorn doesn't believe brain chemistry is the cause of mental illness. What four factors may cause it?

What's the impact of childhood developmental trauma?

What healing techniques help with PTSD?

How does Dr. Alcorn remove intrusive entities?

I was born in 1944 in Cleveland, Ohio, a Libra, the second of three siblings. *Do you feel like a Midwesterner?* I am a dyed-in-the-wool Northern Ohioan. Except for college and my internship, I've lived in the Cleveland Area. Now, I live south of there. I spent four years in New Haven, Connecticut at Yale University getting an under-graduate degree, and I did my medical training in Cleveland, while Berkeley was where I had the internship. I am kind of an oddball because I didn't like California, because I think people are having too much fun.

What's your Myers-Briggs or Enneagram types? I'm an INTJ. My wife, Barbara Stone,* claims we both are Two on the Enneagram, the caregiver, helper type. When I tried to look at the Enneagram, it seems like I have some of each. I spend a lot of my time trying to do things the right way and at the same time struggling against doing it the right way because the right way was wrong. *Is that in terms of medical school?* You name it. Psychiatry was not like other branches in medicine in many ways, but that's kind of where I live, still struggling after 45 years of it. *That makes life interesting, right?* There's never a dull moment.

What was there about your family background that got you into Yale and med school? I had a really good family and my parents were very loving and supportive. They were a little alarmed by me, but they let me be who I am as far as they could stand it. I was raised in what was then called the Congregational Church and is now United Church of Christ. I was quite devoted to that as a teenager, but there were some ripples that caused some difficulty. One was that I become aware of the famous book, *Autobiography of a Yogi* by Paramahansa Yogananda. I got so excited to learn all these wonderful spiritual things happening in India while nobody in my church ever talked about that, and I had been shut up about it. One day I was delivering the newspaper at the parish house and the minister's wife came running out and said, "Bob, I hear you've left the church." I said, "What? I just read a book, that's all." My mother talked about this with her prayer group at the church because she was worried about it, but my parents never got after me about it.

My father once said to me that he was worried about me because I think about things that are so deep and he never knew anybody who thought about those things who was happy. As to how I got to Yale, I used to be really smart until I got old. The guidance counselor in high school said, "You need to be going to the Ivy League." So my dad took me on trip and we interviewed at Princeton, Yale, and Harvard. I liked Yale the best. I won a National Merit Scholarship and Yale sent me a telegram that said, "Congratulations, your admission is assured." Then I found out I wasn't the smartest guy there.

Why did you decide on med school? I wanted to be a writer but I realized that I didn't have a broad enough life experience to write anything interesting and I was really afraid of having a broad interest in things. I didn't want to be an exchange student, for example, because I was afraid to go live in another country. One day I thought if I become a doctor, then I can do wonderful things. Then I found that medical school is where you learn 5,000 new words. You learn fancy terms, like if somebody comes to you with a skin rash then you say you have rosacea; if you give it a Greek-derived name, it sounds like you know something. There is a lot of pretending you know a lot because you have a different language, but there is a lot of great learning involved in it also. It's just very limited because the Flexner Report came out in 1910 and criticized the practice of medicine as unscientific. So everything had to become scientific, which meant we had to throw out any concept of vital energy, which seemed like some kind of weird philosophy to the scientists, along with anything having to do with electricity or magnetism.

For decades, if you had an interest in bio-energy or the magnetic field around the human body or electrical phenomena other than the electrocardiogram and EEG, you were considered to be doing something really crazy. Robert Becker wrote a nice book about that titled *The Body Electric*. He was an orthopedic surgeon who studied how bones know how to heal. He experimented on salamanders because he would cut off a limb and it would grow back. He was trying to figure out how the limb knew how to grow back. He found there was an electrical potential he called the "current of injury." If you distort that current of injury, the limb will grow back at right angles to where it's supposed to be. He was regularly denied research funds because he was doing research that had to do with electricity and the body. He was very bitter about that. Anytime there is an innovation in medicine, at first, the person is ridiculed and then the idea gets accepted and then it becomes the given reality and everybody forgets who came up with it. *Or takes credit for it.*

You said when you were in a residency that a mental patient had "intrusions" and a supervisor told you, "Oh no, we don't think like that." This was in the early '70s in my residency at University Hospital in Cleveland. A young man who had a first psychiatric admission was talking about witchcraft and experiences while the bed was shaking as he was in it. He could see spirits flying around the room and he thought he had been cursed. I got very excited about this as it sounded really interesting. My supervisor said, "I thought you had yourself more together than that," so I learned painfully you don't inquire about things that are generally accepted in non-industrial cultures because our Western attitude is anything that doesn't come from our way of seeing things is superstitious or childish. I learned to keep my mouth shut about that and struggled to find ways to make sense of some of these kinds of experiences.

When I was working with homeless people in Cleveland, I was trying to convince a patient that he should take his pills but he said, "Doc, you don't understand. It's a spiritual war. There is a war in heaven. That's what it's all about." I thought that was a classic symptom of schizophrenia and he really needed meds, but maybe he knew something that the rest of us are not aware of. *Have you had experiences of patients who were classified as schizophrenic and then you helped them clear out the intrusions, the negative entities, and they regained sanity?* Yes, I did a workshop at the Canadian Energy Psychology conference in 2017 called "A Psychiatrist Takes a Shamanic Look at the DSM-5," the Diagnostic and Statistical Manual of the American Psychiatric Association. *The Bible.* I talked about my most wonderful triumph ever.

A young woman in her early 20s was brought to me by her father. She was in treatment with a nurse practitioner. You are supposed to have one thing wrong with you and the rest are ancillary, so when she was diagnosed as bipolar, schizoaffective, panic disorder, bulimia, eating disorder, and PTSD, it started to sound like there is something we are not understanding. When I started with her, she was in a prolonged state of depression and had gained over 150 pounds, right around 300 pounds. She was very lethargic, very inactive, and on six medications. She'd had a number of psychiatric admissions, with some cutting and some suicidal thinking. Her father found me somehow and thought we need another look.

I saw her four or five times and the story that is relevant here is that in her late teens, she started experiencing the presence of a male who wanted to be her boyfriend, and she fell in love with him. She realized only a few months later that nobody else could see him although it was a very real experience for her. He became a negative presence, more demeaning, talking about how ugly she was and stupid, so she ought to kill herself. It is not an unusual kind of story for people experiencing otherworldly kinds of entities. They start out looking friendly and positive and then they turn sour.

She slipped into what others would call a psychosis; she developed an eating disorder and had severe mood swings. In the first session, I did a shamanic kind of an intervention to create sacred space, connecting with helping spirits like guides and angels. We brought this questionable fellow into the space with the aid of Archangel Michael, and he turned out to be a dark force entity, as William Baldwin calls them. (He was one of the giants of this field of spirit removal and the author of *Spirit Releasement Therapy*.) I think they are best thought of as fallen angels. He owned up to what he had been doing and we were able to remove him and hand him over to Michael for redemption to be reformed and give up his dark ways and become an angel again.

Did she speak for him? She was translating what he said. She was in contact with him and I had some perception of him myself, but I am not a profoundly gifted psychic and not as visionary as many people I know. Things turned around and she wanted to start taking walks. She got up off the couch and started moving her body around. The next time I saw her, she had tended to her hair and had some makeup on. We began whittling away at some of the medicines. When her father wanted to know what I found I said he was a demon and we handed him over to the angels. The father started weeping and said, "I knew that's what it was." After four sessions, she was off all medication. She got a job as a bank teller and re-enrolled in college. She checked in with me about six months later because of anxiety, so we did another bit of spirit removal. One more session like that and she got into counseling in college to deal with sort of ordinary psychological issues, but there were no paranormal issues after our four or five sessions.

There are many other cases where it hasn't gone as smoothly. Very often there are layers and layers of intrusion, depending on how long it's been going on. When somebody comes to me at the age of 40 and says, "I've had schizophrenia since I was 18," it is likely they have more than one demon in them since they can bury themselves and hide very deeply. What I am doing is not exorcism: In the training I had in the shamanic world, we call it "compassionate depossession," the term coined by my teacher Betsy Bergstrom in Seattle. She insisted we should not refer to these things as entities but as "suffering beings." Even the nastiest thing attacking one of my clients is a "suffering being" that needs my help maybe more than the client does.

It's a very different attitude if we take the classic Christian view of entities as from the devil so you smack them over the head with the Bible and sprinkle holy water on them and chase them away. No thought is given to where they go. We try to make a difference for the spiritual being who is acting in a nasty way towards the client so they can do something more productive.

What have been the most difficult challenges in your life and how did you cope with them? The first most difficult was when I was three years old and nearly died. I don't remember any of it but it clearly was a very important event. Working with healers who have tried to help me, they sometimes reference this event as having had a profound influence. In understanding shamanic phenomena, there's often the concept of a shamanic illness or shamanic challenge which creates the shaman, so I think that was true for me. I was very sickly and skinny as a child so I got bullied some. I couldn't be on the football team and be a star so I was the trainer. I taped the athletes' ankles instead of playing myself.

The best thing that happened was at age four, I was standing in the living room looking at this piano my parents had bought so my older sister could take piano lessons, and I was marveling at this thing, that seemed wonderful. I saw a horse with wings standing in front of the piano—*Pegasus.* He was glowing white, a luminous being. I felt a lot of love coming from him toward me like he had come to do something for me and I couldn't figure out what. I got excited and I ran into the kitchen and said, "Mommy, why is there a white horse in the living room?" She looked very alarmed and said, "There is no white horse in the living room. It's your imagination." I learned not to have that kind of experience because it would upset my mother and it took a long time for me to even remember that it happened. When I was a teenager, there were a bunch of us who were spiritually minded at the church and we would meet together to pray and meditate. It was upsetting to the youth minister because we didn't go to the dance and we didn't do the youth activities that he was running; we were doing our own thing, which was highly devotional and very Christian. One of my friends told me that the youth minister said: "You know the trouble with Bob? He doesn't want to take anything on faith. He wants to experience God directly." I thought, "Well, what's wrong with that?

When I was 16, I had a profoundly dramatic dream. When I woke up I found that I was lying in bed with my whole body on fire inside. *A kundalini experience?* I don't know what kundalini is so I don't know, maybe. It didn't go rushing from my coccyx up to my brain, it was just there in my bones, and I was terrified and fascinated at the same time. I was so afraid that I prayed to Jesus to make it stop and it did. Recently my wife and I looked into it together and found that it was intended as an initiation experience by my healing and guidance team, but they aborted the process because I was too frightened. Thirty years later I sort of prayed to my guidance team and said, "I am sorry that I stopped you, but let's do it a little more gradually." So that's what's been happening little bits at a time. *How did you and Barbara figure that out? Did you use muscle testing?* We created sacred space and she did a hypnotic procedure with me and then we both compared what we were seeing and it seemed to correspond. She was self-testing with her own finger.

What about other challenges? I've had a lot of difficult experiences but compared to my patients, I've had nothing. I've had a very smooth life. *What about getting divorced?* I am on my third wife so you can imagine there were some bumpy spots. I have three wonderful children with two different women. Barbara and I found each other six years ago so better late than never. *Sometimes we have to go through steps to get to a good marriage.* If I had met Barbara 20 years ago, I would have brushed her off as too wacky for me. It's difficult to move from medical school and psychiatric residency to talking to spirits and understanding the reality of an invisible world to an ordinary state of consciousness. It doesn't fit with the medical or psychiatric training I've had.

I'll give you a little example of what doesn't fit. There is a famous psychiatrist named Bessel van der Kolk who studied trauma for many years and wrote many publications about it. I went to a workshop he taught three or four years ago in which he proposed a new diagnosis to the DSM people called Developmental Trauma Syndrome. He said it's related to PTSD, but it's different if it happens to you before age seven. For the last 15 years, I've been working in a public mental health center. I became "woke" to the presence of sexual assault in so many women who see psychiatrists and how few of these women come into the office saying, "I have a history of being sexually assaulted and I need help with that." Rather, they say, "I am depressed or I have rages or I have panic attacks. I have these strange experiences where I can't remember what I was doing for two hours." They get treated for everything else except their traumatic history while they are dissociating and panicking because of the disruption to their autonomic nervous system caused by those life-threatening events.

When this happens before the age of seven, it's a different phenomenon because the trauma is probably parentally inflicted, which is different than if you were in combat and the bad guys are shooting at you. He proposed this to the DSM committee with 100,000 cases. The committee said we need data about the genetics and the neurotransmitter aspects of this syndrome. We need 20,000 cases and they gave him 30 days to do it. His team brought together 20,000 cases addressing these issues but the committee said we don't think it presented something that is separable from other diagnoses.

The main thing I took from it is that the adult expression of childhood developmental trauma includes everything else in the diagnostic manual and all the other diagnoses come out of that. If you accept that fact, you have to throw out the DSM and start over from a scratch. But they didn't want to throw away 150 years of diagnoses based on description of behavioral patterns for something that recognizes the enormous extent of abuse of children and sexual trauma that pervades our culture. This is not in the realm of the paranormal or spiritual but it shows how difficult it is to move the institutions that have been in place for so long.

We're talking about a paradigm shift, the greatest revolution in science since Copernicus. That shift from materialism to idealism upsets people. I'll give you another example, which gets a little closer to the spiritual side. There was a study done in Camp Pendleton, the Marine Corps Camp in California, published in September 2013 in *Military Medicine,* about the treatment of PTSD studying the effects of Healing Touch and Guided Imagery. The control group was treatment as usual—seeing a psychiatrist, getting put on medicine, and talking with a therapist. The result of the study was that nobody got better in the control group. They measured PTSD on a scale based on a questionnaire and nobody in the control group improved enough to be statistically significant. Total symptoms only went down from 56 to 52 on the questionnaire. The vets in the group where healers put their hands on you and suggested imagining things that sound like a shamanic journey went from 56 to under 40, which was below the threshold for PTSD. About 80% of these 19-year-old leathernecks lying on a couch imagining spirit guides around them no longer had PTSD after six treatments of two-hour sessions!

Why isn't that used everywhere when it was so helpful? When I asked my friend who works at Camp Pendleton as a therapist, how are they treating PTSD after these results, he said the same as usual; the vets see a psychiatrist and psychotherapist. *The EFT people have been doing work with vets with PTSD with good effect and I think EMDR as well.* I use tapping a great deal. The first thing I learned was EFT and since I met Barbara I've learned more sophisticated ways of tapping since EFT is a sort of "one size fits all." *Roger Callahan's Thought Field Therapy algorithms varied according to the problem.* It is more like the Callahan approach and I don't use EMDR particularly. Van der Kolk thinks EMDR is great but doesn't seem to know about tapping. He shows slides in his presentation that claim EMDR is four times more effective than Cognitive Behavioral Therapy. CBT is the gold standard now generally speaking but it doesn't work on PTSD.

In CBT we talk it through, we understand why we feel like this. It looks for cognitive distortions and changing patterns of thought, but PTSD is deeply embedded in the autonomic nervous system, which doesn't speak English. It's like when you are having a panic attack and you try to talk yourself out of it. How does that work? It doesn't. A cartoon shows two pictures; the first one is a man talking to his dog saying "Fido, it's not a good idea for you to pee on the rug and I really want you to go outside. You understand that Fido?" The second frame is what the dog hears "Blah, blah, blah, blah, blah Fido." That's like our autonomic nervous system, which is where tapping works because it changes energy flows in the meridians that get into the brain in a way that the brain understands. I tell my patients your sympathetic nervous system doesn't speak English, it speaks Chinese, so I am going to show you how to speak Chinese to your brain. I had a woman who was an army veteran who had some trauma. She was sitting there in my office sweating profusely to the point where the chair became a puddle. We did some tapping and she immediately stopped sweating. She could control her symptoms from one visit.

Do you think tapping works because of its effect on the acupressure points and meridians, or it's a form of self-hypnosis, a Piezoelectric effect on the bone, or do you have other explanations for why tapping works? This reminds me of a conversation I had with my ex-father-in-law, a physician. He considered himself to be open-minded and spiritual, so he told me how he thinks acupuncture works, having to do with phenomena in the thalamus. I asked him, "Why do you try to think that way about acupuncture, which the Chinese have been doing for 6,000 years, and don't consider what they say about why it works?" He didn't want to think about that because he doesn't believe there are meridians. Well, actually there are. They've been demonstrated now in electron microscopy. It's an explosive understanding to think there really are channels for the flow of information within the connective tissue channels.

The connective tissue is a semiconductor, an information system. I don't think it's self-hypnosis or placebo effect. It's very specific because the studies report you have to tap on the right places. One aspect of EFT that isn't about meridians is called a heart massage. With the right hand, you go clockwise around the center of the chest. That's where the heart chakra is and you are making it rotate clockwise because the energy in your hand entrains the energy of the chakra. When you are screwed up, it's going backwards, so you start by making it go in the right direction. *They have pictures of the meridians. I've seen them when I've had pictures taken of my body by Harry Oldfield.* The BioField Viewer, which I have, was created by Thornton Streeter. It's a way of deciphering photons emitted from the body. In some of those views, there are organizations of shapes of colors around what look like chakras.

Why did you start studying with Rosalyn Bruyere and Sandra Ingerman? When I was in med school, I realized that it was not going to give me true wisdom. I began looking around where could I find something that's more spiritual. I went to a retreat center with my teenaged friends back in the day where they talked about George Ivanovich Gurdjieff and P.D. Ouspensky. I found a book by Gurdjieff that a friend of mine was reading at the same time. We found out there are Gurdjieff groups all over the world. I was involved in a secret organization for many years studying the methods of Gurdjieff, including sacred dance and meditation. After 25 years, I began to realize I wasn't getting the answers I thought I was going to get, but it took me another 10 years to say that's enough.

One of the things that I started doing before I left them was writing down my dreams. I ran across a book titled *Conscious Dreaming* by Robert Moss; it's a wonderful book. They were studying the lucid dreams in indigenous peoples describing how the aboriginals in Australia say the dream time is reality and the rest of it is imagination. As I was writing down dreams they became more frequent, more detailed, and more lengthy. I had a dream where I was all alone in the world walking around Cleveland. I saw a billboard with three words on it: "Move, move, move." In the dream, I said, "What am I supposed to do?" I found myself following an older woman, who was a bit on the heavy side, down into the basement of a house and through a secret passage into another house, up the stairway into the kitchen, where she started teaching me how to cook.

I woke up and I wrote down the dream. In the morning, I cast about on the internet looking for who could this woman be. I saw Rosalyn's website and she looked like the woman in the dream, so I signed up for her workshop. Two months later, I went to Arizona in 1999. I never had any experience of hands-on healing work, which is what she does. They had tables for doing healing work and when they were finished, the man who seemed to be leading that group said: "OK, I think she is cooked." I did not make the connection until I went home and told my wife about it. I told her and then it dawned on me, "Oh my God, I went there to learn how to cook." Now when I tell that story, I get the chills.

Two years later I had a phone reading with a psychic who my second wife recommended. She told me that I am a healer and should be putting my hands on people. I thought that was crazy: Psychiatrists don't touch their patients, how can I do that? She was surprised that big guides came to talk to her about me—St. Germain and Archangel Michael. I tried putting my hands on people and it seemed to work sometimes. Rosalyn has some senior pupils who live in the Cleveland area and I started studying with a couple of them. I went to Rosalyn's workshops for about four years and studied with the others in Cleveland for a little longer than that until I got frustrated because other people in the classes seemed to be more psychic than I was. They could hear their guides talking to them and see them.

Then I found out about the Foundation for Shamanic Studies (FSS). *With Sandra Ingerman?* She was but she split with them. This is Michael Harner's outfit. *In Marin County in the San Francisco Bay Area.* I took their basic workshop to learn how to do shamanic journeying. I needed some individual tutelage from the teacher over lunch, because I wasn't getting it, me and another guy. Then I got it and I started being able to do that. I had a journey during that two-day workshop that foreshadowed something that was going to happen a month later, with a dramatic connection with the Gurdjieff work. The journey showed a great wind in a forest picked me up along with all the other animals and trees and dropped them in another place. To me, that was a metaphor for we were going to change something in a big way.

In 2004, there was a meeting of the board of the Gurdjieff work in Ohio that made it impossible for my wife and me to continue to be board members. It freed me any feeling of obligation to continue and allowed me to pursue other things. After learning the basics of shamanic journeying, I took another of the basic courses from a different teacher from FSS. I took one about how to extract negative energies from people and thought the next step would be soul retrieval—that's where I went to Sandra Ingerman's five-day intensive with a group of 55 people, but just a handful of men and two doctors. One of the men told me, "You really need to learn depossession. You've probably seen a lot of people who were possessed." I told him that in 30 years of practice, I had never seen a single case but I bore in mind the advice of Alcoholics Anonymous that if two or three people tell you the same thing, you probably ought to listen. So I did, and Sandra said to the whole group: if you want to learn depossession, go study with Betsy Bergstrom.

I studied with Betsy for a couple of years: curse unraveling, depossession, mediumship, and a two-year program called Middle World Shamanism. *This is the middle world, where we are now?* Yes, it's about the hidden aspects of the world we are in. The Foundation for Shamanic Studies teaches journeying to the lower world which is where you meet power animals and other helping spirits and the upper world where you meet angels, teachers, and Guides. Harner was quite against teaching middle world stuff, although the native people in the Amazon Valley where he got started with all this did it all the time, mostly in the form of dirty tricks. I believe that Harner was afraid to teach it because he didn't want people to learn how to harm each other and he didn't want to have to clean up the mess. Betsy teaches how to fix all of that. I felt really safe working with her although it was kind of scary doing all this stuff. I went to Rosalyn's five-day workshop on mediumship and I was too frightened really to learn how to do it. The idea of talking to ghosts is terrifying to me, maybe because of what happened when I was three years old when some dark spirits were involved.

During Betsy's first dispossession class, I discovered that I had a spirit in me who had entered me in 1966 when I was in Italy in the Uffizi Gallery in Florence looking at paintings as I had an interest in art history. I was alone in that gallery when somebody attacked me from behind and I had a panic attack. *This was a disembodied someone, right?* It felt like someone attacked me from behind so I had to leave the museum to get air outside. I forgot about it until 41 years later in 2007 when, in Betsy's class, I kept being drawn to thinking about the experience. On the second day, I realized this guy who was in me was listening to the same talks and he had figured out what happened to him and he wanted out. I started to feel his head sort of over to the side of me.

We were in groups of three and this poor woman who was a cook was supposed to depossess me and she froze up because she couldn't imagine she could work on the psychiatrist. Somebody else did it, but it was really very simple. You go into a trance state and you dissociate from the "other" and it becomes more clear who is he and who is me and we could interview him. They interviewed him and I said what he was telling me. We got his name and that he was a British college student who had gone to Florence on holiday and jumped off a building to kill himself because he was in despair. When he went to the world of light, they told me you can't go with him, you have to stay here, and it does seem very attractive up there. I stopped being depressed because he took his despair with him. *You'd been mildly depressed for 40 years?* Yes. They cured it in 20 minutes. I thought there are probably a lot of people who were carrying around somebody they don't even know about. I started trying to do it on anybody who would hold still.

I was amazed that I had been studying with Rosalyn and other people in her lineage who could see into the body but none talked about spirit attachments and possession. None of them who had done healing with me had said, "There is another guy in here.

We've got to do something about that." Maybe they are really good at hiding. When I do this work a common issue is the spirit that's attached to somebody is very deeply in their energy system and trying not to be discovered because the astral plane is a scary place for them. *You and Barbara work with disembodied humans who've passed over but haven't made the transition, as well as the djinn and fallen angels. What entities don't have a human history?* There are four or five basic categories including earth-bound spirits—dead people who haven't crossed into light and dark force entities that are fallen angels or "dark brothers" who are angelic in their nature but have fallen into slavery to the darkness.

The djinn are elemental spirits. They are from the Earth and are different from demons or dark force entities. They live in the earth and they are very powerful; they live a long time, are very wise, very intelligent, and hate us. *Because we are destroying their environment?* Yes, they were here first, and then humans came, and some humans enslaved the djinn. King Solomon, for example, knew a magic way of ensnaring the djinn to make them do what he wanted. They could do magic and still can. It is said when he had them build the Temple of Jerusalem, he was concerned that if he released the ones he had ensnared, that they would come after him. So it says in *The Lesser Key of Solomon* that he sealed the demons up in jars and threw them in the Red Sea. This is the origin of the legend of rubbing a magic lamp and out comes a genie (the English word for them). They are elemental beings. If you rub the lamp and then you get three wishes, the third wish usually ends up screwing you over.

When I think of elementals, I think fire, air, and water spirits and being helpful as a positive part of the whole cycle of life. The djinn are fire elementals. The Quran states that Allah created them from smokeless fire so they are generally considered to be the fire element. When I told this to a physicist who is spiritually inclined, he said, "You mean plasma, the fourth state of matter." He thought maybe that's the state where they live in a sort of a parallel dimension with us. The word *djinn* means the hidden ones; you can't see them unless you are in a very altered state or unless they want to be seen. They can appear if they want to; they can shapeshift into human form and dog form and so on. The elementals are not necessarily friendly; they are not necessarily unfriendly.

Are fairies, elves, and gnomes something different? Some people think that fairies are djinn. Rosemary Ellen Guiley, for example, wrote about the djinn in books like *Guide to Psychic Protection*. She finds a lot of parallels between stories about the fairies and the djinn. Maybe the legends from the British Isles were really talking about the djinn. In my wife Barbara's house we had a fun experience. She said that many times when she comes back from her travels she will find her laminator machine turned on. I thought it sounds like a poltergeist phenomenon, so let's investigate this. We had learned how to work together and so we created sacred space where she is the medium and I am the questioner. I ask Archangel Michael to bring us the spirit was who turned on the laminator. An earth-bound man, age 61, who died, said he wanted some help and was trying to get our attention. He didn't know what to do and we seemed to know about these things.

My usual interview with these spirits is how did you die and why did you get stuck here? Why you didn't go to the light? I like to know who these people are. It occurred to me, how did he know how to turn on the laminator? If you remember the movie *Ghost*, one of the funny things is there is a dead guy who has to learn how to move physical objects although it's hard to do when you don't have a body. The earthbound spirit we were talking with said the leprechaun told me. So I asked Archangel Michael to bring his leprechaun. I told him, "I am very grateful for your willingness to come and talk with us. Since I have never met a leprechaun before, could you tell me about what the leprechaun world is like?" And he said, "Read a book. I don't have time for this. Read Alice Bailey." I apologized for my ignorance and I asked him what was he angry about. He was mad because Barbara had planted a tree right on his house. We apologized and made friends with him but he still would rather be left alone.

Thinking of your patients who are diagnosed as schizophrenic or bipolar, what percentage is due to some kind of intrusion rather than a chemical brain imbalance? We are dealing with a myth here, the myth of the chemical imbalance. There is no chemical imbalance. *If I am short of serotonin* …. That's baloney; the theory that people who are depressed are short of serotonin was disproved in 1984. Any studies measuring serotonin never showed any difference between people who are depressed and people who are not and yet the myth exists that there is a deficiency of a neurotransmitter. The idea that there is some sort of scientifically proved chemical imbalance has not been proved. When I wrote my book *Healing Stories: My Journey from Mainstream Psychiatry Toward Spiritual Healing* in 2009, I looked at the American Psychiatric Association website to see what do they say about bipolar disorder and found they do not speak at all about chemical imbalance.

They do not address the issue of causation, except to say that they think it's genetic but the genetics of bipolar disorder is a very murky business as compared with other kinds of genetic disorders. In bipolar disorder, they talk about maybe 20 or more genes that are involved. The same genes can produce somebody who is a cocaine addict or has Attention Deficit Disorder. So this is not a very convincing science to say that it's genetic. It's further made murky by one of our discoveries that the djinn, in particular, can have an interest in the lineage of a family. The classic example is that you find a djinn attached to the client and the djinn has been alive for a thousand years. When you ask, it might say, "Seven generations ago, the ancestor invoked my aid because he was in love with this beautiful woman and he wanted her affections. I said I will help with that and I put a spell on her and she fell in love with him, but he wouldn't pay up. All I asked for was the first-born child."

That's a classic condensed version of how this works. Because the human reneges on the contract, the djinn thinks he has a right to take it out on all the descendants. You'll see in the history of the family, the first-born child dies young, is very ill, or insanity passes through the generations or other kinds of darkness like addictions.

If you don't believe that there are djinn who could do this sort of thing, you think it must be the genes and DNA, because it's following a family line but it isn't that. I believe that the current diagnostic system is irrelevant for understanding what really happens in mental illness.

Why is it then that someone who is psychotic and takes meds can function? The meds have an impact for many people. Sometimes it does seem they have a normal life, but if you listen carefully to the patients, they don't really like it, particularly anti-depressants. The ones we use now commonly suppress your sexual desire, sometimes they suppress all kinds of feelings, and you feel like you are a dishrag going through life, but you don't want to kill yourself anymore. Schizophrenics very quickly learn: if I tell the doctor what's really going on, they are going to increase my dose. "Yes, I still hear voices. Okay, we are going to raise your Haldol another five," and then they get more side effects, so they don't tell you. Now the situation is you get put into a psychiatric hospital, it's a scary place to be for most patients, they hate it, and they learn very quickly the best way to get out of there is to say you're better.

For nine years, I worked in a homeless center and one of the things we did was emergency evaluations for the whole county. I would see people one time to make a diagnosis, put them on the right meds, and then see them once or twice more, and then refer them to another agency for ongoing care. But in the job I've been in the last 15 years, I have patients I see for a long time, and you start to learn that it doesn't work as well as you thought it did. What we are doing with the anti-psychotic medicines is putting a damper on the whole system. The kind of agitation a spirit can cause to a person, a dark spirit in particular, seems to come under better control in many cases because the whole brain has been ratcheted down like you turn down the volume in a stereo system. But the voices don't go away, they just become a mumble.

A useful book by Shakuntala Modi is titled *Remarkable Healings*. She is a psychiatrist who practices in West Virginia and described 100 cases of spirit attachment. She holds the view that mental illness is caused by five things: First, traumatic events in this life-time, which is becoming more generally accepted as one of the par-adigm shifts. Second is traumatic events in the past life, which will take a while before that becomes generally accepted, as described by Brian Weiss in *Many Lives, Many Masters* and Barbara Stone* in *Invisible Roots*. Third is spirit attachment by dead people, earth-bound spirits. Fourth is spirit attachment by other things—in her case, mostly demons. (Dr. Modi doesn't know about the djinn and she didn't want to hear about it when we tried to talk to her.) Fourth is karma but I don't know if I agree with her. We see lineage issues where you are getting patterns from your ancestors, not from your own past lives, so that's another fork in the road that's possible. We have earth-bound spirits, we have dark force entities, we have djinn. There are some dead animals now and then I see when I run into earth-bound animals. One was a large cat who was shot by hunters in Africa and he got stuck here because he was angry. He somehow ended up attached to a woman in Ohio.

And then there are extraterrestrials (ETs) If we start talking about them, we'll be getting about as far into the woo-woo as I know how to do. I am clearly insane if I talk about that, according to my colleagues, except that John Mack wrote a book about aliens titled *Abduction* while he was a psychiatrist on the faculty at Harvard. More information is coming out about the presence of ETs in our life, like a book by Lt. Col. Philip Corso titled *The Day after Roswell*. He was put in charge of artifacts collected from the craft that crashed in Roswell. He had them in his office in the Pentagon and had to figure out what to do with them. Some of these artifacts led to new technologies such as night-vision goggles, fiber optics, and computer chips. The ETs had things like computer chips in their craft in 1947. Corso was under a non-disclosure agreement which expired after 50 years, so the book came out 50 years after Roswell.

We were turned on to this book by listening to Paul Hellyer who was a former Canadian Minister of Defense. He was skeptical at first until he read Corso's book. In Barbara Stone's work, she discov-ered implants in her clients, mostly energetic rather than physical implants, put there by ETs for a variety of purposes. *To monitor, to observe?* Some scientific, some to help, some to disrupt us. In any case, they are always detrimental to people because when we put something into our energy system, it's going to screw it up. Barbara has devised some ways of removing and disabling them.

This has led us to try to figure out what's going on with these various ET civilizations; it seems that there are many different ones with an interest in planet earth. I read that there are 40 different galactic civilizations who have bases on the moon. *There are different dimensions, is that why we don't see them?* On the dark side of the moon, they can't be seen, and they are underground. There has been direct contact between the government and some of these groups, according to reports I have read. I have no way to verify them.

One of the implications, when you look at the world of dark force entities, is their world is very hierarchical. You find a demon attacking your client and he has a boss, and the boss has a boss, so there is a food chain there. What's happening is the one attached to the client is extracting energy from that person by causing them to be in despair or in rage or in panic as the person leaks energy. When we are like that, we are in a low-energy state, which is nourishment for the dark suffering beings. The one who is doing the dirty work is attached to my client and pulls all this energy out but has to give most of it to its boss, and so on.

At a certain point, you are dealing with what we call an archdemon, but they never see one they have to answer to. Barbara discovered that the boss of the archdemon is usually a reptilian being from another galaxy and another constellation, wherever Draco is. They came here long ago before we were created so they consider this planet theirs and are very powerful, very intelligent, very psychic. Reptilians are kind of intergalactic bandits who have traveled around the universe conquering civilizations and plundering, using their skills and their technology to make themselves and their DNA faster, stronger, and smarter than anything else. They use the fallen angels to do their work, to get the energy they need to live on. They consider humanity as a food source. *They are like psychopaths without guilt or conscience.* Right, it may be some of them had a soul but they seem to have lost them.

This is one thing they can't figure out, is how can we get the soul? They are trying to suck everything out to see if they can get the soul. They steal souls but don't know what to do with them then, but then you are missing a piece of yourself. They are really a very special problem for the shamanic practitioner. We can talk to the archdemons. After being reminded that they are angels, Archangel Michael can talk to them as a brother to brother. They are quite willing to reform if they can be convinced it is safe to do so. I have been advised by high spiritual beings, don't try to talk to the reptilians, leave it to us. We call the Ascended Master, Sanat Kumara to deal with them, as he has at his disposal the Arcturian Civilization, who know how to do this. They will mobilize the reptilians and attach a beam of divine love, then host them up under their mothership but it takes a long time to reform them. I was told that it will take 1000 years, while I can reform an archdemon in 20 minutes. There is a very interesting description of a reptilian in material provided by Corey Goode, a whistleblower who claims to have been in the Secret Space Program and has videos on YouTube.[1] Michael Salla, Ph.D., wrote two books on the US Navy Secret Space Program.[2] Goode tells about going into a barn with an elevator that goes down into the earth, many layers. They descend down into this underground cavern with this fully-armed contingent of Marines and they meet a reptilian, dragon-like creature who is about 14 feet tall with such a menace about his presence that the Marines are shaking in their boots. The reptilian has yellow eyes with vertical pupils like a snake and the pupils start to vibrate back and forth as he does a psychic scan of Corey Goode's soul. Goode was there as an empath for the Secret Space Program.

He also talks about a galactic council that meets in a special place somewhere between Jupiter and Saturn, in a space-time warp. He was assigned to go there for this meeting of the council to read the participants psychically for whoever he was working for at that time. There were two humans and all these other people, just like *Star Trek*. The Intergalactic Federation of Planets is having a meeting where the next item on the agenda is a Royal Dragon reptilian, a very high ranking being who comes with his retinue of reptilians, insectoids, and grays. He said very angrily, "You are wrong to allow this quarantine you've put around the earth and the solar system that prevents us from coming and going freely as we have a right to do." Apparently, this happened within the last 20 years, in that some higher dimensional beings have put us under quarantine so the reptilians who are outside the solar system can't come in and the ones that are here can't leave. He said, "I want you to know that our bosses live in another universe altogether. They are AI beings and you have never seen anything like them and they are coming to get you unless you remove the quarantine." That's where Goode leaves the story.

What I understand about the reptilians is that they have been allowed to exist, although they have a very parasitic nature. I think a lot of them exist only at a certain level of frequency and can't ascend above a certain frequency. The higher beings like the Arcturians and the angels can enter that world. What's happening now in our world is that beings of much higher dimension have entered and have started intervening with our situation here. *What evidence is there for that? We are destroying the planet. We have maybe a decade before we are at two degrees centigrade.* The quarantine is one example. Higher-dimensional beings are incarnating as humans more and more. You know about the crystal children and the rainbow children. More and more of the young people are remembering their past lives and not losing their psychic ability as I did when I was a child.

I had a patient who was discharged from a psych hospital, diagnosed with major depression with psychotic features. That means he is not schizophrenic but there was something crazy about him. So I looked in through the records and the only thing I could find that sounded a little outrageous was that he believed that his seven-year-old son was a reincarnated Tibetan Lama. I talked to this guy and found the life crisis had made him have some suicidal thoughts and got him into the hospital was that he was tired of being an insurance salesman and he wanted to become a sportscaster. This threw him into some kind of an emotional crisis and he had some fleeting suicidal thoughts. So he comes out on an anti-psychotic medicine and antidepressants.

I couldn't contain myself and I asked him, "Is there something special about your son?" and he looked very uncomfortable. He told me he, his wife, and his kid went to another family's house for a potluck dinner and on the coffee table was a big coffee table book about Tibet. It was written in Tibetan and had photographs of places in Tibet. The four-year-old walks over to this book and starts reading it and he says, "Mommy, I remember when I lived there. I remember this guy." They took him to a Tibetan Buddhist monastery in New York and introduced him to the monks who verified that he was speaking Tibetan and could read it and is a reincarnated Tibetan Lama. They took him to meet the Dalai Lama. The psychiatrist in the hospital declared him crazy for believing all that. Kids like that are being born now.

So that means you are hopeful? Whether it's going to work out or not I don't know, but higher beings say, "If you all would just ask us for help and give up trying to kill each other we could fix this ecological crisis in half an hour. We have the technology to transform matter." They could just turn plastic waste in the ocean into water or pure energy, while we have the arrogance to think we are the smartest thing around.

Do you have another book that you're thinking about or has Healing Stories *said what you wanted to say?* If I were to write a book, it would be hard hitting about the inadequacies of the current diagnostic system because it is completely blind to anything spiritual. It's much more fun giving talks and making YouTube videos and people don't read books anyway. My wife is writing a book about ETs, bless her heart.

Is there anything that you would like readers to think about? There is something very special about being human. It's one of the reasons that other civilizations are fascinated with us. We think of being human as kind of shameful. On the other hand, I went to a conference about orbs 10 years ago in Glastonbury and one of the speakers was a theologian named Micheál Ledwith. He spoke about the great spectrum of electromagnetic energy. Humans are able to vibrate at all those frequencies from the lowest to the highest; we're very unique in that way.

Ledwith spoke about the Gospel of John when Jesus was questioned by the rabbis, wanting to know if he is the Messiah. He replied, "By my works, you will know me." They replied, "Come on tell us, what's really the truth?" he said, "I do these things because the father is in me and I am in the father." And they picked up stones to stone him and Jesus said, "Why are you going to stone me?" They said, "Because you are blaspheming. You are saying you are God." And Jesus says to them, "Why would you call this blasphemy when it is in our scriptures?" in Psalm 82. In chapter 14 of John, Jesus tells the apostles, "You can do even greater things than I," so he wasn't claiming exclusive rights to magical healing. This means to me that we are all capable of having the Most High manifest through us.

In Bergstrom's teachings, one of the things we did was to connect to "our true self." Others say call it the "high self," the high consciousness. This is the main thing you have to do if you are doing this kind of dangerous healing work or you are dealing with dark entities—connect your true self to your own divinity. We are all divine in this way. I studied some Hawaiian Huna teachings that uses a prayer called *Pule o Kane*, and our teacher Larry Kessler intoned this prayer as the way of calling in your *aumakua*, the high consciousness. The Hawaiian language has many meanings for each word. You call in your higher consciousness by calling on Kane, Father God. He explained that the aumakua is that portion of the godhead that is available to you as an individual. I do this with my patients and we clear everything out to connect to their true self. Betsy taught us that in connecting to your true self, you are connecting to a power, a source of energy, a source of wisdom that is more powerful than any demon. This is very important for people to learn. It's what we have to do; if people do that enough, we will change the world.

Books and Videos

Healing Stories: My Journey from Mainstream Psychiatry Toward Spiritual Healing, 2010

https://youtu.be/SLrtNawPOtE

Endnotes

1 https://www.bing.com/videos/search?q=Corey+Goode+&&FORM=V DVVXX

2 *US Air Force Secret Space Program: Shifting Extraterrestrial Alliances & Space Force,* 2019

MITCHELL EARL GIBSON, M.D.
LEARNING ABOUT HELPFUL AND HARMFUL ENTITIES

Photo by Kathy Gibson

Questions to Ponder

What influences led Dr. Gibson to be the first person in his family to go to college?

He uses non-traditional methods to assist mentally ill clients. Describe the methods.

According to Dr. Gibson's experiences, what levels of beings exist besides humans and how do they interact with us?

I was born in August of 1959 in Pinehurst, North Carolina. I am an early Virgo. *One of your books includes astrology along with medical diagnoses. How do you think of yourself in terms of being a Virgo? You like to talk? You're sensitive? You care about people?* That's a good summary but there are still a lot of Leo traits in there. I have a big need for fashion and appearance. My moon is in Leo and my rising sign is Pisces. *That probably contributed to your sensitivity, your clairvoyant part?* That's right.

As a person who was raised in the South but went to graduate school elsewhere, do you feel like your development had regional influences? I've traveled to over 60 countries and I've spoken in at least 50 countries. My wife and I have been around the world three or four times and have personal friends all over the world. I grew up in the South but world travel changed me and educated me in a way that really nothing else—not school, not college, not medical school—educated me.

What are some examples of how you are different because you've traveled the world? I've slept in temples in Indonesia. I've met people and loved people in India. I've eaten food in the desert in Dubai. It really makes you see the world more as a home. When I turn on the TV or see a movie I can say I've been there and know people there: It makes the world feel more homey. Growing up in southern North

Carolina is a very provincial place. Most people never travel more than 100 miles from their home. When you say you're going to the Middle East, they think you're in the military. People from north of the Mason-Dixon line are still "Yankees" as in "We don't sell gas to Yankees here." That's what my father used to say. *I was in Cairo during the 2011 revolution and in Lhasa in Tibet as the Chinese were eroding the culture. I understand what you're saying about how expansive travel can be—if you avoid group travel.*

Tell me about the family that you grew up in. What did they do to encourage you to go to medical school and be such a high achiever? I am the first person in my family to go to college. Most people in my family didn't finish high school. My father went as far as the sixth grade. My mother actually finished high school, but she had no schooling after that. My grandfather went to the third grade and my grandmother did not go to school. Everybody was expected to contribute to the huge farm where I grew up. When I said that I wanted to go to college, they said, "How are you going to pay for that?" I knew that I had to get a scholarship and I was going to have to support myself through that. Family was not what I would call supportive.

Studies show that disadvantaged kids have at least one mentor who believes in them, like a teacher or a minister. Did you have someone like that? Yes, fortunately, several mentors recognized that I had this drive. I had good grades and I did a lot of IQ tests that showed I had pretty good IQ. There were a lot of people who were very supportive, including teachers, and one of my pastors. I wanted to go to the Air Force. I didn't initially want to go to college but my high school science teacher Mrs. Sarah Hamilton talked me out of going into the Air Force, God bless her.

How many siblings do you have? I had three older sisters and three brothers so I was smack dab in the middle. *Did any of your siblings go to college?* After I went, two sisters and a brother went. I broke the mold and opened the doorway for them. My two sisters quit, but my brother did finish.

What else contributed to your ambition that was fairly unique in your family? When you look at astrology, it only partially defines a person's interior or their soul. When you look at my chart, it really doesn't tell you why I am who I am and where I get this drive from. I think it comes from somewhere else because when you look at my family, I shouldn't be sitting here. *What about past-life influences?* They would explain a lot more. *Do you have a feeling about them?* When looked at my astrological birth chart, I found that it wasn't explaining me well enough, so I did an extensive search on past lives. I came up with an interesting lineage that better defines me, connected to the god Thoth, a man by the name of Imhotep, and Sivali—a follower of the Buddha. When you look at pictures of them, I look exactly like Sivali and Imhotep. *Thoth and Imhotep are Egyptians.* Thoth has an Egyptian lineage although he is a god that is recognized in a number of pantheons. Imhotep is Greek and Egyptian. Sivali is Thai and Buddhist.

Are you saying that you incarnated as those people or they influenced you in previous incarnations? I incarnated as those people. One of the first past-life memories I had was working with the Buddha and providing food for him when he was going through the forest. I later found out that Sivali was the main person who provided food for the Buddha. I knew that years before I found out who Sivali was. *Being able to help the Buddha is impressive!*

Why do you think your spirit picked being born into a poor black Southern family? I ask myself that question quite a lot. In part because there is a very strong suicide depression gene that runs in that whole area. For me to become a psychiatrist to help with that gave people a nugget of hope that they could get out of that crushing poverty and depression, to not always have to be an itinerant farmer. They saw that somebody could escape that. Even a nugget of hope is worth a lot so that's why I think the gods put me there to show that the condition where your family keeps incarnating in for hundreds and hundreds of years can be beaten. *Maybe also because you had lives of high regard and respect, your spirit wanted to experience humility and not being automatically regarded as somebody exalted.* That would certainly stick. You don't get exalted growing up like that. In my house, we didn't have running water or have electricity for years. I didn't take a shower until I went to college. *You had an outhouse and sponge baths with basins?* I helped build our three outhouses. One of them fell over during a rainstorm. It's a mess to clean up an outhouse. That's how I grew up. *That's definitely humbling.*

Where were you an undergraduate? I went to Florida A&M University in Tallahassee and medical school at North Carolina at Chapel Hill and residency at Albert Einstein Medical Center in Philadelphia. *How did you finish medical training at age 24?* I finished college in three years and worked at Proctor & Gamble for a while. I went to medical school on a governor's scholarship that allowed me to focus just on medicine. I made myself not date and just focus on studying. In my mind, I always had that sense of crushing poverty overshadowing me and said I did not want any part of that. When I looked at the people I went to high school with, most of them didn't finish and a lot of them worked for factories that no longer exist. Most of the people I grew up with are living on $400 or $500 a month even now.

You decided to specialize in psychiatry because of the depression and anxiety in the area that you grew up in? My mother wanted me to be a neurosurgeon. That was the first rotation I took and I absolutely hated it with a capital H. *You didn't like cutting into people's skulls?* As a medical student, you don't really get to do that very much, but what I really hated were the ridiculously long calls and the outrageous time you had to get up every day to go to work. You had to be there at five o'clock in the morning. A 15-hour day was a normal day but you were the big neurosurgeons on campus with the white coats and you worked on people's brains. I thought, "No, screw that. I'm not doing that for a living."

Psychoanalysts Freud and Jung did talk therapy. They tried to figure out the influences on peoples' developmental stages and how that affected them and their unconscious and their dreams. But it seems like now psychiatrists think, "You've got this symptom? Take this drug." That is an artifact of the times. Psychiatrists have to make a living. Insurance companies refuse to pay a psychiatrist for therapy. Even Medicare, if you're going to do therapy with people, you'd be lucky to get $25 for the hour. If you've got two secretaries, that payment is gone. *Is there a rationale for it because psychiatry is about helping people work through their issues, not just masking the symptoms?* Psychiatry is a derivative of psychoanalytic psychotherapy. If you try to follow the psychoanalytic model, it used to be standard in my training to try to see people three times a week for at least a year to even start psychotherapy. Now, insurance companies won't pay you hardly at all for psychotherapy. *You have to be a pill pusher?* You really do, otherwise, you can't keep your doors open. It's the reason that finding a psychiatrist in private practice is very hard now.

Have you explored the energy psychologies, tapping on acupressure points? I have studied EFT and EMDR. *What do you think about their efficacy?* EMDR is fantastically efficacious. When I was practicing medicine, it changed my practice. I saw people recover in minutes from things it would normally take weeks to months of therapy. Once you get the art of it down, it really does transform how you see disease and trauma. *Did you use brain hemisphere sounds or did you use your finger back and forth to activate the hemispheres?* I had the electronic tapping device and a visual scanning device that is like a long light bar they could watch. What I found was most effective was using my fingers waving back and forth in front of their eyes. It's almost like a form of pre-hypnosis.

Francine Shapiro, who developed EMDR, said the reason it works is because it integrates left and right-brain and allows for the release of trauma. Is that your understanding of how it works? I would agree but I would also say that traumas tend to clump together in the brain, not unlike a cluster of grapes. If you can identify at least one of the clumps in the trauma cluster and get it discharged, the others discharge much more easily. I've seen that in dozens and dozens of people. I think the cluster phenomenon isn't hemispheric. *Gary Craig, the founder of EFT, explained you don't have to take down all of the legs of a table to make it collapse.*

A good example of that is I treated a young lady who had fallen off of a boat. She had a skull fracture and concussion as a result and difficulty sleeping and even leaving her house. After one session, all those traumas disappeared after we got to the kernel of what had happened. *Was it simply the trauma of falling off or was there more to it?* For her, it was more about trust. She felt like the people who were close to her should have watched after her more carefully as she was drinking. Once we got to that trust nugget, the whole cascade of that trauma dissolved. She started sleeping and could eat better. A light went on in her head and her brain could work again.

You've worked with sleep disorders. What interested you about that? I was always interested in sleep disorders. I did some sleep disorder training in my residency at Jefferson Medical Center in Philadelphia and I worked with some pretty sophisticated sleep disorder specialists. I saw that sleep is not a restful phenomenon if you look at it scientifically as it's in some ways more complex a state of being than being awake. I was fascinated by how complex sleep is. There is nothing that we do when we are awake that compares to all the things that go on when you are asleep.

Are you a dream recaller, keen on dreams? I was trained in sleep disorders and sleep psychoanalysis so I had quite a bit of training in experiencing and interpreting dreams. That's a big part of psychoanalysis and psychotherapy. *Do you keep a dream journal?* I did for about ten years. I also had a machine called the NovaDreamer created by Dr. Steven LaBerge that allowed me to become lucid in dreams more easily. With that, I was able to record about two years' worth of lucid dreams in addition to normal waking dreams. *What did the machine do? Did it wake you up a little bit?* It was actually an eye-goggle machine that you put over your eyes before you go to sleep. The sensors over the eyelids register when your mind goes into Rapid Eye Movement and then flash a predetermined series of laser sensations in your eyes to waken you in the dream, but not enough to waken you physically.

What is an example of a lucid dream that you had? My experience keeping dream journals is there are patterns that the unconscious is working on. The same theme repeats until it resolves. I spent a lot of time in my lucid dream state with people that I grew up with; there was a lot of unfinished business with them. I stopped that cluster of memories when I moved on to medical school. There was one particular incident in medical school that I worked on for two years in my dreams. It involved me being in intensive care working on some patients and I would always show up late to rounds so I didn't know what was going on with them. I had to work through that for two years. Then I started spending a lot of time with angels, mostly flying with them. It was like I had to deal with those experiences of humanity before I could deal with anything different.

Did the angels take you to different realms? I spent a lot of time in dream school with the angels teaching me things that I had never seen before. They taught me words, art, and science. We usually met in what looked like a stadium in the sky. The angels would fly and swarm around the stadium. When you sat down, you could see the wings go into their bodies. You couldn't tell them from normal humans. They like to dress up like hippies with long hair, jeans, t-shirts, and jackets. *Any females?* You couldn't tell that, you weren't at a football game by the time you sat down with them. I spent years with them learning stuff.

What is an example of something you learned that you would never have known on your own? I did a book called *Regnus Sancti Draconum*, which is what we call Royal Dragons that originated in other dimensions of reality. They are part dragon, part angel and rule over entire domains. I had never heard of them but I wrote a book on four Royal Dragons. *They are benevolent?* Yes. *What is the dragon part? Does that make them very powerful?* Hollywood doesn't give a good depiction of what a real dragon is like. A real dragon is a huge being on an average of 50 to 60 feet tall. The dragon in *Game of Thrones* is probably closer to a real dragon than most dragons you see in movies. They can speak better than we can in over 100 languages and are also extremely psychic and telepathic in their ability to manipulate reality. They can make you see what they want you to see. A dragon can be flying above you but they can make themselves look like an airplane. They also can turn into people; a cross between a dragon and a human is called a drake. I learned that drakes exist.

They taught me a lot about the life of dragons and how interwoven they are in human society yet we don't even know about them.

They are other dimensional? They have an interdimensional reality, which means they exist partly in the physical world, partly in the astral world, and partly in the extradimensional world which is beyond our reality. They have the capacity to exist in all of those states at one time. Humans can, but it's difficult for us. We don't like to focus on more than a couple of states at a time—that being sleep and dreams. They have the ability to extend their reality and consciousness way beyond that.

The world is really in dire straits with the destruction of the environment and the big increase in the number of autocrats in the world, the US, Brazil, Philippines, Russia, Hungary, etc. Do the angels and Royal Dragons intervene in any way to help us? I had the same questions about why the world is the way it is. The higher beings I've talked with have a strict code not to intervene on problems human beings create for themselves. If, for instance, nature got out of hand or there were famines that were worldwide that weren't our fault—caused by disease— they would help. But, if we're killing ourselves or denying food to our neighbors for political reasons or problems that we cause, they stand back. They say we have to evolve enough to recognize that we're causing our own problems and take action when we can, which we tend not to do.

Scientists are saying maybe we have a decade before the environment is made inhospitable to millions of people. Could you ask the angels, "Could you help us out a little bit down here?" We had the capacity with scientists such as Nikola Tesla and electrical engineer Charles Steinmetz to use free energy to make cars and to power entire cities with no pollution. We allowed a handful of people to choose fossil fuels, which interferes with the environment and causes global warming. We could have prevented that but we didn't. We didn't rebel against those things which were clearly destroying our environment. So, your concerns about what is going to happen in the world in the next 10 to 15 years are legitimate. They have confirmed to me that disasters, because of our choices, are going to be allowed to happen which includes flooding, famines, and global diseases. *They're happening now.*

The thing that bothers them the most is that so many people theorize about problems in the world but too many people stand back and let a handful of very bad people have their way with the planet. It's not enough to theorize and complain; if you really want to change things you have to get out there and get your hands dirty, but not enough people are willing to do that. So, the people who are wealthy and powerful do what they want. *If you were going to get your hands dirty, what would you do?* I probably do it covertly and I would probably use magic. *Are you still in touch with the angelic beings and the Royal Dragons?* Because of them, I've written over 50 books. I've given over 100 seminars in many countries all over the world, which allowed me to stop practicing medicine in 2005. I work with them in meditation with very close relationships on both sides of the veil.

Overall, are you hopeful or pessimistic about our future as a species? The human race is a very difficult race but it's also a very promising race. We allow hundreds of thousands of children to die every year of starvation and disease when we have the capacity to heal them. We allow more of the sex trade now than we did a hundred years ago. A hundred million people died in WW II but most people couldn't tell you the real reason it started. Yeah, Hitler was involved, but why did so many people have to die to stop one person, one country? We could have stopped that long before that. I'm hopeful, but I know human nature, both from my training and my own personal experience. Sometimes, humans need to learn lessons *through consequences of our actions.* Unfortunately, the human race learns best through consequences. We make excuses for bad things and then we believe them.

In your book Signs of Mental Illness, *you talk about astrological and psychiatric breakthroughs.* When I was working in psychiatry, I noticed that during certain times of the year, I would have more suicide attempts than normal. I noticed people would come in with anxiety disorders in waves and other cycles that didn't really make any sense. Yes, there was a full moon cycle, but I saw so many waves that it made me wonder is there a reason for the waves of anxious people or waves of manic depressives? I started noting patients' birthdays and looked at hundreds of charts, comparing diagnoses and planetary positions, using a computer. I found that depressed people tend to have certain things that I could look for in their charts, as did schizophrenics. When I plotted movements of stars and planets in the sky, I could tell when I was going to get a wave of anxious people or a wave of suicides or schizophrenics. I could also look at a person's birth chart and tell the disease or mental illnesses to which they would be susceptible.

Does it have to do with squares and oppositions in their charts? Those are two-dimensional movements in the sky. If you look at the sky as a plate, squares and oppositions all move around in circular patterns on that plate. The sky is actually three-dimensional. When you look at the two-dimensional squares and oppositions and then the extra-dimensional plane of declinations and conjunctions etc., you recognize a three-dimensional synergy with planets and stars and constellations that affects every one of us. When you put those in a computer program, it very beautifully shows waves of energy connected to waves of conditions.

So we could look at a baby's natal chart and say, "We really need to work in this area to resolve this weakness." Have you done that with your children? One of the greatest civilizations, that is very adept at that is the Tibetans. They can look at a person's birth chart and tell you the same thing. They use a different system than I do, but it's the same theory. The sky is a living three-dimensional entity. You can tell a lot about a person's personality and psyche through looking at the stars in the sky the correct way. I looked at my kids and at my wife. I looked at people I was dating. When a client came in that was difficult, I often got insight on how to treat him or her by looking at the birth chart. *Have any other psychoanalysts used this tool?* Carl Jung was a brilliant astrologer. He often used astrological charts to help give him insight into his clients. There are a number of colleagues that use the birth chart.

In the course of your medical training, you started getting clairvoyant insights into your patients. How did that come about? I was introduced to Kabbalah in Los Angeles in 1998. I learned a prayer called the *Ana beKo'ach.* I knew a lot of prayers because I grew up in the church. But the first time I said that prayer, I felt a tingle like electricity go through my entire nervous system, like somebody hit me with lightning. So I memorized it and over the two or three years I used it, my etheric neural system turned on. I started developing more intense psychic and spiritual abilities, particularly clairvoyance. On a scale from one to ten, it was maybe a two before and it went up to an eight or nine after by memorizing that prayer and saying it on a regular basis. I since learned that the god Thoth wrote that prayer to help create the world.

You had initiations from Shree Mataji Nirmala Devi and from Indira Devi before the Kabbalah prayer? Yes, in 1994 I went to visit her ashram in Puna, India. She placed energy inside me that felt like living water as though somebody opened up the top of my head and poured down a cross between water and electricity. When I first experienced that, it made me vomit, have diarrhea, and made my vision hyper-alert. I started seeing glowing light around everybody. That lasted two months before it settled down. Ma or Idiri Devi was the wife of the ambassador to England from India. She was a billionaire in India. Her family didn't like the fact that she was studying spirituality but she was a very powerful and very advanced Indian saint and teacher. *What else did she teach besides giving darshan that initiated you?* She wrote over 40 books, most of them in her own language. She talked about the goddess Lakshmi and the goddess Mat. She also wrote about higher consciousness and life on other planets. Only one of her books has ever been translated into English.

The combination of your past-life experiences, the initiation, and the prayer heightened your clairvoyant abilities? Those things heightened it but the biggest accelerator of my consciousness was learning to take in sunlight. Nothing compared to that. *How do you take in sunlight consciously?* I had a teacher named Gene Savoy who was a self-taught archaeologist, a real-life Indiana Jones. He spent a lot of time in South America where he discovered that in a couple of South American cultures a priest would use parabolic mirrors to take in sunlight and communicate with beings in the sun. He learned to do it and enlivened his nervous system. He wrote a book called *Project X* in which he talked about his experiences with these mirrors and beings and taking in sunlight at different times of the day. I was skeptical because I thought sunlight will blind you if you look at the sun the wrong way. But I got parabolic mirrors and followed his instructions. I met him and worked with him. I found that taking it in the right way, especially starting with sunrise sun, sunlight accelerates consciousness and the growth of your nervous system in a way that nothing else does. I attribute sunlight to the vast majority of what I consider my consciousness.

Do you take it in through your eyes or through your whole body? You can take it in a number of ways. You can take it in just by sitting outside. All the light that is on this planet is sunlight. Light does come in through the stars, through quasars and some of the larger nebula, but what we see is sunlight. When you sit outside, you take in sunlight through your skin. If we didn't do that, we wouldn't have enough of the 19 separate vitamins that we get from taking in sunlight, Vitamin D being the most famous. Melatonin is another hormone we need from taking in sunlight. You can take it in through your skin and you can take it in through your eyes. You can take it in through your acupuncture points. When I take in sunlight, I have a solar box with mirrors and crystals. My main tool has a golden parabolic mirror like the Incas used. It changes the polarity of sunlight so it doesn't hurt your eyes. What Gene Savoy taught me absolutely works.

When you look at the sun, there is an attunement process that goes on for a couple of years after you start where you begin to see the sun pulsing and vibrating. It's like a big gigantic heart. After about two or three years, you begin to see a dark spot in the middle of the sun. You focus on that spot for a little while and start saying certain prayers and that spot opens in your consciousness in your third eye. You begin to see cities in the sun, golden cities paved with something that looks like gold but it's not gold. You see things that look like heaven, but you also see cities that look like Incan, Mayan, and Aztec temples in the sun. Civilizations still live there. The Incas and Maya, I believe, fashioned their cities after these civilizations that they saw in the sun. They said they fashioned their cities after being in the sun with gods that came out of the sky. I think they established a relationship with these higher beings and used that relationship to fashion their civilizations, which are quite advanced even compared to our civilizations now.

People can use clairvoyance to help other people, but do you find that you also get guidance about your next step or the person you should marry, etc.? Yes, very much so. *Did you have a feeling that you were going to meet your wife before you met her?* I met my wife online. We both had been online, meeting people and dating, but I was sick of it by the time I met her. I changed my profile to just a picture of myself and a poem by Kahlil Gibran. I said if anybody wants to meet me and get to know me, they are going to recognize who I am through this poem. She did. She said, "I like a man who likes Gibran," and I said, "That's my kind of woman." *Is she a scientist like you?* No, not at all. She emotes more and is more of a very highly developed empath, which is a good balance for me.

Did your art inspiration also come from higher guidance? When I go into meditation, when I go into the sun, I go to art galleries where I see a lot of art, some of which I just don't have the skill to bring back. But they said you can bring back whatever you remember so that's where my art comes from. I have sold literally thousands of pieces of art all over the world. When you look at it you can say, "That's not from here."

If you were going to tell people to read two of your books to help you on their path, which would you pick? I write at different levels. I write accelerated texts designed to help speed up consciousness and help people communicate with higher beings. I write novels, traditional books like a J.K. Rowling. I write books called power books which are books of spells and incantations meant for people who are more serious about their spiritual growth at a much higher level. If I was going to recommend just my regular novels and traditional books, I would say *Nine Insights for a Highly Successful Life* and *First Darkness*.

As someone with medical training, I would assume that you are interested in the spiritual bodies, the anatomy of spirit. Barbara Brennan describes the seven layers of the auras and the chakras in her books. How do you describe our energy bodies? I have some pretty sophisticated aura equipment that actually enables you to see not only the auras but the chakras and the petals in 3-D in the living body. There are more than seven chakras. You can also see that there are different inclusions [*see Robert Alcorn** *and Barbara Stone*]* in the body and in the aura that can help you understand disease at a whole different level. I use the Win Aura Star Interactive system that can measure acupuncture points and help you see the points. I also have the 3D aura imaging software system that allows you to examine the body energetically in ways that aren't well known at this point. I used that equipment to help me explore what works energetically and what doesn't. That's where a lot of recordings and some of my books came from.

Spiritual protection is something that I'm very much into. Maybe 15 or so years ago, I found that most of the tools for spiritual protection don't do a good job. A person would come in and say look at my aura and check my medallion, my cross, whatever, and I would show them entities inside their aura despite their protective tools. Over the years, I learned what worked and what didn't work to actually protect people. If you put on a protective device, you shouldn't be able to see those things in an aura. That's how we started offering medallions and certain spiritual tools.

For people who don't want to wear something, what do you suggest for protection? We found the average human being has about 10 to 15 attaching spirits. A lot of those spirits over time tend to cause disease in the body. Prayers help. Meditation helps, but it's difficult for us to hold concentration long enough to keep them out, especially when we're sleeping. To have some sort of protective tool is almost a necessity for the average human being as we are food to them. They feed on us. I designed a tool that has the miracle prayer built into it. I turned it into a binary code so a person can wear this when they need extra protection. We have our best protection in our medallions that people can wear anytime. *If people want to get it, they can go to TYBRO.com.*

Our strongest protective tool is a very specific combination of Hebrew letters. It's about two inches across and you can wear it under your clothing. It's designed to prevent spirits from getting into your aura. It's one of the things we tested and it works very well. *What do the letters mean?* It's called the Angels of Sanctification Medallion. There is also a computer program underneath the letters. If you look at it very closely, you will see something like a circuit board under the letters, which is an etheric computer program. The letters represent each of the angels of sanctification and connect their energy to the energy of the medallion which connects to your aura. It penetrates the energy of your aura and allows the protective energy to be amplified and protects you just by putting it on. That was developed because of years of working with devices that worked and some that didn't work. We found out that it's important to connect with the energy of higher, more perfect beings in order to protect your aura here. Just thinking it and hoping it with the human mind just doesn't work.

You said you work with others. Angels primarily. *Do you think that lower-level astral entities are just like bacteria that want to feed on human energy or do they want to do evil?* There are entire classes of entities that look just like us except they are astral and not physical. They are not bacteria, though they may use bacteria to infect a body, but they are highly intelligent and in many cases, highly evolved. A lot of people make the mistake of underestimating their abilities. *What is their intent?* They are not human. They are not beings that exist in the way that you and I would understand as people. But their intent is to further and expand their own lifespans at our expense. *They are parasites.* Very much so.

Some people talk about reptilians as having a lot of control in human history. Is this the same kind of entity? Reptilians are on a lower order of parasitic entities that affect the human race. There are races far more insidious than reptiles. Reptiles just get a lot of the press, but they are bit players. These beings think in terms of centuries. They don't mind having a plan to take 50 years to unfold. Human lifespan to them is nothing; that would be like crushing an ant or a gnat. *But if they get rid of us, then they wouldn't have their food to eat.* The plan is not to get rid of us. Do you ever see a child play with insects? At the end of the day, the child loses interest in the insects over time and goes onto something else. To these beings that are old, evolved and advanced, we are their playthings. Their goal is to play with us as long as we're interesting. That's it. There is no big plan to wipe us all out because what's the interest in that? Their goal is to play with us, to toy with us to see what we can tolerate, what we can't tolerate. To see what will help us and what we want. We're just interesting and that's it.

These are different than the grays, the ETs that people say do operations and scientific experiments on abductees. I believe that at any one time there are 50 to 60 different races playing with the human race. *Do you think that's because there aren't many human forms in the universe? The universe is so vast there must be other humanoid forms they can play with.* There are many races they play with. Ours is just one. *Some people have hope that the Pleiadeans will help us or evolved ETs like that. Do you think that's realistic?* One of the difficulties we have is that we do so much to ourselves that invites those insidious energies into our domain. It's like going into a troubled neighborhood and putting up a grocery store. One of the problems you are going to run into is that people will shoplift and rob the grocery store so that eventually you'll have to close it, even though you are trying to bring food. A simple analogy like that is very applicable to the human race. For instance, if a race bought very high technology, it would turn into a bidding war to see if someone could weaponize it or make a profit off of it. It would never reach the masses because of that.

What is your next book? What are you currently interested in learning about? My next book is going to be called *Dragon Summonings*. It's going to teach people how to summon the major groupings and orders of dragons that I believe are real and still live on this planet. *It's encouraging that you see them as helpful to us.* I do see some of them as helpful. Some of them aren't. *So, we have to be careful what we summon.* That's why I'm writing these books on summoning. There are people on the left hand of the pact that will teach you how to summon the dark ones that will also grant you power. *Do you use your abilities to pray for the good of the planet?* I mostly pray for popcorn and chocolate. Whenever I can, I try to help as much as I can.

Consciousness is the key concept in the new scientific paradigm. I think consciousness is our best currency in the entire universe. Humans have not spent nearly enough time developing consciousness. We don't understand that in order to have any kind of a place in the universe, we need to develop consciousness. *How do you define that?* It's the ability to make choices. The brighter your consciousness, the more choices you can make. There are some choices that we don't understand because we don't have the consciousness to comprehend them.

Are your children more evolved because you have all this knowledge that most people don't have? Both my children just finished college and work for my wife and I. We have a film production company where we produce TV shows and films. They are editors and photographers and answer the phones. Like any young person, they rebelled and didn't want to come to the seminars at first. But they kept seeing all these people coming to our seminars and asking us questions. And then they got curious and that curiosity hooked them. Now, they want to know everything we know. When you tell them enough about what's going to happen in a relationship before they even meet the guy, they start paying attention. They said, "How did you know that?" I said, "I looked at his chart. I looked at his aura." Now they want to know how to do that. *When you see people, do you automatically see their auras or do you have to focus?* I don't do therapy or do medicine anymore but I do have the ability to see auras. Over time, I've learned to turn it on or off. If I get really tired, it's harder to turn it on or off, but if I'm well-rested, it's very easy to control.

Is quantum physics useful for you in explaining why we can do prayer from a distance, clairvoyance, or precognition? Very much so. Quantum entanglement and quantum resonance and the concept that the universe responds to us individually. Things don't exist until we focus on them. These concepts are at the core of what I work with and how I teach. *How do you define quantum resonance?* It's a phenomenon at the core of quantum physics that says once an item has contact with another item, they are forever entangled energetically. When two people share thoughts, that entangles them. When two people share words, that entangles them. *If you separate entangled particles, they influence each other. What do you think is the explanation for how they can connect at a distance instantaneously?* There is no distance. There is no time. There is no separation. I believe that we live in a tremendously sophisticated program, not unlike a computer program, but far more sophisticated. All of our thoughts, all human consciousness, are part of the network of what I call participles or binary code that live within that program. Everything is connected to everything else through this massively sophisticated program. This is like *The Matrix* films.

Do you think there is an intelligent force behind it that some people call God? I think God is something bigger than we can comprehend and that this program is one of trillions of programs running simultaneously, all of which have nothing to do with God. God is bigger than these programs. *You're saying there is like an Earth program and a Mars program? What are the levels of programs that you are thinking of?* If you went to a beach and you picked up one individual grain of sand, there are more molecules within that grain of sand than there are stars in the universe. If you look at all the grains of sand as a totality, you've got more molecules than exist in the entire universe, but you are just looking at one beach, one grain of sand, one type of sand. You haven't taken into account the trees, or the water, or the bacteria in the sand. The programs are nothing more than single grains of sand, single grains of consciousness, in a large sea of consciousness.

Are we evolution or devolving? Some evolving, some devolving, some stagnant. They are all over the place. I believe that we are a stagnant race and in some ways, devolving. There are a few levels of evolving consciousness, but the vast majority of consciousness here is angry, violent, and devolving, much more so than we would even like to think about. *I read that 85,000 babies starved to death in Yemen in the last three years; there's no excuse for that.*

Is there anything else that you think would be useful to readers to know about that you've found important to you? Learn a divine world prayer. We have a number of those on our website. We give one away. The main one we use is the miracle prayer because it changes your connection and consciousness with the universe. Sit in the sunlight and take in sun on a regular basis. Also, get one spiritual tool that has power, like a medallion, like one of our spiritual crosses. Get something that has power and use that while you pray, put it under your pillow while you sleep. It's transformative.

Books

Divine Solar Magic, 2010
Nine Insights for a Happy and Successful Life, 2011
Rare Latin Incantations, 2012
Healing Spells, 2012
Solaris, 2013
The First Darkness, 2013
Rare Waters Rare Herbs, 2014
Regnus Sancti Draconum, 2014
Defense Against The Dark Arts, 2015
Aotava, 2016
The New Emerald Tablets, 2016
Metaparables, 2016
Ars Immortals, 2016
Reincarnation and Ascension, 2017
Dark Orders, 2019
Two Souls, 2019
The Temple, 2019

Websites

www.tybro.com

JOHN G. RYAN, M.D.
UNITY FIELD HEALING DNA

Photo by Melanie Provencher

Questions to Ponder

What did Dr. Ryan's visions teach him about our DNA? What form did the visions take?

He believes a major revolution in consciousness is occurring, which he calls ascension. Describe the process and how it impacts us. Who is helping us in the process?

What healing process does he teach?

I was born on the east coast of Canada, in the province of Newfoundland, by the Atlantic Ocean, on a little island pretty much in the ocean with the whales. My birthday is 30 June 1964, a Cancer. I am ISFJ. *What did that mean to you to grow up around the ocean?* When I was a baby, my family moved from where I was born to Nova Scotia. They had lived there for about eight generations, probably part of the original Irish immigration to Canada, and developed a fishing community. My dad was one of the first in his family to get an advanced education and became a marine engineer. So, the whole family moved off to Nova Scotia, which is the next province west of Newfoundland. It was a small town of about 10,000 people, a really nice community.

As you said, Canadians are known to be nice, but on the East Coast, I believe it is exceptionally so. The people are so heart-based, kind in their nature, a wonderful place to grow up and living on the ocean was incredible. I didn't know how powerful that was until I moved inland. Today I live in Ontario, more in the central part of the country. However, when you are on the ocean, a wonderful tempering of energy that takes place because you are near open space where you can go for a walk on the shore and encounter the ocean, which has a calming and nurturing effect. An expansiveness of mind that is natural to being near the water.

I was number six of seven children. *Did you get treated like the baby that the others wanted to direct and take care of or were they busy?* I think all of us were fairly independent and we let each other be their own person in lots of ways. So, in a strange way, I grew up with a lot of space because my older siblings were much closer together; they were all within two years of each other.

Were your parents Irish Catholic? Yes, my mom particularly was fairly religious. She was raised in an environment where the church was a big part of the community, especially when they lived on the island where everybody was part of the church. Everything in the community was dictated by religion. When my parents moved to Nova Scotia, the church made a big imprint on our upbringing. For the most part, we went to church every week and prayer was part of our life; however, it wasn't the greatest overshadowing influence. There is a whole other aspect of family life that was not religious but it created more of a community. It was important to be honest and to have integrity, to be kind, to do good for other people—that was well indoctrinated in us as young kids. My parents demonstrated this by their own example because it's the way they were as people. So, I learned more from seeing than hearing—like most people.

You didn't come away with the sin and guilt and shame like some kids who are raised in the Catholic tradition? I've met a lot of people who had that influence who were able to break free from that thinking later in life. Personally, I didn't have that same struggle. *Do you still identify as a Catholic?* I think it's sort of in your DNA in a way; it's part of my heritage going back as far as we are aware. But even as a child, I didn't really see myself as religious as I always identified more spiritually. I questioned things at church, including doctrine that made no sense to me. I would challenge that kind of thinking to my parents or to the priests. My spirituality was always a little bit more open and free. It was such an innate natural part of me, that I didn't think much about it. As I got older, I didn't continue going to church, but the system of being a good person, the morality and the integrity stayed important.

What's an example of something that you challenged your priest about? As a young boy I asked the priest about celibacy, "Why can only men represent God and why can't a man representing God also have a human counterpart who they could love and participate within a family?" I think the rule of celibacy followed a time of corruption when there was a lot of polygamy and abuse. *It's also less expensive to support a single person.* But it's shortsighted and I think in modern day it's not necessarily the best for people involved. It's very possible to have human relationships based in love and still be an emissary of a greater cause or a spiritual purpose.

When did you decide that you wanted to be a physician? I always knew I wanted to be a doctor or involved in healing in some capacity. As a little boy, my father worked on the marine ferries that went between the two island provinces. As kids, we would sometimes go for a crossing to spend a day with dad on the boat. The captain asked me when I was four or five years old, "What do you want to be when you grow up?" I said, "I want to be a doctor" and I never really looked back. I met some really wonderful physicians when I was a kid who were such a big part of the community, which added fuel to the fire. I finished high school when I was 17, did a three-year bachelor's degree in Biology and when I was 20 or 21 I started medical school.

You *were so certain, do you think there were past-life roots in your desire to be a physician?* Yes, today I do, but I didn't think about spiritual or esoteric topics until I got into my 20s. A lot of it was triggered when I lost my dad at the end of medical school. I had experiences where I became aware of a transpersonal reality and I knew beyond a doubt that he lived past his death. He gave these very special signs to my mother at the funeral and all kinds of bizarre things started to happen. It was the first time I had ever encountered anything like that in my own personal life, which triggered me to start to ask lots of questions.

What are examples of your father's contact with your family after he crossed over? My mother and my dad were very close and my father was ill for almost a year before he passed. I woke up one night about a week before he passed with a very strong intuition that he was going to be leaving the next Friday. I went to work that day at the hospital, and as fate would have it, I admitted three patients who had the same medical diagnosis as my father. Presenting these cases to the team later, I burst into tears. The senior physician took me aside and said, "It's time you go home and be with your family." It was an incredible "gift of consciousness" to experience being treated that way by the senior M.D. My whole family came home and were all there with my dad when he passed the next Friday as I foresaw!

My mom became obsessed with this idea that it had to rain on his funeral on Monday. She wasn't really a superstitious person but it became such a powerful thing that talk of this needing to happen overtook planning my father's wake. She explained, "I always believed that if it rained on the day that he interred, it's a sign that his soul has passed in peace." When Monday came, it was a beautiful sunny day in July and there was no sign of rain. At the cemetery, when the priest said the last "amen" in his prayer, out of the sky came three massive raindrops, the size of golf balls and splattered on the coffin in a straight line pinging over his head, pinging his belly and again at the feet. It was as if they baptized us as they made a splash. *They were just on your father's coffin?* Exactly. And as it happened I saw my mother take a huge breath and literally saw peace descend on her. We were all thinking this is a miracle. I remember thinking, "I don't know if there is a God, I don't know if this was my father's doing, but there is some spiritual force that's part of our reality and it knows when to intervene and to be there in a way that can heal."

We've all had different kinds of moments like this that are perfectly tailor-made to teach us things. I saw the power of faith to create and the power of love to manifest. It was a catalyst moment and I began to ask really serious questions like what do I believe about the universe, about spirituality, and about life? I had left behind a lot of strict beliefs and religious thinking, but I hadn't really found a new path of spirituality that felt aligned with who I was. This was one of those pivotal moments that changes everything forever.

Around that time, I began to live what is termed today a kundalini awakening. I began to have energy movements and strange OBEs at the end of my medical studies around 1987 and 1988. I didn't know what was happening but was in a scientific environment. I knew that what I was living outside of the parameters of anything that could be explained by religious or scientific systems of thinking I knew, so I began to search. It led me on a spiritual quest, exposing me to ideas that were revolutionary in my thinking at the time. It led me to experiences that taught me about the reality of energy, the power of consciousness and the nature of consciousness-based healing. I learned through this part of my journey how we are truly guided when our spirit and our mind are open. I lived many synchronicities and intuitive experiences that brought me to answers I could never have found with my rational or logical mind. Through this, I learned to trust my intuition and discovered that I experience synchronicities when I trusted it and thus learned to follow it powerfully. As much as I had been taught the scientific method, here I was having this whole other education in a very esoteric way of life. The two merged together over time.

What kind of books have been especially influential in your spiritual understanding? I have always loved the true teachings of Jesus, the mysticism and how he was teaching us to be multidimensional over 2000 years ago by lesson and by demonstration. Buddhist teachings have been very powerful to me, I love a lot of writings by the Dalai Lama. The work of Lee Carroll channeling Kryon has been very powerful and helpful for me. Gregg Braden's writings are a powerhouse of incredible information and Bruce Lipton's books are another tremendous resource. I've found if you use your intuition you will always be led to the right next book for you!

As I lived this kundalini experience, I knew I was living something profound and powerful, but I had no idea why I was living it. I had not heard of the word kundalini and I wasn't familiar with the human energy system. One day I had an intuition to go to a bookstore, which almost felt like I was being commanded to go from inside of myself. The New Age kind of a bookstore was located in an old house with lots of rooms filled with books. As I entered the store, I thought, "How am I ever going to find what I need in this place?" As my eyes panned across the bookstore, a book on the bookshelf got big as my eyes crossed over it! I gave my head a shake and it happened again. The book was called *The Spontaneous Awakening of Kundalini* by Gopi Krishna. I was overwhelmed for as I read the back cover I thought, "This is exactly what's happening to me."

I had moments where I would pop out of my body in full consciousness and see my body. At times the roof would disappear from the house and I would see the stars! I could see the sky and travel in my energy body outside my physical body in full consciousness. As I read the book, it brought me a lot of comfort because I thought, "This is actually a real phenomenon." It's been mapped, somebody has lived it, somebody has explained it. To find a book like a needle in a haystack was an incredible synchronicity.

Do you think that you have spiritual guides help us or was it a vibrational intention that attracted you to go to the bookstore? I believe that we do have guides, but it's hard for us to conceptualize what they really are. I think a lot of the wisdom that flows through us is innate to our own higher self. As we open to greater aspects of consciousness and more of our own multidimensional or quantum reality, there is a lot of wisdom we all carry in our soul fabric that's innate to who we are as an experiential being. So some of the guidance is really from our higher self; we are our own guide in that way. However, we are also part of a system. If you need to fix a pipe you call a plumber; you rely on people who have other areas of expertise to help make something balanced and whole—our guidance system is like that. We attract attributes of consciousness that are strong in other souls or other teachers and they become part of our energy makeup as we journey forward through our own evolution of understanding and development.

There are helpers in both bodies and in inter-dimensional bodies? Absolutely. If you think about synchronicity, how do we create it? We may put out a strong intention to create something. We don't know the factors that need to come together to make it possible for that to happen so we are relying on a big system. It's like we are here living in our mind, but above us is a whole plane of consciousness where all of this is being worked out. We are led to these discoveries and synchronistic moments as part of a greater plan or system of consciousness.

As you evolve in your being in both consciousness and energy, an awakening tends to happen in the body and in the mind. You can think of kundalini as a spiritual energy, part of who you are. People in Eastern religious traditions will describe it as dormant, coiled up at the base of the spine. As you go through your awakening, this energy starts to expand and to move through all of your bodies—the physical, mental, emotional and spiritual bodies—that are part of us as a whole energy being. It begins to open us up in consciousness so that we can integrate more of our own spiritual essence or our soul. It's an energetic expansion, so energy and consciousness go hand-in-hand, consciousness governs energy and is a type of energy. When kundalini is awakening it's like our energy system is being stretched and remodeled so that we can carry more energy and consciousness within our body.

Kundalini is a form of chi or subtle energy, as Einstein called it? Yes, in a way. A lot of people who have experienced kundalini awakening have spent lots of time meditating or doing spiritual practices. But in modern times, many people will experience it rather spontaneously. I believe what's happening right now on the planet is a lot of people who've had these experiences previously are being born and living very normal lives and this awakening happens spontaneously because of their past-life experience or Akashic history [*Hindu concept of stored information like a cosmic internet*].[1] There are a lot of people who are spiritually inclined, who have wisdom or insight and part of their journey is to have this awakening. Some people live it all at once, like a really powerful ka-boom and other people live it in slow incremental doses like little waves. *Some people think they are going crazy, so if it's too extreme, it can be really difficult.* Yes, and there are many examples of people who were overwhelmed by the experience and knocked out of balance for years where they had no orientation or understanding of how they could function or cope. So it can be offsetting, particularly if it's not understood or nurtured in a healthy or wise way.

Is there an environment that evokes this awakening? It all started to happen for me when I started to ask questions. When I was in medical school, a professor was explaining the "healing cascade" that defines all the biochemical processes that happen when you cut yourself. As he was explaining this very complex biochemistry, I thought, "How does the body know how to do this? Where is the intelligence that knows how to govern all of these processes?" I was sitting there and kept asking and asking. I went into this really strange altered state as if I entered in the field of healing consciousness and I understood there is an intelligence that knows how to direct the body and how to direct life in different ways. It was almost like I merged with that field and energy for a few minutes. This was an incredible experience because I could feel the love and the expansiveness in that state. I thought that must be what's it like when people meditate or go into this bigger field.

Was the answer to your question DNA? Yes, ultimately, but it is part of an even fuller system. Within everything that exists in form, there is quantum information that governs its physical presence on the planet. The body has an intelligence coded in it that knows how to make it and to heal it. Our DNA interfaces with that body intelligence. Imagine if we could more fully access it! Every species that exists on the planet has a formative consciousness. As humans, we have this divine DNA that is powerfully conscious.

Is that intelligence more than the soul or the spirit that exists before we're born? It's part of that. As I went through all of this, I became interested in energy and consciousness as a force of healing. I began to have experiences where I would see energy, see auras, and energy fields in nature. Because of my own experiences, I knew when people talked about things like auras and chakras they weren't making it up. I learned a lot about energy healing through many synchronicities and I met people who taught me about the energy body and the power of consciousness. I began to understand how all the spiritual systems and healing tie together and how spiritual wisdom is part of the healing fabric of humanity. Later in life, I began to have more visionary-type experiences, often in a meditation, usually in a very powerful part of the planet like a sacred site, or sometimes when in a big group of conscious people—like in a seminar. I would be shown things about DNA or quantum DNA through a series of visions. I came to understand that this is an invocative way of healing, available to human beings who seek to heal.

The shapes that you saw in your visions already exist in the Unity Field? Correct. As my third eye opened, I saw what looked like a dark-blue star-lit sky. A dot of light came down from the top and it opened up into a pyramid that was like a shell of light. Down through the pyramid came another dot of light and formed another pyramid and it happened a third time. In the third pyramid, a dot of light came that opened into a circle that opened into two smaller circles in the bigger circle and then the smaller circles developed two circles and the whole thing became activated, like it was plugged in. *It's like a mandala?* Yes. In another vision a little bit later, it became active within the DNA structure that I was shown—people can read about it on my website with pictures to help viewers really understand. *Then you saw a crop circle that was very similar.* Yes.

I had another vision in December of 2012 which is an auspicious date because it goes back to the Mayan end times prophecy. I was in Arkansas in a conference of about 500 conscious healers. We were on the big crystal bed that is Mount Ida. In this setting, I had another one of these meditating experiences. In this one, I was shown a crystalline staircase. I was at the bottom of the staircase. If anybody has done shamanic visioning, you can have an intentional interaction with what you are seeing. My intention was to go up the stairs to see what's on the other side, but as I tried to do this, it was like I ran into a glass wall and I ricocheted it so powerfully that I almost tipped backward physically in my chair in the room. I thought, "I guess I am not going to take these stairs by intention or by walking up."

The whole energy disappeared but came back like a screen refresh. A DNA symbol lay on the stairs and I knew what the vision was communicating: the way you go up to this next level of reality is through the vibration of your DNA. This big cosmic DNA came back that I had seen in a couple of other meditations and I could see the light pattern inside the DNA molecule. A little bubble was moving around in the big quantum DNA space, to clean up the DNA. As it moved around, there were little reactions like explosions of light in the DNA molecule. I was shown that the pattern works inside this quantum space of DNA to help recalibrate it to help it heal the human body. After that, I was led to create the audio sessions and to develop a formula or a modality of a system that people could use to work with the energy.

Please correct me if this is not an accurate summary of your Unity Field theory. A galactic cycle of ascension or rapid evolutionary change began December 21, 2012, that galactically requires humans to shift our consciousness. That shift occurred for us during the Harmonic Convergence on August 27, 1987. The way the shift occurs in our energy field is through the quantum field of information or the unity field around our DNA. It includes all our past lives in what the Hindus call the Akashic records. We can draw on in this information for the knowledge that's stored there and we're also supported by an evolving planetary crystalline grid. First, define Unity Field.

"Unity Field" came to me through a visionary experience shown to me in a meditation. I give a summary in my book of what I was shown in a conscious meditation. In terms of the visual teaching, I don't have these experiences every day; these tend to happen sporadically, usually when I am to be shown new information. I am shown visuals that I end up decoding. I am usually taught something that's meaningful to the work I am doing. It's like my third eye opens and I can see visions in my mind's eye. Many people today have this type of experience in a meditation or shamanic journey, but although not everyone has this type of experience everybody can understand what it is to dream where you see things in your head that you are not seeing with your eyes. This is happening while I am conscious in my body. I was shown experiences that explained what happens when we incarnate and the energy that we bring from our soul to be part of our reality as a person. This field of energy has always been quantumly linked to our soul. The energy between us and our higher spiritual nature is now expanding. When people talk about a DNA expansion or quantum DNA awakening or 12 strands of DNA, they address this process.

A decision point depended on the spiritual maturity of humanity and so the ascension on December 21st, 2012 is the date when we entered into a new time cycle. *The Aquarian Age?* Yes, in essence, but on a much bigger galactic scale since the Aquarian age is only one small cycle within a 26,000 years cycle. December 12th earmarks the convergence of many time cycles at a single point in time. One of them is the shift from the Piscean to the Aquarian age but on a galactic level this precession of equinoxes, this rotation of the Earth through the constellations, will take 26,000 years to go through all the cycles. That is the point when the Earth's alignment returns to the galactic center, so on a time scale of galactic proportions, we are ending a cycle and beginning another. At the end of this cycle, what's determined is whether during the evolution of humanity, we have matured enough spiritually or in consciousness to be able to sustain rapid rise in ascension status. The process is going from a consciousness based in duality with dark and light struggle into one of a more harmonious nature where the unity of life, the unity of humanity with the nature kingdoms, with the Earth, the greater galactic system, starts to become a faction of consciousness. To be a human being is different in this energy that we're growing into.

The harmonic convergence of August 21, 1987, was the test date to figure out now whether humanity is able to go through rapid ascension of consciousness. The truth is if we weren't ready, it would have meant a decline of our civilization as has happened many times on our planet already. *Atlantis, Lemuria?* Yes, but this was a very special one because the Earth is poised to move into a part of the galaxy where there's a very strong stream of energy and consciousness. We've never been in this part of the galactic alignment with what's called the "photon belt" and other names. The Earth is going to start receiving high vibrational fluxes of energy through the sun because of humanity. The ascension was triggered because humanity is conscious enough to sustain this rapid change.

Current history doesn't look very conscious so is there a tipping point of a percent who are on a spiritual path and can carry it for the rest? It's more of a collective ratio or an aggregate of energy; it might be 30% or 32%. In response to that, the energy grids of the Earth were adjusted. The Earth has an electromagnetic field that looks like a donut of energy that's shaped around the Earth with the North Pole and the South Pole. *The toroid.* Yes, so the electromagnetic grid of the Earth was strengthened to be able to receive this influx of new energy and new consciousness light.

Did this happen automatically or was it guided by entities like the Sirians? It was guided by entities. For example, Kyron is channeled through Lee Carroll. Kyron is a magnetic master, part of the spiritual team that came to help the Earth build up the energy to move through this transition. The magnetic field was set by pre-2012. As we move into this new energy space, other grids are expanded, such as the crystalline grid and the Gaia grid. Human beings are intimately in resonance with the Earth so as the Earth's electromagnetic posture is being shifted, so is the fundamental electromagnetic field of every human being. This shift in the magnetic grid is opening up elements of energy and consciousness within our energy structure. It's not something that science can yet see or prove and all of this information ends up coming through channeled sources of people who receive it.

HeartMath researchers like Rollin McCraty* are measuring how the electromagnetic field correlates with human coherence in the heart rate. Yes, although you can't measure these things directly, you can measure the influence or the consequences of these things. They're measuring changes in baseline heart rate variability and big events like the twin towers in New York or the death of Princess Diana that touch the lives of billions of people in one way or another. *As measured by RNGs in Roger Nelson's* Global Consciousness Project at Princeton.*

As the rest of these grids open, this ties into the quantum field of DNA. This is based on the visions where I was shown how the energy field around the DNA molecule is structured and how it relates to the soul's energy. When the soul comes to incarnate in the human body it brings with it an energy field that merges with the developing physical baby. As the DNA of the little zygote and the energy field merged with the genetics of that little cell, it stays with you through your life. We also bring in elements from the spiritual realm such as attributes, maybe a quotient of karma and certain skills to form the elements for a particular incarnation.

As the energy grids are opening and expanding, human beings have much more open access to this multidimensional aspect of themselves. We see people having memories of past-life experiences or they have OBEs, NDEs, and elements of consciousness where they bilocate. Somebody will see the person in one form and yet they're physically present in another place. All of that is a direct result of the quantum field around the DNA being activated by the shift. *What about people like autocrats who are sociopaths, narcissistic, and don't seem to have the brain wiring to evolve in this spiritual correction?* Because the Earth is a planet of free will, we have the choice between doing something enlightened and doing something dark or unenlightened.

Do you use your ability to see energy fields and your intuition to help you in your practice as a radiologist? Of all things in medicine, radiology is really one element of medicine that already sees the world of healing in terms of energy. We don't think this way typically, but we actually use energy technology and rely on the energetic nature of the human body to see inside the body. These images are made by sound waves, radiofrequency and magnetic fields, and radiation, which have an energetic interaction with the body! Yes, when I read a CT or an MRI scan, intuition guides that process a lot. Often, before I finish reading a scan, I'll close my eyes and ask, "Is there anything else I need to see?" Sometimes I get a hit, look again, and see something that I didn't see the first time. (*Radiologist Larry*

Burk* said the same thing.) Sometimes I will be compelled to offer a prayer or a healing intention as I am going through the scan.

What about your own personal shadow? What have been the most difficult points in your life and how did you cope? Although I make light of it today, a lot of the things I lived were very challenging and difficult. When I had the kundalini awakening experience I was scared [*like Richard Moss**]. *You probably thought you were going crazy.* Yes, all types of questions and fears surfaced like do I have a brain tumor or am I psychotic? A social stigma exists since a lot of my beliefs formed from personal experiences are very unorthodox. When I share them with people, many are open-minded but others can't help but judge, because they do not have any personal frame of reference to understand what I am sharing. Also, through the journey, everyone encounters the "bits of your ego" in your own personality that must be integrated or healed. You see what you do to create anxiety, where you judge other people, how you mask or hide who you are or you are tested to see if you capable of being hurt by someone you love and forgiving them. This is all part of the overall ascension process. That work never really ends as I still find myself judging something or being dismissive of something, etc. If there is anything I am missing in my ascensional journey, life hands me a magical wand to learn from. LOL! This is true for all of us.

Some people talk about the physician attitude, that in med school physicians are trained to be authoritarian, the gods in the white coats who should be obeyed absolutely, but you don't seem to have succumbed to it. Actually, a lot of physicians are not like that. Historically yes, but as medicine evolves a lot of change is happening and some of it is driven by patients who stand up and say, "It has to be better, I need more respect, I need to be a participant in this story, I need to make decisions that are self-appropriate," and medicine has adapted.

The earth now is in the process of birthing a whole new consciousness. With this, human beings are being catalyzed into what you might call an ascended civilization, one that understands the principles of spiritual truth. You begin to understand what spiritual gurus have taught through time, like the way you treat another human being has energy consequences, both for them and you. You learn to unravel your mistakes through forgiveness and through compassion. You learn "to be in the world but not of the world." You learn to exist in a 3D reality, but what governs the way you live in that reality is from a multidimensional reality or plane of consciousness. The wisdom of the Christ teachings or the Buddha's teachings are revealed because the nature of life expands to include a vast spiritual reality which can be termed quantum or multidimensional. As Christ taught, "Love your neighbor as yourself" becomes the way because you understand a bigger view.

As humanity integrates these principles, our whole world is moving forward into a higher plane of reality and consciousness. We live in an energy system that can only be understood in galactic terms. The evolution of the earth falls within a time cycle. For example, the Mayans knew this, naming December 21, 2012, as the end of a time cycle. This also marks a new beginning cycle. Simply speaking, the energy of the earth and human consciousness is transitioning into a new kind of an energy reality.

Of course, if you look at the daily news, it seems like that's all wishful thinking! So much chaos is happening in all our societal systems but the reason for this is that everything in the old energy system has to transition into the new. Things that don't vibrationally match where we are going will have to disintegrate, often through being exposed or revealed. For example, anything that is founded in corruption or dishonesty in business, or health care, or politics is going to be challenged. Today there is chaos in all the systems as we're identifying problems in order to begin the process of healing and formatting our reality in a new and more enlightened way.

Like the Jungian shadow coming up to light to be revealed and cleaned out? Exactly, that is what's happening on a big scale in terms of social systems and structure, but more importantly, it's happening on a personal level where people are living their own personal transformation. As we are being propelled through this transformation, we are awakening to all kinds of knowledge and information that wasn't available to us 50 years ago unless you were part of a special spiritual teaching system or a mystery school. Today people are talking about energy, consciousness, their chakras and doing yoga—signs are everywhere.

Some people talk about ascension as wanting to leave the body, but it sounds like you are talking about ascension as changing the way people live in this body on earth. Absolutely, it's an ascension vibration and coherence of energy and a rise in consciousness into a higher vibrational reality. This actually means an integration of higher vibrational energy and consciousness. As much as we experience an ascension, it's also a descension as your soul comes more fully into your body. You begin to understand your multidimensional nature, that you are part of a collective system of life and humanity is a family that extends beyond the earth! We discover that humans have a powerful force of consciousness that we can use to create and to heal things. As we remember multidimensional experiences, we become aware that we've lived other lifetimes. We are aware of *two* experiences at the same time, which by definition is a multidimensional experience.

As we open up to the energy of memories of other lifetimes, sometimes there is a healing that takes place. For example, if you have to go through emotions that were part of your death or an experience in another lifetime, this clears the charge of this energy as an influence on your well-being. Vicariously many things happen because as you clear those energies you become innately aware that you do not die, you discover that you are here on purpose, and by divine design. Because we don't die per se, we live a little bit more fearlessly and more openly. Also, not just the trauma, but also the wisdom of these other lifetimes is also available to you. As you open up to this bigger you, you see that you have gifts, abilities, and talents that may not be aware of until this all begins to happen. Think how many people you know who have through major metamorphoses in this lifetime.

As we move into this new energy, children are changing. If you look at children today compared to children a generation ago, sometimes you say it's not even the same species—these kids are so different. We sometimes find them "entitled" and "disinterested" because they are not interested in things that don't have integrity and they have an innate sense of worth. You can reach them through respect and relate to them in an authentic way rather than in an authoritarian way because they're wired differently. There is a lot of conflict because in the old energy you were told what to do, but the kids today won't have it. It's a rebelliousness on the surface but the truth is, it's changing human nature.

This is reflected in the younger generation of physicians I see. I teach a lot and I see an incredible open-mindedness in them. It's actually magical to see that they are very open in thinking; they are not judgmental the way physicians were two or three generations ago. *I've been doing research on global youth attitudes and have a series of books about it and I think what you say is absolutely true. Globally, they are much more egalitarian and accepting and not willing to put up with corruption, lies, and pretenses.* Right, and youth insist on having more balance in their life and money is not the most important thing to them. Their whole frame of reference is very different from the culture we are leaving behind.

The question is how long does this ascension take in the face of the rapid pace at which we are destroying our life forms? So much about the last cycle was naïve. Particularly this was true in the sense that, apart from indigenous cultures, humanity didn't understand its "integration" or oneness with the planet. As we become more conscious, or awakened, we realize the validity of the beautiful indigenous saying, "We all live downstream." You can't poison the water and not be affected by it. As we move into the new energy, we are going to be given the ability to do new things, such as develop the technology to utilize free energy, clean up plastics, provide clean water to all people, etc. This is all happening now. *People say they have invented free energy devices and they end up with men in black suits carrying them off because they don't want to disrupt the capitalist economic system.* Absolutely correct but now inventions can be placed on a chip or conveyed through technology that you can easily share so it harder to keep them a secret. A lot of the things that seem futuristic will become as innate in the future as the internet or a Wi-Fi zone is to us today, things that were incomprehensible 25 or 30 years ago.

As you read the news it's hard to be encouraged; do you have hope in the short run? Yes, it's so important for the message of hope to be spread. We are living through a powerful transition from an old energy into a new energy and change leads to chaos. Everything that is part of the old system that doesn't belong in the new system has to be reintegrated. We need to evolve into a more conscious unified collective, which will take the course of a couple of generations. If you look at life today and you look at life two generations ago, it's already a different world. We haven't ever been more conscious of problems like racism, sexism, and inequality than we are today. People who were already aligned with the change will be ahead of the curve and be frustrated that it's not changing fast enough. People who were attached to the old ideas will slowly open their minds to seeing it differently. Especially when change has a spiritual impetus behind it, the earth is being compelled to make this transformation. Since energy follows consciousness, we end up inhibiting the evolution if we focus on the problems. To paraphrase Buckminster Fuller, rather than fight with the old, let's get busy creating the new.

Many are concerned about the scientific report that we have a decade to turn around climate change and I wonder if your higher guides have suggested that there's any remedy for that because we're trashing the environment. This is a very tough issue. We'll develop technology that can produce clean non-polluting energy. *Cold fusion, zero-point energy.* Exactly. When people ask me what they can do, I say, "Today it might be to go to the coffee shop and to make sure that barista has a better day." When you go to work, don't engage in gossip and negativity, change the world one encounter at a time. Those elements of daily actions change the fabric of life. We need to retake our power to create from consciousness and from a place of balance and wellbeing.

Let's talk about your book, Unity Field Healing, Volume 1, Foundations of Energy Medicine and Quantum Healing. The inspiration for the book came to me as I talked to people about healing through energy and consciousness. I found that I was unable to recommend a book to explain energy and consciousness-based healing and how all of that ties into the new energy paradigm. The book discusses what you need to know to understand the power of energy healing and why medicine has a hard time with this concept of quantum healing.

I discuss our energy system and the bodies and chakras as part of the energy matrix. We talk about ascension and how our energy is capable of healing through the quantum field of information that is part of our DNA, creating a whole new potential to bring healing and change. I self-published the book (originally titled *The Missing Pill*) and it sold thousands of copies. Last year, the book was picked up by Ariane. a Canadian publisher, in both English and French.

Does the DNA exist on a spiritual template before we are born or are we talking about DNA that's purely part of our physical body? It does exist before you are born and you bring with you the bits and pieces that are relevant to this lifetime. Imagine, for example, that you've lived a hundred thousand times and you've been a man, a woman, a healer, a teacher, a prostitute, a spiritual person. Through the journey, you've lived so much that you have wisdom about the nature of life and gifts you have acquired in those lifetimes. You narrow that experience to something that's meaningful to an incarnation. For example, if you are going to be a mother, have two children and be a nurse and live in a community with a family with people who are part of your soul group, the information and attributes you bring in will be tailored to that experience.

You may also choose to deal with several elements of your personal karma, things that you may have done in another lifetime around which you want to neutralize the energy. As a soul, you bring with you the attributes to help walk you through the journey of an incarnation. You also have a quantum connection to the genetics of your parents, so your mother and father's DNA is also part of your make-up, with an overlay of that energy as part of your reality. Indigenous people say that the sins of a father will affect seven generations and in a quantum way that energy is carried in one's genetics. That's also true of good things, which is important to understand.

As we go through ascension and open up to this multidimensional part of us, it's contained in what I was shown as a big quantum DNA molecule or field. In this quantum space, every lifetime you ever lived is stored in what is like a quantum library. We can actually go back into that space and bring that information forward within the awareness of the person that we are today. When we do that, we are creating a multidimensional experience. When you open to this field of information, you have within you the memory of a lifetime where you didn't have a current problem such as an illness. You know in this fuller memory what it is to be healthy and happy in your body and you can seed this energy in your life today. People use the term "mining the Akash" going into that quantum energy and bringing new possibilities forward into this lifetime and allow it to help us to heal or transform—you see beautiful examples of it all the time. Every spontaneous remission is a demonstration of this potential!

When I was shown these visions, I was shown a template of a light pattern that I call The Unity Field Healing Template that looks like a series of interlocking eights. It appears as spheres within spheres. What I saw in the meditation was this pattern working inside the quantum field of energy that is our quantum DNA structure, vibrating there to recalibrate the DNA. These visions led to the system of healing that I was inspired or instructed to develop. The work came forward first as a series of audio guided meditations, recorded with my voice and background music, in three sessions. In the first session, you are attuned to your own spiritual DNA axis. This is a self-attunement where you are tuning to your own greater spiritual or quantum nature. The second session is an attunement to the actual template, the pattern of light that I was shown as a living light geometry.

Session three is for tailored intentional work. When we put an intention into the third session, we can be very specific or we can be very open about the goal. So, for example, someone is anxious all the time but the person may not understand that the anxiety stems from their own ascension as their energy is being stirred and touching on the memory of other lifetimes where fearful things that happened to them. The body has a reflexive protection that says don't do this, it always ends badly or it stirs a stored emotional memory. The energetic basis to healing is to clear out the fear that creates that reflexive anxiety.

However, it is not all about healing as it's really about creation; healing is "creating health." Healing is getting over things from the past, but we can also create actions for the future that inspire us toward a more balanced, joy-filled, soul-inspired reality. *People can download them from your website.* It has been amazing because people have now done the sessions for a couple of years and the stories that people tell me are really powerful. The sessions are a tool of high intensity support. What's happening is such a natural thing, it's innate. However, if you broke your leg and you wanted to heal, you could sit for six weeks or you could wear a cast and the bone will heal quickly, efficiently and remain aligned. This work helps people to create the space to do that inner work, a meditative work, in a powerful transformative way. Each session takes about 30 minutes through a guided process that takes you on a journey where the energetic changes occur within that process.

Would you say that the three sessions are like epigenetics in that you are using spiritual intention and attunement to change how the DNA manifests? Yes, but to me, epigenetics is more of the study of how psychology and social systems affect genetic expression. *This is like a spiritual epigenetics?* Yes, it has a different orientation, but it's the same principle. You really nailed it there, spiritual epigenetics. It's calling upon a higher order within yourself to recalibrate your health and your life. *So at this time, spirit—even without your conscious intention—is realigning your spiritual and physical DNA for a higher purpose in ascension?* Yes, but understand it is your soul's intention even if you are not fully conscious of what is taking place.

With Unity Field Healing, the work continued to develop. People kept saying to me, "When are you going to teach people to do this?"

People were aware there was a healing modality in addition to the audios that would be developed. I have learned that when spirit is sending you a message, it will send many people to say the same thing to you over the course of time. I woke up one morning and knew how to teach it; it all came as a download of information it seems! Over the course of a month or two, I put together a teaching program and then started to initiate practitioners to use the tools; over a hundred practitioners have been attuned to do the work. Many of them have been in healing practices doing Reiki, etc. What I found quite phenomenal is about 30% to 40% of the people who wanted to do the training have no healing experience. An elementary teacher told me, "It has so profoundly affected the way I relate to the children that it shows up in everything I do. Working with the children is so natural in this new space." I realized that you can manifest this energy and consciousness in different ways and there are so many ways we heal.

In the beginning, to attune them I would do a physical energy process but now the work is done in a meditative way. What I see happening in my mind's eye is these light beings come into the space standing with each person and people have had very vivid experiences with them. The Collective said, "We'll begin to do transmissions," which is a group meditation that leads into a channeled message. The people in the group receive attunements while we do the meditation together and then the channeled message helps us understand the process. I created a YouTube video so people can still do the transmission in another space in time.

You are teaching how to access the light template in order to activate the DNA in a more evolved way? Yes. What happens is the energetic response is unique to the intention. I had a lady who was having chest pain; after the session, she said, "It's like I can breathe in my chest for the first time that I can remember." She was dumbfounded! And two days later, she got a phone call from her sister who she hadn't spoken to in decades and they went through a process of healing. It was like the energetic change took place mirrored by a response of psychological events. You begin to see how so many things are interconnected and you are making the space for the transformation in the sessions.

Do you think Quantum Mechanics underlies all of this? I do, all of it. In this vision, the template came as a structure and introduced itself to me in that meditation. I did another meditation a few months later, where the template came back and activated in a brand new way with all kinds of light coming out of the template, different colors and vibrations. My body was reacting to the energy like I was undergoing adjustments and energy experiences. My limbs would flick, or my head and neck would straighten, or I'd need to stretch my chest to let a kink out of my body. I realized the energy was healing me in some way. At this point in time, I didn't know it was a healing system that I was being shown. I was just having these meditative experiences. *That were like the kundalini experience?* Exactly.

Traditionally placebo effect has been dismissed. But it's a huge effect of belief. Are you hearing more discussion of mind-body interaction? Yes, when a new medication is to be tested to see if it is effective for the treatment of a certain condition, it has to be more effective than placebo. The question is: what drives 40% of people to be effective healers in their own right with no medication? In the new advances in psychology and epigenetics, subjects like neuroplasticity, mind-body medicine, and life-extension studies are being integrated into medical studies. Science is very cognizant today of frames of reality that support health and well-being. If you are under constant stress and anxiety, it has a toll on the immune system and nervous system and the ability to heal and be well.

Bruce Lipton and others are doing a lot of epigenetics research to demonstrate how certain genes are more likely to express in a certain environment. This means your genetics does not define your full risk of health and disease the way we used to believe in our early understanding of genetics. We are starting to blend together our understanding of how psychology and healing all tied together and it will become a much bigger part of medicine in the future.

Is your feeling that your download is orchestrated by some intelligent beings? Yes. I believe that it's part of an overall plan that is supported by other conscious beings in our galactic network. It is a natural part of an evolution that we are going through supported by other star systems too. They are certainly involved in helping us go through this ascension process in ways that we don't necessarily fully understand. *The crop symbol seems be evidence of that since it is so much like your template?* Exactly. I understood it was a universal pattern, so it's not something we can own or possess. This information is available to people and it comes in different ways.

In March 2019, you had a vision of the Sirian Blue White Collective who are helping with the evolutionary shift in consciousness. They are from Sirius, the brightest star in the night sky. What form do they take in your visions? They call themselves "masters of light, geometry, and sound." Why did they select you as their Ambassador? The geologist Gregg Braden says that our DNA, maybe two millennia ago, was consciously changed by some higher force so that we could be more intuitive and intelligent (but others say there is no evidence of this change). So does Lee Carroll whose information was channeled from Kryon. He talks about our second chromosome that is bigger than most other chromosomes because it's actually two chromosomes that were fused into one. It's believed that we had 24 pairs of chromosomes that became 23 pairs. Some people believe that this was part of the Pleiadean seeding of life on our planet and they can be thought of as our spiritual parents who were instrumental in bringing the divine element of DNA and consciousness to the earth as it evolved. The conscious and divine part of human beings was woven into the DNA at this time and people believe it coincides with the period of time when 23 chromosome pairs were made from 24 pairs.

In March of 2019, you started communicating with the Sirian Blue White Collective, who are helping us. I never really thought much about off-planet beings, but in a meditation a group of light beings came and presented themselves to me in an array, like a choir standing on the stage in light form. They communicated telepathically, as a thought form, that they are from Sirius. Sirian Blue White

Collective was the name they gave me to use. I started to see beings take shape within the overall energy field. They told me that they've always worked with humanity as part of humans' evolution on the Earth. They're coming forth now to help us understand the nature of ascension and the DNA transformation that we're going through. They're masters of light, sound, and geometry that work within the quantum space of DNA and they told me that they are behind the Unity Field healing work.

As this was all unfolding, I hosted Lee Carol in 2018 at a workshop where I received a personal channel from Kryon who told me that the visions that I'm being shown to help understand the DNA work are new and correct. One day I'll be shown in more scientific ways. *Did Lee Carol know that you were having these transmissions?* No, he didn't know anything about the Sirians but he said as the channel, "That help you're getting from your Sirians is real." To have that validation or confirmation is tremendously supportive when you're processing things like this because you don't know if you're losing your mind or if it's expanding.

Sirus is the brightest star in the sky but no humanoid form could live on a star so where do the Sirians live? They live in an energy field. The Earth, in essence, is an energy field. Their civilization has gone through ascension so they are luminous like as when we're in spirit. When we leave our physical body and return to the realm of the spiritual presence, we're multidimensional too. We have these aspects that we understand that we're limited to while we're incarnate in the human form.

Do you think that beings are associated with our sun? Yes, I do and this is something that people have often talked about In old channeled information in terms of Helios and Vesta, the masculine and feminine attributes of the solar system. In nature, there are fairies and sylphs and different elemental beings that help energy take form. It's invisible to us like all the energy fields we don't see with our physical senses: the etheric body, emotional body, mental body, etc. outside the realm of sensory perception. As we develop the technology to understand and see quantum things, we're going to start seeing some of these spirits through that quantum technology, like the structure of the light fields that are part of DNA. *Some people can video the auric field of plants and humans.*

On the other side, are we opposed by beings that don't want spiritual evolution? That's not how the information has been presented to me. What I do know for sure is that there's nothing more powerful than a person who understands their luminous autonomy, a sovereignty of being. There's a force field that's part of what keeps negativity in at bay. The more you move into the space of love and authentic love consciousness, that's an ascended vibration. It's someone who has presence, who has courage, who is kind, who is non-judgmental, who has the strength to hold these attributes in form even when they're challenged by the environment around them to do so. The whole process of evolution is an ascendance from fear into love.

Kryon said that you were Lemurian. Do you have any remembrance of that? Is that one of the reasons you're able to work with the Sirians? I have little tiny memories of things that connect me to that time and space. When I first went to Hawaii before I knew that it was the Lemurian island, I had a profound feeling about being there. Later when I started to learn more about the Lemurian history I felt the deep connection to it. I've had memories of other lifetimes and places that don't exist on the world today in any frame that I understand. I don't know whether those are dream experiences or vivid memories or recalls from other lifetimes in civilizations that no longer have a historical record on the planet.

Or it could be other dimensions or other planets. It doesn't have to be Earth? That's right. What Kyron specifically said was, "You were born at the time and worked in the temple of rejuvenation. That original incarnation is the information that's encoded in your DNA because it was what you worked with in that space and time. So it's like a memory and I guess that's why I have these visions or have these experiences of seeing things and understanding them. It's like a recall or pulling upon the Akashic memory.

Is there anything else that you or the Sirian Blue White Collective would like to add? It's a message of hope because we're going through a process of enlightenment and if you think about light, what does it do? If you've had a room that's been sealed off in the house for a very long time and it's collected dust and cobwebs and you shine light in there, you see things that you didn't even know existed. It's a wonderful metaphor for describing what's happening right now on the planet. People are so unsettled and nervous and think we're going down a terrible pathway when you turn on the news and it's tragedy after tragedy and horror after horror. We're becoming more aware of what's happening. The first step of that revelation is to see what needs to change. All of these social uprisings come along with the knowledge of what's been wrong up to this point in time.

We hurt each other because of our fear-based perception and we divide ourselves into factions because we don't understand the collective nature of the human experience. When you think in terms of collective vibration consciousness, you're holding a balance for the collective. You're holding a posture of consciousness that helps the whole of humanity move forward in a different way. Maintaining that high vibration, maintaining that force of consciousness becomes a sacred responsibility, something that you take very seriously to heart. The future is very bright with developments like non-traditional forms of medicine, energy-based healing, and consciousness-based healing strategies. We're becoming more aware of our creative ability, our intuition, the synchronicities that support us living in the framework of the new energy. There's so much to learn and get excited about.

What do you do for fun to nurture yourself? What I do for fun changes. There have been some consistencies like I am in a relationship and I have a beautiful Great Dane, who I adore! A lot of my fun around experiences with my family. I love to go on trips and learn new things. I love learning about energy and consciousness and love being inspired by other speakers and authors. This is all a very rich part of my life and I love to teach.

Books

Harp of the One Heart: Poetic Songs of Ascension, 2013

The Missing Pill: The Rise of Energy-Based Healing and Conscious BioSpiritual Transformation, 2014

Unity Field Healing: Foundations of Energy Medicine and Quantum Healing, 2018

www.unityfieldhealing.com

Endnotes

1 https://www.eastern-spirituality.com/glossary/spirituality-terms/a-definitions/akasha

BARBARA STONE, PH.D.
SOUL DETECTIVE

Photo by Vicki Bosler-Kilmer

Questions to Ponder

How did Dr. Stone discover she had breast cancer and what did she learn from it?

What energy psychology tools does the author use in her therapy sessions?

She finds that trauma can not only stem from life experiences, but also from past-life traumas and from attached entities. Give examples.

I was born in Elkhart, Indiana, in 1948, a Sagittarian, the second of three girls. My grandparents on my mother's side were Amish while my grandmother on my father's side was Methodist. My parents joined the Mennonite Church and I was raised in this pacifist belief system. My mother did her doctoral dissertation on the Myers Briggs, so we heard a lot about it! I am an ENFJ on the Myers Briggs. On the Enneagram, I am a Two, the Helper, in recovery!

Tell us about themes in your childhood that led you to become a therapist? What was your family's attitude to religion and spirituality? How has yours evolved? As a child, I wanted to be a missionary doctor and go to Africa. The pastor at our church had been a missionary in Africa, and it felt like a way I could go into the darkest place in the world and bring healing. Service was very important in the Mennonite value system. Now, I am grateful that I did not go into medicine and get locked into the medical model that largely discounts the spiritual aspect of a person. I am working as a doctor on the soul level now, where we use energy therapies to heal from the inside rather than applying an outside intervention of a drug.

In the '70s, I started reading about other religions and other forms of spirituality. I had been taught that the Buddhists did not believe in God. When I read about Buddhism, I found they believed

God was in everything—every plant, rock, person, flower, etc. After my divorce, I went inside to my direct link with the Divine, through Jesus, the face God wears for me. Only now I call him by his Hebrew name, Yeshua. He is my main spiritual guide. I also love the work of Carl Jung. Studying at the Jung Institute was amazing and magical, but I did not become a Jungian analyst. I came back home before that happened and I am glad now that I didn't because the Jungian model is to go to analysis four or five times a week for five to ten years and then you are done. Living in Europe was an education in itself for me and my children.

It's a radical idea in the history of humanity that each person can link directly to God. What we were taught is that we have to go through an intermediary, for instance, in the Catholic church, only the pope has a pipeline to talk to God. The pope tells the cardinals what God says, they tell the bishops, they tell the priests, and they tell the parishioners. Somebody like Joan of Arc who talks directly to God is burned at the stake. That's not approved of because there is a hierarchy, a controlling human behavior. The concept of True Self is that every person has a spark of the Creator within them, a link to divinity, to Source by whatever name you want to call it. That Source is pure unconditional love. You don't have to earn it; it's just there because we are creations of the divine. When we plug in directly to Source for guidance, then we will be guided to what's truly best for our own lives; we'll stand in our power, and that's the safest place to be. No dark entity can overcome when you are standing in your power; no ET, no nothing. When you are in your power, you have your divine right to sovereignty.

What happens after death is a big topic in my book *Invisible Roots*. My belief is that consciousness, the immortal spirit, survives the death of the physical body. Sometimes the spirit gets stuck between the worlds, but the goal is to move from this dimension into the higher dimension of the World of Light. The Higher Self, the True Self, is the piece of Divinity accessible to each human. As a direct link to Source, it's the most reliable guidance for our lives because it comes from within and connects us to higher realms that can see the overview and the future.

What have been your most difficult challenges and how did you cope? The hardest thing I ever went through was the decision to leave my marriage to the father of my two children when they were four and seven. I was in a Mennonite church, which disapproved of divorce very strongly. Only one person in the whole church was divorced after her husband ran off to Europe with his secretary and she did not remarry until he died. I thought if I could be a good wife and obey and follow the rules, that the marriage would work. But it didn't. I had the feeling that I was going to die if I didn't get out of that situation. It was hard because it hurt my children who loved their father and the separation from him was hard on them. That was when I went inside for the first time in my life and connected directly to spirit and asked what to do. My inner guidance said that I had permission to leave, so I did.

I think the problems that led up to that divorce seeded my breast cancer that came about a decade later, as it takes about 10 years for one mutated cancer cell to grow into a tumor of one centimeter, the size where you can find it. Cancer was hard, but it did not have the social stigma that divorce had, and the trauma was mitigated by a spiritual healing the night before my surgery. I found the lump myself and that was an amazing synchronicity. My daughter and I were taking ballet classes. One night nobody else came, but I wanted to dance anyway because being an ex-Mennonite who was not allowed to dance, I enjoyed it doubly. Our teacher looked sad that night, so I did my social work thing of listening to her. She told us that her mom had been pregnant with her when she was diagnosed with breast cancer. The doctor said, "Abort, get chemotherapy, and save your life." Her mother said, "No, I will give life to my child." She did and she died not too long after my ballet teacher was born. Her older sister had the same situation, gave birth to her child, and had recently died. All of a sudden, breast cancer got real to me.

I had a mammogram several months before that because I had remarried one month before. That mammogram was fine. But I went home after the class, did a self-test, and found the lump. How Spirit kept everybody else away from my dance class that night, I don't know. I caught the lump just in time before it had a chance to metastasize to the rest of the body. The night before my surgery, when I knew it was malignant, I prayed for help. I was 42 at the time and when a young person has cancer, it's worse than when an older person gets it. I was a health nut; I exercised and ate well and meditated. But, in a young person, the cancer has more vitality, grows faster, and spreads faster, plus it was estrogen negative, which meant that hormone therapies wouldn't work.

The night after surgery, I dreamed about being ill from cancer and not being able to do things. In the dream I was told, "Write about your experience and title the book *Cancer as Initiation*. I took that advice, journaling about every step in my healing process. The diagnosis came while I was midstream in my doctoral program in Clinical Psychology at Pacifica Graduate Institute and I wrote my dissertation on the emotional aspects of surviving cancer. The popular form of that dissertation, without all the literature review, is my book *Cancer As Initiation: Surviving the Fire*.

I saw my funeral as a possibility at that moment when I found the lump. Up until then, I had been thinking, "Life on this planet is just too hard; people are too mean to each other and I'd like to go back home." But when I got my ticket home with this lump in my breast, I changed my mind. I thought, "I don't want to go home that way. Cancer is not a fun way to die." So, the night before surgery, I prayed for help and in my mind's eye, I saw Jesus, because Jesus is a face that love wears for me. He stood in front of me and communicated a message—a clear, complete thought, "I now heal your soul." I felt a tap on my sternum and I felt a deep wound, a pain in my soul, heal. I was filled with joy and I absolutely knew with my soul healed that my body would follow suit. That was 27 years ago. I am 69 and I've had time to witness the birth of five grandchildren, and I love my life. I am so grateful. So that was my first experience with tapping when Jesus tapped on my chest.

What did your dreams teach you during the cancer struggle? I was in Jungian analysis. Two themes that came up were snakes and pregnancy. There were snakes all around the house; the snake is the symbol of the Greek god of healing called Asclepius. He has a pole with a snake wrapped around it. The snake is a symbol of the kundalini energy that rises around the spine with the two intertwined snakes. I didn't know about Asclepius at the time and the snakes were kind of scary. But a deep soul healing was in progress. The other repeated dream I had was that I was pregnant. I couldn't figure that one out until I was doing the study for my thesis and researched the physiology of cancer. What does the tumor do to escape the immune system attack? It mimics the chemistry of the fetus, saying, "I'm a baby. Don't get rid of me." And of course, the immune system isn't going to get rid of the baby, so I kept dreaming I had a baby in there. But as a metaphor, I started a different life after cancer. My biggest lesson—and if everybody who's reading this wants to get the lesson without the cancer, I'll tell you the secret: It was to love myself. I know how to love other people but I didn't know how to receive love and I had to learn that.

What have your three marriages taught you? It was three months after I married my second husband when I got the diagnosis. To get through breast cancer, three factors are most important for survival: One is financial stability. Having to worry about money detracts from the healing you can do; second is prior health history. If you weren't healthy before cancer, it's not likely to improve your health, and I was in good health before that. The third factor is having a transpersonal experience of healing. In my case, Jesus touched my heart and healed me. I had all three of those going for me. My second husband was very supportive and provided financial stability. But we grew apart and there came a time when we had to go separate ways.

I was single for 12 years after that second divorce before I met my third husband; this is his third marriage too. Actually, the third marriage statistics are better than the first and better than the second—a 75% endurance rate. We are both grownups now, and we have a common mission. He is a psychiatrist named Robert Alcorn.* He also has shamanistic training, so he understands there is a spiritual world behind what looks like mental disorders. Sometimes it's the attachment of somebody else's energy, somebody who died and got stuck between the worlds and is attached to that person. Sometimes it's a curse or a hex; sometimes it's past-life trauma or the invasion of an outside entity. We work together and learn from each other and the connection is delightful.

My husband is a remarkable man. Robert has a well-developed feminine side, the ability to feel. He's brilliant too, but he nurtured his feeling side and was called by his dreams to study with a hands-on energy healer where he learned how to read energy with his hands and how to send energy. Plus, he's had a deep desire to talk to Spirit directly. His life is about spirituality, as seen in his natal chart. His sun sign and his spiritual planet, Neptune, are right on top of each other. He is Mr. Spirituality. My dream man was someone I could pray with, so every day we pray together. We talk about what we need and give thanks for what we have. We help each other with our cases and if one of us gets something attached to us, the other one helps. It's really a soulmate relationship and it's a great treasure in my life. I can't live in fear of losing him, so every day I say, "Thank you for one more day of marriage." We've been married two-and-a-half years.

Was it love at first sight with your soulmate? The first time we crossed paths was at an ISSSEEM (International Society for the Study of Subtle Energies and Energy Medicine) conference where he came to my talk. I saw him in the hallway and thought, "What a distinguished-looking person." But there were 100 people at my talk, and we were both in other relationships and didn't connect there. I heard about him through colleagues who told me he had a video where he was helping a woman release the spirit of her great-grandmother, with a photograph of the spirit as it came out. I thought, "Wow. This is my kind of man!" I had written a book on earthbound spirit release. Also, I read an article about him in *Bridges* magazine where he described his work. One of my Soul Detective students who had also been in a shamanism class with Robert called me up and said, "Dr. Alcorn is going to speak at a meeting of the Ohio Metaphysical Society and I want to schedule him at a time when you can come," because I was going to Costa Rica in the winter. I came to his talk, and it was amazing!

I thought he was married because we traded books afterward and his was dedicated to his wife. A psychic gave me a reading and said, "There's someone out there who would be perfect for you and it would be a long-term relationship. Your work would support each other and his name is Robert." I thought about how to tactfully find out if he was still married. I emailed Dr. Alcorn to ask, "How is it for your wife with you being a traditionally-trained psychiatrist to publish a book about working with spirits?" He saw right through my question and he wrote back, "I am no longer married. My divorce is final and I am available." I responded, "I happen to be available too," and he asked me out.

After I had cancer I prayed—and don't ever do this if you don't want to take the consequences—"God, you gave me back my life. I dedicate my life to you. Use me as you will, not what would be the most comfortable for me, but what's most needed." A woman I call Paula came into my practice who told me she was the survivor of Satanic ritual abuse and told me horrifying stories. Then she asked me to write her story but it took me 20 years to complete that book. Paula pushed me to learn energy therapies because talk therapy didn't work for her, and her personality was fractured, which back then we called Multiple Personality Disorder, now named Dissociative Identity Disorder. I went to a support group to find out how to deal with dissociation and they told me to learn energy therapies. I started learning them to help myself with the vicarious traumatization I got from listening to Paula's stories and to help her heal.

You call your methods of energy psychology becoming a Soul Detective. With the energy therapies, we can often clear one trauma in one session. It doesn't take as long as the Jungian healing model. Jung's work gave me a real appreciation for what's going on in the subconscious mind that I can discover from a person's dreams. Energy psychology gave me a way to read what's going on in the subconscious mind with muscle testing. You have someone hold out their arm and test muscle strength. A locked muscle indicates a statement is true and an unlocked muscle indicates the statement is not true. Jung's research was behind the lie detector test to find out what's true and what's not true. Now we have more streamlined ways to get to that information.

How accurate is muscle testing when it can be influenced by many causes? Muscle testing is an art. Very definitely, objectivity is difficult and many factors go into increasing accuracy. One factor is where a person is on David Hawkins' scale of consciousness explained in his book *Power vs. Force* that goes from downer emotions like shame, fear, and guilt to upper emotions like courage, reason, love, joy, and peace. The higher your spiritual vibration and the more you are free of those downer emotions, the more accurate your testing gets. If you have a client living in fear who tries to muscle test, the client may be reversed, so testing will not be accurate.

The second factor is that a therapist and a client both need to be blank slates, without bias about what the answer is to a statement like "chocolate is good for me." If you have a bias, your muscle testing will lean in the direction of that bias. Also, if you have a toxic load in your system, such as from alcohol, or you are too hot, too cold, too tired, or for me when I get too hungry, I can feel my system move into reversal. Then I don't get anything right with my testing. I know when I feel "hangry" (for hungry and angry), that I can't test under those circumstances. A person also needs to be well-hydrated. All vectors of the human energy field need to be centered. Cross crawling and other corrections from Educational Kinesiology [*like Brain Gym or Donna Eden's work*] can help restore balance to the system.

In the diagnostic procedure, we do a lot of muscle testing for where is the right point to tap next or muscle testing for what negative life beliefs may be blocking the whole process. Then there is the technique of applying the right amount of pressure. With intuitive

414

people, sometimes we think we know the answer before we test, but we have to put that aside and just be a blank slate. There was a study done by Monti, *et al* with machines applying the pressure: They discovered that when a person was giving a response that was congruent with what they believed was true, the muscle was 17% stronger than one that was not true, and it held 59% longer.[1] Workshops are available to teach good muscle-testing technique.

What instruction do you give your client when testing? I say, "Meet my pressure" or "hold" or "hold firm." I don't say "resist" because resistance is a dirty word in psychotherapy; it means you are trying to sabotage your results. *How do you teach people to self-test?* Probably my favorite self-test is lifting the knee on your dominant side a few inches off the floor, push on it with your dominant hand, and say a true statement like, "My name is Barbara Stone." Another easy one is the tilt test where you stand in your center and you say a true statement, such as, "This is November," and the body goes forward for something that's true. If you say, "This is April," the body goes back for something that's not true. But before you start testing yourself, you need to be sure you are centered, your motives are pure, and you have no bias about the outcome.

Did energy therapies work for Paula? Nothing worked initially for Paula, because I found out later that as a cult survivor, she was programmed that anything that was supposed to help her would make her feel worse. There was a reversal programming put into her system, so when I tried to have her circle her heart clockwise (down on the left and up on the right) while saying, "I totally love and accept myself," she said, "I don't love myself. I hate myself." Later, I learned one could say, "I really want to feel better. I wish I could feel better." Or one could just circle the heart without saying anything. What worked for Paula was Reiki. Somehow that flew under the radar of the cult programing so Reiki hands-on healing worked for her. I got introduced to earthbound spirits through her. Paula's father was a cult member and had died before we started working together. One day she came in and the room got freezing cold and Paula said, "My father's spirit is attached to me." I was thinking some holy four-letter words; "We've got a ghost here!" I knew an earthbound spirit was present because the room was so cold; this ghost was a satanic cult member, not just a regular ghost.

I prayed, "Help, I need some help here." Perfect peace came into the room, the feeling I associate with the presence of my guardian angels. Then I knew what to do. I didn't have any courses in ghost-busting in my doctoral program or my master's social work program, but I had heard about a Gestalt therapy technique where you put an empty chair for somebody you want to work with who's not there. So I said, "If Dad came to therapy today, let's talk to Dad." We pulled up an empty chair for him and Paula intuited a conversation between the two of them. She did some forgiveness work that day. What happens if you are a therapist and you deal with something out of the ordinary and it's successful? The spirit guides of that person let the guides of others know, "Go to this person." Soon earthbound spirits started popping up in my practice all over the place and I had to figure out, "What am I going to do with these ghosts?"

What was the dad's attitude as a spirit? He had some remorse at that point. He was a little different after he died. I started having my clients with attachments tap for the problems of the earthbound spirit and it worked. It's like the ghost has melded into your system and when you tap, the earthbound spirit gets the benefit because of being attached. My strategy is not to just say, "Go to the light," but to heal the trauma that prevented them from going. I have my client channel intuitively what's going on with this person, do the tapping and then help the earthbound one cross to the light. I notice that when a spirit crosses over, a golden hue comes in the room, a feeling of deep peace and joy, sometimes with tears of joy. It's the most delicious feeling to see someone who's been stuck here go into the next world and reconnect with their loved ones. I first learned about earthbound spirits from my direct experience with Paula's father. I also had to learn how to deal with dark forces.

I had always prayed, "God keep those evil spirits away from me. I don't want to deal with them." But then I read William Baldwin's book, *Healing Lost Souls: Releasing Unwanted Spirits from Your Energy*

Body.[2] Baldwin had a session with a female client in which a deep voice came out and said, "Leave her alone. She is mine!" Baldwin recognized a dark force entity in her. He asked the entity, "What's your job with this person? Who do you work for, the darkness or the light?" Then Baldwin would have the spirit find the spark of the creator's light in their own center, focus on it, expand it and then offer the entity a better job working for the light. His process worked to actually transform that spirit. Some traditional Christian churches do not believe that dark force entity transformation is possible. They think demons are unredeemable, so you have to cast them out, throw them in hell and lock them up forever. In Jungian terms, that process would be like dissociating from your shadow. You split it off, lock it up. The Baldwin method goes into the shadow, bringing light into the darkness to get that fallen angel reconnected to source so they can start being a good angel again. I added a few things to the protocol like finding out how the dark force entity got in because if you don't heal the entry wound, more entities will invade. I also realized I needed to be centered and be in sacred space to do that work.

I think it is hilarious when I am interviewing a dark force entity, asking for its purpose, and it will say, "My job is to cause as much pain and suffering as possible." I'll reply, "You are really good at that. We are going to get you a job promotion, and I know you are going to be good at your next job." I am feeding the ego of the entity by praising what a good job it is doing of creating pain and suffering, since the entities have huge egos and the praise makes a connection. They have been told the light is dangerous and could burn them up. When the fallen angels discover they've been lied to about the light and that it's really wonderful, they get mad that they've been lied to. To see that transformation of "I am big and bad" to the fallen angel realizing the creator still loves it and wants it back is such a beautiful, joyful event! The intervention makes more light on our planet and gives us all hope.

What do you teach in your Soul Detective classes? In addition to clearing past life trauma, releasing curses and hexes, healing soul loss, and helping earthbound spirits and obsessive spirits (ghosts with an agenda to hurt you), we also work with djinn, popularly known as genies, which are fire elemental spirits. We also work with other elemental spirits, angry fairies, and leprechauns. I hesitate to say this because in the psychological community it's considered crazy, but I have found invasive programs from extraterrestrials. One of the four ET species that the former Canadian Minister of Defense Paul Hellyer talked about was the insectoid races and I have had things that look like insects invade my clients. Since I have little familiarity with these insectoid races, when they come up, I ask for spiritual help to deal with them. It's all about energy; they want to steal my client's energy. We try to connect them to a better energy source so they leave my client alone.

Some of my knowledge of ETs comes from my practice, dealing with clients who have had interaction with ETs. Some comes from clients who have had lifetimes in different cultures, on different stars, in different ET races. Some of the information is from reading and some is from direct experience. I believe that whales came from another planet, so they may be ETs. I've been going for eight years to swim in the wild with humpback whales.

Have you worked with abductees? The first ET abductee that I worked with showed me the scar on his arm where the Greys had put in an implant to track him. He told me they would take him and his sister up on the ship and do experiments on them. He made friends with one of them. That ET talked about how they were trying to hybridize a race and that his abduction was a scientific endeavor not meant to hurt him or his sister. The Greys used a magnet to try to wipe his memory of the abduction, but it never quite completely wiped the memory out for this man. When he walked into a walk-in freezer, he'd have a flashback because the cold reminded him of how cold the temperature was on the spaceship. This client had some trouble functioning in this world, knowing about this other ET race and their technology, but he was an amazing man.

When I have a problem while in sacred space with a client, now I ask for volunteers. Who in the company of heaven knows how to deal with this particular problem? Sometimes somebody from the Pleiades will come; sometimes there is a volunteer from the angelic realm with a certain expertise; sometimes an ET comes; sometimes a 10th dimensional person comes, so I take whatever help I can get.

The next book I am working on, *Star Civilizations 101,* deals with the ET origins of our species and interactions with other ET races on this planet. The worst thing about the ET problem is fear, but I believe whales came here from a different planet named Oceania, they carry the records of our civilization—and they're not scary. When I was snorkeling with a mother whale I called Minerva, I sent her love and she sent what felt like a pop around my energy field that changed me from being self-critical, to being self-accepting. Her message was, "Be all you can be." That message is for all humans, not just me. According to the work of Zecharia Sitchin, sheep were brought here from the planet Niburu when civilization was developing so we'd have meat and wool.[3] I talk about different ET races and what interaction they've had with people and in my forthcoming book, I also cover the Grays, Tall Whites, Andromedans, and others.

Do you think the ETs can help us? This question is addressed in a documentary called *Thrive* by Foster Gamble and his wife Kimberly. This documentary brought me hope, particularly their report of some pilots who were carrying a nuclear warhead, when an ET craft appeared and disarmed their nuclear warhead. In the Cuban missile crisis of the early 60s, the United States had a bunch of nuclear warheads aimed at Cuba, when an ET appeared at the base and disarmed them all. The ETs know that nuclear blasts damage our atmosphere terribly and they also cause a rip in time and space that affects all the planets in our solar system and in our galaxy. It's not just that if we decide to blow ourselves up, we are gone. No, nuclear war has a ripple effect of damage to other civilizations too. It's as if those ETs said, "You guys are like a little kid playing with a laser gun. You don't know how to use that weapon, and we are not going to let you." They have also possibly foiled nuclear tests, making them fizzle.

I feel like there are many benevolent presences that care about us and are giving us more time so that we can mature and learn how to get along with each other through non-violent means. That approach is very much in line with my Mennonite pacifist thinking. If I were to shoot my enemy dead, his spirit is going to follow me around and try to make trouble for me. It's much better if I make a friend out of my enemy.

The woman I call Paula in *Transforming Fear into Gold* asked me to write her story, which she called, "I Want This Nightmare to End." Hearing what goes on in Satanic cults, I felt like I was in the deepest, darkest place in the world. I faced a lot of fear and learned to transform it. Writing the book took 20 years. I sandwiched her story between two other parts of the book. The first part is "Transforming the Dark Side," where I give the Soul Detective protocol on how to convert what we might call fallen angels to get them reconnected to Source and back to their jobs of serving the Light. The last part of the book is titled "Hope for Humanity" and shows how the dark patterns got into our society and how we can rise above them. It goes into how we were programmed to be a slave species and how we can step out of those programs into the fullness of our True Selves. Instead of looking to our hierarchy for answers—the priest, the bishop, the cardinal, the pope—we can go directly to Source, each person plugging into their True Self. That is the safest place to be, standing in your own power, directly connected to Source.

Do you think fallen angels are real? How did these angels fall from their connection to Source? I think that a reptilian race may be feeding on our suffering and the Reptilians have done dirty tricks to God's angels. The Reptilians somehow disconnect them from Source and use them to cause more suffering. When Reptilians come up in my practice, I use an intervention of asking the Arcturians to help because Arcturus was once invaded by Reptilians and they found a way to deal with the Reptilians. They send them a tractor beam of unconditional love. They zap them with love and Reptilians can't resist this beam of love because the one thing they don't have is love. The Arcturians kind of wafted the Reptilians off the planet with their unconditional love.

Dr. Mitchell Gibson* mentions working with dragons; what's your observation? From the work of an energy healer and inventor Brian Besko, I have come to see the Dragons as a different race from the Reptilians. Brian says the Dragons were the ones who created the universe. According to what I understand of what he said, the Reptilians were able to capture and chain some of them, pinning them to energy points on the earth's gridwork beneath churches. Brian and his sister started setting them free and got very sick at first. This is a wild story but one he told at the American Dowser's Society. The gridwork goes to the Vatican but he was not able to release the dragons there. We have had personal experience with a Golden Dragon who is a spiritual helper for us.

Invisible Roots: How Healing Past Life Trauma Can Liberate Your Present is the second book and *Transforming Fear into Gold* is the third book I've written. *Invisible Roots* gives the Soul Detective protocol for past-life trauma. If someone knows muscle testing and centering, they could use that protocol with their clients. I describe 10 case histories where the origin of the problem was a past-life trauma. The second topic is earthbound spirits. Past-life trauma is my trauma, while earthbound spirits are somebody else's past-life trauma. If there's a ghost or an earthbound spirit, it's a wayward spirit that couldn't get to the light because to get to heaven, you can't take any baggage. When people die filled with negative emotions, they are too heavy to float up to the higher dimension. *Invisible Roots* gives a protocol for helping earthbound spirits cross to the light.

My first client with a past-life trauma had a phobia of driving on the road in traffic, so it took her a long time to get to my house because she had to go via back roads. I had learned Roger Callahan's five-minute phobia cure. We tap under the eyes to rebalance the stomach meridian, under the arms to rebalance spleen meridian, and under the collar bone to rebalance kidney meridian.[4] We tapped away her phobia and she left. When she came back the next week, her phobia was back. We repeated the tapping process. It still had not cleared after repeating the treatment three times. That's a sign of past-life trauma when you do the treatments that normally fix something and they are not fixed.

I asked her, "What do you think about reincarnation? Do you think we might have other lives?" She said, "I don't know, but I am willing to check it out." I suggested, "Let's muscle test and see if there's past-life trauma behind this phobia" and her body indicated there was. Through muscle testing, we found out that in the past life, she was a girl of about 16 going out to meet her lover. Petticoats flying, she gets in her buggy. It's raining out and she comes around a corner where another buggy is on the path and they crash. She is thrown out, her lung is damaged, and over the course of three days, she dies thinking, "I didn't get to get married, I didn't get to connect with my lover, I am only 16, I've been cheated." In this lifetime, she didn't have her fear of driving on the highway until she saw her mother dying of a lung disease. We did a healing for that past-life trauma, letting her know that in this life, she got to marry and have children. We crossed the 16-year-old into the light.

Then my client said to me, "I have a horse and buggy but I only drive it around the driveway; I never drive it on the road." We desensitized that fear and decided to test it out. I did a Roger Callahan intervention where I got in the car with her, she tapped for her fear on the interstate highway. I said, "If you need to stop and tap, we can do that." As we drove, she tapped under her eye the whole time and desensitized her fear. That phobia never came back because we got to the origin of it from that past life. Unexplained phobias are a big sign that past-life trauma could be involved.

I muscle test to get the framework for a past life. First, I test for gender in that life, how long did they live, cause of death, the date of birth, and place of birth. Then I ask the client to go to the happiest time in that life as a way to get into the memory. We really want the worst time, but if you try to go directly there, it's just too traumatic. So we go around the backdoor to get a link to that Akashic Record and the client channels his or her own past life. Once they get that framework, they can link in to what happened and do the healing work to resolve it.

Do you know about some of your past lives? I grew up a Mennonite, so I didn't believe in reincarnation, which was considered a heresy. I was in dream analysis and in one of my dreams, a scribe read to me a list of who I had been in past lives. One of the names on that list was Simone de Beauvoir, the French author who wrote *The Second Sex.* I looked her up and she was still living. I thought, "That proves my dream is wrong. She can't be a past life because she is still alive." Since then I've learned we can overlap lifetimes so that parallel lives are going on at the same time. I am this little Mennonite girl and Simone is in a sexual threesome with Jean-Paul Sartre and another woman. Simone de Beauvoir wrote a book that rocked French society on its heels and she stood up for the value of women. I knew I had to write a book this lifetime.

My work goes outside the box of traditional society and I have had some opposition for that, especially around the ET material. Some people are so unwilling to accept that there might be other intelligent life and that it might be impacting ours that they deny the whole ET topic and ridicule people who have had ET experiences or believe it might be true. I try to keep open to what my clients bring me and go with it whether it's metaphor or true. What we are after is healing the emotions; it doesn't matter if the past life was literal or figurative. I did some work with de Beauvoir because she hadn't crossed to the light; when I got her to the light, I could breathe easier. She didn't have a concept of a transpersonal world. I believe she died sad, alone and angry, full of nicotine and not filled with joy. She was too heavy to float up to heaven.

How do you view meridians and chakras in your work? The Chinese tradition of 5,000 years mapped the meridian energy lines and the Indian system mapped it in the chakra wheels of energy. I respect the work of Barbara Brennan. I love her diagrams of chakras in the energy field in her book *Hands of Light. Me too.*

How do you work with energy cords? I am a mom with a cord of love from my heart to my family members. The mother cords of love are never going to stop and I also consciously cord to my guardian angel. I say, "Guardian angel, I need some help here. Please send me a beam of help." That's a positive energetic cord. If I would send a control cord from my solar plexus to my grown children and try to make them do what I think they should do with their lives, that would not be appropriate, so cords can be beneficial or detrimental. People who are very depleted energetically and hungry for energy might cord somebody who is high energy. It's like the needy person sticks a straw in your solar plexus and sucks on it. When that situation comes up in my practice, I try to identify where the cords are. Then I ask a Being of Light to disconnect the detrimental cord and to heal both parties. If I try to remove a cord from my client who is getting sucked dry and I pull that cord out myself, the person on the other end might cord me, so I ask a Being of Light to do it. I might have a client ask his or her guardian angel to unplug the cord from his solar plexus and to plug it into the heart of the sender's guardian angel so that person could get the energy needed.

How do you protect from negative intentions? Sending curses and hexes or a death spell are dangerous things to do for two reasons: If you curse somebody else, you wind up cursing yourself too. That's just a law of energy. That's why it's good to bless other people because that rains down blessings upon your own life. Also, sending a death spell, the evil eye, only works if the targeted person believes it is going to work.

When I was in Rwanda, our translator had six siblings. (Create Global Healing is a non-profit humanitarian healing venture put together by my friend and colleague Lori Leyden, Ph.D. In 2009, I had the privilege to go with her team on a humanitarian mission to do healing work with energy therapies in Rwanda with orphans who were survivors of the 1994 genocide.)

Our translator's father asked for something from his ancestors and they said, "We'll give it to you if you sacrifice a bull to us." So his father said, "Okay, deal." He got the thing he wanted but then he reneged on sacrificing a bull because it was expensive. After that, all six of his other siblings died within a year due to different causes. He felt those deaths happened because of a curse from his father's ancestors who were angry that his father didn't give them the bull. I asked him, "You are obviously not dead. Why didn't this curse didn't fall on you? He replied, "Oh, that's easy. The blood of Jesus Christ covers me, and that curse couldn't touch me." So his faith made him immune to the curse. He didn't believe it could touch him and he was very much alive.

If practitioners want to curse somebody, they have to remote view your energy field to find a crack in your armor where they can send in the curse. So, a way to avoid curses is to heal your own wounds, deal with your feelings, resolve your traumas, forgive yourself and everybody else. My colleague Judith Swack* has a curse protocol that she has available in an online training.[5]

You work with ancestral wounds. What are they? The family as a whole has a soul. For example, if somebody in the family died of diabetes and their life had not been sweet enough, that person carries the wound that life is bitter. If that person's spirit didn't get to the light, then the DNA, which is passed down energetically, affects everybody in the lineage. My grandfather died of diabetes, as did my uncle. If I ate a normal American diet of sweet rolls and Coca-Cola, I would be diabetic, so I don't eat white sugar. If anybody in your DNA lineage has a wound, you may feel the effects, but we can do healing for people in our ancestral lineage.

Epigenetics research found that genes change with our environment. Yes, certainly the work of Dawson Church showed that it's not just the genes we have, but which ones we express. This happens on the physical level and also on the emotional level to manifest disease. When emotional trauma is in your lineage, that resonates in the soul of the whole family. One can ask to heal everyone in this lineage, in this DNA stream, of a trauma. William Tiller taught us that the meridian system is a coupled system, like there's a train going to heaven, and you just jump on one of the cars and you go to heaven. Gary Craig, the founder of EFT, talked about the coupling phenomenon as "borrowing benefits." Every time we do a healing, I like to multiply the benefits, to broadcast that coupled system for healing that variety of mental disorder to invite everybody else to jump on the train.

Our planet has a cloud of darkness around it of the spirits of the people who have been killed in wars and were terrified and have still not crossed over. As we lift that cloud of earthbound spirits and multiply the benefits, the cloud dissipates and more light can come into the planet. This astral cloud of trauma around our planet is something that we all breathe and feel. Jung called it the collective unconscious. There is a web of life and each person is like an intersection in that web.

The world situation seems to be getting worse rather than better, as with the rise of autocratic rulers, increasing inequality, and ongoing wars. Is there any reason to be hopeful? More people are waking up to who we really are. The first step is to turn off the TV and don't listen to the news! I don't go into the negativity of the news, because the news is designed to create fear and trauma. Plus, it's addictive; you want to see what's going to happen next and it gets you upset. I spend my spare time working in my yard, tending my flowers, making crafts and pendulums, cooking, reading, and writing, but I don't have time to let the news feed me scary thoughts.

I also believe that there has to be a higher plan somewhere. What I've seen in my own life is that every time something bad happens, it gets turned around for good. I believe that is happening now. Dr. Christine Page teaches that we have a window from 2012 to 2028, when we can collectively make a shift from third-dimensional power struggles up to the fourth dimension where love rules, then to the fifth dimension where we create with thought. What I see in my practice is that people heal faster and my students learn faster. When I first started teaching students self-testing, only a few got it right away, and now everybody gets it right away. How does that happen? It's the 100th monkey effect. Everybody who does their own healing puts another drop in the ocean of healing that everybody shares. People are waking up, saying, "I don't want somebody telling me everything I have to do. I want to think for myself, I want to check in to see what's really right for my soul and follow that!"

Books

Cancer As Initiation: Surviving the Fire, 1994

Invisible Roots: How Healing Past Life Trauma Can Liberate Your Present, 2008

Transforming Fear into Gold, 2012

Endnotes

1 Monti, D., Sinnott, J., Marchese, M., et al. (1999). "Muscle test comparisons of congruent and incongruent self-referential statements," *Perceptual and Motor Skills* 88, 1019-1

2 Baldwin, W. (2003). *Healing Lost Souls: Releasing Unwanted Spirits from your Energy Body.* Hampton Roads.

3 Sitchin, Z. (2002). *The Lost Book of Enki.* Rochester, VT: Bear & Co.

4 William Tiller's book *Science and Human Transformation: Subtle Energies, Intentionality and Consciousness* (1997) discusses how the points on the meridian system are antennae that couple to the nervous system (p. 117).

5 https://hblu.org/

Conclusion

The visionary scientists' research expands our sources of knowledge beyond logic and what we can see visually to intuition, ESP, dreams, precognition, remote viewing, synchronicities, non-human guides and a higher intelligence. Jim Carpenter names this other-dimensional source of information "First Sight" and Robert and Suzanne Mays believe that psi phenomenon occur on the fifth dimension. Many people who have NDEs report reviewing their life lessons with the help of loving guides and sometimes receive accurate information about their futures. Mediums and channelers get information from formerly incarnated spirits or higher dimensional beings like Seth and Abraham.

The materialist worldview limits our access to information only to what we can learn from our five senses. Skeptics like Susan Blackmore maintain that extraordinary experiences like hers can be explained by brain functions. I'm convinced there's more than the little brain by the psi research with statistical results far beyond probability, case studies, and my own access of information from beyond my thought process. Many of the visionary scientists meditate in order to go beyond their thoughts to quiet inspiration and peace.

Not only do we connect with non-physical information, psychokinesis and psychonnuroimunolgy shows that thoughts and intentions can influence matter. Numerous lab experiments use only intention to change cell growth, the rate at which yeast release oxygen, change direction of plasma, and so on. This ability could be developed to enhance health, as evidenced by the placebo effect, intercessory prayer, and one multiple personality having a disease and the other not having it, in the same body. Not only did William Bengston's students and trainees heal mice injected with cancer, he is researching how to capture the healing signals to share without healers present. He found that cancer cells do change in response to these signals sent through speakers. The non-materialist paradigm adds consciousness or spirit that we should explore and use as humans with more potential than the dominant paradigm recognizes.

Made in the USA
San Bernardino, CA
26 May 2020